Five
Thousand
Quotations
for all
occasions

Five Thousand Quotations for all occasions

Arranged and Edited by LEWIS C. HENRY

DOUBLEDAY & COMPANY, INC.
Garden City, New York

PRINTED IN THE UNITED STATES

INTRODUCTION

THIS book brings together in convenient form a rich selection of useful and interesting quotations, on literally hundreds of topics, from the works of writers, thinkers, orators, and leaders down through the ages and the world over, including outstanding utterances of our own day. The reader will find page after page filled with wise sayings, witty remarks, tersely phrased observations, and sparkling epigrams, which may be read for their own sake or used effectively in the preparation of speeches or written material whenever the occasion arises.

All the quotations have been grouped under appropriate subject headings. These headings are in alphabetical order in the book, and under each heading the quotations are arranged alphabetically according to author.

To find an appropriate quotation dealing with some particular topic or for use on a particular occasion, the reader should turn to the heading which would most likely represent the subject and there select the passage which best fills his need. Since the same subject may be identified by a number of possible headings, we have included a large number of alternative headings in their alphabetical place, with cross references to the headings under which the quotations are actually grouped. In addition, the reader can easily find quotations on related subjects by referring to the cross references which are in parentheses at the end of almost every entry. If you do not find a heading on a specific topic, as, for example, the name of a particular flower or bird, look under the more general heading; thus under "Flowers" you will find entries on roses, poppies, and other individual varieties, as well as on the subject as a whole.

Those readers who want to locate and verify a quotation with which they are already familiar and of which they know the author, will find the Index at the end of the book very convenient, as it lists all the pages containing passages from individual writers and speakers. This Index also contains concise biographical information about all the persons quoted in the book. In cases where the author's name is not known, the quotation sought should be looked up under the subject heading with which the quotation primarily deals.

It is the editor's hope that this book will serve many useful purposes as a handy reference volume, and that readers will also find leisure-time pleasure in browsing among these 5000 carefully selected, varied, and choice quotations.

L.C.H.

ABILITY

Behind an able man there are always other able men.
> CHINESE PROVERB

I add this also, that natural ability without education has oftener raised man to glory and virtue, than education without natural ability.
> CICERO—*Oratio Pro Licinio Archia*

As we advance in life, we learn the limits of our abilities.
> FROUDE—*Short Studies on Great Subjects*

We judge ourselves by what we feel capable of doing, while others judge us by what we have already done.
> LONGFELLOW

Ability is of little account without opportunity.
> NAPOLEON

They are able because they think they are able.
> VERGIL—*Aeneid*

(See also ACTION, CHARACTER, GENIUS, PERSEVERANCE, POWER, SELF-RELIANCE, SUCCESS, TALENT.)

ABSENCE

Absence makes the heart grow fonder.
> THOMAS HAYNES BAYLY—*Isle of Beauty*

Absent in body, but present in spirit.
> I CORINTHIANS. V. 3

Achilles absent, was Achilles still.
> HOMER—*Iliad*

Let no one be willing to speak ill of the absent.
> PROPERTIUS—*Elegiae*

(See also FAREWELL, MEMORY, PARTING.)

ABUNDANCE
See RICHES

ABUSE
See RIDICULE

ACCIDENT

Accidents will occur in the best regulated families.
> DICKENS—*David Copperfield*

At first laying down, as a fact fundamental,
That nothing with God can be accidental.
> LONGFELLOW—*Christus*

(See also CALAMITY, CHANCE, DANGER, DESTINY, FATE.)

ACQUAINTANCE

A wise man knows everything; a shrewd one, everybody.
> ANONYMOUS

1

Sudden acquaintance brings repentance.

    THOMAS FULLER

If a man is worth knowing at all, he is worth knowing well.

    ALEXANDER SMITH—*Dreamthorp*

(See also ASSOCIATE, FRIEND.)

ACTING

The most difficult character in comedy is that of the fool, and he must be no simpleton that plays that part.

    CERVANTES

When an actor has money, he doesn't send letters but telegrams.

    ANTON CHEKHOV

The drama's laws, the drama's patrons give.
For we that live to please, must please to live.

    SAMUEL JOHNSON—*Prologue*

The play's the thing.

    SHAKESPEARE—*Hamlet*. Act II. Sc. 2

(See also DRAMA, ELOQUENCE, ORATORY.)

ACTION

Let us do or die.

    BURNS—*Address to the Unco Guid*

The best way to keep good acts in memory is to refresh them with new.

    Attributed to CATO by BACON —*Apothegms*

Whatsoever thy hand findeth to do, do it with thy might.

    ECCLESIASTES. IX. 10

Did nothing in particular
And did it very well.

    W. S. GILBERT—*Lord Mountararat*

He started to sing as he tackled the thing
    That couldn't be done, and he did it.

    EDGAR A. GUEST—*It Couldn't Be Done*

Do well and right, and let the world sink.

    HERBERT—*Country Parson*

Trust no future, howe'er pleasant!
    Let the dead past bury its dead!
Act,—act in the living Present!
    Heart within and God o'erhead.

    LONGFELLOW—*Psalm of Life*

Let us then be up and doing,
    With a heart for any fate;
Still achieving, still pursuing,
    Learn to labor and to wait.

    LONGFELLOW—*Psalm of Life*

Every man feels instinctively that all the beautiful sentiments in the world weigh less than a single lovely action.

    LOWELL

Go, and do thou likewise.

    LUKE. X. 37

He nothing common did, or mean,
Upon that memorable scene.

    MARVELL—*Horatian Ode*. Upon Cromwell's Return from Ireland

So much to do; so little done.
CECIL RHODES—*Last Words*

I took the canal zone and let Congress debate, and while the debate goes on the canal does also.
THEODORE ROOSEVELT

Get good counsel before you begin: and when you have decided, act promptly.
SALLUST—*Catilina*

He that is overcautious will accomplish little.
SCHILLER—*Wilhelm Tell*

What's done can't be undone.
SHAKESPEARE—*Macbeth*. Act V. Sc. I

Heaven ne'er helps the men who will not act.
SOPHOCLES—*Fragment*

Theirs not to make reply,
Theirs not to reason why,
Theirs but to do and die.
TENNYSON—*Charge of the Light Brigade*

Out of the strain of the doing,
Into the peace of the done.
JULIA WOODRUFF—*Gone*

(See also DECISION, DEEDS, LABOR, RESOLUTION, WORK.)

ADAM AND EVE

Whilst Adam slept, Eve from his side arose:
Strange his first sleep would be his last repose.
ANONYMOUS

When Adam dolve, and Eve span,
Who was then the gentleman?
JOHN BALL—*Wat Tyler's Rebellion*

Adam and Eve had many advantages, but the principal one was that they escaped teething.
S. L. CLEMENS (MARK TWAIN)
—*Pudd'nhead Wilson*

When Eve upon the first of men
The apple pressed with specious cant,
Oh! what a thousand pities then
That Adam was not adamant.
HOOD—*Adam and Eve*

Adam ate the apple, and our teeth still ache.
HUNGARIAN PROVERB

In Adam's fall—
We sinned all.
NEW ENGLAND PRIMER

(See also BIBLE, HISTORY, MAN, MATRIMONY, SCRIPTURE, WOMAN.)

ADMIRATION

Admiration is a very short-lived passion, that immediately decays upon growing familiar with its object.
ADDISON—*The Spectator*

Our polite recognition of another's resemblance to ourselves.
BIERCE—*The Devil's Dictionary*

Distance is a great promoter of admiration!
DIDEROT

We always love those who admire us, and we do not always love those whom we admire.
LA ROCHEFOUCAULD

For fools admire, but men of sense approve.
POPE—*Essay on Criticism*

(See also APPLAUSE, FAME, PRAISE.)

ADVENTURE
See DARING

ADVERSITY

Adversity introduces a man to himself.
ANONYMOUS

God brings men into deep waters, not to drown them, but to cleanse them.
AUGHEY

Constant success shows us but one side of the world; adversity brings out the reverse of the picture.
COLTON

There is no education like adversity.
DISRAELI

Prosperity is a great teacher; adversity is a greater. Possession pampers the mind; privation trains and strengthens it.
HAZLITT

Sweet are the uses of adversity;
Which, like the toad, ugly and venomous,
Wears yet a precious jewel in his head.
SHAKESPEARE—*As You Like It.*
Act II. Sc. I

(See also AFFLICTION, CALAMITY, GRIEF, MISERY, MISFORTUNE, SUFFERING, TRIAL, TROUBLE.)

ADVERTISING

When business is good it pays to advertise; when business is bad you've got to advertise.
ANONYMOUS

You can tell the ideals of a nation by its advertisements.
DOUGLAS—*South Wind*

Advertisements contain the only truths to be relied on in a newspaper.
JEFFERSON—*Letter to Nathaniel Macon*

(See also BUSINESS.)

ADVICE

Never give advice in a crowd.
ARAB PROVERB

Never give advice unless asked.
GERMAN PROVERB

Whatever advice you give, be short.
HORACE—*Ars Poetica*

Old men are fond of giving good advice, to console themselves for being no longer in a position to give bad examples.
LA ROCHEFOUCAULD

We give advice, but we do not inspire conduct.
LA ROCHEFOUCAULD

Good counsel has no price.
MAZZINI

Never advise anyone to go to war or to marry.
SPANISH PROVERB

Many receive advice, only the wise profit by it.
SYRUS

Admonish your friends privately, but praise them openly.
SYRUS

(See also EXPERIENCE, PRUDENCE, TEACHING.)

AFFECTATION

Affectation is the product of false-hood.
CARLYLE

We are never so ridiculous from the habits we have as from those we affect to have.
LA ROCHEFOUCAULD

Affectation hides three times as many virtues as charity does sins.
HORACE MANN

(See also APPEARANCE, VANITY.)

AFFECTION
See FRIENDSHIP

AFFLICTION

The eternal stars shine out as soon as it is dark enough.
CARLYLE

Whom the Lord loveth he chasten-eth.
HEBREWS. XII. 6

Be still, sad heart, and cease repining,
Behind the clouds the sun is shining;
Thy fate is the common fate of all;
Into each life some rain must fall,—
Some days must be dark and dreary.
LONGFELLOW

(See also ADVERSITY, GRIEF, MISERY, MISFORTUNE, SUFFERING, TROUBLE.)

AGE

It is always in season for old men to learn.
AESCHYLUS—Age

To know how to grow old is the master work of wisdom, and one of the most difficult chapters in the great art of living.
AMIEL

Old wood best to burn, old wine to drink, old friends to trust, and old authors to read.
Quoted by BACON—Apothegm

Youth is a blunder; Manhood a strug-gle; Old Age a regret.
DISRAELI—Coningsby

At 20 years of age the will reigns; at 30 the wit; at 40 the judgment.
FRANKLIN—Poor Richard's Al-manac

If wrinkles must be written upon our brows, let them not be written upon the heart. The spirit should not grow old.
JAMES A. GARFIELD

The riders in a race do not stop short when they reach the goal. There is a little finishing canter be-fore coming to a standstill. There is time to hear the kind voice of friends and to say to one's self: "The work is done."
HOLMES II—Speech on his 91st birthday

Study until twenty-five, investigation until forty, profession until sixty, at which age I would have him retired on a double allowance.
WILLIAM OSLER

In youth the days are short and the years are long; in old age the years are short and the days long.
PANIN

The days of our years are threescore years and ten; and if by reason of strength they be fourscore years, yet is their strength labour and sorrow; for it is soon cut off, and we fly away.
PSALMS. I. 3

The first forty years of life give us the text; the next thirty supply the commentary on it.
SCHOPENHAUER

Age cannot wither her, nor custom stale
Her infinite variety.
SHAKESPEARE—Antony and Cleopatra. Act II. Sc. 2

An old man is twice a child.
SHAKESPEARE—Hamlet. Act II. Sc. 2

The old believe everything: the middle-aged suspect everything: the young know everything.
WILDE

(See also BABYHOOD, CHILDHOOD, LIFE, TIME, YOUTH.)

AGRICULTURE

Earth is here so kind, that just tickle her with a hoe and she laughs with a harvest.
JERROLD—A Land of Plenty

A field becomes exhausted by constant tillage.
OVID

Praise a large domain, cultivate a small estate.
VERGIL—Georgics

Blessed be agriculture! if one does not have too much of it.
CHARLES DUDLEY WARNER—My Summer in a Garden

When tillage begins, other arts follow. The farmers, therefore, are the founders of human civilization.
DANIEL WEBSTER—Remarks on Agriculture

(See also COUNTRY LIFE, FARMING, FRUIT, GARDEN, HARVEST, NATURE.)

AMBITION

When you are aspiring to the highest place, it is honorable to reach the second or even the third rank.
CICERO—De Oratore

Hitch your wagon to a star.
EMERSON—Society and Solitude

Most people would succeed in small things if they were not troubled with great ambitions.
LONGFELLOW—Drift-Wood

Better to reign in hell than serve in heaven.
MILTON—Paradise Lost

When that the poor have cried, Caesar hath wept:
Ambition should be made of sterner stuff:
Yet Brutus says he was ambitious;
And Brutus is an honourable man.
SHAKESPEARE—Julius Caesar. Act IV. Sc. 3

If you wish to reach the highest, begin at the lowest.
SYRUS—*Maxims*

Ambition destroys its possessor.
THE TALMUD—*Yoma*

Ambition has but one reward for all:
A little power, a little transient fame,
A grave to rest in, and a fading name!
WILLIAM WINTER—*The Queen's Domain*

(See also APPLAUSE, DESIRE, FAME, GLORY, REPUTATION, SUCCESS, ZEAL.)

AMERICA

Don't sell America short.
ANONYMOUS

So at last I was going to America! Really, really going, at last! The boundaries burst. The arch of heaven soared. A million suns shone out for every star. The winds rushed in from outer space, roaring in my ears, "America! America!"
MARY ANTIN—*The Promised Land*

O beautiful for patriot dream
 That sees beyond the years
Thine alabaster cities gleam
 Undimmed by human tears!
America! America!
 God shed His grace on thee,
And crown thy good with brotherhood
 From sea to shining sea!
KATHARINE LEE BATES—*America the Beautiful*

Hail, Columbia! happy land!
Hail, ye heroes! heavenborn band!
Who fought and bled in Freedom's cause.
JOSEPH HOPKINSON—*Hail Columbia*

America is a tune. It must be sung together.
GERALD STANLEY LEE—*Crowds*

Thou, too, sail on, O Ship of State!
Sail on, O Union, strong and great!
Humanity with all its fears,
With all the hopes of future years,
Is hanging breathless on thy fate!
LONGFELLOW—*Building of the Ship*

Only those Americans who are willing to die for their country are fit to live.
DOUGLAS MACARTHUR

This generation of Americans has a rendezvous with destiny.
F. D. ROOSEVELT—Speech, 1936

In the United States there is more space where nobody is than where anybody is. This is what makes America what it is.
GERTRUDE STEIN—*The Geographical History of America*

I pledge allegiance to the flag of the United States and to the Republic for which it stands, one nation, indivisible, with liberty and justice for all.
JAMES B. UPHAM AND FRANCIS BELLAMY—*Pledge to the Flag*

I was born an American; I live an American; I shall die an American.
DANIEL WEBSTER

American liberty is a religion. It is a thing of the spirit. It is an aspiration on the part of the people for not only a free life but a better life.
WENDELL L. WILLKIE—
Speech, 1941

Some Americans need hyphens in their names, because only part of them has come over; but when the whole man has come over, heart and thought and all, the hyphen drops of its own weight out of his name.
WOODROW WILSON

America is God's crucible, the great Melting-Pot where all the races of Europe are melting and reforming! . . . The real American has not yet arrived. He is only in the crucible, I tell you—he will be the fusion of all races, the common superman.
ISRAEL ZANGWILL

(See also DEMOCRACY, EQUALITY, FLAG, FREEDOM, HUMANITY, INDEPENDENCE, LIBERTY, PARTY, PATRIOTISM, POLITICS, RIGHTS, SLAVERY, STATESMANSHIP, UNION, WAR.)

AMUSEMENT

If those who are the enemies of innocent amusements had the direction of the world, they would take away the spring, and youth, the former from the year, the latter from human life.
BALZAC

You can't live on amusement. It is the froth on water,—an inch deep, and then the mud!
GEORGE MACDONALD

The real character of a man is found out by his amusements.
SIR JOSHUA REYNOLDS

(See also ACTING, DANCING, DRAMA, FESTIVITIES, FISHING, GAMBLING, SPORT.)

ANARCHISM

Anarchism is the name given to a principle or theory of life and conduct under which society is conceived without government—harmony in such a society being obtained not by submission to law or by obedience to any authority, but by free agreements concluded between the various groups, territorial and professional, freely constituted for the sake of production and consumption, as also for the satisfaction of the infinite variety of needs and aspirations of a civilized being.
PETER KROPOTKIN—Article on Anarchism in *Encyclopedia Britannica*

Anarchism may be described as the doctrine that all the affairs of men should be managed by individuals or voluntary associations, and that the State should be abolished.
BENJAMIN R. TUCKER—*State Socialism and Anarchism*

ANCESTRY

A degenerate nobleman, or one that is proud of his birth, is like a turnip. There is nothing good of him but that which is underground.
BUTLER—*Characters*

My father was a creole, his father a Negro, and his father a monkey; my family, it seems, begins where yours left off.

> DUMAS, on being asked "Who was your father?"

Breed is stronger than pasture.

> GEORGE ELIOT

Noble ancestry makes a poor dish at table.

> ITALIAN PROVERB

There is no king who has not had a slave among his ancestors, and no slave who has not had a king among his.

> HELEN KELLER—Story of My Life

People who take no pride in the noble achievements of remote ancestors will never achieve anything worthy to be remembered with pride by remote descendants.

> MACAULAY

Whoever serves his country well has no need of ancestors.

> VOLTAIRE

(See also AGE, HEREDITY, POSTERITY.)

ANGER

Men often make up in wrath what they want in reason.

> W. R. ALGER

An angry man opens his mouth and shuts up his eyes.

> CATO

Never answer a letter while you are angry.

> CHINESE PROVERB

When angry, count four; when very angry, swear.

> SAMUEL L. CLEMENS (MARK TWAIN)—Pudd'nhead Wilson

Heav'n has no rage, like love to hatred turn'd,
Nor Hell a fury, like a woman scorn'd.

> CONGREVE

Beware the fury of a patient man.

> DRYDEN—Absalom and Achitophel

Anger is momentary madness, so control your passion or it will control you.

> HORACE—Epistles

Anger blows out the lamp of the mind. In the examination of a great and important question, every one should be serene, slow-pulsed, and calm.

> INGERSOLL

He that is slow to anger is better than the mighty; and he that ruleth his spirit than he that taketh a city.

> PROVERBS. XVI. 32

(See also HATE, PASSION, REVENGE.)

ANIMALS

Animals are such agreeable friends; they ask no questions, pass no criticisms.

> GEORGE ELIOT

If 't were not for my cat and dog, I think I could not live.

> EBENEZER ELLIOTT

A mule has neither pride of ancestry nor hope of posterity.
INGERSOLL

Men show their superiority inside; animals, outside.
RUSSIAN PROVERB

(See also CAT, DOG, FOX, HORSE, LAMB, LION, MOUSE, SHEEP.)

ANTICIPATION
See EXPECTATION

APOLOGY

No sensible person ever made an apology.
EMERSON

Apology is only egotism wrong side out.
HOLMES

(See also COURTESY, EXCUSE, MANNERS, PARDON.)

APPEARANCE

O wad some power the giftie gie us
To see oursel's as ithers see us!
BURNS—*To a Louse*

All that glisters is not gold.
CERVANTES—*Don Quixote*

Polished brass will pass upon more people than rough gold.
CHESTERFIELD

Handsome is that handsome does.
FIELDING—*Tom Jones*

By outward show let's not be cheated.
An ass should like an ass be treated.
GAY—*Fables*

Things are seldom what they seem,
Skim milk masquerades as cream.
W. S. GILBERT—*H.M.S. Pinafore*

Men in general judge more from appearances than from reality. All men have eyes, but few have the gift of penetration.
MACHIAVELLI

Whited sepulchres, which indeed appear beautiful outward, but are within full of dead men's bones.
MATTHEW. XXIII. 27

She looks as if butter wouldn't melt in her mouth.
SWIFT—*Polite Conversation*

(See also BEAUTY, CLOTHES, FASHION, HYPOCRISY, MANNERS, WORTH.)

APPETITE

Animals feed, man eats; the man of intellect alone knows how to eat.
BRILLAT-SAVARIN

All philosophy in two words,—sustain and abstain.
EPICTETUS

Put a knife to thy throat, if thou be a man given to appetite.
PROVERBS. XXIII. 2

If you are surprised at the number of our maladies, count our cooks.
SENECA

(See also COOKING, EATING, HUNGER, PASSION.)

APPLAUSE

The echo of a platitude.
BIERCE—*The Devil's Dictionary*

Applause is the spur of noble minds,
the end and aim of weak ones.
COLTON—*Lacon*

About the only person we ever heard
of that wasn't spoiled by being lion-
ized was a Jew named Daniel.
G. D. PRENTICE

(See also ADMIRATION, COMPLI-
MENT, FLATTERY, HONOR, POPU-
LARITY, PRAISE, REPUTATION,
SUCCESS, VANITY.)

APPRECIATION
See GRATITUDE

ARCHITECTURE

Old houses mended,
Cost little less than new before they're
ended.
COLLEY CIBBER

Architecture is frozen music.
GOETHE

Ah, to build, to build!
That is the noblest of all the arts.
LONGFELLOW—*Michelangelo*

(See also ART, BUILDING, CITY.)

ARGUMENT

Arguments out of a pretty mouth
are unanswerable.
ADDISON

Many can argue; not many converse.
ALCOTT

Wise men argue causes, and fools
decide them.
ANACHARSIS

When Bishop Berkeley said, "there
was no matter,"
And proved it—'twas no matter what
he said.
BYRON—*Don Juan*

Neither irony nor sarcasm is argument.
RUFUS CHOATE

I am bound to furnish my antagonists with arguments, but not with
comprehension.
DISRAELI

How agree the kettle and the earthen
pot together?
ECCLESIASTICUS. XIII. 2

Strong and bitter words indicate a
weak cause.
VICTOR HUGO

Insolence is not logic; epithets are
the arguments of malice.
INGERSOLL

Myself when young did eagerly fre-
quent
Doctor and Saint, and heard great
argument
About it and about: but evermore
Came out by the same door where in
I went.
OMAR KHAYYÁM—*Rubaiyat*

Never argue at the dinner table, for
the one who is not hungry always
gets the best of the argument.
WHATELY

When people agree with me I always feel that I must be wrong.
WILDE—*The Critic as an Artist*

(See also CONTROVERSY, ELOQUENCE, LOGIC, ORATORY, REASON, SPEECH, TALK, WIT, WORD.)

ARISTOCRACY
See NOBILITY

ARMY
See SOLDIER

ART

What is art? Nature concentrated.
BALZAC

Art is I; science is we.
CLAUDE BERNARD

Nature hath made one world, and art another.
SIR THOMAS BROWNE

Art for art's sake.
VICTOR COUSIN

Art, as far as it is able, follows nature, as a pupil imitates his master; thus your art must be, as it were, God's grandchild.
DANTE—*Inferno*

What is the good of prescribing to art the roads that it must follow. To do so is to doubt art, which develops normally according to the laws of Nature, and must be exclusively occupied in responding to human needs.
DOSTOYEVSKY

Art is the stored honey of the human soul, gathered on wings of misery and travail.
DREISER—*Life, Art and America*

A photograph is a portrait painted by the sun.
DUPIN

Every artist was first an amateur.
EMERSON

A picture is a poem without words.
HORACE

Art hath an enemy called ignorance.
BEN JONSON

It's clever, but is it art?
KIPLING—*The Conundrum of the Workshops*

Art is not an end in itself, but a means of addressing humanity.
M. P. MOUSSORGSKY

Great art is as irrational as great music. It is mad with its own loveliness.
GEORGE JEAN NATHAN—*House of Satan*

Art is a kind of illness.
GIACOMO PUCCINI

Art is indeed not the bread but the wine of life.
JEAN PAUL RICHTER

Art is difficult, transient is her reward.
SCHILLER

The artist does not see things as they are, but as he is.
ALFRED TONNELLE

(See also ARCHITECTURE, DANCING, LITERATURE, MUSIC, PAINTING, POETRY, SCULPTURE, SONG.)

ASSOCIATE

My friends! There are no friends.
ARISTOTLE

When a dove begins to associate with crows its feathers remain white but its heart grows black.
GERMAN PROVERB

If you always live with those who are lame, you will yourself learn to limp.
LATIN PROVERB

He that walketh with wise men shall be wise.
PROVERBS. XIII. 20

(See also FRIEND.)

ASTRONOMY
See STARS

ATHEISM

I am an atheist, thank God!
ANONYMOUS

I don't believe in God because I don't believe in Mother Goose.
CLARENCE DARROW

The fool hath said in his heart, There is no God.
PSALMS. CIV. 1

That the universe was formed by a fortuitous concourse of atoms, I will no more believe than that the accidental jumbling of the alphabet would fall into a most ingenious treatise of philosophy.
SWIFT

By night an atheist half believes in God.
YOUNG

(See also CREATION, DOUBT, GOD, RELIGION, SCIENCE.)

AUDACITY

Audacity, more audacity, always audacity.
DANTON, during French Revolution

Fortune favors the audacious.
ERASMUS

(See also BRAVERY, COURAGE, DARING, VALOR.)

AUTHORITY

Every great advance in natural knowledge has involved the absolute rejection of authority.
HUXLEY—*Lay Sermons*

All authority belongs to the people.
JEFFERSON

The highest duty is to respect authority.
POPE LEO XIII

(See also GOVERNMENT, INFLUENCE, LAW, POWER.)

AUTHORSHIP

The pen is the tongue of the mind.
CERVANTES—*Don Quixote*

The author who speaks about his own books is almost as bad as a mother who talks about her own children.
DISRAELI

An incurable itch for scribbling takes possession of many, and grows inveterate in their insane breasts.
JUVENAL—*Satires*

He who writes prose builds his temple to Fame in rubble; he who writes verses builds it in granite.
BULWER-LYTTON

You do not publish your own verses, Laelius; you criticise mine. Pray cease to criticise mine, or else publish your own.
MARTIAL

The ink of the scholar is more sacred than the blood of the martyr.
MOHAMMED—*Tribute to Reason*

(See also BOOKS, CRITICISM, JOURNALISM, LITERATURE, NEWSPAPER, PEN, PLAGIARISM, PRESS, QUOTATION, READING, WRITING.)

AUTUMN

The melancholy days have come, the
  saddest of the year,
Of wailing winds, and naked woods,
  and meadows brown and sear.
  BRYANT—*The Death of the Flowers*

The year's in the wane;
  There is nothing adoring;
The night has no eve,
  And the day has no morning;
  Cold winter gives warning!
  HOOD—*Autumn*

O, it sets my heart a clickin' like the
  tickin' of a clock,
When the frost is on the punkin and
  the fodder's in the shock.
  JAMES WHITCOMB RILEY—
  When the Frost Is on the Punkin

(See also MONTHS, NATURE, SEASONS.)

AVARICE

If you wish to remove avarice you must remove its mother, luxury.
CICERO—*De Oratore*

Avarice is generally the last passion of those lives of which the first part has been squandered in pleasure, and the second devoted to ambition.
SAMUEL JOHNSON

The avaricious man is kind to no person, but he is most unkind to himself.
JOHN KYRLE

                    That disease
Of which all old men sicken, avarice.
  THOMAS MIDDLETON — *The Roaring Girl*

The lust of avarice has so totally seized upon mankind that their wealth seems rather to possess them than they possess their wealth.
PLINY

(See also ECONOMY, GOLD, MAMMON, MONEY.)

AVIATION

Bombardment from the air is legitimate only when directed at a military objective, the destruction or injury of which would constitute a distinct military disadvantage to the belligerent.
THE HAGUE CONVENTION

What can you conceive more silly and extravagant than to suppose a man racking his brains, and studying night and day how to fly?
WILLIAM LAW—*A Serious Call to a Devout and Holy Life* (1728)

He rode upon a cherub, and did fly; yea, he did fly upon the wings of the wind.
PSALMS. XVIII. 10

The birds can fly,
An' why can't I?
TROWBRIDGE — *Darius Green and His Flying Machine.* (1869)

(See also PROGRESS, SCIENCE.)

BABYHOOD

Here we have a baby. It is composed of a bald head and a pair of lungs.
EUGENE FIELD—*The Tribune Primer*

Where did you come from, baby dear?
Out of the Everywhere into here.
GEORGE MACDONALD — Song in *At the Back of the North Wind*

Rock-a-bye-baby on the tree top,
When the wind blows the cradle will rock,
When the bough bends the cradle will fall,
Down comes the baby, cradle and all.
OLD NURSERY RHYME

Out of the mouth of babes and sucklings hast thou ordained strength.
PSALMS. VIII. 2

Sweetest li'l feller, everybody knows;
Dunno what to call him, but he's mighty lak' a rose;
Lookin' at his mammy wid eyes so shiny blue
Mek' you think that Heav'n is comin' clost ter you.
FRANK L. STANTON—*Mighty Lak' a Rose*

Beat upon mine, little heart! beat, beat!
Beat upon mine! you are mine, my sweet!
All mine from your pretty blue eyes to your feet,
My sweet!
TENNYSON—*Romney's Remorse*

Hush, my dear, lie still and slumber,
Holy angels guard thy bed!
Heavenly blessings without number
Gently falling on thy head.
ISAAC WATTS—*A Cradle Hymn*

(See also AGE, BIRTH, CHILDHOOD, MOTHER, YOUTH.)

BACHELOR

A bachelor is one who enjoys the chase but does not eat the game.
ANONYMOUS

A bachelor is a souvenir of some woman who found a better one at the last minute.
ANONYMOUS

The best works, and of greatest merit for the public, have proceeded from the unmarried or childless men.
BACON—*Essays*

A single man has not nearly the value he would have in a state of union. He is an incomplete animal. He resembles the odd half of a pair of scissors.
FRANKLIN

By persistently remaining single a man converts himself into a permanent public temptation.
WILDE—*The Importance of Being Earnest*

(See also MATRIMONY, WOOING.)

BANK

A banker is a man who lends you an umbrella when the weather is fair, and takes it away from you when it rains.
ANONYMOUS

Banking establishments are more dangerous than standing armies.
JEFFERSON—Letter to Gerry

(See also BORROWING, BUSINESS, CREDITOR, GOLD, LENDING, MONEY.)

BARGAIN

It takes two to make a bargain.
ENGLISH PROVERB

It's a bad bargain where nobody gains.
ENGLISH PROVERB

The best of a bad bargain.
PEPYS—Diary

(See also BUSINESS, ECONOMY.)

BEAUTY

There is no cosmetic for beauty like happiness.
LADY BLESSINGTON

She walks in beauty like the night
Of cloudless climes and starry skies;
And all that's best of dark and bright
Meet in her aspect and her eyes:
Thus mellowed to that tender light
Which heaven to gaudy day denies.
BYRON—She Walks in Beauty

That which is striking and beautiful is not always good, but that which is good is always beautiful.
NINON DE L'ENCLOS

The dimple that thy chin contains
has beauty in its round,
That never has been fathomed yet by
myriad thoughts profound.
HAFIZ—Odes

Nothing is beautiful from every point of view.
HORACE—Carmina

The beautiful attracts the beautiful.
LEIGH HUNT

A thing of beauty is a joy forever.
KEATS—Endymion

Beauty is truth, truth beauty.
KEATS—Ode on a Grecian Urn

Beauty is the first present Nature gives to women, and the first it takes away.
MÉRÉ

Beauty is power; a smile is its sword.
CHARLES READE

Remember that the most beautiful things in the world are the most useless; peacocks and lilies, for instance.
RUSKIN

The saying that beauty is but skin deep is but a skin deep saying.
RUSKIN—Personal Beauty

What is really beautiful needs no adorning. We do not grind down the pearl upon a polishing stone.
SATAKA

Truth exists for the wise, beauty for the feeling heart.
SCHILLER—Don Carlos

(See also APPEARANCE, ART, FACE, NATURE, POETRY, WOMAN.)

BED

In bed we laugh, in bed we cry;
And born in bed, in bed we die;
The near approach a bed may show
Of human bliss to human woe.
Isaac De Benserade

As you make your bed you must lie in it.
English Proverb

Rise with the lark and with the lark to bed.
James Hurdis—*The Village Curate*

The bed has become a place of luxury to me! I would not exchange it for all the thrones in the world.
Napoleon

(See also REPOSE, REST, SLEEP.)

BEE

The bee is more honored than other animals, not because she labors, but because she labors for others.
St. Chrysostom

The bee that hath honey in her mouth hath a sting in her tail.
Lyly—*Euphues*

How doth the little busy bee
  Improve each shining hour,
And gather honey all the day
  From every opening flower.
Isaac Watts—*Against Idleness*

(See also NATURE.)

BEGGING

Beggars must be no choosers.
Beaumont and Fletcher—*Scornful Lady*

Set a beggar on horseback, and he will ride a gallop.
Burton—*Anatomy of Melancholy*

Better a living beggar than a buried emperor.
La Fontaine

Borrowing is not much better than begging.
Lessing—*Nathan the Wise*

(See also BORROWING, CHARITY, GIFT, HUMANITY, HUNGER, POVERTY.)

BEGINNING

Well begun is half done.
Horace

He that climbs a ladder must begin at the first round.
Scott—*Kenilworth*

It is the beginning of the end.
Talleyrand

The first step, my son, which one makes in the world, is the one on which depends the rest of our days.
Voltaire

(See also CAUSE, RESULT.)

BELIEF

Men willingly believe what they wish.
Julius Caesar

Believe only half of what you see and nothing that you hear.
Dinah Mulock Craik

No iron chain, or outward force of any kind, could ever compel the soul of man to believe or to disbelieve: it is his own indefeasible light, that judgment of his; he will reign and believe there by the grace of God alone!

CARLYLE — *Heroes and Hero Worship*

A man must not swallow more beliefs than he can digest.

HAVELOCK ELLIS—*The Dance of Life*

He that believeth not shall be damned.

MARK. XVI. 16

Nothing is so firmly believed as what we least know.

MONTAIGNE

(See also ATHEISM, DOCTRINE, FAITH, GOD, KNOWLEDGE, OPINION, RELIGION, .SUPERSTITION, TRUST.)

BELLS

The tocsin of the soul—the dinner bell.

BYRON—*Don Juan*

Those evening bells! those evening bells!
How many a tale their music tells!

MOORE—*Those Evening Bells*

Ring in the valiant man and free,
The larger heart, the kindlier hand;
Ring out the darkness of the land;
Ring in the Christ that is to be.

TENNYSON—*In Memoriam*

Ring out the old, ring in the new,
Ring, happy bells, across the snow.

TENNYSON—*In Memoriam*

Curfew must not ring tonight.

ROSA H. THORPE

(See also MUSIC, SOUND.)

BIBLE

I call the Book of Job, apart from all theories about it, one of the grandest things ever written with pen.

CARLYLE

The Bible is a window in this prison-world, through which we may look into eternity.

TIMOTHY DWIGHT

A Bible and a newspaper in every house, a good school in every district —all studied and appreciated as they merit—are the principal support of virtue, morality and civil liberty.

FRANKLIN

The inspiration of the Bible depends upon the ignorance of the gentleman who reads it.

INGERSOLL—Speech, 1881

The English Bible—a book which, if everything else in our language should perish, would alone suffice to show the whole extent of its beauty and power.

MACAULAY

The story of the whale swallowing Jonah, though a whale is large enough to do it, borders greatly on the marvelous; but it would have approached nearer to the idea of miracle if Jonah had swallowed the whale.

THOMAS PAINE—*The Age of Reason*

(See also FAITH, RELIGION, REVELATION, SCRIPTURE.)

BIGOTRY
See OPINION

BIOGRAPHY

Biography is the only true history.
CARLYLE

One anecdote of a man is worth a volume of biography.
CHANNING

Lives of great men all remind us
  We can make our lives sublime,
And, departing, leave behind us
  Footprints on the sands of time.
LONGFELLOW—*A Psalm of Life*

To be ignorant of the lives of the most celebrated men of antiquity is to continue in a state of childhood all our days.
PLUTARCH

Every great man nowadays has his disciples, and it is always Judas who writes the biography.
WILDE—*The Critic as Artist*

(See also BOOKS, FAME, HISTORY, LITERATURE.)

BIRDS

A bird in the hand is worth two in the bush.
CERVANTES—*Don Quixote*

The crack-brained bobolink courts his crazy mate,
Poised on a bulrush tipsy with his weight.
HOLMES—*Spring*

Sweet bird! thy bower is ever green,
  Thy sky is ever clear;
Thou hast no sorrow in thy song,
  No winter in thy year.
JOHN LOGAN—*To the Cuckoo*

The swallow is come!
The swallow is come!
  O, fair are the seasons, and light
Are the days that she brings,
With her dusky wings,
  And her bosom snowy white!
LONGFELLOW—*Hyperion*

Birds of a feather will flock together.
MINSHEU

O thrush, your song is passing sweet,
But never a song that you have sung
Is half so sweet as thrushes sang
When my dear love and I were young.
WILLIAM MORRIS—*Other Days*

And the Raven, never flitting,
  Still is sitting, still is sitting
On the pallid bust of Pallas
  Just above my chamber door;
And his eyes have all the seeming
  Of a demon's that is dreaming,
And the lamplight o'er him streaming
  Throws his shadow on the floor,
And my soul from out that shadow,
  That lies floating on the floor,
Shall be lifted—nevermore.
POE—*The Raven*

Art thou the bird whom Man loves best,
The pious bird with the scarlet breast,
  Our little English Robin;
The bird that comes about our doors
When autumn winds are sobbing?
WORDSWORTH—*The Redbreast Chasing the Butterfly*

(See also DOVE, LARK, NIGHTIN-GALE, SWAN.)

BIRTH

Born on Monday, fair in the face;
Born on Tuesday, full of God's grace;

Born on Wednesday, sour and sad;
Born on Thursday, merry and glad;
Born on Friday, worthily given;
Born on Saturday, work hard for your living;
Born on Sunday, you will never know want.

ANONYMOUS

Man alone at the very moment of his birth, cast naked upon the naked earth, does she abandon to cries and lamentations.

PLINY THE ELDER — *Natural History*

(See also AGE, BABYHOOD, FATHER, MOTHER, PARENT.)

BIRTHDAY

JANUARY

By her who in this month is born,
No gems save *Garnets* should be worn;
They will insure her constancy,
True friendship and fidelity.

FEBRUARY

The February born will find
Sincerity and peace of mind;
Freedom from passion and from care,
If they the *Pearl* (*also green amethyst*) will wear.

MARCH

Who in this world of ours their eyes
In March first open shall be wise;
In days of peril firm and brave,
And wear a *Bloodstone* to their grave.

APRIL

She who from April dates her years,
Diamonds should wear, lest bitter tears
For vain repentance flow; this stone,
Emblem of innocence is known.

MAY

Who first beholds the light of day
In Spring's sweet flowery month of May
And wears an *Emerald* all her life,
Shall be a loved and happy wife.

JUNE

Who comes with Summer to this earth
And owes to June her day of birth,
With ring of *Agate* on her hand,
Can health, wealth, and long life command.

JULY

The glowing *Ruby* should adorn
Those who in warm July are born,
Then will they be exempt and free
From love's doubt and anxiety.

AUGUST

Wear a *Sardonyx* or for thee
No conjugal felicity.
The August-born without this stone
'Tis said must live unloved and lone.

SEPTEMBER

A maiden born when Autumn leaves
Are rustling in September's breeze,
A *Sapphire* on her brow should bind,
'Twill cure diseases of the mind.

OCTOBER

October's child is born for woe,
And life's vicissitudes must know;
But lay an *Opal* on her breast,
And hope will lull those woes to rest.

NOVEMBER

Who first comes to this world below
With drear November's fog and snow
Should prize the *Topaz'* amber hue—
Emblem of friends and lovers true.

DECEMBER

If cold December gave you birth,
The month of snow and ice and
    mirth,
Place on your hand a *Turquoise* blue,
Success will bless whate'er you do.
ANONYMOUS

(See also BIRTH.)

BLESSING

God bless me and my son John,
Me and my wife, him and his wife,
Us four, and no more.
ANONYMOUS

Blessings never come in pairs; misfortunes never come alone.
CHINESE PROVERB

God bless us every one.
DICKENS—*Christmas Carol*

We mistake the gratuitous blessings
of heaven for the fruits of our industry.
L'ESTRANGE

BLINDNESS

In the country of the blind the one-
eyed man is king.
ERASMUS

If the blind lead the blind, both shall
fall into the ditch.
MATTHEW. XV. 14

There's none so blind as they that
won't see.
SWIFT—*Polite Conversation*

(See also DARKNESS, EYE, NIGHT.)

BLISS

Alas! by some degree of woe
    We every bliss must gain;
The heart can ne'er a transport know,
    That never feels a pain.
GEORGE LYTTLETON—*Song*

The sum of earthly bliss.
MILTON—*Paradise Lost*

Every one speaks of it,—who has
known it?
MME. NECKER

Condition, circumstance, is not the
    thing;
Bliss is the same in subject or in king.
POPE—*Essay on Man*

(See also CONTENTMENT, HAPPI-
NESS, HEART, JOY, PLEASURE.)

BLOOD

Whoso sheddeth man's blood, by man
shall his blood be shed.
GENESIS. IX. 6

Blood is thicker than water.
    Attributed to COMMODORE
    TATTNALL

The blood of the martyrs is the seed
of the church.
TERTULLIAN

The old blood is bold blood, the wide
world round.
    BYRON WEBBER—*Hands across
    the Sea*

BOASTING
See VANITY

BOATING
See SHIP

BODY

A healthy body is a guest-chamber
for the soul; a sick body is a prison.
BACON—*The Advancement of
Learning*

Your body is the temple of the Holy
Ghost.
I CORINTHIANS. VI. 19

No knowledge can be more satisfactory to a man than that of his own frame, its parts, their functions and actions.
JEFFERSON—Letter to Thomas Cooper

We are bound to our bodies like an oyster to its shell.
PLATO—*Phaedrus*

If any thing is sacred, the human body is sacred.
WHITMAN—*I Sing the Body Electric*

(See also DISEASE, HEALTH, MEDICINE, MIND, SOUL.)

BOLDNESS
See AUDACITY

BOOKS

Some books are to be tasted, others to be swallowed, and some few to be chewed and digested.
BACON—*Of Studies*

Laws die, Books never.
BULWER-LYTTON—*Richelieu*

All that Mankind has done, thought, gained or been: it is lying as in magic preservation in the pages of Books. They are the chosen possession of men.
CARLYLE — *Heroes and Hero Worship*

God be thanked for books. They are the voices of the distant and the dead, and make us heirs of the spiritual life of past ages.
CHANNING

A book is the only immortality.
RUFUS CHOATE

Beware of the man of one book.
ISAAC D'ISRAELI—*Curiosities of Literature*

Of making many books there is no end; and much study is a weariness of the flesh.
ECCLESIASTES. XII. 12

If you would understand your own age, read the works of fiction produced in it. People in disguise speak freely.
ARTHUR HELPS

My desire is . . . that mine adversary had written a book.
JOB. XXXI. 35

Everywhere I have sought rest and found it not except sitting apart in a nook with a little book.
THOMAS À KEMPIS

Except a living man there is nothing more wonderful than a book! a message to us from . . . human souls we never saw. . . . And yet these arouse us, terrify us, teach us, comfort us, open their hearts to us as brothers.
KINGSLEY

The writings of the wise are the only riches our posterity cannot squander.
LANDOR

A good book is the precious life-blood of a master-spirit, embalmed and treasured up on purpose to a life beyond life.
MILTON—*Areopagitica*

As good almost kill a man as kill a good book: who kills a man kills a reasonable creature, God's image; but he who destroys a good book kills reason itself, kills the image of God, as it were, in the eye.
MILTON—*Areopagitica*

A best-seller is the gilded tomb of a mediocre talent.
> LOGAN P. SMITH—*Afterthoughts*

The Bookshop has a thousand books,
All colors, hues, and tinges,
And every cover is a door
That turns on magic hinges.
> NANCY BYRD TURNER — *The Bookshop*

All the known world, excepting only savage nations, is governed by books.
> VOLTAIRE

Camerado, this is no book.
Who touches this, touches a man.
> WHITMAN—*So Long*

There is no such thing as a moral or an immoral book. Books are well written or badly written. That is all.
> WILDE—*The Picture of Dorian Gray*

(See also AUTHORSHIP, BIOGRAPHY, CRITICISM, EDUCATION, HISTORY, LEARNING, PEN, PLAGIARISM, PRESS, READING, STORY-TELLING, WRITING.)

BORE

A bore is one who, when you ask him "How are you?" tells you.
> ANONYMOUS

Bore: a person who talks when you wish him to listen.
> BIERCE—*The Devil's Dictionary*

Society is now one polished horde,
Formed of two mighty tribes, the *Bores* and *Bored*.
> BYRON—*Don Juan*

He says a thousand pleasant things,—
But never says "Adieu."
> J. G. SAXE—*My Familiar*

(See also MANNERS, STUPIDITY.)

BORROWING

Debt is a bottomless sea.
> CARLYLE

Borrowing from Peter to pay Paul.
> CICERO

The borrower is servant to the lender.
> PROVERBS. XXII. 7

Neither a borrower nor a lender be:
For loan oft loses both itself and friend,
And borrowing dulls the edge of husbandry.
> SHAKESPEARE—*Hamlet*. Act I. Sc. 3

Who goeth a borrowing
Goeth a sorrowing.
> TUSSER

(See also BEGGING, CREDITOR, DEBT, LENDING, PLAGIARISM.)

BOSTON

If you hear an owl hoot: "To whom" instead of "To who," you can make up your mind he was born and educated in Boston.
> ANONYMOUS

And this is good old Boston,
The home of the bean and the cod,
Where the Lowells talk to the Cabots,
And the Cabots talk only to God.
> J. C. BOSSIDY—*On the Aristocracy of Harvard*

Then here's to the City of Boston,
The town of the cries and the groans,
Where the Cabots can't see the Kabotschniks,
And the Lowells won't speak to the Cohns.
> FRANKLIN P. ADAMS—Revised

BOY

One boy is more trouble than a dozen girls.
ENGLISH PROVERB

Boys will be boys.
ENGLISH PROVERB

A boy is, of all wild beasts, the most difficult to manage.
PLATO

(See also CHILDHOOD, MAN, YOUTH.)

BRAVERY

How sleep the brave, who sink to rest,
By all their country's wishes blest!
WILLIAM COLLINS

Bravery is a cheap and vulgar quality, of which the brightest instances are frequently found in the lowest savages.
CHATFIELD

None but the brave deserves the fair.
DRYDEN

Many brave men lived before Agamemnon; but, all unwept and unknown, are lost in the distant night, since they are without a divine poet (to chronicle their deeds).
HORACE—*Odes*

True bravery is shown by performing without witness what one might be capable of doing before all the world.
LA ROCHEFOUCAULD

Physical bravery is an animal instinct; moral bravery is a much higher and truer courage.
WENDELL PHILLIPS

(See also AUDACITY, COURAGE, DARING, HERO, NAVY, SOLDIER, VALOR, WAR.)

BREAD

Man doth not live by bread only.
DEUTERONOMY. VIII. 4

Cast thy bread upon the waters: for thou shalt find it after many days.
ECCLESIASTES. XI. 1

Bread is the staff of life.
ENGLISH SAYING

I know on which side my bread is buttered.
HEYWOOD—*Proverbs*

Better is half a loaf than no bread.
HEYWOOD—*Proverbs*

Oh, God! that bread should be so dear,
And flesh and blood so cheap!
HOOD—*The Song of the Shirt*

Jesus said unto them, I am the bread of life: he that cometh to me shall never hunger; and he that believeth on me shall never thirst.
JOHN. VI. 35

Give us this day our daily bread.
MATTHEW. VI. 11

What man is there of you, whom if his son ask bread, will he give him a stone?
MATTHEW. VII. 9

I won't quarrel with my bread and butter.
SWIFT—*Polite Conversation*

(See also CHARITY, EATING, FESTIVITIES, SPIRIT.)

BREVITY

Let thy speech be short, comprehending much in few words.
ECCLESIASTICUS. XXXII. 8

The more you say, the less people remember. The fewer the words, the greater the profit.
FÉNELON

The fewer words, the better prayer.
LUTHER

The wisdom of nations lies in their proverbs, which are brief and pithy.
WILLIAM PENN

God helps the brave.
SCHILLER—*Wilhelm Tell*

Brevity is the soul of wit.
SHAKESPEARE—*Hamlet.* Act II. Sc. 2

(See also ORATORY, TALK, WORD.)

BRIBERY

The universe would not be rich enough to buy the vote of an honest man.
ST. GREGORY

Every man has his price.
SIR ROBERT WALPOLE

Few men have virtue to withstand the highest bidder.
WASHINGTON—*Moral Maxims*

(See CORRUPTION, CRIME, GOLD, PARTY, POLITICS, STATESMANSHIP.)

BRITAIN
See ENGLAND

BROOK
See NATURE

BROTHERHOOD

While there is a lower class I am in it. While there is a criminal class I am of it. While there is a soul in prison I am not free.
EUGENE V. DEBS—*Labor and Freedom*

Am I my brother's keeper?
GENESIS. IV. 9

A new commandment I give unto you, That ye love one another; as I have loved you, that ye also love one another.
JOHN. XIII. 34

The crest and crowning of all good, Life's final star, is Brotherhood.
EDWIN MARKHAM—*Brotherhood*

When man to man shall be a friend and brother.
GERALD MASSEY

(See also ASSOCIATE, FRIEND, FRIENDSHIP, GOLDEN RULE, HUMANITY, MAN.)

BUILDING

Old houses mended
Cost little less than new before they're ended.
COLLEY CIBBER

Never build after you are five and forty; have five years' income in hand before you lay a brick; and always calculate the expense at double the estimate.
KETT

(See also ARCHITECTURE, CITY.)

BUSINESS

Nation of shopkeepers.
    Attributed to SAMUEL ADAMS

Anybody can cut prices, but it takes brain to produce a better article.
    P. D. ARMOUR

The fundamental principles which govern the handling of postage stamps and of millions of dollars are exactly the same. They are the common law of business, and the whole practice of commerce is founded on them. They are so simple that a fool can't learn them; so hard that a lazy man won't.
    P. D. ARMOUR

Business is religion, and religion is business. The man who does not make a business of his religion has a religious life of no force, and the man who does not make a religion of his business has a business life of no character.
    MALTBIE BABCOCK

The nature of business is swindling.
    AUGUST BEBEL

There are two times in a man's life when he should not speculate: when he can't afford it, and when he can.
    SAMUEL L. CLEMENS (MARK TWAIN)

They (corporations) cannot commit treason, nor be outlawed, nor excommunicated, for they have no souls.
    COKE—The Case of Sutton's Hospital

The business of America is business.
    CALVIN COOLIDGE

Business is like oil. It won't mix with anything but business.
    J. GRAHAM

Whose merchants are princes.
    ISAIAH. XXII. 8

A man's success in business today turns upon his power of getting people to believe he has something that they want.
    GERALD STANLEY LEE—Crowds

Wist ye not that I must be about my Father's business?
    LUKE. II. 49

We demand that big business give people a square deal; in return we must insist that when anyone engaged in big business honestly endeavors to do right, he shall himself be given a square deal.
    THEODORE ROOSEVELT

That which is everybody's business, is nobody's business.
    IZAAK WALTON—Compleat Angler

Call on a business man at business times only, and on business, transact your business and go about your business, in order to give him time to finish his business.
    WELLINGTON

The way to stop financial "joy-riding" is to arrest the chauffeur, not the automobile.
    WOODROW WILSON

It is not the crook in modern business that we fear, but the honest man who does not know what he is doing.
    OWEN D. YOUNG

(See also CAPITAL AND LABOR, COMMERCE, LABOR, OCCUPATION, WORK.)

BUTTERFLY
See NATURE

CALAMITY

A calamity that affects everyone is only half a calamity.
ITALIAN PROVERB

When any calamity has been suffered the first thing to be remembered is, how much has been escaped.
SAMUEL JOHNSON

Calamity is the test of integrity.
RICHARDSON

(See also ACCIDENT, GRIEF, MISERY, MISFORTUNE, SUFFERING, TROUBLE.)

CALUMNY

Calumniate, calumniate; there will always be something which sticks.
BEAUMARCHAIS—*Barber of Seville*

One triumphs over calumny only by disdaining it.
MME. DE MAINTENON

There are calumnies against which even innocence loses courage.
NAPOLEON

Calumny is a vice of curious constitution; trying to kill it keeps it alive; leave it to itself and it will die a natural death.
THOMAS PAINE

Cutting honest throats by whispers.
SCOTT

To persevere in one's duty and to be silent is the best answer to calumny.
WASHINGTON

(See also GOSSIP, REPUTATION, SCANDAL, SLANDER.)

CANDOR
See TRUTH

CANT
See HYPOCRISY

CAPITAL

Capital is that part of wealth which is devoted to obtaining further wealth.
ALFRED MARSHALL

What capital does for production is to afford the shelter, protection, tools, and materials which the work requires, and to feed and otherwise maintain the laborers during the process. Whatever things are destined for this use—destined to supply productive labour with these various prerequisites—are Capital.
JOHN STUART MILL—*The Principles of Political Economy*

Capital is that part of the wealth of a country which is employed in production, and consists of food, clothing, tools, raw materials, machinery, etc., necessary to give effect to labour.
DAVID RICARDO—*Principles of Political Economy and Taxation*

CAPITAL AND LABOR

Capital is a result of labor, and is used by labor to assist it in further production. Labor is the active and initial force, and labor is therefore the employer of capital.
HENRY GEORGE—*Progress and Poverty*

Labor is prior to, and independent of, capital. Capital is only the fruit of labor, and could never have existed if labor had not first existed. Labor is the superior of capital, and deserves much the higher consideration.

LINCOLN—*Message to Congress, 1861*

Each needs the other: capital cannot do without labor, nor labor without capital.

POPE LEO XIII

Capital is dead labor that, vampire-like, lives only by sucking living labor, and lives the more, the more labor it sucks.

KARL MARX—*Capital*

Capital is condensed labor. It is nothing until labor takes hold of it. The living laborer sets free the condensed labor and makes it assume some form of utility or beauty. Capital and labor are one, and they will draw nearer to each other as the world advances in intellect and goodness.

DAVID SWING

(See BUSINESS, LABOR, OCCUPA-TION, WORK.)

CARDS
See GAMBLING

CARE

To carry care to bed is to sleep with a pack on your back.

HALIBURTON

The night shall be filled with music
  And the cares that infest the day
Shall fold their tents like the Arabs,
  And as silently steal away.

LONGFELLOW — *The Day Is Done*

Old Care has a mortgage on every estate,
And that's what you pay for the wealth that you get.

J. G. SAXE—*Gifts of the Gods*

Providence has given us hope and sleep as a compensation for the many cares of life.

VOLTAIRE

Care to our coffin adds a nail, no doubt;
And every Grin, so merry, draws one out.

JOHN WOLCOT—*Expostulatory Odes*

(See also CAUTION, CONDUCT, DIS-CRETION, ECONOMY, PRUDENCE.)

CARELESSNESS

Carelessness does more harm than a want of knowledge.

FRANKLIN

For want of a nail the shoe was lost; for want of a shoe the horse was lost; and for want of a horse the rider was lost; being overtaken and slain by the enemy, all for want of care about a horseshoe nail.

FRANKLIN—*Poor Richard's Almanac*

The wife of a careless man is almost a widow.

HUNGARIAN PROVERB

(See also STUPIDITY.)

CAT

Ding, dong, bell,
Pussy's in the well;
Who put her in?

Little Tommy Green.
Who pulled her out?
Little Johnny Stout.
ANONYMOUS

When the cat's away the mice will play.
ENGLISH PROVERB

It has been the providence of nature to give this creature nine lives instead of one.
PILPAY—*Fable*

There is not room to swing a cat.
SMOLLETT—*Humphrey Clinker*

A cat may look at a king.
JOHN HEYWOOD—*Proverbs*

(See also ANIMALS.)

CAUSE

There is one basic cause of all effects.
GIORDANO BRUNO

In war events of importance are the result of trivial causes.
JULIUS CAESAR

Christian Science explains all cause and effect as mental, not physical.
MARY BAKER EDDY—*Science and Health*

God befriend us, as our cause is just!
SHAKESPEARE—*Henry IV*. Pt. I. Act V. Sc. 1

Everything in nature is a cause from which there flows some effect.
SPINOZA

The first springs of great events, like those of great rivers, are often mean and little.
SWIFT

(See also BEGINNING, LOGIC, REASON.)

CAUTION

If your lips would keep from slips
Five things observe with care:
To whom you speak, of whom you speak,
And how, and when, and where.
ANONYMOUS

Hasten slowly.
AUGUSTUS CAESAR

A wise man does not trust all his eggs to one basket.
CERVANTES—*Don Quixote*

When you go to buy use your eyes, not your ears.
CZECH PROVERB

Be slow of tongue and quick of eye.
CERVANTES

The cautious seldom err.
CONFUCIUS

Among mortals second thoughts are wisest.
EURIPIDES

Little boats should keep near shore.
FRANKLIN

Caution is the eldest child of wisdom.
VICTOR HUGO

Drink nothing without seeing it, sign nothing without reading it.
SPANISH PROVERB

It is a good thing to learn caution by the misfortunes of others.
SYRUS

(See also CARE, PRUDENCE.)

CELIBACY
See BACHELOR

CENSORSHIP

Every burned book enlightens the world.
EMERSON—*Compensation*

I am mortified to be told that, in the United States of America, the sale of a book can become a subject of inquiry, and of criminal inquiry too.
JEFFERSON

If there had been a censorship of the press in Rome we should have had today neither Horace nor Juvenal, nor the philosophical writings of Cicero.
VOLTAIRE

(See also CRITICISM, DICTATOR, FREEDOM, LAW, PRESS.)

CENSURE
See CRITICISM

CHANCE

Chance happens to all, but to turn chance to account is the gift of few.
BULWER-LYTTON

Although men flatter themselves with their great actions, they are not so often the result of a great design as of chance.
LA ROCHEFOUCAULD

Chance never helps those who do not help themselves.
SOPHOCLES

(See also CIRCUMSTANCE, OPPORTUNITY.)

CHANGE

Never swap horses crossing a stream.
AMERICAN PROVERB

Earth changes, but thy soul and God stand sure.
BROWNING—*Rabbi Ben Ezra*

I am not now
That which I have been.
BYRON—*Childe Harold*

There is a certain relief in change, even though it be from bad to worse; as I have found in travelling in a stagecoach, that it is often a comfort to shift one's position and be bruised in a new place.
IRVING—*Tales of a Traveller*

Can the Ethiopian change his skin, or the leopard his spots?
JEREMIAH. XIII. 23

The world goes up and the world goes down,
  And the sunshine follows the rain;
And yesterday's sneer and yesterday's frown
  Can never come over again.
KINGSLEY—*Songs*

All things must change
To something new, to something strange.
LONGFELLOW

Revolutions are not made; they come.
WENDELL PHILLIPS

Life may change, but it may fly not;
Hope may vanish, but can die not;
Truth be veiled, but still it burneth;
Love repulsed,—but it returneth.
SHELLEY—*Hellas*

The old order changeth, yielding place to new.
TENNYSON—*The Passing of Arthur*

Everything changes but change.
ZANGWILL

(See also CHOICE, EVOLUTION, VARIETY.)

CHAOS
See RUIN

CHARACTER

When wealth is lost, nothing is lost;
When health is lost, something is lost;
When character is lost, all is lost!
ANONYMOUS

It is in general more profitable to reckon up our defects than to boast of our attainments.
CARLYLE—*Signs of the Times*

Every one is as God made him, and often a great deal worse.
CERVANTES—*Don Quixote*

The great hope of society is individual character.
CHANNING

You must look into people as well as at them.
CHESTERFIELD

Character is not cut in marble; it is not something solid and unalterable. It is something living and changing, and may become diseased as our bodies do.
GEORGE ELIOT

Human improvement is from within outward.
FROUDE

Talent is nurtured in solitude; character is formed in the stormy billows of the world.
GOETHE—*Torquato Tasso*

O Douglas, O Douglas!
Tender and true.
SIR RICHARD HOLLAND—*The Duke of the Howlat*

In death a hero, as in life a friend!
HOMER—*Iliad*

Gentle of speech, beneficent of mind.
HOMER—*Odyssey*

Wise to resolve, and patient to perform.
HOMER—*Odyssey*

Only what we have wrought into our character during life can we take away with us.
HUMBOLDT

The heart to conceive, the understanding to direct, or the hand to execute.
JUNIUS—*City Address and the King's Answer*

Every man has three characters—that which he exhibits, that which he has, and that which he thinks he has.
ALPHONSE KARR

E'en as he trod that day to God, so walked he from his birth,
In simpleness and gentleness and honor and clean mirth.
KIPLING—*Barrack Room Ballads*

Oh, East is East, and West is West, and never the twain shall meet
Till earth and sky stand presently at God's great judgment seat;
But there is neither East nor West, border nor breed nor birth

When two strong men stand face to
    face, tho' they come from the
    ends of the earth!
        KIPLING—*Ballad of East and
        West*

In this world a man must either be
anvil or hammer.
        LONGFELLOW—*Hyperion*

Not in the clamor of the crowded
    street,
Not in the shouts and plaudits of
    the throng,
But in ourselves, are triumph and
    defeat.
        LONGFELLOW—*The Poets*

It is by presence of mind in untried
emergencies that the native metal
of a man is tested.
        LOWELL—*My Study Windows*

Who knows nothing base,
Fears nothing known.
        OWEN MEREDITH—*A Great
        Man*

In men whom men condemn as ill
I find so much of goodness still,
In men whom men pronounce divine
I find so much of sin and blot
I do not dare to draw a line
Between the two, where God has not.
        JOAQUIN MILLER—*Byron*

His heart as far from fraud as
heaven from earth.
        SHAKESPEARE—*Two Gentlemen
        of Verona*. Act II. Sc. 7

The true greatness of nations is in
those qualities which constitute the
greatness of the individual.
        CHARLES SUMNER

It is in men as in soils where sometimes there is a vein of gold which
the owner knows not of.
        SWIFT

Fame is what you have taken,
    Character's what you give;
When to this truth you waken,
    Then you begin to live.
        BAYARD TAYLOR—*Improvisa-
        tions*

(See also ABILITY, DECENCY, DIG-
NITY, FAME, INFLUENCE, NOBILITY,
QUALITY, REPUTATION, WORTH.)

CHARITY

It is more blessed to give than to
receive.
        ACTS. XX. 35

Charity is the perfection and ornament of religion.
        ADDISON

Every charitable act is a stepping
stone toward heaven.
        HENRY WARD BEECHER

My poor are my best patients. God
pays for them.
        BOERHAAVE

Though I have all faith, so that I
could remove mountains, and have
not charity, I am nothing.
        I CORINTHIANS. XIII. 2

Charity suffereth long and is kind;
charity envieth not; charity vaunt-
eth not itself, is not puffed up.
        I CORINTHIANS. XIII. 4

And now abideth faith, hope, charity, these three; but the greatest of
these is charity.
        I CORINTHIANS. XIII. 13

Better to expose ourselves to ingratitude than fail in assisting the unfortunate.

Du Coeur

You are indeed charitable when you give, and while giving, turn your face away so that you may not see the shyness of the receiver.

Kahlil Gibran—*Sand and Foam*

What we frankly give, forever is our own.

George Granville

As the purse is emptied the heart is filled.

Victor Hugo

That charity which longs to publish itself, ceases to be charity.

Hutton

He who waits to do a great deal of good at once, will never do anything.

Samuel Johnson

Prayer carries us half way to God, fasting brings us to the door of His palace and alms-giving procures us admission.

The Koran

I was an hungred, and ye gave me meat; I was thirsty, and ye gave me drink: I was a stranger, and ye took me in.

Matthew. XXV. 35

Organized charity, scrimped and iced,
In the name of a cautious, statistical Christ.

John Boyle O'Reilly—*In Bohemia*

Charity shall cover the multitude of sins.

I Peter. IV. 8

Our charity begins at home,
And mostly ends where it begins.

Horace Smith—*Horace in London*

Giving is true having.

Spurgeon

Defer not charities till death. He who does so is rather liberal of another man's substance than his own.

Stretch

(See also BEGGING, FRIENDSHIP, GIFT, HUMANITY, KINDNESS, LIBERALITY, MERCY, PHILANTHROPY.)

CHASTITY
See INNOCENCE

CHEERFULNESS

I exhort you to be of good cheer.

Acts. XXVII. 22

He who sings frightens away his ills.

Cervantes

The creed of the true saint is to make the best of life, and make the most of it.

Chapin

A cheerful look makes a dish a feast.

Herbert—*Jacula Prudentum*

Cheer up, the worst is yet to come.

Philander Johnson

Let us be of good cheer, remembering that the misfortunes hardest to bear are those which never happen.

Lowell

A good laugh is sunshine in a house.
THACKERAY

(See CONTENTMENT, GOOD-HUMOR,
HAPPINESS, JOY, MERRIMENT,
PLEASURE.)

CHILDHOOD

Do ye hear the children weeping, O
my brothers?
E. B. BROWNING—*The Cry of
the Children*

A little curly-headed, good-for-noth-
ing,
And mischief-making monkey from
his birth.
BYRON—*Don Juan*

When I was a child, I spake as a
child, I understood as a child, I
thought as a child; but when I became a man, I put away childish
things.
I CORINTHIANS. XIII. 11

Better to be driven out from among
men than to be disliked of children.
R. H. DANA—*The Idle Man*

Children should be seen and not
heard.
ENGLISH PROVERB

Spare the rod and spoil the child.
ENGLISH PROVERB

Wynken, Blynken and Nod one
night
Sailed off in a wooden shoe—
Sailed on a river of crystal light
Into a sea of dew.
EUGENE FIELD—*Wynken,
Blynken and Nod*

Teach your child to hold his tongue,
He'll learn fast enough to speak.
FRANKLIN—*Poor Richard's
Maxims*

I think that saving a little child
And bringing him to his own,
Is a derned sight better business
Than loafing around the throne.
JOHN HAY—*Little Breeches*

It is a wise child that knows his
own father.
HOMER—*Odyssey*

Children have neither past nor future; and that which seldom happens to us, they rejoice in the present.
LA BRUYÈRE

There was a little girl,
And she had a little curl,
Right in the middle of her fore-
head;
When she was good she was very,
very good,
When she was bad she was horrid.
LONGFELLOW

Suffer the little children to come
unto me, and forbid them not; for
of such is the kingdom of God.
MARK. X. 14

Rachel weeping for her children,
and would not be comforted, because
they are not.
MATTHEW. II. 18

The childhood shows the man,
As morning shows the day.
MILTON—*Paradise Regained*

The children in Holland take pleasure in making
What the children in England take pleasure in breaking.
OLD NURSERY RHYME

The wildest colts make the best horses.
PLUTARCH—*Life of Themistocles*

A wise son maketh a glad father.
PROVERBS. X. 1

Train up a child in the way he should go; and when he is old he will not depart from it.
PROVERBS. XXII. 6

It is a wise father that knows his own child.
SHAKESPEARE—*Merchant of Venice*. Act II. Sc. 2

It is very nice to think
  The world is full of meat and drink
With little children saying grace
  In every Christian kind of place.
STEVENSON—*Child's Garden of Verses*

The best way to make children good is to make them happy.
WILDE

How dear to this heart are the scenes of my childhood,
When fond recollection presents them to view.
SAMUEL WOODWORTH—*The Old Oaken Bucket*

The child is father of the man.
WORDSWORTH—*My Heart Leaps Up*

(See also BABYHOOD, BOY, DAUGHTER, MOTHER, YOUTH.)

CHOICE

I do not choose to run for President in 1928.
CALVIN COOLIDGE

Betwixt the devil and the deep sea.
ERASMUS—*Adagia*

For many are called, but few are chosen.
MATTHEW. XXII. 14

There's small choice in rotten apples.
SHAKESPEARE—*Taming of the Shrew*. Act I. Sc. 1

When to elect there is but one,
  'Tis Hobson's Choice; take that or none.
THOMAS WARD—*England's Reformation*

(See also CHANGE, OPPORTUNITY, TASTE, VARIETY.)

CHRIST

Star unto star speaks light, and world to world
Repeats the passage of the universe
To God; the name of Christ—the one great word
Well worth all languages in earth or heaven.
BAILEY

In every pang that rends the heart
The Man of Sorrows had a part.
MICHAEL BRUCE—*Gospel Sonnets*

The sages and heroes of history are receding from us, and history contracts the record of their deeds into a narrower and narrower page. But

time has no power over the name and deeds and words of Jesus Christ.
CHANNING

As to Jesus of Nazareth, my opinion of whom you particularly desire, I think the system of morals and His religion, as He left them to us, is the best the world ever saw, or is likely to see.
FRANKLIN

Jesus Christ the same yesterday, and today, and forever.
HEBREWS. XIII. 8

Jesus . . . was made a little lower than the angels.
HEBREWS. II. 9

Thou hast conquered, O Galilean.
Attributed to JULIAN THE APOSTATE

All His glory and beauty come from within, and there He delights to dwell, His visits there are frequent, His conversation sweet, His comforts refreshing; and His peace passing all understanding.
THOMAS À KEMPIS—*Imitation of Christ*

The foxes have holes, and the birds of the air have nests; but the Son of man hath not where to lay his head.
MATTHEW. VIII. 20

Alexander, Caesar, Charlemagne and I myself have founded empires; but upon what do these creations of our genius depend? Upon force. Jesus alone founded His empire upon love; and to this very day millions would die for Him.
NAPOLEON

If the life and death of Socrates were those of a sage, the life and death of Jesus were those of a God.
ROUSSEAU

(See also CHRISTIANITY, CHRISTMAS, DOCTRINE, EASTER, GOD, RESURRECTION, SIN.)

CHRISTIAN

Onward, Christian soldiers,
Marching as to war,
With the cross of Jesus
Going on before.
BARING-GOULD

It is more to the honor of a Christian soldier, by faith to overcome the world, than by a monastical vow to retreat from it; and more for the honor of Christ, to serve Him in a city than to serve Him in a cell.
MATTHEW HENRY

A Christian is God Almighty's gentleman.
J. C. and A. W. HARE—
Guesses at Truth

Servant of God, well done! Well hast thou fought
The better fight.
MILTON—*Paradise Lost*

To be like Christ is to be a Christian.
WILLIAM PENN—Last words

Whatever makes men good Christians, makes them good citizens.
DANIEL WEBSTER—Speech at Plymouth

(See also CHRIST, CHRISTIANITY, CHURCH, MARTYR.)

CHRISTIANITY

Christianity is completed Judaism, or it is nothing.
DISRAELI

His Christianity was muscular.
DISRAELI—*Endymion*

Christianity ruined emperors, but saved peoples.
ALFRED DE MUSSET

Christianity is a battle, not a dream.
WENDELL PHILLIPS

I desire no other evidence of the truth to Christianity than the Lord's Prayer.
MME. DE STAËL

Christianity, with its doctrine of humility, of forgiveness, of love, is incompatible with the state, with its haughtiness, its violence, its punishment, its wars.
TOLSTOY

(See also BIBLE, CHRIST, DOCTRINE, FAITH, RELIGION, REPENTANCE, RESURRECTION, SCRIPTURE.)

CHRISTMAS

O little town of Bethlehem,
  How still we see thee lie!
Above thy deep and dreamless sleep
  The silent stars go by.
PHILLIPS BROOKS—*O Little Town of Bethlehem*

No Santa Claus! Thank God, he lives, and he lives forever. A thousand years from now, Virginia, nay, ten times ten thousand years from now, he will continue to make glad the heart of childhood.
FRANCIS P. CHURCH—*Is There a Santa Claus?*

God rest ye, little children; let nothing you affright,
For Jesus Christ, your Saviour, was born this happy night;
Along the hills of Galilee the white flocks sleeping lay,
When Christ, the Child of Nazareth, was born on Christmas day.
DINAH MULOCK CRAIK—*Christmas Carol*

I heard the bells on Christmas Day
Their old, familiar carols play,
  And wild and sweet
  The words repeat
Of peace on earth, good-will to men!
LONGFELLOW—*Christmas Bells*

For unto you is born this day in the city of David a Saviour, which is Christ the Lord.
LUKE. II. 11

Let's dance and sing and make good cheer,
For Christmas comes but once a year.
G. MACFARREN (Before 1580)

Holy night, peaceful night,
  Wondrous Star, lend thy light!
With the angels let us sing
  Alleluia to our King,
  Jesus the Saviour is here.
Translated from JOSEPH MOHR, 1818

'Twas the night before Christmas, when all through the house
Not a creature was stirring—not even a mouse:
The stockings were hung by the chimney with care,
In hopes that St. Nicholas soon would be there.
CLEMENT C. MOORE—*A Visit from St. Nicholas*

At Christmas play, and make good
   cheer,
For Christmas comes but once a
   year.
   TUSSER

Hark the herald angels sing,
"Glory to the new-born king."
Peace on earth, and mercy mild,
God and sinners reconciled!
   CHARLES WESLEY—*Christmas
   Hymn*

Blow, bugles of battle, the marches
   of peace;
East, west, north, and south let the
   long quarrel cease;
Sing the song of great joy that the
   angels began,
Sing the glory of God and of good-
   will to man!
   WHITTIER—*Christmas Carmen*

(See also CHRIST, CHRISTIANITY.)

CHURCH

The nearer the church, the further
from God.
   BISHOP ANDREWES—Sermon on
   the Nativity before James I

Oh! St. Patrick was a gentleman
   Who came of decent people;
He built a church in Dublin town,
   And on it put a steeple.
   HENRY BENNETT

Whenever God erects a house of
   prayer
The devil always builds a chapel
   there;
And 'twill be found, upon examina-
   tion,
The latter has the largest congrega-
   tion.
   DANIEL DEFOE—*True Born
   Englishman*

Division has done more to hide
Christ from the view of men than
all the infidelity that has ever been
spoken.
   GEORGE MACDONALD

It was founded upon a rock.
   MATTHEW. VII. 25

I never weary of great churches. It
is my favourite kind of mountain
scenery. Mankind was never so hap-
pily inspired as when it made a
cathedral.
   STEVENSON—*Inland Voyage*

See the Gospel Church secure,
   And founded on a Rock!
All her promises are sure;
   Her bulwarks who can shock?
Count her every precious shrine;
   Tell, to after-ages tell,
Fortified by power divine,
   The Church can never fail.
   CHARLES WESLEY

The itch of disputing is the scab of
the churches.
   SIR HENRY WOTTON—*A Panegyric to King Charles*

(See also BELLS, CHRIST, CHRIS-
TIANITY, CLERGYMAN, RELIGION,
WORSHIP.)

CIRCUMSTANCE

The long arm of coincidence.
   HADDON CHAMBERS—*Captain
   Swift*

Man is not the creature of circumstances,
Circumstances are the creatures of
   men.
   DISRAELI—*Vivian Grey*

Circumstances alter cases.
HALIBURTON—*The Old Judge*

The happy combination of fortuitous circumstances.
SCOTT

The circumstances of others seem good to us, while ours seem good to others.
SYRUS—*Maxims*

(See also CHANCE, DESTINY, EVENTS, FATE, FORTUNE, LIFE, OPPORTUNITY.)

CITIZEN

I am a citizen, not of Athens or Greece, but of the world.
Attributed to SOCRATES

Paul said, I am a man which am a Jew of Tarsus, a city in Cilicia, a citizen of no mean city.
ACTS. XXI. 39

(See also DEMOCRACY, GOVERNMENT, LIBERTY, PEOPLE.)

CITY

This poor little one-horse town.
S. L. CLEMENS (MARK TWAIN) —*The Undertaker's Story*

If you would know and not be known, live in a city.
COLTON

God made the country, and man made the town.
COWPER—*The Task*

Cities force growth, and make men talkative and entertaining, but they make them artificial.
EMERSON

I always seem to suffer some loss of faith on entering cities.
EMERSON

In the busy haunts of men.
FELICIA D. HEMANS—*Tale of the Secret Tribunal*

Far from gay cities, and the ways of men.
HOMER—*Odyssey*

Ye are the light of the world. A city that is set on a hill cannot be hid.
MATTHEW. V. 14

The people are the city.
SHAKESPEARE—*Coriolanus* Act III. Sc. 1

It is men who make a city, not walls or ships.
THUCYDIDES

(See also BOSTON, LONDON, NEW YORK CITY, ROME.)

CIVILIZATION

Mankind's struggle upwards, in which millions are trampled to death, that thousands may mount on their bodies.
CLARA L. BALFOUR

We think our civilization near its meridian, but we are yet only at the cock-crowing and the morning star.
EMERSON—*Politics*

A sufficient measure of civilization is the influence of good women.
EMERSON

The path of civilization is paved with tin cans.
ELBERT HUBBARD

Nations, like individuals, live and die; but civilization cannot die.
MAZZINI

Civilization, or that which is so called, has operated two ways to make one part of society more affluent and the other part more wretched than would have been the lot of either in a natural state.
THOMAS PAINE

(See also PROGRESS, WORLD.)

CLEANLINESS

All will come out in the washing.
CERVANTES—*Don Quixote*

He that toucheth pitch shall be defiled therewith.
ECCLESIASTICUS. XIII. I

Wash you, make you clean.
ISAIAH. I. 16

God loveth the clean.
THE KORAN

If dirt was trumps, what hands you would hold!
LAMB—*Lamb's Suppers*

Certainly this is a duty, not a sin. "Cleanliness is indeed next to godliness."
JOHN WESLEY

(See also APPEARANCE, HEALTH, PURITY.)

CLERGYMAN

Politics and the pulpit are terms that have little agreement.
BURKE

If you would lift me you must be on a higher ground.
EMERSON

As a career, the business of an orthodox preacher is about as successful as that of a celluloid dog chasing an asbestos cat through Hell.
ELBERT HUBBARD

The life of a conscientious clergyman is not easy. I have always considered a clergyman as the father of a larger family than he is able to maintain. I would rather have chancery suits upon my hands than the cure of souls.
SAMUEL JOHNSON

I do not envy a clergyman's life as an easy life, nor do I envy the clergyman who makes it an easy life.
SAMUEL JOHNSON

The defects of a preacher are soon spied.
LUTHER

(See also CHURCH, PREACHING.)

CLEVERNESS

Cleverness is serviceable for everything, sufficient for nothing.
AMIEL—*Journal*

Cleverness is not wisdom.
EURIPIDES

Be good, sweet maid, and let who will be clever.
KINGSLEY—*A Farewell*

(See also ABILITY, CHARACTER, GENIUS, TALENT, WIT.)

CLOTHES

The woman shall not wear that
which pertaineth unto a man,
neither shall a man put on a woman's
garment; for all that do so are
abomination unto the Lord thy God.
DEUTERONOMY. XXII. 5

Good clothes open all doors.
THOMAS FULLER—*Gnomologia*

Whenas in silks my Julia goes,
Then, then, methinks, how sweetly
flows
The liquefaction of her clothes!
HERRICK—*Hesperides*

The clothes make the man.
LATIN PROVERB

Costly thy habit as thy purse can
buy,
But not express'd in fancy; rich, not
gaudy;
For the apparel oft proclaims the
man.
SHAKESPEARE—*Hamlet*. Act I.
Sc. 3

The soul of this man is his clothes.
SHAKESPEARE—*All's Well that
Ends Well*. Act II. Sc. 5

She wears her clothes as if they
were thrown on her with a pitch-
fork.
SWIFT—*Polite Conversation*

Do not conceive that fine clothes
make fine men, any more than fine
feathers make fine birds. A plain,
genteel dress is more admired, ob-
tains more credit in the eyes of the
judicious and sensible.
WASHINGTON—Letter, 1783

(See also APPEARANCE, DRESS,
FASHION, JEWEL, SHOEMAKING,
VANITY.)

CLOUDS
See STORM

COLOR

Colors speak all languages.
ADDISON—*The Spectator*

Blue is true,
Yellow's jealous,
Green's forsaken,
Red's brazen,
White is love,
And black is death.
ANONYMOUS

The purest and most thoughtful
minds are those which love color the
most.
RUSKIN—*The Stones of Venice*

(See also ART, BEAUTY, PAINTING,
STYLE, TASTE.)

COMFORT
See CONTENTMENT

COMMERCE

More pernicious nonsense was never
devised by man than treaties of
commerce.
DISRAELI

Commerce links all mankind in one
common brotherhood of mutual dependence and interests.
JAMES A. GARFIELD

Commerce is the equalizer of the
wealth of nations.
GLADSTONE

Whatever has a tendency to promote the civil intercourse of nations
by an exchange of benefits is a subject as worthy of philosophy as of
politics.
THOMAS PAINE

(See also BUSINESS.)

COMMON SENSE

Common sense is very uncommon.
HORACE GREELEY

Common sense is in spite of, not the result of, education.
VICTOR HUGO

Common sense is instinct, and enough of it is genius.
H. W. SHAW

(See also INTELLECT, JUDGMENT.)

COMMUNISM

From each according to his ability, to each according to his needs.
Attributed to LOUIS BLANC

What is a Communist? One who hath yearnings
For equal division of unequal earnings.
Idler or bungler, or both, he is willing,
To fork out his copper and pocket your shilling.
EBENEZER ELLIOTT

The Communist is a Socialist in a violent hurry.
G. W. GOUGH—*The Economic Consequences of Socialism*

The theory of Communism may be summed up in one sentence: Abolish all private property.
KARL MARX AND FRIEDRICH ENGELS—*The Communist Manifesto*

Communism is the theory which teaches that the labor and the income of society should be distributed equally among all its members by some constituted authority.
SIR R. H. INGLIS PALGRAVE

Communism is the exploitation of the strong by the weak. In communism, inequality springs from placing mediocrity on a level with excellence.
PROUDHON

As soon as classes have been abolished, and the dictatorship of the proletariat has been done away with, the (Communist) party will have fulfilled its mission and can be allowed to disappear.
JOSEPH STALIN—Speech, 1924

(See also CAPITAL AND LABOR, EQUALITY, LABOR.)

COMPANIONSHIP

Tell me thy company and I will tell thee what thou art.
CERVANTES—*Don Quixote*

We have been born to associate with our fellow-men, and to join in community with the human race.
CICERO

Two's a company, three's a crowd.
ENGLISH PROVERB

We are in the same boat.
POPE CLEMENT I—To the Church of Corinth

The right hands of fellowship.
GALATIANS. II. 9

No man can be provident of his time who is not prudent in the choice of his company.
JEREMY TAYLOR

(See also FRIEND, FRIENDSHIP, SOLITUDE, SYMPATHY.)

COMPARISON

Comparisons are odious.
ARCHBISHOP BOIARDO—
Orlando Innamorato

Some say, compared to Bononcini,
That Mynheer Handel's but a
ninny;
Others aver, that he to Handel
Is scarcely fit to hold a Candle:
Strange all this difference should be,
'Twixt Tweedle-dum and Tweedle-
dee!
JOHN BYROM

The bee and the serpent often sip
from the selfsame flower.
METASTASIO—*Morte d'Abele*

(See also JUDGMENT, LIKE, QUAL-
ITY, WORTH.)

COMPASSION
See PITY

COMPENSATION

There is a day of sunny rest
For every dark and troubled night;
And grief may hide an evening
guest,
But joy shall come with early light.
BRYANT

Cast thy bread upon the waters; for
thou shalt find it after many days.
ECCLESIASTES. XI. 1

If the poor man cannot always get
meat, the rich man cannot always
digest it.
HENRY GILES

'Tis always morning somewhere in
the world.
RICHARD HENGEST HORNE—
Orion

Nothing is pure and entire of a piece.
All advantages are attended with
disadvantages. A universal compensation prevails in all conditions of being and existence.
HUME

The prickly thorn often bears soft
roses.
OVID

I believe that every right implies a
responsibility; every opportunity, an
obligation; every possession, a duty.
JOHN D. ROCKEFELLER, JR.—
Speech, 1941

No evil is without its compensation.
SENECA

(See also COMPARISON, LIFE,
RETRIBUTION.)

COMPLAINING

Constant complaint is the poorest
sort of pay for all the comforts we
enjoy.
FRANKLIN

Those who complain most are most
to be complained of.
MATTHEW HENRY

The usual fortune of complaint is
to excite contempt more than pity.
SAMUEL JOHNSON

Complaint is the largest tribute
Heaven receives.
SWIFT

(See also DISCONTENT, SATISFAC-
TION.)

COMPLIMENT

Compliments are only lies in court
clothes.
ANONYMOUS

When two people compliment each other with the choice of anything, each of them generally gets that which he likes least.

POPE

Compliments and flattery oftenest excite my contempt by the pretension they imply; for who is he that assumes to flatter me? To compliment often implies an assumption of superiority in the complimenter. It is, in fact, a subtle detraction.

THOREAU

(See also ADMIRATION, APPLAUSE, FLATTERY, HONOR, PRAISE.)

COMPROMISE

All government—indeed, every human benefit and enjoyment, every virtue and every prudent act—is founded on compromise and barter.

EDMUND BURKE—Speech on Conciliation

Compromise makes a good umbrella, but a poor roof; it is a temporary expedient, often wise in party politics, almost sure to be unwise in statesmanship.

LOWELL

Better bend than break.

SCOTTISH PROVERB

(See also JUDGMENT.)

CONCEIT

Conceited men often seem a harmless kind of men, who, by an overweening self-respect, relieve others from the duty of respecting them at all.

HENRY WARD BEECHER

No man was ever so much deceived by another as by himself.

GREVILLE

The art of making much show with little substance.

MACAULAY

Seest thou a man wise in his own conceit? There is more hope of a fool than of him.

PROVERBS. XXVI. 12

(See also EGOTISM, PRIDE, SELFISHNESS, SELF-LOVE, VANITY.)

CONDUCT

It is not enough that you can form, nay, and follow, the most excellent rules for conducting yourself in the world. You must also know when to deviate from them, and where lies the exception.

GREVILLE

Be swift to hear, slow to speak, slow to wrath.

JAMES. I. 19

The integrity of men is to be measured by their conduct, not by their professions.

JUNIUS

(See also CARE, MANNERS.)

CONFESSION

Open confession is good for the soul.

SCOTTISH PROVERB

To confess a fault freely is the next thing to being innocent of it.

SYRUS

(See also REPENTANCE.)

CONFIDENCE

He who believes in nobody knows
that he himself is not to be trusted.
AUERBACH

For they can conquer who believe
they can.
DRYDEN

The confidence which we have in
ourselves gives birth to much of that
which we have in others.
LA ROCHEFOUCAULD

Society is built upon trust.
SOUTH

Be courteous to all, but intimate
with few; and let those few be well
tried before you give them your confidence.
WASHINGTON—Letter, 1783

(See also BELIEF, DECISION, EGO-
TISM, FAITH, SELF-RELIANCE.)

CONGRESS

Every man in it is a great man, an
orator, a critic, a statesman; and
therefore every man upon every question must show his oratory, his
criticism, and his political abilities.
JOHN ADAMS—Letter to his wife

Fleas can be taught nearly anything
that a Congressman can.
S. L. CLEMENS (MARK TWAIN)
—What Is Man?

Some statesmen go to Congress and
some go to jail. It is the same thing,
after all.
EUGENE FIELD—Tribune Primer

(See also DEMOCRACY, GOVERN-
MENT, LAW, POLITICS.)

CONQUEST

How grand is victory, but how dear!
BOUFFLERS

He who surpasses or subdues mankind must look down on the hate of
those below.
BYRON

I came, I saw, I conquered.
JULIUS CAESAR

To rejoice in conquest is to rejoice
in murder.
LAO-TSZE

The more acquisitions the government makes abroad, the more taxes
the people have to pay at home.
THOMAS PAINE

Self-conquest is the greatest of victories.
PLATO

A conqueror, like a cannon-ball,
must go on. If he rebounds, his career is over.
WELLINGTON

(See also DEFEAT, GLORY, PEACE,
SOLDIER, SUCCESS, TYRANNY,
VICTORY, WAR.)

CONSCIENCE

Nor ear can hear nor tongue can tell
The tortures of that inward hell!
BYRON

Liberty of conscience (when people
have consciences) is rightly considered the most indispensable of liberties.
HADDON CHAMBERS

The only incorruptible thing about us.
FIELDING

A good conscience is a continual Christmas.
FRANKLIN

There is no pillow so soft as a clear conscience.
FRENCH PROVERB

A still, small voice.
I KINGS. XIX. 12

Conscience is a sacred sanctuary where God alone may enter as judge.
LAMENNAIS

I am more afraid of my own heart than of the pope and all his cardinals. I have within me the great pope, self.
LUTHER

Conscience is the guardian in the individual of the rules which the community has evolved for its own preservation.
WILLIAM SOMERSET MAUGHAM—*The Moon and Sixpence*

Thus conscience does make cowards of us all;
And thus the native hue of resolution
Is sicklied o'er with the pale cast of thought;
And enterprises of great pith and moment,
With this regard, their currents turn awry,
And lose the name of action.
SHAKESPEARE—*Hamlet.* Act III. Sc. 1

The soft whispers of the God in man.
YOUNG

(See also CHARACTER, GUILT, REPENTANCE, SUICIDE.)

CONSERVATISM

A statesman who is enamored of existing evils, as distinguished from the Liberal, who wishes to replace them with others.
BIERCE—*The Devil's Dictionary*

We are reformers in spring and summer; in autumn and winter we stand by the old; reformers in the morning, conservers at night. Reform is affirmative, conservatism negative; conservatism goes for comfort, reform for truth.
EMERSON

A conservative is a man who will not look at the new moon, out of respect for that "ancient institution," the old one.
DOUGLAS JERROLD

What is conservatism? Is it not adherence to the old and tried, against the new and untried?
LINCOLN, 1860

A Conservative is a man with two perfectly good legs who, however, has never learned to walk.
F. D. ROOSEVELT, 1939

(See also CAUTION, LIBERAL, PRUDENCE.)

CONSISTENCY

A foolish consistency is the hobgoblin of little minds, adored by

little statesmen and philosophers and divines.
EMERSON—*Self-Reliance*

Shoemaker, stick to your last.
PLINY

Inconsistency is the only thing in which men are consistent.
HORACE SMITH—*Tin Trumpet*

(See also NEWNESS, REPUTATION.)

CONSOLATION
See SYMPATHY

CONSTITUTION

What's the Constitution among friends?
Attributed to CONGRESSMAN TIMOTHY CAMPBELL, of New York

Constitutions should consist only of general provisions; the reason is that they must necessarily be permanent, and that they cannot calculate for the possible change of things.
ALEXANDER HAMILTON

We are under a Constitution, but the Constitution is what the judges say it is.
CHARLES EVANS HUGHES—Speech

In questions of power let no more be heard of confidence in man, but bind him down from mischief by the chains of the constitution.
JEFFERSON—*Kentucky Resolutions*

A good constitution is infinitely better than the best despot.
MACAULAY

Our Constitution is so simple and practical that it is possible always to meet extraordinary needs by changes in emphasis and arrangement without loss of essential form.
F. D. ROOSEVELT—Inaugural Address, 1933

There is a higher law than the Constitution.
SEWARD—Speech in Senate

It is very doubtful whether man is enough of a political animal to produce a good, sensible, serious and efficient constitution. All the evidence is against it.
GEORGE BERNARD SHAW—Address in New York, 1933

(See also AMERICA, GOVERNMENT, LAW.)

CONTEMPT
See CRITICISM

CONTENTION
See ARGUMENT

CONTENTMENT

Enjoy your own life without comparing it with that of another.
CONDORCET

Contentment is, after all, simply refined indolence.
HALIBURTON

Those who want much, are always much in need; happy the man to whom God gives with a sparing hand what is sufficient for his wants.
HORACE—*Carmina*

I earn that I eat, get that I wear, owe no man hate, envy no man's

happiness; glad of other men's good, content with my harm.
SHAKESPEARE—*As You Like It.*
Act III. Sc. 2

He is well paid that is well satisfied.
SHAKESPEARE—*Henry VI.* Pt.
III. Act III. Sc. 1

It is not for man to rest in absolute contentment.
SOUTHEY

(See also BLISS, HAPPINESS, PEACE, REPOSE, SATISFACTION.)

CONTRAST
See VARIETY

CONTROVERSY

No great advance has ever been made in science, politics, or religion, without controversy.
LYMAN BEECHER

If a cause be good, the most violent attack of its enemies will not injure it so much as an injudicious defence of it by its friends.
COLTON

(See also ARGUMENT, QUARRELING.)

CONVERSATION

Debate is masculine; conversation is feminine.
ALCOTT

Never hold any one by the button or the hand in order to be heard out; for if people are unwilling to hear you, you had better hold your tongue than them.
CHESTERFIELD

Conversation enriches the understanding, but solitude is the school of genius.
GIBBON

Silence is one great art of conversation.
HAZLITT

Conceit causes more conversation than wit.
LA ROCHEFOUCAULD

The less men think, the more they talk.
MONTESQUIEU

(See also ELOQUENCE, LANGUAGE, ORATORY, SPEECH, TALK, WIT, WORD.)

COOKING

The discovery of a new dish does more for human happiness than the discovery of a new star.
BRILLAT-SAVARIN

We may live without friends; we may live without books;
But civilized man cannot live without cooks.
BULWER-LYTTON

Too many cooks spoil the broth.
ENGLISH PROVERB

God sends meat, and the Devil sends cooks.
JOHN TAYLOR—*Works*

(See also APPETITE, EATING, HUNGER.)

CORRUPTION

Just for a handful of silver he left us,
Just for a ribbon to stick in his
coat.
BROWNING—*The Lost Leader*

The time to guard against corruption
and tyranny is before they shall have
gotten hold of us. It is better to keep
the wolf out of the fold than to trust
to drawing his teeth and talons after
he shall have entered.
JEFFERSON—*Notes on Virginia*

If the chief party, whether it be the
people, or the army, or the nobility,
which you think most useful and of
most consequence to you for the con-
servation of your dignity, be corrupt,
you must follow their humor and in-
dulge them, and in that case honesty
and virtue are pernicious.
MACHIAVELLI—*The Prince*

The more corrupt the state, the more
laws.
TACITUS

(See also BRIBERY, CRIME, GOVERN-
MENT, GUILT.)

COST
See WORTH

COUNTRY LIFE

I consider it the best part of an education to have been born and brought
up in the country.
ALCOTT

The town is man's world, but this
(country life) is of God.
COWPER—*The Task*

The country for a wounded heart.
ENGLISH PROVERB

(See also AGRICULTURE, ANIMALS,
BIRDS, CITY, CONTENTMENT, FLOW-
ERS, HOME, NATURE, TREE.)

COURAGE

Often the test of courage is not to
die but to live.
ALFIERI—*Orestes*

A man of courage is also full of faith.
CICERO

Watch ye, stand fast in the faith,
quit you like men, be strong.
I CORINTHIANS. XVI. 13

When moral courage feels that it is
in the right, there is no personal
daring of which it is incapable.
LEIGH HUNT

Fortune and Love befriend the bold.
OVID

Women and men of retiring timidity
are cowardly only in dangers which
affect themselves, but the first to
rescue when others are endangered.
JEAN PAUL RICHTER

Hail, Caesar, those who are about to
die salute thee.
SUETONIUS

(See also AUDACITY, BRAVERY,
HERO, NAVY, SOLDIER, VALOR,
WAR.)

COURTESY

The small courtesies sweeten life; the
greater ennoble it.
BOVEE

A moral, sensible, and well-bred man
Will not affront me, and no other
can.
COWPER

Life is not so short but that there is
always time enough for courtesy.
EMERSON—*Social Aims*

To speak kindly does not hurt the
tongue.
FRENCH PROVERB

(See also FRIENDSHIP, GENTLEMAN,
MANNERS.)

COURTSHIP
See WOOING

COW

I never saw a Purple Cow,
I never hope to see one:
But I can tell you, anyhow
I'd rather see than be one.
GELETT BURGESS—*The Purple
Cow*

There was an old man who said,
"How
Shall I flee from this horrible cow?
I will sit on this stile, and continue
to smile,
Which may soften the heart of that
cow."
EDWARD LEAR—*The Book of
Nonsense*

(See also ANIMALS.)

COWARD

One who in a perilous emergency
thinks with his legs.
BIERCE—*The Devil's Dictionary*

He who fights and runs away
May live to fight another day.
But he who is in battle slain,
Can never rise to fight again.
GOLDSMITH

A cowardly act! What do I care about
that? You may be sure that I should
never fear to commit one if it were
to my advantage.
NAPOLEON

A cowardly cur barks more fiercely
than it bites.
QUINTUS CURTIUS RUFUS

All men would be cowards if they
durst.
EARL OF ROCHESTER

(See also FEAR, WAR.)

CREATION

In the beginning God created the
Heaven and the earth. And the earth
was without form, and void; and
darkness was upon the face of the
deep. And the Spirit of God moved
upon the face of the waters. And
God said, Let there be light; and
there was light.
GENESIS. I. 3

Nature they say, doth dote,
And cannot make a man
Save on some worn-out plan,
Repeating us by rote.
LOWELL—Ode at Harvard Com-
memoration

All are but parts of one stupendous
whole,
Whose body Nature is, and God the
soul.
POPE

It is easier to suppose that the universe has existed from all eternity than to conceive a Being beyond its limits capable of creating it.
SHELLEY—*Queen Mab*

The world embarrasses me, and I cannot dream
That this watch exists and has no watchmaker.
VOLTAIRE

(See also BEGINNING, EVOLUTION, GOD, LIFE, NATURE, WORLD.)

CREDIT

In God we trust; all others must pay cash.
AMERICAN SAYING

He that hath lost his credit is dead to the world.
HERBERT—*Outlandish Proverbs, 1639*

No man's credit is as good as his money.
E. W. HOWE—*Sinner Sermons*

Ah, take the cash, and let the credit go.
OMAR KHAYYÁM—*Rubaiyat*

A pig bought on credit is forever grunting.
SPANISH PROVERB

(See also BUSINESS, CONFIDENCE, DEBT, MONEY, TRUST.)

CREDITOR

It takes a man to make a devil; and the fittest man for such a purpose is a snarling, waspish, red-hot, fiery creditor.
HENRY WARD BEECHER

Creditors have better memories than debtors.
FRANKLIN

(See also BORROWING, BUSINESS, CONFIDENCE, DEBT, MONEY, TRUST.)

CREDULITY

Better be too credulous than too skeptical.
CHINESE PROVERB

Let us believe neither half of the good people tell us of ourselves, nor half the evil they say of others.
J. PETIT-SENN

You believe that easily which you hope for earnestly.
TERENCE

I wish I was as sure of anything as Macaulay is of everything.
WILLIAM WINDHAM

CRIME

Providence sees to it that no man gets happiness out of crime.
ALFIERI—*Orestes*

Disgrace does not consist in the punishment, but in the crime.
ALFIERI—*Antigone*

Society prepares the crime; the criminal commits it.
BUCKLE

It is not the thief who is hanged, but one who was caught stealing.
CZECH PROVERB

One crime is everything; two nothing.
MME. DELUZY

Whoever profits by the crime is guilty of it.

FRENCH PROVERB

Many commit the same crimes with a very different result. One bears a cross for his crime; another a crown.

JUVENAL—*Satires*

If poverty is the mother of crimes, want of sense is the father.

LA BRUYÈRE

We enact many laws that manufacture criminals, and then a few that punish them.

TUCKER—*Instead of a Book*

Yet each man kills the thing he loves,
By each let this be heard,
Some do it with a bitter look,
Some with a flattering word,
The coward does it with a kiss,
The brave man with a sword.

WILDE—*Ballad of Reading Gaol*

(See also BRIBERY, CORRUPTION, EVIL, GUILT, JUDGMENT, JUSTICE, LAW, MURDER, PRISON, PUNISHMENT, SIN, TREACHERY.)

CRISIS

In great straits, and when hope is small, the boldest counsels are the safest.

LIVY

The nearer any disease approaches to a crisis, the nearer it is to a cure.

THOMAS PAINE

(See also CIRCUMSTANCE, EVENTS, HISTORY.)

CRITICISM

The rule in carving holds good as to criticism; never cut with a knife what you can cut with a spoon.

CHARLES BUXTON

Said the pot to the kettle, "Get away, blackface."

CERVANTES—*Don Quixote*

If the present criticises the past, there is not much hope for the future.

WINSTON CHURCHILL—Speech, 1941

Critics are the men who have failed in literature and art.

DISRAELI

It is much easier to be critical than to be correct.

DISRAELI

Even the lion has to defend himself against flies.

GERMAN PROVERB

What a blessed thing it is that nature, when she invented, manufactured and patented her authors, contrived to make critics out of the chips that were left!

HOLMES

I had rather be hissed for a good verse than applauded for a bad one.

VICTOR HUGO

As a bankrupt thief turns thief-taker in despair, so an unsuccessful author turns critic.

SHELLEY—*Fragments of Adonais*

Of all the cants which are canted in this canting world—though the cant of hypocrites may be the worst—the cant of criticism is the most tormenting.

LAURENCE STERNE — *Tristram Shandy*

(See also ARGUMENT, AUTHORSHIP, BOOKS, JUDGMENT, OPINION, READING, SATIRE.)

CROSS
See RELIGION

CRUELTY

Man's inhumanity to man
Makes countless thousands mourn!
BURNS — *Man Was Made to Mourn*

It is not linen you're wearing out,
But human creatures' lives.
HOOD—*Song of the Shirt*

All cruelty springs from weakness.
SENECA

I must be cruel, only to be kind.
SHAKESPEARE—*Hamlet.* Act III.
Sc. 4

(See also REVENGE, TYRANNY, WAR, WOUND, WRONG.)

CULTURE

Reading makes a full man, conference a ready man, and writing an exact man.
BACON

Culture, with us, ends in headache.
EMERSON—*Experience*

Culture is what your butcher would have if he were a surgeon.
MARY PETTIBONE POOLE — *A Glass Eye at the Keyhole*

(See also ART, KNOWLEDGE, LEARNING, STUDY.)

CUNNING
See DECEPTION

CURE
See MEDICINE

CURIOSITY

Curiosity killed the cat.
AMERICAN PROVERB

Ask me no questions, and I'll tell you no fibs.
GOLDSMITH — *She Stoops to Conquer*

Curiosity is one of the permanent and certain characteristics of a vigorous intellect.
SAMUEL JOHNSON

(See also INQUISITIVENESS, SECRECY.)

CURSING
See PROFANITY

CUSTOM

Men commonly think according to their inclinations, speak according to their learning and imbibed opinions; but generally act according to custom.
BACON

There is no tyrant like custom, and no freedom where its edicts are not resisted.
BOVEE

Other times, other customs.
ITALIAN PROVERB

Ancient custom has the force of law.
LEGAL MAXIM

Custom is the law of fools.
VANBRUGH

(See also FASHION, HABIT, MANNERS, SOCIETY.)

CYNICISM

The cynic is one who never sees a good quality in a man, and never fails to see a bad one. He is the human owl, vigilant in darkness and blind to light, mousing for vermin, and never seeing noble game. The cynic puts all human actions into two classes—openly bad and secretly bad.
    HENRY WARD BEECHER

A cynic is a man who knows the price of everything, and the value of nothing.
    WILDE — *Lady Windermere's Fan*

(See also DOUBT, PREJUDICE, SNEER, WORTH.)

DANCING

On with the dance! let joy be un-confin'd;
No sleep till morn, when Youth and Pleasure meet.
    BYRON—*Childe Harold*

No man in his senses will dance.
    CICERO

Come and trip it as ye go,
On the light fantastic toe.
    MILTON—*L'Allegro*

They who love dancing too much seem to have more brains in their feet than in their head.
    TERENCE

(See also AMUSEMENT, ART.)

DANGER

We triumph without glory when we conquer without danger.
    CORNEILLE—*The Cid*

The pitcher that goes too often to the well is broken at last.
    ENGLISH PROVERB

Danger for danger's sake is senseless.
    LEIGH HUNT

A timid person is frightened before a danger, a coward during the time, and a courageous person afterwards.
    JEAN PAUL RICHTER

(See also ACCIDENT, CALAMITY.)

DARING

Who dares nothing, need hope for nothing.
    SCHILLER—*Don Carlos*

No one reaches a high position without daring.
    SYRUS

(See also AUDACITY, BRAVERY, COURAGE, VALOR.)

DARKNESS

Darkness which may be felt.
    EXODUS. X. 21

It is always darkest just before the day dawneth.
    THOMAS FULLER

(See also BLINDNESS, EVIL, IGNORANCE, LIGHT, NIGHT, OBSCURITY.)

DAUGHTER

My son is my son till he have got him a wife,
But my daughter's my daughter all the days of her life.
    THOMAS FULLER

If thy daughter marry well, thou
hast found a son; if not, thou hast
lost a daughter.
> QUARLES

(See also CHILDHOOD, FATHER,
MOTHER, PARENT, YOUTH.)

DAWN
See MORNING

DAY

Think that day lost whose (low)
    descending sun
Views from thy hand no noble action
    done.
> JACOB BOBART—Krieg's Album
> in British Museum

Well, this is the end of a perfect
    day,
    Near the end of a journey, too;
But it leaves a thought that is big and
    strong,
    With a wish that is kind and true.
For mem'ry has painted this perfect
    day
    With colors that never fade,
And we find at the end of a perfect
    day,
    The soul of a friend we've made.
> CARRIE JACOBS BOND—A Per-
> fect Day

What a day may bring a day may
take away.
> THOMAS FULLER

Monday for wealth,
Tuesday for health,
Wednesday the best day of all:
Thursday for crosses,
Friday for losses,
Saturday no luck at all.
> OLD ENGLISH RHYME

Boast not thyself of tomorrow; for
thou knowest not what a day may
bring forth.
> PROVERBS. XXVII. 1.

One glance of Thine creates a day.
> ISAAC WATTS

(See also LIGHT, MORNING, SUN-
RISE, TODAY, TOMORROW.)

DEATH

Call no man happy till he is dead.
> AESCHYLUS—Agamemnon

Though this may be play to you,
'Tis death to us.
> AESOP—Fables

But whether on the scaffold high,
    Or in the battle's van,
The fittest place where man can die
    Is where he dies for man.
> MICHAEL J. BARRY—The Place
> to Die

Earth to earth, ashes to ashes, dust to
dust, in sure and certain hope of the
resurrection.
> Book of Common Prayer

In the midst of life we are in death.
> Book of Common Prayer

Man that is born of a woman hath
but a short time to live, and is full
of misery. He cometh up, and is cut
down, like a flower; he fleeth as it
were a shadow, and never continueth
in one stay.
> Book of Common Prayer

Death, so called, is a thing which
    makes men weep,
And yet a third of life is pass'd in
    sleep.
> BYRON—Don Juan

O death, where is thy sting? O grave, where is thy victory?
I CORINTHIANS. XV. 55

Every moment of life is a step towards death.
CORNEILLE

Sit the comedy out, and that done, When the Play's at an end, let the Curtain fall down.
THOMAS FLATMAN—*The Whim*

Why fear death? It is the most beautiful adventure in life.
CHARLES FROHMAN

Now I am about to take my last voyage, a great leap in the dark.
THOMAS HOBBES

The Lord gave, and the Lord hath taken away; blessed be the name of the Lord.
JOB. I. 21

The young may die, but the old must!
LONGFELLOW—*Christus*

There is no Death! What seems so is transition;
This life of mortal breath
Is but a suburb of the life elysian,
Whose portal we call Death.
LONGFELLOW—*Resignation*

There is no such thing as death.
In nature nothing dies.
From each sad remnant of decay
Some forms of life arise.
CHARLES MACKAY

We begin to die as soon as we are born, and the end is linked to the beginning.
MANILIUS

There is no death! the stars go down
To rise upon some other shore,
And bright in Heaven's jeweled crown,
They shine for ever more.
JOHN L. McCREERY

Strange—is it not?—that of the myriads who
Before us passed the door of Darkness through,
Not one returns to tell us of the road
Which to discover we must travel too.
OMAR KHAYYÁM—*Rubaiyat*

Till tired, he sleeps, and life's poor play is o'er.
POPE—*Essay on Man*

Yet a little sleep, a little slumber, a little folding of the hands to sleep.
PROVERBS. VI. 10

I am going to seek a great perhaps; draw the curtain, the farce is played.
Attributed to RABELAIS

Is death the last sleep? No, it is the last final awakening.
SCOTT

I have a rendezvous with Death
At some disputed barricade.
ALAN SEEGER

I am dying, Egypt, dying.
SHAKESPEARE—*Antony and Cleopatra*. Act IV. Sc. 15

                    To die:—to sleep:
No more; and, by a sleep to say we end
The heart-ache and the thousand natural shocks
That flesh is heir to, 'tis a consummation
Devoutly to be wished.
SHAKESPEARE—*Hamlet*. Act III. Sc. 1

Nothing in his life
Became him like the leaving it.
SHAKESPEARE—*Macbeth*. Act I.
Sc. 4

If I must die
I will encounter darkness as a bride,
And hug it in mine arms.
SHAKESPEARE — *Measure for
Measure*. Act III. Sc. 1

Death lies on her, like an untimely
frost
Upon the sweetest flower of all the
field.
SHAKESPEARE—*Romeo and Juliet*. Act IV. Sc. 5

First our pleasures die—and then
Our hopes, and then our fears—and
when
These are dead, the debt is due,
Dust claims dust—and we die too.
SHELLEY—*Death*

Sunset and evening star,
   And one clear call for me!
And may there be no moaning of the
   bar
   When I put out to sea.
TENNYSON—*Crossing the Bar*

Twilight and evening bell,
   And after that the dark!
And may there be no sadness of fare-
well
   When I embark.
TENNYSON—*Crossing the Bar*

God's finger touched him, and he
slept.
TENNYSON—*In Memoriam*

Nothing can happen more beautiful
than death.
WALT WHITMAN—*Starting
from Paumanok*

For he who lives more lives than one
More deaths than one must die.
WILDE—*Ballad of Reading Gaol*

(See also EPITAPH, ETERNITY, GRAVE,
HEAVEN, HELL, IMMORTALITY, MON-
UMENT, MORTALITY, MOURNING,
MURDER, RESURRECTION, SLEEP,
SUICIDE.)

DEBATE
See ARGUMENT

DEBT

A church debt is the devil's salary.
HENRY WARD BEECHER

Wilt thou seal up the avenues of
ill?
Pay every debt as if God wrote the
bill!
EMERSON

A national debt, if it is not excessive,
will be to us a national blessing.
HAMILTON

Debt is the worst poverty.
M. G. LICHTWER

Owe no man anything.
ROMANS. XII. 8

He that dies pays all debts.
SHAKESPEARE — *Tempest*. Act
III. Sc. 2

If you want the time to pass quickly,
just give your note for 90 days.
R. B. THOMAS—*Farmers' Almanack*

(See also BEGGING, BORROWING,
CREDITOR, MONEY.)

DECEIT
See DECEPTION

DECENCY

No law reaches it, but all right-minded people observe it.
CHAMFORT

Decency renders all things tolerable.
DE GERANDO

(See also CHARACTER, QUALITY, REPUTATION, WORTH.)

DECEPTION

A delusion, a mockery, and a snare.
LORD DENMAN

We are never deceived; we deceive ourselves.
GOETHE

Which I wish to remark—
    And my language is plain,—
That for ways that are dark
    And for tricks that are vain,
The heathen Chinee is peculiar.
    BRET HARTE—*Plain Language from Truthful James*

Hateful to me as are the gates of hell,
Is he who, hiding one thing in his heart,
Utters another.
    HOMER—*Iliad*

"Will you walk into my parlour?"
    Said a spider to a fly;
" 'Tis the prettiest little parlour
    That ever you did spy."
    MARY HOWITT — *The Spider and the Fly*

It is double pleasure to deceive the deceiver.
    LA FONTAINE

You can fool some of the people all of the time, and all of the people some of the time, but you cannot fool all of the people all the time.
LINCOLN

One is easily fooled by that which one loves.
MOLIÈRE—*Tartuffe*

(See also FALSEHOOD, HYPOCRISY, LYING, TREACHERY.)

DECISION

And her *yes*, once said to you,
    Shall be Yes for evermore.
        E. B. BROWNING—*The Lady's Yes*

Once to every man and nation comes
        the moment to decide,
In the strife of Truth with Falsehood, for the good or evil side.
    LOWELL—*The Present Crisis*

Here I stand; I can do no otherwise.
God help me. *Amen.*
    LUTHER

(See also ACTION, DEEDS, IRRESOLUTION, JUDGMENT, RESOLUTION.)

DEEDS

We have left undone those things which we ought to have done; and we have done those things which we ought not to have done.
BOOK OF COMMON PRAYER

Little deeds of kindness, little words of love,
Make our earth an Eden like the heaven above.
    JULIA F. CARNEY—*Little Things*

Whatever is worth doing at all is worth doing well.
CHESTERFIELD

Give me the ready hand rather than the ready tongue.
GARIBALDI

Noble deeds that are concealed are most esteemed.
PASCAL

Heaven ne'er helps the man who will not help himself.
SOPHOCLES

(See also ACTION, GOODNESS, LABOR, WORK.)

DEFEAT

It is defeat that turns bone to flint; it is defeat that turns gristle to muscle; it is defeat that makes men invincible.
HENRY WARD BEECHER—*Royal Truths*

What is defeat? Nothing but education, nothing but the first step to something better.
WENDELL PHILLIPS

Defeat should never be a source of discouragement, but rather a fresh stimulus.
SOUTH

(See also FAILURE.)

DEFENSE
See WAR

DELAY

All delays are dangerous in war.
DRYDEN

Do not delay,
Do not delay: the golden moments fly!
LONGFELLOW—*Masque of Pandora*

Late, late, so late! but we can enter still.
Too late, too late! ye cannot enter now.
TENNYSON—*Idylls of the King*

(See also IDLENESS, PROCRASTINATION.)

DELICACY
See FRAILTY

DELIGHT
See JOY

DELUSION
See ERROR

DEMOCRACY

When everybody is somebody, then nobody is anybody.
ANONYMOUS

Democracy arose from men thinking that if they are equal in any respect they are equal in all respects.
ARISTOTLE—*Politics*

The tyranny of a multitude is a multiplied tyranny.
EDMUND BURKE

It would be folly to argue that the people cannot make political mistakes. They can and do make grave mistakes. They know it, they pay the penalty, but compared with the mistakes which have been made by every kind of autocracy they are unimportant.
CALVIN COOLIDGE

Democracy is based upon the conviction that there are extraordinary possibilities in ordinary people.
HARRY EMERSON FOSDICK—
Democracy

While democracy must have its organization and controls, its vital breath is individual liberty.
CHARLES EVANS HUGHES—
Speech, 1939

Democracy is the government of the people, by the people, for the people.
LINCOLN

Democracy means not "I am as good as you are," but "You are as good as I am."
THEODORE PARKER

All the ills of democracy can be cured by more democracy.
ALFRED E. SMITH—Speech, 1933

I believe in Democracy because it releases the energies of every human being.
WOODROW WILSON

The world must be made safe for democracy.
WOODROW WILSON—War Address to Congress, 1917.

(See also AMERICA, EQUALITY, FREE-DOM, GOVERNMENT, INDEPEND-ENCE, LIBERTY, PARTY, PEOPLE, POLITICS, RIGHTS, STATESMAN-SHIP, WAR.)

DEMAGOGUE

The qualities necessary to a demagogue are these: to be foul-mouthed, base-born, a low, mean fellow.
ARISTOPHANES

Demagogues and agitators are very unpleasant, but they are incidents to a free and constitutional country, and you must put up with these inconveniences or do without many important advantages.
DISRAELI—Speech

A wise fellow who is also worthless always charms the rabble.
EURIPIDES

In every age the vilest specimens of human nature are to be found among demagogues.
MACAULAY—*History of England*

Every one that was in distress, and every one that was in debt, and every one that was discontented, gathered themselves unto him; and he became a captain over them.
I SAMUEL. XXII. 2

(See also ELOQUENCE, MOB, ORATORY, PEOPLE.)

DEPENDENCE

There is no one subsists by himself alone.
FELLTHAM

People may live as much retired from the world as they please; but sooner or later, before they are aware, they will find themselves debtor or creditor to somebody.
GOETHE

He who imagines he can do without the world deceives himself much; but he who fancies the world cannot do without him is still more mistaken.
LA ROCHEFOUCAULD

(See also FAITH, INDEPENDENCE, SELF-RELIANCE, TRUST.)

DESIRE

It is easier to suppress the first desire than to satisfy all that follow it.
FRANKLIN

Our desires always increase with our possessions. The knowledge that something remains yet unenjoyed impairs our enjoyment of the good before us.
SAMUEL JOHNSON

He who desires naught will always be free.
E. R. LEFEBVRE LABOULAYE

Ah love! could you and I with Him conspire
To grasp this sorry scheme of things entire,
Would not we shatter it to bits—and then
Re-mold it nearer to the heart's desire!
OMAR KHAYYÁM—*Rubaiyat*

There are two tragedies in life. One is not to get your heart's desire. The other is to get it.
GEORGE BERNARD SHAW—*Man and Superman*

(See also ANTICIPATION, HOPE, LOVE, PASSION, WISH.)

DESPAIR

All hope abandon, ye who enter here.
DANTE—*Inferno*

Despair is the conclusion of fools.
DISRAELI

Despair doubles our strength.
ENGLISH PROVERB

(See also AFFLICTION, FEAR, GRIEF, MISERY, MISFORTUNE, SORROW.)

DESPOTISM

Despotism can no more exist in a nation until the liberty of the press be destroyed than the night can happen before the sun is set.
COLTON

It is the old practice of despots to use a part of the people to keep the rest in order.
JEFFERSON

I will believe in the right of one man to govern a nation despotically when I find a man born into the world with boots and spurs, and a nation with saddles on their backs.
ALGERNON SIDNEY

(See also DICTATOR, FORCE, GOVERNMENT, TYRANNY.)

DESTINY

Destiny is not a matter of chance, it is a matter of choice; it is not a thing to be waited for, it is a thing to be achieved.
W. J. BRYAN—Speech, 1899

No living man can send me to the shades
Before my time; no man of woman born,
Coward or brave, can shun his destiny.
HOMER—*Iliad*

We are but as the instrument of Heaven.
Our work is not design, but destiny.
OWEN MEREDITH — *Clytemnestra*

Every man meets his Waterloo at last.
WENDELL PHILLIPS

There is a divinity that shapes our
ends,
Rough-hew them how we will.
SHAKESPEARE—*Hamlet.* Act V.
Sc. 2

(See also FATE, FORTUNE, LUCK.)

DEVIL

The devil was sick, the devil a monk
would be;
The devil was well, the devil a monk
was he.
ANONYMOUS

Here is the devil-and-all to pay.
CERVANTES—*Don Quixote*

How art thou fallen from heaven,
O Lucifer, son of the morning!
ISAIAH. XIV. 12

Resist the Devil, and he will flee
from you.
JAMES. IV. 7

Get thee behind me, Satan.
MARK. VIII. 33

The Devil and me, we don't agree;
I hate him; and he hates me.
SALVATION ARMY HYMN

He will give the devil his due.
SHAKESPEARE—*Henry IV.* Pt.
I. Act I. Sc. 2

The prince of darkness is a gentle-
man.
SHAKESPEARE—*King Lear.* Act
III. Sc. 4

The devil can cite Scripture for his
purpose.
SHAKESPEARE — *Merchant of
Venice.* Act I. Sc. 3

(See also CHURCH, HELL,
PUNISHMENT.)

DEVOTION
See RELIGION

DEW

'Tis of the tears which stars weep,
sweet with joy.
BAILEY—*Festus*

Every dew-drop and rain-drop had a
whole heaven within it.
LONGFELLOW—*Hyperion*

(See also FLOWERS, NATURE, RAIN.)

DICTATOR

We have nothing to fear in this
country from a dictatorship. It cannot live here. We are not organized
to carry it on. We have no desire for
it.
ALFRED E. SMITH—Speech,
1933

In your dread of dictators you established a state of society in which
every ward boss is a dictator, every
financier a dictator, every private employer a dictator, all with the liveli-
hood of the workers at their mercy,
and no public responsibility.
GEORGE BERNARD SHAW—Ad-
dress in New York City, 1933

(See also DEMOCRACY, FREEDOM,
GOVERNMENT, TYRANNY.)

DIFFICULTY

The best way out of a difficulty is
through it.
ANONYMOUS

The three things most difficult are—
to keep a secret, to forget an injury,
and to make good use of leisure.
CHILO

Many things difficult to design prove
easy to performance.
SAMUEL JOHNSON

(See also IMPOSSIBILITY, TRIAL,
TROUBLE.)

DIGNITY

As vivacity is the gift of woman,
gravity is that of man.
ADDISON

There is a healthful hardiness about
real dignity that never dreads con-
tact and communion with others,
however humble.
WASHINGTON IRVING

All celebrated people lose dignity on
a close view.
NAPOLEON

(See also APPEARANCE, CHARACTER,
GREATNESS, HONOR, NOBILITY,
PRIDE.)

DIPLOMACY

A diplomat is a man who remembers
a lady's birthday but forgets her age.
ANONYMOUS

When a diplomat says yes he means
perhaps; when he says perhaps he
means no; when he says no he is no
diplomat.
ANONYMOUS

I have discovered the art of deceiving diplomats. I speak the truth, and
they never believe me.
DI CAVOUR

Diplomacy is to do and say
The nastiest thing in the nicest way.
ISAAC GOLDBERG—The Reflex

(See also GOVERNMENT, POLICY,
STATESMANSHIP, TACT.)

DISAPPOINTMENT

The best-laid schemes o' mice an'
men,
Gang aft a-gley,
And leave us nought but grief and
pain,
For promised joy.
BURNS—To a Mouse

Disappointment is the nurse of wisdom.
SIR BOYLE ROCHE

Disappointments are to the soul what
a thunder-storm is to the air.
SCHILLER

(See also DISCONTENT, FAILURE,
SORROW.)

DISCIPLINE
See ORDER

DISCONTENT

Who is not satisfied with himself
will grow; who is not sure of his own
correctness will learn many things.
CHINESE PROVERB

Men would be angels;
Angels would be gods.
POPE

Now is the Winter of our discon-
tent.
SHAKESPEARE—Richard III.
Act 3. Sc. 1

I was born to other things.
TENNYSON—In Memoriam

Discontent is the first step in the
progress of a man or a nation.
WILDE—Woman of No Im-
portance

(See also COMPLAINING, DISAP-
POINTMENT, SORROW.)

DISCRETION

Discretion in speech is more than eloquence.
BACON

A sound discretion is not so much indicated by never making a mistake as by never repeating it.
BOVEE

Great ability without discretion comes almost invariably to a tragic end.
GAMBETTA

Let your own discretion be your tutor: suit the action to the word, the word to the action.
SHAKESPEARE—*Hamlet.* Act III. Sc. 2

The better part of valour is discretion.
SHAKESPEARE—*Henry IV.* Pt. I. Act V. Sc. 4

(See also CARE, JUDGMENT, PRUDENCE, WISDOM.)

DISCUSSION
See ARGUMENT

DISEASE

Disease is the retribution of outraged Nature.
HOSEA BALLOU

Disease is an experience of so-called mortal mind. It is fear made manifest on the body.
MARY BAKER EDDY—*Science and Health*

Desperate diseases require desperate remedies.
ENGLISH PROVERB

Some remedies are worse than the disease.
SYRUS

(See also HEALTH, MEDICINE, QUACK, SICKNESS.)

DISGRACE

No one can disgrace us but ourselves.
J. G. HOLLAND

Whatever disgrace we may have deserved, it is almost always in our power to re-establish our character.
PLAUTUS

(See also CONSCIENCE, GUILT, HONOR, SHAME.)

DISPLAY
See VANITY

DISSENSION
See CONTROVERSY

DISTRUST

A usurper always distrusts the whole world.
ALFIERI

Doubt the man who swears to his devotion.
MME. LOUISE COLET

Women distrust men too much in general, and too little in particular.
COMMERSON

What loneliness is more lonely than distrust?
GEORGE ELIOT—*Middlemarch*

(See also DOUBT, INCREDULITY, SUSPICION.)

DOCTOR
See MEDICINE

DOCTRINE

Doctrine is nothing but the skin of truth set up and stuffed.
HENRY WARD BEECHER

How absurd to try to make two men think alike on matters of religion, when I cannot make two timepieces agree!
CHARLES V

In religion as in politics it so happens that we have less charity for those who believe half our creed, than for those who deny the whole of it.
COLTON

You can and you can't,
You will and you won't;
You'll be damn'd if you do,
You'll be damn'd if you don't.
LORENZO DOW—(Definition of Calvinism)

"Orthodoxy, my Lord," said Bishop Warburton, in a whisper,—"orthodoxy is my doxy,—heterodoxy is another man's doxy."
JOSEPH PRIESTLEY—Memoirs

(See also BELIEF, CHRISTIANITY, CHURCH, FAITH, PRAYER, RELIGION.)

DOG

Do not disturb the sleeping dog.
ALESSANDRO ALLEGRI

Every dog is entitled to one bite.
ANONYMOUS

Who loves me will love my dog also.
ST. BERNARD OF CLAIRVAUX

You're only a dog, old fellow; a dog,
and you've had your day;
But never a friend of all my friends
has been truer than you alway.
JULIAN S. CUTLER—Roger and I

I agree with Agassiz that dogs possess something very like a conscience.
DARWIN—The Descent of Man

A living dog is better than a dead lion.
ECCLESIASTES. IX. 4

Oh, the saddest of sights in a world of sin
Is a little lost pup with his tail tucked in!
ARTHUR GUITERMAN—Little Lost Pup

Fox-terriers are born with about four times as much original sin in them as other dogs.
JEROME K. JEROME—Three Men in a Boat

The more one comes to know men, the more one comes to admire the dog.
JOUSSENEL

The dogs eat of the crumbs which fall from their masters' table.
MATTHEW. XV. 27

The cowardly dog barks more violently than it bites.
QUINTUS CURTIUS RUFUS

Every dog must have his day.
SWIFT

Gentlemen of the Jury: The one, absolute, unselfish friend that man can have in this selfish world, the one that never deserts him, the one that never proves ungrateful or treacherous, is his dog.

> SENATOR GEORGE GRAHAM VEST—*Eulogy on the Dog*

(See also ANIMALS, FLEA.)

DOUBT

Who never doubted, never half believed.
Where doubt there truth is—'tis her shadow.

> BAILEY—*Festus*

Galileo called doubt the father of invention; it is certainly the pioneer.

> BOVEE

Of that there is no manner of doubt—
No probable, possible shadow of doubt—
  No possible doubt whatever.

> W. S. GILBERT—*The Gondoliers*

We know accurately only when we know little; with knowledge doubt increases.

> GOETHE

When in doubt, win the trick.

> HOYLE

I respect faith, but doubt is what gets you an education.

> WILSON MIZNER

And he that doubteth is damned if he eat.

> ROMANS. XIV. 23

To be, or not to be, that is the question:
Whether 'tis nobler in the mind to suffer
The slings and arrows of outrageous fortune;
Or to take arms against a sea of troubles,
And by opposing end them?

> SHAKESPEARE—*Hamlet.* Act III. Sc. 1

              Our doubts are traitors
And make us lose the good we oft might win
By fearing to attempt.

> SHAKESPEARE—*Measure for Measure.* Act I. Sc. 5

There lives more faith in honest doubt,
Believe me, than in half the creeds.

> TENNYSON—*In Memoriam*

I'm from Missouri; you must show me.

> COLONEL WILLARD D. VANDIVER

(See also DISTRUST, SUSPICION.)

DOVE

See how that pair of billing doves
With open murmurs own their loves
And, heedless of censorious eyes,
Pursue their unpolluted joys:
No fears of future want molest
The downy quiet of their nest.

> LADY MARY WORTLEY MONTAGU

Oh that I had wings like a dove! for then would I fly away, and be at rest.

> PSALMS. LV. 6

(See also BIRDS.)

DRAMA

The drama's laws the drama's patrons give,
For we that live to please, must please to live.
SAMUEL JOHNSON

The business of the dramatist is to keep himself out of sight, and to let nothing appear but his characters. As soon as he attracts notice to his personal feelings, the illusion is broken.
MACAULAY

Of all imitators, dramatists are the most perverse, the most unconscionable, or the most unconscious, and have been so time out of mind.
POE—*Marginalia*

The drama is the book of the people.
WILMOT

(See also ACTING, LITERATURE.)

DREAMS

If there were dreams to sell,
Merry and sad to tell,
And the crier rung his bell,
    What would you buy?
T. L. BEDDOES—*Dream-Pedlary*

I dreamt that I dwelt in marble halls,
With vassals and serfs at my side.
ALFRED BUNN—*Bohemian Girl: Song*

Again let us dream where the land lies sunny
And live, like the bees, on our hearts' old honey,
Away from the world that slaves for money--
    Come journey the way with me.
MADISON CAWEIN—*Song of the Road*

Abou Ben Adhem (may his tribe increase!)
Awoke one night from a deep dream of peace.
LEIGH HUNT—*Abou Ben Adhem*

Your old men shall dream dreams, your young men shall see visions.
JOEL. II. 28

There's a long, long trail a-winding
Into the land of my dreams,
Where the nightingales are singing
And the white moon beams;
There's a long, long night of waiting
Until my dreams all come true,
Till the day when I'll be going down that
Long, long trail with you.
STODDARD KING—*There's a Long, Long Trail*

For dhrames always go by conthraries, my dear.
SAMUEL LOVER

                We are such stuff
As dreams are made on, and our little life
Is rounded with a sleep.
SHAKESPEARE—*The Tempest.* Act IV. Sc. 1

(See also IMAGINATION, SLEEP, VISION.)

DRESS

If a woman were about to proceed to her execution, she would demand a little time to perfect her toilet.
CHAMFORT

Eat to please thyself, but dress to please others.
FRANKLIN

(See also APPEARANCE, CLOTHES, FASHION.)

DRINKING

There was an old hen
And she had a wooden leg,
And every damned morning
She laid another egg;
She was the best damned chicken
On the whole damned farm—
And another little drink
Wouldn't do us any harm.
AMERICAN FOLKSONG

It's a long time between drinks.
ANONYMOUS

He is a drunkard who takes more
than three glasses, though he be not
drunk.
EPICTETUS

Drink today, and drown all sorrow;
You shall perhaps not do it tomor-
row.
JOHN FLETCHER—*The Bloody
Brother*

Woe unto them that rise up early
in the morning, that they may follow
strong drink; that continue until
night, till wine inflame them.
ISAIAH. V. 11

The habit of using ardent spirits by
men in office has occasioned more injury to the public, and more trouble
to me, than all other causes. Were
I to commence my administration
again, the first question I would ask
respecting a candidate for office
would be, Does he use ardent spirits?
JEFFERSON

I would appeal to Philip, she said,
but to Philip sober.
VALERIUS MAXIMUS

Drink! for you know not whence
you came, nor why:
Drink! for you know not why you
go, nor where.
OMAR KHAYYÁM—*Rubaiyat*

All excess is ill, but drunkenness is
of the worst sort. It spoils health,
dismounts the mind, and unmans
men. It reveals secrets, is quarrel-
some, lascivious, impudent, dangerous and bad.
WILLIAM PENN

There St. John mingles with my
friendly bowl
The feast of reason and the flow of
soul.
POPE—*Second Book of Horace*

Drunkenness is temporary suicide:
the happiness that it brings is merely
negative, a momentary cessation of
unhappiness.
BERTRAND RUSSELL—*The Conquest of Happiness*

Water is the only drink for a wise
man.
THOREAU—*Walden*

(See also INTEMPERANCE, SONG,
TEMPERANCE, TOASTS, WINE AND
SPIRITS.)

DUTY

To do my duty in that state of life
unto which it shall please God to
call me.
Book of Common Prayer

So nigh is grandeur to our dust,
So near is God to man.
When Duty whispers low, *Thou
must,*
The youth replies, *I can.*
EMERSON—*Voluntaries*

No personal consideration should stand in the way of performing a public duty.
ULYSSES S. GRANT

It is thy duty oftentimes to do what thou wouldst not; thy duty, too, to leave undone that thou wouldst do.
THOMAS À KEMPIS

Let us have faith that right makes might, and in that faith let us, to the end, dare to do our duty as we understand it.
LINCOLN

England expects every man to do his duty.
NELSON

Theirs not to make reply,
Theirs not to reason why,
Theirs but to do and die.
TENNYSON—*The Charge of the Light Brigade*

Not once or twice in our rough island story,
The path of duty was the way to glory.
TENNYSON—*Ode on the Death of the Duke of Wellington*

(See also CHARACTER, MORALITY, SERVICE.)

EARLY RISING

Next to temperance, a quiet conscience, a cheerful mind and active habits, I place early rising as a means of health and happiness.
TIMOTHY FLINT

Early to bed and early to rise,
Makes a man healthy, wealthy and wise.
FRANKLIN—*Poor Richard's Almanac*

(See also MORNING, SUNRISE.)

EARNESTNESS

A man in earnest finds means, or, if he cannot find, creates them.
WILLIAM ELLERY CHANNING

Earnestness is the salt of eloquence.
VICTOR HUGO

Earnestness is enthusiasm tempered by reason.
PASCAL

(See also SINCERITY.)

EARTH
See NATURE

EASTER

Tomb, thou shalt not hold Him longer;
Death is strong, but Life is stronger;
Stronger than the dark, the light;
Stronger than the wrong, the right;
Faith and Hope triumphant say
Christ will rise on Easter Day.
PHILLIPS BROOKS—*An Easter Carol*

Hail, Day of days! in peals of praise
Throughout all ages owned,
When Christ, our God, hell's empire trod,
And high o'er heaven was throned.
FORTUNATUS (Bishop of Poitiers)

Come, ye saints, look here and wonder,
See the place where Jesus lay;
He has borne our sins away;
Joyful tiding,
Yes, the Lord has risen today.
THOMAS KELLY

Hallelujah! Hallelujah!
On the third morning He arose,

Bright with victory o'er his foes.
  Sing we lauding,
  And applauding,
Hallelujah!
    From the Latin of the 12th
    Century

In the bonds of Death He lay
  Who for our offense was slain;
But the Lord is risen today,
  Christ hath brought us life again,
Wherefore let us all rejoice,
Singing loud, with cheerful voice,
Hallelujah!
    LUTHER

"Christ the Lord is risen today,"
Sons of men and angels say.
Raise your joys and triumphs high;
Sing, ye heavens, and earth reply.
    CHARLES WESLEY

(See also CHRIST, CHURCH, RE-
LIGION, RESURRECTION.)

EATING

Eat, drink, and be merry, for tomorrow ye diet.
    WILLIAM GILMORE BEYMER

Tell me what you eat, and I will
tell you what you are.
    BRILLAT-SAVARIN—Physiologie
    du Gout

Better halfe a loafe than no bread.
    CAMDEN—Remaines

The proof of the pudding is in the
eating.
    CERVANTES—Don Quixote

Thou shouldst eat to live; not live
to eat.
    CICERO

The nearer the bone, the sweeter
the meat.
    ENGLISH PROVERB

When I demanded of my friend
    what viands he preferred,
He quoth: "A large cold bottle, and
    a small hot bird!"
    EUGENE FIELD—The Bottle
    and the Bird

I want every peasant to have a
chicken in his pot on Sundays.
    HENRY IV of France

A cheerful look makes a dish a
feast.
    HERBERT—Jacula Prudentum

Let us eat and drink; for tomorrow
we shall die.
    ISAIAH. XXII. 13

For a man seldom thinks with more
earnestness of anything than he does
of his dinner.
    SAMUEL JOHNSON

Man shall not live by bread alone.
    MATTHEW. IV. 4

The way to a man's heart is through
his stomach.
    MRS. SARAH PAYSON PARTON—
    Willis Parton

Better is a dinner of herbs where
love is, than a stalled ox and hatred
therewith.
    PROVERBS. XV. 17

He hath eaten me out of house and
home.
    SHAKESPEARE—Henry IV. Pt.
    II. Act II. Sc. 1

There is no love sincerer than the love of food.
> GEORGE BERNARD SHAW—*Man and Superman*

They say fingers were made before forks, and hands before knives.
> SWIFT—*Polite Conversation*

Bread is the staff of life.
> SWIFT—*Tale of a Tub*

(See also APPETITE, COOKING, FESTIVITIES, FRUIT, HUNGER.)

ECCENTRICITY
See INDIVIDUALITY

ECONOMY

Buy not what you want, but what you have need of; what you do not want is dear at a farthing.
> CATO—*The Censor*

He who will not economize will have to agonize.
> CONFUCIUS

After order and liberty, economy is one of the highest essentials of a free government. . . . Economy is always a guarantee of peace.
> CALVIN COOLIDGE—Speech, 1923

Beware of little expenses; a small leak will sink a great ship.
> FRANKLIN

No man is rich whose expenditure exceeds his means; and no one is poor whose incomings exceed his outgoings.
> HALIBURTON

Have more than thou showest,
Speak less than thou knowest.
> SHAKESPEARE—*King Lear.* Act I. Sc. 4

(See also AVARICE, CARE, MONEY PRUDENCE, THRIFT.)

EDUCATION

Education commences at the mother's knee, and every word spoken within the hearsay of little children tends towards the formation of character.
> HOSEA BALLOU

Education makes a people easy to lead, but difficult to drive; easy to govern, but impossible to enslave.
> Attributed to LORD BROUGHAM

"Reeling and Writhing, of course, to begin with," the Mock Turtle replied, "and the different branches of Arithmetic—Ambition, Distraction, Uglification and Derision."
> LEWIS CARROLL—*Alice in Wonderland*

What greater or better gift can we offer the republic than to teach and instruct our youth?
> CICERO

Training is everything. The peach was once a bitter almond; cauliflower is nothing but cabbage with a college education.
> SAMUEL L. CLEMENS (MARK TWAIN)

The foundation of every state is the education of its youth.
> DIOGENES

The things taught in schools and colleges are not an education, but the means of education.
> EMERSON—*Journal, 1831*

Education is the process of driving a set of prejudices down your throat.
MARTIN H. FISCHER

If a man empties his purse into his head, no one can take it from him.
FRANKLIN

Schoolhouses are the republican line of fortifications.
HORACE MANN

'Tis education forms the common mind;
Just as the twig is bent the tree's inclined.
POPE—*Moral Essays*

Education does not mean teaching people what they do not know. . . . It is a painful, continual and difficult work to be done by kindness, by watching, by warning, by precept, and by praise, but above all—by example.
RUSKIN

There is nothing so stupid as an educated man, if you get off the thing that he was educated in.
WILL ROGERS

Education is an admirable thing, but it is well to remember from time to time that nothing that is worth knowing can be taught.
WILDE—*The Critic as Artist*

(See also ART, BOOKS, CULTURE, KNOWLEDGE, LEARNING, SCIENCE, STUDENT, STUDY, TEACHING.)

EFFICIENCY

He did nothing in particular,
And did it very well.
W. S. GILBERT—*Iolanthe*

The best carpenters make the fewest chips.
GERMAN PROVERB

(See also EXPERT, GENIUS, PERSEVERANCE, TALENT, WORK.)

EGOTISM

The reason why lovers are never weary of one another is this—they are always talking of themselves.
LA ROCHEFOUCAULD

Do you wish men to speak well of you? Then never speak well of yourself.
PASCAL

Nothing is more to me than myself.
STIRNER—*The Ego and His Own*

(See also APPEARANCE, INDIVIDUALITY, SELF-RELIANCE, VANITY.)

ELOQUENCE

Eloquence is the poetry of prose.
BRYANT

The manner of your speaking is full as important as the matter, as more people have ears to be tickled than understandings to judge.
CHESTERFIELD

Noise proves nothing. Often a hen who has merely laid an egg cackles as if she laid an asteroid.
SAMUEL L. CLEMENS (MARK TWAIN)

Thoughts that breathe and words that burn.
GRAY

True eloquence consists in saying all that is necessary, and nothing but what is necessary.
LA ROCHEFOUCAULD

(See also CONVERSATION, HUMOR, LANGUAGE, ORATORY, SPEECH, TALK, TONGUE, WIT, WORD.)

EMPLOYMENT
See OCCUPATION

EMULATION
See IMITATION

ENCOURAGEMENT
See PRAISE

ENDURANCE

Endurance is patience concentrated.
CARLYLE

What can't be cured must be endured.
ENGLISH PROVERB

Endurance is the prerogative of woman, enabling the gentlest to suffer what would cause terror to manhood.
WIELAND

(See also PATIENCE, PERSEVERANCE, STRENGTH, SUFFERING.)

ENEMY

They love him most for the enemies that he has made.
GENERAL E. S. BRAGG—Nominating Speech for Cleveland, 1884

Man is his own worst enemy.
CICERO

He who has a thousand friends has not a friend to spare,
And he who has one enemy will meet him everywhere.
EMERSON—*Translations*

None but yourself who are your greatest foe.
LONGFELLOW

If thine enemy hunger, feed him; if he thirst, give him drink.
ROMANS. XII. 20

My prayer to God is a very short one "Oh Lord, make my enemies ridiculous!" God has granted it.
VOLTAIRE

A man cannot be too careful in the choice of his enemies.
WILDE—*Picture of Dorian Gray*

(See also HATE, JEALOUSY, QUARRELING, REVENGE, WAR.)

ENERGY
See STRENGTH

ENGLAND

If I should die, think only this of me:
  That there's some corner of a foreign field
That is forever England.
RUPERT BROOKE—*The Soldier*

Oh, to be in England,
  Now that April's there.
BROWNING—*Home Thoughts from Abroad*

In England there are sixty different religions, and only one sauce.
MARQUIS CARACCIOLI

Be England what she will,
With all her faults, she is my country still.
CHARLES CHURCHILL—*The Farewell*

I have nothing to offer but blood, toil, tears and sweat.
WINSTON CHURCHILL—Speech, May 28, 1940

We shall go on to the end, we shall fight in France, we shall fight on the seas and oceans, we shall fight with growing confidence and growing strength in the air, we shall defend our Island whatever the cost may be, we shall fight on the landing grounds, we shall fight in the fields and in the streets, we shall fight in the hills; we shall never surrender, and even if, which I do not for a moment believe, this Island or a large part of it were subjugated and starving, then our Empire beyond the seas, armed and guarded by the British Fleet, would carry on the struggle, until, in God's good time, the New World, with all its power and might steps forth to the rescue and the liberation of the old.
WINSTON CHURCHILL—Speech, June 4, 1940

Let us therefore brace ourselves to our duties, and so bear ourselves that, if the British Empire and its Commonwealth last for a thousand years, men will still say, "This was their finest hour."
WINSTON CHURCHILL—Speech, June 18, 1940

Long, dark months of trials and tribulations lie before us. Not only great dangers, but many more misfortunes, many shortcomings, many mistakes, many disappointments will surely be our lot. Death and sorrow will be the companions of our journey; hardship our garment; constancy and valor our only shield. We must be united, we must be undaunted, we must be inflexible. Our qualities and deeds must burn and glow through the gloom of Europe until they become the veritable beacon of its salvation.
WINSTON CHURCHILL—Speech, October 8, 1940

Never in the field of human conflict was so much owed by so many to so few.
WINSTON CHURCHILL, 1941, referring to England's debt to its Royal Air Force.

O, it's a snug little island!
A right little, tight little island!
THOMAS DIBDIN—*The Snug Little Island*

The English nation is never so great as in adversity.
DISRAELI—Speech, 1857

We are indeed a nation of shopkeepers.
DISRAELI—*The Young Duke*

For he might have been a Rooshian
A French or Turk or Proosian,
Or perhaps Itali-an.
But in spite of all temptations
To belong to other nations,
He remains an Englishman.
W. S. GILBERT—*H.M.S. Pinafore*

What have I done for you,
England, my England?
What is there I would not do,
England, my own?
W. E. HENLEY—*England, My
England*

Winds of the World give answer!
They are whimpering to and
fro—
And what should they know of
England who only England
know?—
KIPLING—*English Flag*

This royal throne of kings, this
scepter'd isle,
This earth of majesty, this seat of
Mars,
This other Eden, demi-paradise,
This fortress built by nature for her-
self
Against infection and the hand of
war;
This happy breed of men, this little
world,
This precious stone set in the silver
sea.
SHAKESPEARE—*Richard II.* Act
II. Sc. 1

There is nothing so bad or so good
that you will not find Englishmen
doing it; but you will never find an
Englishman in the wrong. He does
everything on principle. He fights
you on patriotic principles; he robs
you on business principles; he en-
slaves you on imperial principles.
GEORGE BERNARD SHAW—*The
Man of Destiny*

An Englishman thinks he is moral
when he is only uncomfortable.
GEORGE BERNARD SHAW

When Britain first at Heaven's
command,
Arose from out the azure main,
This was the charter of the land,
And Guardian angels sung this
strain;
"Rule Britannia! rule the waves;
Britons never will be slaves."
JAMES THOMSON—*Masque of
Alfred*

Froth at the top, dregs at bottom,
but the middle excellent.
VOLTAIRE—*Description of the
English Nation*

(See also DEMOCRACY, FLAG,
FREEDOM, LONDON, WAR.)

ENJOYMENT
See PLEASURE

ENTHUSIASM

In things pertaining to enthusiasm
no man is sane who does not know
how to be insane on proper occasions.
HENRY WARD BEECHER

Nothing is so contagious as enthusiasm; it moves stones, it charms
brutes. Enthusiasm is the genius of
sincerity and truth accomplishes no
victories without it.
BULWER-LYTTON

Nothing great was ever achieved
without enthusiasm.
EMERSON—*On Circles*

The world belongs to the Enthusiast who keeps cool.
WILLIAM McFEE—*Casuals of
the Sea*

The sense of this word among the
Greeks affords the noblest definition
of it: enthusiasm signifies God in us.
MME. DE STAËL

Enthusiasm is that temper of the mind in which the imagination has got the better of the judgment.
BISHOP WARBURTON—*Divine Legation*

(See also AMBITION, CHARACTER, ENERGY, STRENGTH, YOUTH, ZEAL.)

ENVY

As a moth gnaws a garment, so doth envy consume a man.
ST. CHRYSOSTOM

Thou shalt not covet thy neighbor's house, thou shalt not covet thy neighbor's wife, nor his manservant, nor his maidservant, nor his ox, nor his ass, nor anything that is thy neighbor's.
EXODUS. XX. 17

The hen of our neighbor appears to us a goose, says the Oriental proverb.
MME. DELUZY

It is better to be envied than pitied.
HERODOTUS

Envy, to which th' ignoble mind's a slave,
Is emulation in the learn'd or brave.
POPE—*Essay on Man*

It is the practice of the multitude to bark at eminent men, as little dogs do at strangers.
SENECA—*Of a Happy Life*

When men are full of envy they disparage everything, whether it be good or bad.
TACITUS

(See also DOUBT, HATE, JEALOUSY, SUSPICION.)

EPITAPH

A tomb now suffices him for whom the whole world was not sufficient.
Epitaph on Alexander the Great

O man! whosoever thou art, and whensoever thou comest, for come I know thou wilt, I am Cyrus, founder of the Persian empire. Envy me not the little earth that covers my body.
Epitaph of Cyrus

Let there be no inscription upon my tomb. Let no man write my epitaph. No man can write my epitaph. I am here ready to die. I am not allowed to vindicate my character; and when I am prevented from vindicating myself, let no man dare calumniate me. Let my character and motives repose in obscurity and peace, till other times and other men can do them justice.
ROBERT EMMET—Speech on his Trial, 1803

The body of Benjamin Franklin, Printer, (Like the cover of an old book, its contents torn out and stript of its lettering and gilding), Lies here, food for worms; But the work shall not be lost, for it will (as he believed) appear once more in a new and more elegant edition, revised and corrected by the author.
BENJAMIN FRANKLIN—Epitaph on Himself, written in 1728

Life is a jest, and all things show it, I thought so once, but now I know it.
GAY—*My Own Epitaph*

Here lies one whose name was writ in water.
Engraved on Keats's tombstone

I strove with none, for none was
  worth my strife;
Nature I loved, and after Nature,
  Art;
I warmed both hands before the fire
  of life;
It sinks, and I am ready to depart.
  LANDOR—Epitaph on Himself

Requiescat in pace.
  May he rest in peace.
  Order of the Mass

Excuse my dust.
  DOROTHY PARKER—Her Own
  Epitaph

Under the wide and starry sky,
Dig the grave and let me lie;
Glad did I live and gladly die,
And I laid me down with a will.
This be the verse you grave for me:
"Here he lies, where he longed to
  be;
Home is the sailor, home from the
  sea,
And the hunter home from the hill."
  STEVENSON—Engraved on his
  tombstone

Green sod above lie light, lie light—
Good night, dear heart, good night,
  good night.
  On the tombstone of Susy
  Clemens by Mark Twain

Here in this place sleeps one whom
  love
Caused, through great cruelty, to fall;
A little scholar, poor enough,
Whom François Villon men did call.
No scrap of land or garden small
He owned. He gave his goods away,
Table and trestles, baskets—all;
For God's sake say for him this Lay.
  FRANÇOIS VILLON—His own
  Epitaph

The poet's fate is here in emblem
  shown,
He asked for bread, and he received
  a stone.
  SAMUEL WESLEY—On Butler's
  Monument in Westminster
  Abbey

If you would see his monument look
around.
  Inscription on the tomb of Sir
  Christopher Wren in St. Paul's,
  London

(See also DEATH, GRAVE, MONU-
MENT, SATIRE, WIT.)

EQUALITY

Men are made by nature unequal.
It is vain, therefore, to treat them
as if they were equal.
  FROUDE—*Party Politics*

The equal right of all men to the
use of land is as clear as their equal
right to breathe the air—it is a right
proclaimed by the fact of their existence. For we cannot suppose that
some men have a right to be in this
world, and others no right.
  HENRY GEORGE

We hold these truths to be self-evident: that all men are created equal;
that they are endowed by their Creator with inalienable rights; that
among these are life, liberty and the
pursuit of happiness.
  JEFFERSON

Your levellers wish to level down
as far as themselves, but they cannot bear levelling up to themselves.
  SAMUEL JOHNSON—*Boswell's
  Life of*

For the colonel's lady an' Judy O'Grady
Are sisters under their skins.
> KIPLING—*Barrack Room Ballads*

Fourscore and seven years ago, our fathers brought forth on this continent a new nation, conceived in liberty, and dedicated to the proposition that all men are created equal.
> LINCOLN—*Gettysburg Address*

Let's go hand in hand, not one before another.
> SHAKESPEARE—*Comedy of Errors*. Act V. Sc. 1

The trickling rain doth fall
Upon us one and all;
The south-wind kisses
The saucy milkmaid's cheek,
The nun's, demure and meek,
Nor any misses.
> E. C. STEDMAN—*A Madrigal*

(See also DEMOCRACY, FREEDOM, RIGHTS, UNION.)

ERROR

To stumble twice against the same stone is a proverbial disgrace.
> CICERO

The cautious seldom err.
> CONFUCIUS

An error gracefully acknowledged is a victory won.
> CAROLINE L. GASCOIGNE

When every one is in the wrong, every one is in the right.
> LA CHAUSSÉE

The man who makes no mistakes does not usually make anything.
> EDWARD J. PHELPS—Speech at Mansion House

To err is human, to forgive divine.
> POPE—*An Essay on Criticism*

Error will slip through a crack, while truth will stick in a doorway.
> H. W. SHAW

(See also EVIL, FALSEHOOD, FAULT, FOLLY, SIN, TRUTH.)

ETERNITY

This is eternal life; a life of everlasting love, showing itself in everlasting good works; and whosoever lives that life, he lives the life of God, and hath eternal life.
> KINGSLEY

The thought of eternity consoles for the shortness of life.
> MALHERBE

In time there is no present,
In eternity no future,
In eternity no past.
> TENNYSON—*The "How" and "Why"*

(See also DEATH, FUTURE, HEAVEN, HELL, IMMORTALITY, RESURRECTION, SOUL, TIME, TOMORROW.)

EVENING

The curfew tolls the knell of parting day,
  The lowing herd winds slowly o'er the lea,
The ploughman homeward plods his weary way,
  And leaves the world to darkness and to me.
> GRAY—*Elegy in a Country Churchyard*

Day hath put on his jacket, and
around
His burning bosom buttoned it with
stars.
HOLMES—*Evening*

One by one the flowers close,
Lily and dewy rose
Shutting their tender petals from the
moon.
CHRISTINA G. ROSSETTI—*Twilight Calm*

(See also DARKNESS, DAY, NATURE,
NIGHT, SHADOW, STAR, SUNSET,
TWILIGHT.)

EVENTS

Coming events cast their shadows
before.
CAMPBELL

Events of great consequence often
spring from trifling circumstances.
LIVY

(See also CIRCUMSTANCE, HISTORY,
LIFE.)

EVIDENCE

One eye-witness is of more weight
than ten hearsays.
PLAUTUS

Facts are stubborn things.
SMOLLETT

Some circumstantial evidence is very
strong, as when you find a trout in
the milk.
THOREAU

(See also FACTS, PROOF.)

EVIL

Evil events from evil causes spring.
ARISTOPHANES

Evil and good are God's right hand
and left.
BAILEY—*Prelude to Festus*

Touch not; taste not; handle not.
COLOSSIANS. II. 21

Evil communications corrupt good
manners.
I CORINTHIANS. XV. 33

Of two evils choose the least.
ERASMUS

Woe unto them that call evil good,
and good evil.
ISAIAH. V. 20

What is evil?—Whatever springs
from weakness.
NIETZSCHE—*The Antichrist*

Never throw mud. You may miss
your mark; but you must have dirty
hands.
JOSEPH PARKER

Ill gotten is ill spent.
PLAUTUS

Be not overcome of evil, but overcome evil with good.
ROMANS. XII. 21

Evil often triumphs, but never conquers.
JOSEPH ROUX

The evil that men do lives after
them;
The good is oft interred with their
bones.
SHAKESPEARE—*Julius Caesar.*
Act III. Sc. 2

As sure as God is good, so surely there is no such thing as necessary evil.
SOUTHEY

(See also BRIBERY, CORRUPTION, DEVIL, ERROR, FALSEHOOD, HATE, MISCHIEF, REVENGE, SIN, WICKEDNESS.)

EVOLUTION

There is no more reason to believe that man descended from some inferior animal than there is to believe that a stately mansion has descended from a small cottage.
W. J. BRYAN, 1925

Some call it Evolution,
    And others call it God.
    W. H. CARRUTH—Each in His Own Tongue

I have called this principle, by which each slight variation, if useful, is preserved, by the term of Natural Selection.
DARWIN—Origin of Species

Or ever the knightly years were gone
    With the old world to the grave,
I was a king in Babylon
    And you were a Christian Slave.
    W. E. HENLEY—Echoes

Children, behold the Chimpanzee;
He sits in the ancestral tree
From which we sprang in ages gone.
I'm glad we sprang: had we held on,
We might, for aught that I can say,
Be horrid Chimpanzees today.
    OLIVER HERFORD—The Chimpanzee

When you were a tadpole and I was
    a fish in the Palaeozoic time
And side by side in the sluggish tide,
    we sprawled in the ooze and
    slime.
    LANGDON SMITH—Evolution

(See also CHANGE, LIFE, NATURE, PROGRESS, SCIENCE, WORLD.)

EXAMPLE

Lives of great men all remind us
    We can make our lives sublime,
And, departing, leave behind us
    Footprints on the sands of time.
    LONGFELLOW—A Psalm of Life

None preaches better than the ant, and she says nothing.
FRANKLIN

Example is more efficacious than precept.
SAMUEL JOHNSON

Children have more need of models than of critics.
JOUBERT

(See also EDUCATION, EXPERIENCE, IMITATION, INFLUENCE, LEARNING, TEACHING.)

EXCELLENCE

If a man has good corn, or wood, or boards, or pigs to sell, or can make better chairs or knives, crucibles, or church organs, than anybody else, you will find a broad, hard-beaten road to his house, though it be in the woods.
EMERSON—Journal, 1855

Excellent things are rare.
PLATO—The Republic

(See also MOUSE-TRAP, QUALITY, SUCCESS, WORTH.)

EXCUSE

An excuse is worse and more terrible
than a lie; for an excuse is a lie
guarded.
POPE

And oftentimes, excusing of a fault
Doth make the fault the worse by the
excuse,—
As patches, set upon a little breach,
Discredit more in hiding of the fault
Than did the fault before it was so
patched.
SHAKESPEARE—*King John.* Act
IV. Sc. 2

(See also APOLOGY, FORGIVENESS,
PARDON.)

EXPECTATION

I have known him (Micawber) come
home to supper with a flood of tears,
and a declaration that nothing was
now left but a jail; and go to bed
making a calculation of the expense
of putting bow-windows to the house,
"in case anything turned up," which
was his favorite expression.
DICKENS—*David Copperfield*

Everything comes if a man will only
wait.
DISRAELI—*Tancred*

Blessed are those that nought expect,
For they shall not be disappointed.
WALCOT—*Ode to Pitt*

(See also AMBITION, CONFIDENCE,
DESIRE, HOPE, TRUST, WISH.)

EXPERIENCE

Experience is the best of schoolmas-
ters, only the school-fees are heavy.
CARLYLE—*Miscellaneous Essays*

Only so much do I know, as I have
lived.
EMERSON—*The American
Scholar*

A burnt child dreads the fire.
ENGLISH PROVERB

Experience is the extract of suffering.
ARTHUR HELPS

I have but one lamp by which my
feet are guided, and that is the lamp
of experience.
PATRICK HENRY

One thorn of experience is worth a
whole wilderness of warning.
LOWELL—*Among My Books*

Experience is the name men give to
their follies or their sorrows.
ALFRED DE MUSSET

Men are wise in proportion, not to
their experience, but to their capacity
for experience.
GEORGE BERNARD SHAW—*Max-
ims for Revolutionists*

Is there anyone so wise as to learn
by the experience of others?
VOLTAIRE

Experience is the fool's best teacher;
the wise do not need it.
WELSH PROVERB

(See also EXAMPLE, FOLLY, KNOWL-
EDGE, LEARNING, LIFE, PROGRESS,
SUFFERING, TRIAL.)

EXPERT

An expert is one who knows more
and more about less and less.
NICHOLAS MURRAY BUTLER

The shoemaker makes a good shoe because he makes nothing else.
EMERSON—*Letters and Social Aims*

An expert is a person who avoids the small errors as he sweeps on to the grand fallacy.
BENJAMIN STOLBERG

(See also EFFICIENCY, GENIUS, TALENT)

EXTRAVAGANCE
See WEALTH

EXTREME

Mistrust the man who finds everything good, the man who finds everything evil, and still more, the man who is indifferent to everything.
LAVATER

In everything the middle course is best; all things in excess bring trouble.
PLAUTUS

Avoid Extremes; and shun the fault of such
Who still are pleas'd too little or too much.
POPE—*Essay on Criticism*

(See also MODERATION, OPINION, WISDOM.)

EYE

A gray eye is a sly eye,
And roguish is a brown one;
Turn full upon me thy eye,—
Ah, how its wavelets drown one!

A blue eye is a true eye;
Mysterious is a dark one,
Which flashes like a spark-sun!
A black eye is the best one.
W. R. ALGER—*Oriental Poetry*

Among the blind the one-eyed man is king.
ANONYMOUS

The mind has a thousand eyes,
And the heart but one;
Yet the light of a whole life dies
When love is done.
F. W. BOURDILLON—*Light*

The love light in her eye.
HARTLEY COLERIDGE

In the twinkling of an eye.
I CORINTHIANS. XV. 52

He kept him as the apple of his eye.
DEUTERONOMY. XXXII. 10

The eyes believe themselves; the ears believe other people.
GERMAN PROVERB

Drink to me only with thine eyes,
And I will pledge with mine.
BEN JONSON

As President, I have no eyes but constitutional eyes; I cannot see you.
LINCOLN to the South Carolina Commissioners

I dislike an eye that twinkles like a star. Those only are beautiful which, like the planets, have a steady, lambent light,—are luminous, but not sparkling.
LONGFELLOW—*Hyperion*

Alack, there lies more peril in thine eye
Than twenty of their swords.
SHAKESPEARE—*Romeo and Juliet*. Act II. Sc. 2

Her eyes are homes of silent prayer.
TENNYSON—*In Memoriam*

(See also BLINDNESS, DARKNESS, LIGHT, LOVE.)

FACE

A fair face without a fair soul is like a glass eye that shines and sees nothing.
BLACKIE

There was but one beloved face on earth,
And that was shining on him.
BYRON—*The Dream*

He had a face like a benediction.
CERVANTES

A cheerful face is nearly as good for an invalid as healthy weather.
FRANKLIN

The worst of faces still is human.
LAVATER

Was this the face that launch'd a thousand ships,
And burnt the topless towers of Ilium?
Sweet Helen, make me immortal with a kiss.—
Her lips suck forth my soul; see, where it flies!—
MARLOWE—*Dr. Faustus*

"What is your fortune, my pretty maid?"
"My face is my fortune, sir," she said.
NURSERY RHYME

Lift thou up the light of thy countenance upon us.
PSALMS. IV. 6

A countenance more in sorrow than in anger.
SHAKESPEARE—*Hamlet*. Act. I. Sc. 2

God has given you one face, and you make yourselves another.
SHAKESPEARE—*Hamlet*. Act III. Sc. 1

(See also APPEARANCE, BEAUTY, EYE, MOUTH, NOSE, SMILE, WOMAN.)

FACTS

I grow daily to honor facts more and more, and theory less and less.
CARLYLE

There are no eternal facts, as there are no absolute truths.
NIETZSCHE — *Human, All-too-Human*

Facts are stubborn things.
SMOLLETT

Every fact that is learned becomes a key to other facts.
E. L. YOUMANS

(See also EVIDENCE, SCIENCE.)

FAILURE

A failure establishes only this, that our determination to succeed was not strong enough.
BOVEE

In the lexicon of youth, which
Fate reserves for a bright manhood, there is no such word
As—*fail!*
BULWER-LYTTON—*Richelieu*

But to him who tries and fails and dies,
I give great honor and glory and tears.
JOAQUIN MILLER—*For Those Who Fail*

How are the mighty fallen!
II SAMUEL. I. 25

Here's to the men who lose!
What though their work be e'er so
nobly plann'd
And watched with zealous care;
No glorious halo crowns their ef-
forts grand—
Contempt is Failure's share!
G. L. SCARBOROUGH—*To the
Vanquished*

Failure is more frequently from want
of energy than want of capital.
DANIEL WEBSTER

(See also ERROR, RUIN, SUCCESS.)

FAIRIES

When the first baby laughed for the
first time, the laugh broke into a million pieces, and they all went skipping about. That was the beginning
of fairies.
BARRIE—*Peter Pan*

Nothing can be truer than fairy wisdom. It is as true as sunbeams.
DOUGLAS JERROLD

Fairies, black, grey, green, and white,
You moonshine revellers, and shades
of night.
SHAKESPEARE—*Merry Wives of
Windsor*. Act V. Sc. 5

(See also ILLUSION, IMAGINATION,
SPIRIT, VISION.)

FAIR PLAY

Thou shouldst not decide until thou
hast heard what both have to say.
ARISTOPHANES—*The Wasps*

All is fair in love and war.
ENGLISH PROVERB

What is sauce for the goose is sauce
for the gander.
ENGLISH PROVERB

(See also CHARACTER, HONESTY,
JUDGMENT, JUSTICE, VIRTUE.)

FAITH

Faith is the continuation of reason.
WILLIAM ADAMS

The person who has a firm trust in
the Supreme Being is powerful in his
power, wise by his wisdom, happy by
his happiness.
ADDISON

Faith is to believe what we do not
see; and the reward of this faith is to
see what we believe.
ST. AUGUSTINE

An outward and visible sign of an
inward and spiritual grace.
BOOK OF COMMON PRAYER

We walk by faith, not by sight.
II CORINTHIANS. V. 7

All I have seen teaches me to trust
the Creator for all I have not seen.
EMERSON

Faith is the substance of things hoped
for, the evidence of things not seen.
HEBREWS. XI. 1

Let us have faith that right makes
might; and in that faith, let us, to the
end, dare to do our duty as we understand it.
LINCOLN

Here I stand. I can do no otherwise.
God help me. Amen.
LUTHER at Diet of Worms

Be thou faithful unto death.
REVELATION. II. 10

There lives more faith in honest doubt,
Believe me, than in half the creeds.
TENNYSON

I have fought a good fight, I have finished my course, I have kept the faith.
II TIMOTHY. IV. 7

Faith is the force of life.
TOLSTOY

I can believe anything, provided it is incredible.
WILDE—*The Picture of Dorian Gray*

(See also BELIEF, CONFIDENCE, DOCTRINE, GOD, RELIGION, TRUST.)

FALL
See AUTUMN

FALSEHOOD

There is no such thing as white lies; a lie is as black as a coalpit, and twice as foul.
HENRY WARD BEECHER

So near is falsehood to truth that a wise man would do well not to trust himself on the narrow edge.
CICERO

Falsehood is so easy, truth so difficult.
GEORGE ELIOT

Round numbers are always false.
SAMUEL JOHNSON

False in one thing, false in everything.
Law Maxim

Falsehoods not only disagree with truths, but usually quarrel among themselves.
DANIEL WEBSTER

(See also DECEPTION, HYPOCRISY, LYING, SLANDER.)

FAME

I awoke one morning and found myself famous.
BYRON—From Moore's *Life of Byron*

To many fame comes too late.
CAMOENS

If you would not be forgotten as soon as you are dead, either write things worth reading or do things worth writing.
FRANKLIN

Men think highly of those who rise rapidly in the world; whereas nothing rises quicker than dust, straw, and feathers.
HARE

The fame of great men ought always to be estimated by the means used to acquire it.
LA ROCHEFOUCAULD

I do not like the man who squanders life for fame; give me the man who living makes a name.
MARTIAL—*Epigrams*

Fame is but the breath of the people, and that often unwholesome.
ROUSSEAU

Fame is the perfume of heroic deeds.
SOCRATES

No true and permanent Fame can be founded except in labors which promote the happiness of mankind.
CHARLES SUMNER—*Fame and Glory*

What a heavy burden is a name that has become too famous.
VOLTAIRE

In fame's temple there is always a niche to be found for rich dunces, importunate scoundrels, or successful butchers of the human race.
ZIMMERMANN

(See also APPLAUSE, GLORY, HERO, HONOR, MONUMENT, NAME, REPUTATION.)

FAMILIARITY

Familiarity breeds contempt
ANONYMOUS

Though familiarity may not breed contempt, it takes off the edge of admiration.
HAZLITT

The living together for three long, rainy days in the country has done more to dispel love than all the perfidies in love that have ever been committed.
ARTHUR HELPS

Familiarity is a magician that is cruel to beauty, but kind to ugliness.
OUIDA

(See also COMPANIONSHIP, FRIENDSHIP, KNOWLEDGE.)

FAMILY

The happiest moments of my life have been the few which I have passed at home in the bosom of my family.
JEFFERSON

There is little less trouble in governing a private family than a whole kingdom.
MONTAIGNE

None but a mule denies his family.
MOROCCAN PROVERB

The family is more sacred than the state.
POPE PIUS XI

(See also BABYHOOD, BOY, CHILDHOOD, DAUGHTER, FATHER, HOME, MOTHER, PARENT.)

FANATICISM

The downright fanatic is nearer to the heart of things than the cool and slippery disputant.
CHAPIN

The false fire of an overheated mind.
COWPER

Fanaticism is the child of false zeal and of superstition, the father of intolerance and of persecution.
J. W. FLETCHER

What is fanaticism today is the fashionable creed tomorrow, and trite as the multiplication table a week after.
WENDELL PHILLIPS

(See also ENTHUSIASM, ZEAL.)

FANCY
See VISION

FAREWELL

Fare thee well! and if for ever,
Still for ever, fare thee well.
BYRON—*Fare Thee Well*

Sweets to the sweet; farewell!
SHAKESPEARE—*Hamlet*. Act. V.
Sc. 1

(See also ABSENCE, PARTING.)

FARMING

Some people tell us that there ain't
no Hell,
But they never farmed, so how can
they tell?
ANONYMOUS

Those who labor in the earth are the
chosen people of God, if He ever had
a chosen people, whose breasts He
has made His peculiar deposit for
substantial and genuine virtue.
JEFFERSON—*Notes on Virginia*

A farmer is always going to be rich
next year.
PHILEMON

Farming is a most senseless pursuit,
a mere laboring in a circle. You sow
that you may reap, and then you reap
that you may sow. Nothing ever
comes of it.
STOBAEUS

The farmer works the soil,
The agriculturist works the farmer.
EUGENE F. WARE—*The Kansas
Bandit*

Let us never forget that the cultiva-
tion of the earth is the most important labor of man. When tillage begins, other arts follow. The farmers,
therefore, are the founders of civilization.
DANIEL WEBSTER

(See also AGRICULTURE, COUNTRY
LIFE, NATURE.)

FASHION

The fashion of this world passeth
away.
I CORINTHIANS. VII. 31

Fashion is only the attempt to realize
art in living forms and social intercourse.
HOLMES

A fashionable woman is always in
love—with herself.
LA ROCHEFOUCAULD

A glass of fashion and the mould of
form,
The observ'd of all observers.
SHAKESPEARE—*Hamlet*. Act III.
Sc. 1

I see that the fashion wears out more
apparel than the man.
SHAKESPEARE — *Much Ado
About Nothing*. Act III. Sc. 3

Fashion is a form of ugliness so in-
tolerable that we have to alter it every
six months.
WILDE

(See also APPEARANCE, CLOTHES,
CUSTOM, DRESS, SOCIETY, VANITY.)

FATE

The bow is bent, the arrow flies,
The wingèd shaft of fate.
IRA ALDRIDGE—*On William
Tell*

Here's a sigh to those who love me,
    And a smile to those who hate;
And whatever sky's above me,
    Here's a heart for every fate.
        BYRON—*To Thomas Moore*

He has gone to the demnition bow-
wows.
        DICKENS—*Nicholas Nickleby*

We make our fortunes and we call
them fate.
        DISRAELI

'Tis Fate that flings the dice,
    And as she flings
Of kings makes peasants,
    And of peasants kings.
        DRYDEN

A strict belief in fate is the worst of
slavery, imposing upon our necks an
everlasting lord and tyrant, whom we
are to stand in awe of night and day.
        EPICURUS

Thou must (in commanding and
winning, or serving and losing, suffering or triumphing) be either anvil
or hammer.
        GOETHE

Though men determine, the gods do
dispose: and oft times many things
fall out between the cup and the lip.
        ROBERT GREENE

The Moving Finger writes; and hav-
    ing writ,
Moves on; nor all your Piety nor
    Wit
    Shall lure it back to cancel half a
        Line,
Nor all your Tears wash out a Word
    of it.
        OMAR KHAYYÁM—*Rubaiyat*

The die is cast.—Exclamation of Caesar as he crossed the Rubicon.
        SUETONIUS

(See CHANCE, DESTINY, FORTUNE,
    GOD, GODS, LIFE, LUCK,
    PROVIDENCE.)

FATHER

A father is a banker provided by
nature.
        FRENCH PROVERB

The fathers have eaten sour grapes,
and the children's teeth are set on
edge.
        JEREMIAH. XXXI. 29

Call no man your father upon the
earth: for one is your Father, which
is in heaven.
        MATTHEW. XXIII. 9

It is a wise father that knows his own
child.
        SHAKESPEARE — *The Merchant
        of Venice. Act II. Sc. 2*

The child is father of the man.
        WORDSWORTH

(See also BABYHOOD, CHILDHOOD,
    PARENT.)

FAULT

There is so much good in the worst
    of us,
And so much bad in the best of us,
That it ill behooves any of us
To find fault with the rest of us.
        ANONYMOUS

The greatest of faults, I should say, is
to be conscious of none.
        CARLYLE — *Heroes and Hero
        Worship*

The defects of great men are the consolation of the dunces.
ISAAC D'ISRAELI

We keep on deceiving ourselves in regard to our faults, until we at last come to look upon them as virtues.
HEINE

He who overlooks a fault, invites the commission of another.
SYRUS—*Maxims*

(See also ERROR, GUILT.)

FEAR

Fear makes us feel our humanity.
DISRAELI

Fear always springs from ignorance.
EMERSON—*The American Scholar*

The meek, the terrible meek, the fierce agonizing meek, are about to enter into their inheritance.
CHARLES R. KENNEDY—*The Terrible Meek*

From a distance it is something; and nearby it is nothing.
LA FONTAINE

They are slaves who fear to speak
For the fallen and the weak.
LOWELL—*Stanzas on Freedom*

The fear of the Lord is the beginning of knowledge.
PROVERBS. I. 7

The only thing we have to fear is fear itself.
F. D. ROOSEVELT — Inaugural Address, 1933

(See also COWARD, DESPAIR, DOUBT.)

FESTIVITIES

Why should we break up
Our snug and pleasant party?
Time was made for slaves,
But never for us so hearty.
JOHN B. BUCKSTONE—*Billy Taylor*

Let us have wine and woman, mirth and laughter,
Sermons and soda-water the day after.
BYRON—*Don Juan*

Then I commended mirth, because a man hath no better thing under the sun, than to eat, and to drink, and to be merry.
ECCLESIASTES. VIII. 15

The feast of reason, and the flow of soul.
POPE—*Book of Horace*

Feast, and your halls are crowded;
Fast, and the world goes by.
ELLA WHEELER WILCOX—*Solitude*

(See also AMUSEMENT, DRINKING, EATING, PLEASURE, SPORT.)

FICTION
See BOOKS

FIDELITY
See FAITH

FIGHT
See CONTROVERSY

FIRE

Your own property is concerned when your neighbor's house is on fire.
HORACE

The burnt child dreads the fire.
BEN JONSON—*The Devil Is an Ass*

There can no great smoke arise, but there must be some fire.
LYLY

All the fat's in the fire.
MARSTON—*What You Will*

FIRMNESS

That which is called firmness in a king is called obstinacy in a donkey.
LORD ERSKINE

When firmness is sufficient, rashness is unnecessary.
NAPOLEON

(See also DECISION, OBSTINACY, RESOLUTION, STRENGTH.)

FISH

As lacking in privacy as a goldfish.
ANONYMOUS

She is neither fish, nor flesh, nor good red herring.
HEYWOOD—*Proverbs*

Master, I marvel how the fishes live in the sea.
Why, as men do a-land: the great ones eat up the little ones.
PERICLES

We have here other fish to fry.
RABELAIS—*Works*

(See also FISHING.)

FISHING

When the wind is in the East,
Then the fishes bite the least;
When the wind is in the West,
Then the fishes bite the best;
When the wind is in the North,
Then the fishes do come forth;
When the wind is in the South,
It blows the bait in the fish's mouth.
ANONYMOUS

There are as good fish in the sea as ever came out of it.
ENGLISH PROVERB

To fish in troubled waters.
MATTHEW HENRY — *Commentaries*. Psalm LX

You must lose a fly to catch a trout.
HERBERT—*Jacula Prudentum*

A fishing-rod was a stick with a hook at one end and a fool at the other.
SAMUEL JOHNSON

Angling is an innocent cruelty.
GEORGE PARKER

Angling may be said to be so like the mathematics that it can never be fully learnt.
IZAAK WALTON—*The Compleat Angler*

We may say of angling as Dr. Boteler said of strawberries: "Doubtless God could have made a better berry, but doubtless God never did"; and so, (if I might be judge,) God never did make a more calm, quiet, innocent recreation than angling.
IZAAK WALTON—*The Compleat Angler*

(See also FISH.)

FLAG

If any one attempts to haul down the American flag, shoot him on the spot.
JOHN A. DIX—*Speeches and Addresses*

When Freedom from her mountain height
  Unfurled her standard to the air,
She tore the azure robe of night,
  And set the stars of glory there.
JOSEPH RODMAN DRAKE—*The American Flag*

Oh! say can you see by the dawn's early light
What so proudly we hail'd at the twilight's last gleaming,
Whose broad stripes and bright stars, thro' the perilous fight,
O'er the ramparts we watch'd, were so gallantly streaming;
And the rocket's red glare, the bombs bursting in air,
Gave proof thro' the night that our flag was still there!
CHORUS
Oh! say, does that star-spangled banner yet wave,
O'er the land of the free and the home of the brave.
FRANCIS SCOTT KEY—*The Star-Spangled Banner*

Cheers for the sailors that fought on the wave for it,
Cheers for the soldiers that always were brave for it,
Tears for the men that went down to the grave for it,
  Here comes the Flag!
ARTHUR MACY—*The Flag*

The flag of our Union forever!
GEORGE P. MORRIS—*The Flag of Our Union*

Your flag and my flag,
  And how it flies today
In your land and my land
  And half a world away!
Rose-red and blood-red
  The stripes forever gleam;
Snow-white and soul-white—
  The good forefathers' dream;
Sky-blue and true-blue, with stars to gleam aright—
The gloried guidon of the day, a shelter through the night.
WILBUR D. NESBIT—*Your Flag and My Flag*

I pledge allegiance to the flag of the United States and to the republic for which it stands, one nation, indivisible, with liberty and justice for all.
The Pledge of Allegiance to the Flag

Yes, we'll rally round the flag, boys, we'll rally once again,
  Shouting the battle-cry of Freedom,
We will rally from the hillside, we'll gather from the plain,
  Shouting the battle-cry of Freedom.
GEORGE F. ROOT—*Battle Cry of Freedom*

Let it rise! let it rise, till it meet the sun in his coming: let the earliest light of the morning gild it, and the parting day linger and play on its summit.
DANIEL WEBSTER

"Shoot, if you must, this old gray head,
But spare your country's flag," she said.
WHITTIER—*Barbara Frietchie*

(See also AMERICA, ENGLAND, PATRIOTISM, SOLDIER, TOASTS, VICTORY, WAR.)

FLATTERY

Imitation is the sincerest (form) of
flattery.
COLTON—*Lacon*

Men are like stone jugs—you may lug
them where you like by the ears.
SAMUEL JOHNSON

A man that flattereth his neighbor
spreadeth a net for his feet.
PROVERBS. XXIX. 5

Their throat is an open sepulchre;
they flatter with their tongue.
PSALMS. V. 9

It is easy to flatter; it is harder to
praise.
JEAN PAUL RICHTER

O, that men's ears should be
To counsel deaf, but not to flattery!
SHAKESPEARE—*Timon of Ath-
ens*. Act I. Sc. 2

(See also APPLAUSE, COMPLIMENT,
IMITATION, PRAISE, VANITY.)

FLEA

Great fleas have little fleas upon their
backs to bite 'em,
And little fleas have lesser fleas, and
so ad infinitum.
And the great fleas themselves, in
turn, have greater fleas to go on;
While these again have greater still,
and greater still, and so on.
AUGUSTUS DE MORGAN — *A
Budget of Paradoxes*

I do honour the very flea of his dog.
BEN JONSON—*Every Man in His
Humour*

(See also DOG.)

FLIRTATION

Flirtation, attention without inten-
tion.
MAX O'RELL—*John Bull and
His Island*

Men seldom make passes
At girls who wear glasses.
DOROTHY PARKER

It is the same in love as in war; a
fortress that parleys is half taken.
MARGUERITE DE VALOIS

(See also KISS, LOVE, WOMAN,
WOOING.)

FLOWERS

I like not lady-slippers,
Nor yet the sweet-pea blossoms,
Nor yet the flaky roses,
Red or white as snow:
I like the chaliced lilies,
The heavy Easter lilies,
The gorgeous tiger-lilies,
That in our garden grow.
T. B. ALDRICH—*Tiger Lilies*

Flowers may beckon towards us, but
they speak toward heaven and God.
HENRY WARD BEECHER

Flowers have an expression of countenance as much as men or animals.
Some seem to smile; some have a sad
expression; some are pensive and
diffident; others again are plain, honest and upright, like the broad-faced
sunflower and the hollyhock.
HENRY WARD BEECHER — *A
Discourse on Flowers*

Where fall the tears of love the rose
    appears,
And where the ground is bright with
    friendship's tears,
Forget-me-not, and violets, heavenly
    blue,
Spring glittering with the cheerful
    drops like dew.
        BRYANT—Trans. of N. Muller's
        Paradise of Tears

The snowdrop and primrose our
    woodlands adorn,
And violets bathe in the wet o' the
    morn.
        BURNS—*My Nannie's Awa'*

I know not which I love the most,
    Nor which the comeliest shows,
The timid, bashful violet
    Or the royal-hearted rose:

The pansy in her purple dress,
    The pink with cheek of red,
Or the faint, fair heliotrope, who
    hangs,
    Like a bashful maid her head.
        PHOEBE CARY—*Spring Flowers*

                Flowers are words
Which even a babe may understand.
        BISHOP COXE—*The Singing of
        Birds*

The buttercups, bright-eyed and
    bold,
Held up their chalices of gold
To catch the sunshine and the dew.
        JULIA C. R. DORR—*Centennial
        Poem*

The lotus flower is troubled
    At the sun's resplendent light;
With sunken head and sadly
    She dreamily waits for the night.
        HEINE—*Book of Songs*

But ne'er the rose without the thorn.
        HERRICK—*The Rose*

I remember, I remember
    The roses, red and white,
The violets, and the lily-cups,
    Those flowers made of light!
The lilacs, where the robin built,
    And where my brother set
The laburnum on his birthday,—
    The tree is living yet.
        HOOD—*I Remember, I Remember*

Underneath large blue-bells tented
Where the daisies are rose-scented,
And the rose herself has got
Perfume which on earth is not.
        KEATS—*Bards of Passion and of
        Mirth*

O flower-de-luce, bloom on, and let
    the river
    Linger to kiss thy feet!
O flower of song, bloom on, and
    make forever
    The world more fair and sweet.
        LONGFELLOW—*Flower-de-Luce*

Violet! sweet violet!
Thine eyes are full of tears;
    Are they wet
    Even yet
With the thought of other years?
        LOWELL—*Song*

And I will make thee beds of roses,
And a thousand fragrant posies.
        MARLOWE — *The Passionate
        Shepherd to His Love*

O lovely lily clean,
O lily springing green,
O lily bursting white,
Dear lily of delight,
Spring in my heart agen
That I may flower to men.
        MASEFIELD—*Everlasting Mercy*

Consider the lilies of the field, how they grow; they toil not, neither do they spin.
MATTHEW. VI. 28

In Flanders' fields the poppies blow
Between the crosses, row on row,
That mark our place, and in the sky,
The larks, still bravely singing, fly
Scarce heard among the guns below.
JOHN McCRAE—*In Flanders' Fields*

Flowers of all hue, and without thorn the rose.
MILTON—*Paradise Lost*

Blue thou art, intensely blue;
Flower, whence came thy dazzling hue?
MONTGOMERY — *The Gentianella*

'Tis the last rose of summer,
Left blooming alone.
MOORE—*Last Rose of Summer*

Yet no—not words, for they
But half can tell love's feeling;
Sweet flowers alone can say
What passion fears revealing:
A once bright rose's wither'd leaf,
A tow'ring lily broken,—
Oh, these may paint a grief
No words could e'er have spoken.
MOORE—*The Language of Flowers*

Steals timidly away,
Shrinking as violets do in summer's ray.
MOORE—*Lalla Rookh*

Those virgin lilies, all the night
Bathing their beauties in the lake,
That they may rise more fresh and bright,
When their beloved sun's awake.
MOORE—*Lalla Rookh*

Where flowers degenerate man cannot live.
NAPOLEON

"Of what are you afraid, my child?" inquired the kindly teacher.
"Oh, sir! the flowers, they are wild," replied the timid creature.
PETER NEWELL—*Wild Flowers*

Say it with flowers.
PATRICK F. O'KEEFE—Slogan for the Society of American Florists

I sometimes think that never blows so red
The Rose as where some buried Caesar bled;
That every Hyacinth the Garden wears
Dropt in her Lap from some once lovely Head.
OMAR KHAYYÁM—*Rubaiyat*

Each Morn a thousand Roses brings, you say;
Yes, but where leaves the Rose of Yesterday?
OMAR KHAYYÁM—*Rubaiyat*

One thing is certain and the rest is lies;
The Flower that once has blown for ever dies.
OMAR KHAYYÁM—*Rubaiyat*

The beauteous pansies rise
  In purple, gold, and blue,
  With tints of rainbow hue
Mocking the sunset skies.
      THOMAS J. OUSELEY—*The Angel of the Flowers*

If of thy mortal goods thou art bereft,
And from thy slender store two
  loaves alone to thee are left,
Sell one, and with the dole
Buy hyacinths to feed thy soul
    SADI—*Gulistan*

But who will watch my lilies,
  When their blossoms open white?
By day the sun shall be sentry,
  And the moon and the stars by
  night!
    BAYARD TAYLOR—*The Garden of Roses*

When lilacs last in the door-yard
  bloom'd,
And the great star early droop'd in
  the western sky in the night,
I mourn'd—and yet shall mourn with
  ever-returning spring.
    WALT WHITMAN

Let us crown ourselves with rosebuds
before they be withered.
    WISDOM OF SOLOMON. II. 8

To me the meanest flower that blows
  can give
Thoughts that do often lie too deep
  for tears.
    WORDSWORTH — *Intimations of Immortality*

FLY

It is easier to catch flies with honey
than with vinegar.
    ENGLISH PROVERB

A fly sat on the chariot wheel
And said "What a dust ‾ raise."
    LA FONTAINE

Baby bye
Here's a fly,
Let us watch him, you and I,
  How he crawls
  Up the walls
  Yet he never falls.
    THEODORE TILTON—*Baby Bye*

FOLLY

The folly of one man is the fortune
of another.
    BACON—*Of Fortune*

To swallow gudgeons ere they're
  catch'd.
And count their chickens ere they're
  hatch'd.
    BUTLER—*Hudibras*

To stumble twice against the same
stone, is a proverbial disgrace.
    CICERO—*Epistles*

He who lives without committing
any folly is not so wise as he thinks.
    LA ROCHEFOUCAULD

Answer a fool according to his folly.
    PROVERBS. XXVI. 5

He has spent all his life in letting
down empty buckets into empty
wells, and he is frittering away his
age in trying to draw them up again.
    SYDNEY SMITH—*Lady Holland's Memoir*

**(See also ERROR, EXPERIENCE,
FOOL, IGNORANCE, STUPIDITY,
VANITY, WISDOM.)**

FOOL

A fool always finds one still more
foolish to admire him.
BOILEAU

Young men think old men are fools;
but old men know young men are
fools.
GEORGE CHAPMAN—*All Fools*

Hain't we got all the fools in town
on our side? And ain't that a big
enough majority in any town?
S. L. CLEMENS (MARK TWAIN)
—*Huckleberry Finn*

Nobody can describe a fool to the
life, without much patient self-
inspection.
FRANK MOORE COLBY—*Essays*

A fool and his money are soon parted.
ENGLISH PROVERB

It is in the half fools and the half
wise that the greatest danger lies.
GOETHE

A learned fool is more foolish than an
ignorant fool.
MOLIÈRE

The right to be a cussed fool
Is safe from all devices human,
It's common (ez a gin'l rule)
To every critter born of woman.
LOWELL—*The Biglow Papers*

For fools rush in where angels fear
to tread.
POPE—*Essay on Criticism*

Even a fool, when he holdeth his
peace, is counted wise.
PROVERBS. XVII. 28

The fool hath said in his heart, There
is no God.
PSALMS. XIV. 1

If you wish to avoid seeing a fool
you must first break your looking-
glass.
RABELAIS

The fool doth think he is wise, but
the wise man knows himself to be a
fool.
SHAKESPEARE—*As You Like It.*
Act V. Sc. 1

A fool's bolt is soon shot.
SHAKESPEARE—*Henry V.* Act
III. Sc. 7

Lord, what fools these mortals be!
SHAKESPEARE — *Midsummer
Night's Dream.* Act II. Sc. 2

He who thinks himself wise, O heavens! is a great fool.
VOLTAIRE

There is a tide in the affairs of men
Which, taken at the flood, leads on
to fortune.
SHAKESPEARE — *Julius Caesar.*
Act 4. Sc. 3

O fortune, fortune! all men call thee
fickle.
SHAKESPEARE—*Romeo and Juliet.* Act 3. Sc. 5

(See also FOLLY, IGNORANCE, JEST-
ING, MIND.)

FORCE

The power that is supported by force
alone will have cause often to tremble.
KOSSUTH

Force is all-conquering, but its victories are short-lived.
LINCOLN

Force and not opinion is the queen of the world; but it is opinion that uses the force.
PASCAL

(See also DECISION, POWER, STRENGTH.)

FORESIGHT

In life, as in chess, forethought wins.
CHARLES BUXTON

If a man take no thought about what is distant, he will find sorrow near at hand.
CONFUCIUS

Forethought we may have, undoubtedly, but not foresight.
NAPOLEON

Look ere thou leap, see ere thou go.
TUSSER

(See also DISCRETION, EXPERIENCE, JUDGMENT, WISDOM.)

FORGETFULNESS

There is nothing new except what is forgotten.
MLLE. BERTIN

There is no remembrance which time does not obliterate, nor pain which death does not terminate.
CERVANTES

The pyramids themselves, doting with age, have forgotten the names of their founders.
FULLER—*Holy and Profane States*

And when he is out of sight, quickly also he is out of mind.
THOMAS À KEMPIS

God of our fathers, known of old,
    Lord of our far-flung battle-line,
Beneath whose awful Hand we hold
    Dominion over palm and pine—
Lord God of Hosts, be with us yet,
Lest we forget—lest we forget!

The tumult and the shouting dies,
    The captains and the kings depart;
Still stands thine ancient sacrifice,
    A humble and a contrite heart.
Lord God of Hosts, be with us yet,
Lest we forget—lest we forget.
KIPLING—*Recessional Hymn*

The world forgetting, by the world forgot.
POPE—*Eloisa to Abélard*

I am forgotten as a dead man out of mind: I am like a broken vessel.
PSALMS. XXXI. 12

If I forget thee, O Jerusalem, let my right hand forget her cunning.
PSALMS. CXXXVII. 5

Who is the Forgotten Man? He is the clean, quiet, virtuous, domestic citizen, who pays his debts and his taxes and is never heard of out of his little circle.
WILLIAM GRAHAM SUMNER—
The Forgotten Man

(See also ABSENCE, MEMORY, THOUGHT, TIME.)

FORGIVENESS

God pardons like a mother, who kisses the offense into everlasting forgetfulness.
HENRY WARD BEECHER

Good, to forgive;
Best to forget.
> BROWNING—*La Saisiaz*

It is easier to forgive an enemy than a friend.
> MME. DOROTHEE DELUZY

His heart was as great as the world, but there was no room in it to hold the memory of a wrong.
> EMERSON—*Letters and Social Aims*

Bear and forbear.
> EPICTETUS

Forgive us our trespasses, as we forgive them that trespass against us.
> MATTHEW. VI. 12 (The Lord's Prayer)

To err is human, to forgive, divine.
> POPE—*Essay on Criticism*

Forgive others often, yourself never.
> SYRUS

It is manlike to punish but godlike to forgive.
> PETER VON WINTER

(See also CHARITY, HUMANITY, PARDON, TOLERATION.)

FORTUNE

Fortune makes him fool, whom she makes her darling.
> BACON

It is fortune, not wisdom, that rules man's life.
> CICERO

Fortune truly helps those who are of good judgment.
> EURIPIDES

The bitter dregs of Fortune's cup to drain.
> HOMER—*Iliad*

Fortunes made in no time are like shirts made in no time; it's ten to one if they hang long together.
> DOUGLAS JERROLD

Men are seldom blessed with good fortune and good sense at the same time.
> LIVY

Fortune and Love befriend the bold.
> OVID

Every man is the architect of his own fortune.
> SALLUST

(See also CHANCE, LUCK, OPPORTUNITY, PROVIDENCE, RICHES, SUCCESS, WEALTH.)

FOX

A sleeping fox counts hens in his dreams.
> RUSSIAN PROVERB

The little foxes, that spoil the vines.
> SONG OF SOLOMON. IV. 15

(See also ANIMALS.)

FRAILTY

This is the porcelain clay of human kind.
> DRYDEN—*Don Sebastian*

All men are frail; but thou shouldst reckon none so frail as thyself.
> THOMAS À KEMPIS

Frailty, thy name is woman!
> SHAKESPEARE—*Hamlet*. Act I. Sc. 2

An amiable weakness.
R. B. Sheridan—*The School for Scandal*

(See also WOMAN.)

FRANCE

Forty million Frenchmen can't be wrong.
Anonymous

France, freed from that monster, Bonaparte, must again become the most agreeable country on earth. It would be the second choice of all whose ties of family and fortune give a preference to some other one, and the first choice of all not under those ties.
Jefferson, 1814

Ye sons of France, awake to glory!
Hark! Hark! what myriads bid you rise!
Your children, wives, and grandsires hoary,
Behold their tears and hear their cries!
Rouget de Lisle—*The Marseilles Hymn*

France always has plenty men of talent, but it is always deficient in men of action and high character.
Napoleon

FRAUD
See DECEPTION

FREEDOM

The cause of freedom is the cause of God.
Samuel Bowles

Personal liberty is the paramount essential to human dignity and human happiness.
Bulwer-Lytton

Hereditary bondsmen! Know ye not
Who would be free themselves must strike the blow?
Byron—*Childe Harold*

And Freedom shrieked as Kosciusko fell!
Campbell—*Pleasures of Hope*

In a free country there is much clamor, with little suffering; in a despotic state there is little complaint, with much grievance.
Carnot

Freedom suppressed and again regained bites with keener fangs than freedom never endangered.
Cicero

When Freedom from her mountain height
Unfurled her standard to the air,
She tore the azure robe of night,
And set the stars of glory there.
Joseph Rodman Drake

For what avail the plough or sail,
Or land, or life, if freedom fail?
Emerson—*Boston*

Ay, call it holy ground,
The soil where first they trod;
They have left unstained, what there they found,—
Freedom to worship God.
Felicia D. Hemans—*Landing of the Pilgrim Fathers*

In the beauty of the lilies Christ was born across the sea,
With a glory in His bosom that transfigures you and me;
As He died to make men holy, let us die to make men free,
While God is marching on.
Julia Ward Howe—*Battle Hymn of the Republic*

I am for freedom of religion and against all maneuvers to bring about a legal ascendancy of one sect over another.

JEFFERSON, 1799

And ye shall know the truth, and the truth shall make you free.

JOHN. VIII. 32

Freedom is that faculty which enlarges the usefulness of all other faculties.

KANT

No amount of political freedom will satisfy the hungry masses.

LENIN—Speech, 1917

. . . That this nation, under God, shall have a new birth of freedom.

LINCOLN—*Gettysburg Address*

Those who deny freedom to others deserve it not for themselves and under a just God cannot long retain it.

LINCOLN

Many politicians are in the habit of laying it down as a self-evident proposition that no people ought to be free till they are fit to use their freedom. The maxim is worthy of the fool in the old story who resolved not to go into the water till he had learned to swim.

MACAULAY

Since the general civilization of mankind I believe there are more instances of the abridgment of the freedom of the people by gradual and silent encroachments of those in power than by violent and sudden usurpations.

MADISON

The only freedom which deserves the name is that of pursuing our own good in our own way, so long as we do not attempt to deprive others of theirs or impede their efforts to obtain it.

JOHN STUART MILL

None can love freedom heartily but good men; the rest love not freedom but license.

MILTON

Countries are well cultivated, not as they are fertile but as they are free.

MONTESQUIEU

I would rather sit on a pumpkin, and have it all to myself, than to be crowded on a velvet cushion.

THOREAU—*Walden*

Only free peoples can hold their purpose and their honor steady to a common end, and prefer the interests of mankind to any narrow interest of their own.

WOODROW WILSON—War Address to Congress, 1917

We must be free or die, who speak
the tongue
That Shakespeare spake; the faith
and morals hold
Which Milton held.

WORDSWORTH

(See also AMERICA, DEMOCRACY, ENGLAND, HUMANITY, INDEPENDENCE, LIBERTY, PATRIOTISM, RIGHTS, SLAVERY, WAR.)

FRIEND

Prosperity makes friends and adversity tries them.
ANONYMOUS

A friend is one who dislikes the same people that you dislike.
ANONYMOUS

A true friend is one soul in two bodies.
ARISTOTLE

Chance makes our parents, but choice makes our friends.
DELILLE

The best way to keep your friends is to never owe them anything and never lend them anything.
PAUL DE KOCK

Forsake not an old friend, for the new is not comparable unto him. A new friend is as new wine: when it is old thou shalt drink it with pleasure.
ECCLESIASTICUS. IX. 10

Animals are such agreeable friends —they ask no questions, they pass no criticisms.
GEORGE ELIOT—Mr. Gilfil's Love-Story

The only way to have a friend is to be one.
EMERSON—Of Friendship

A friend in need is a friend indeed.
ENGLISH PROVERB

There are three faithful friends: an old wife, an old dog, and ready money.
FRANKLIN

If you have a friend worth loving,
Love him. Yes, and let him know
That you love him, ere life's evening
Tinge his brow with sunset glow.
Why should good words ne'er be said
Of a friend till he is dead?
DANIEL W. HOYT—A Sermon in Rhyme

I desire so to conduct the affairs of this administration that if at the end, when I come to lay down the reins of power, I have lost every other friend on earth, I shall at least have one friend left, and that friend shall be down inside of me.
LINCOLN—Reply to Missouri Committee of Seventy (1864)

Friends are like melons. Shall I tell you why?
To find one good, you must a hundred try.
CLAUDE MERMET

A man that hath friends must show himself friendly; and there is a friend that sticketh closer than a brother.
PROVERBS. XVIII. 24

I am wealthy in my friends.
SHAKESPEARE—Timon of Athens. Act II. Sc. 2

A friend must not be injured, even in jest.
SYRUS

Reprove your friends in secret, praise them openly.
SYRUS

God save me from my friends, I can protect myself from my enemies.
MARSHAL DE VILLARS

(See also ASSOCIATE, COMPANIONSHIP, FRIENDSHIP.)

FRIENDSHIP

Great souls by instinct to each other
   turn,
Demand alliance, and in friendship
   burn.
   ADDISON—*The Campaign*

                                 Hand
Grasps at hand, eye lights eye in
   good friendship,
And great hearts expand
And grow one in the sense of this
   world's life.
   BROWNING—*Saul*

Should auld acquaintance be forgot,
   And never brought to mind?
Should auld acquaintance be forgot,
   And days o' auld lang syne?
   BURNS—*Auld Lang Syne*

The highest compact we can make
with our fellow is,—Let there be
truth between us two forevermore.
. . . It is sublime to feel and say
of another, I need never meet, or
speak, or write to him; we need not
reinforce ourselves or send tokens of
remembrance; I rely on him as on
myself; if he did thus or thus, I
know it was right.
   EMERSON—*Essays*

Friendship, peculiar boon of Heaven,
   The noble mind's delight and
      pride,
To men and angels only given,
   To all the lower world denied.
   SAMUEL JOHNSON—*Friendship*

Forsooth, brethren, fellowship is
heaven and lack of fellowship is
hell; fellowship is life and lack of
fellowship is death; and the deeds
that ye do upon the earth, it is for
fellowship's sake that ye do them.
   WILLIAM MORRIS—*Dream of
   John Ball*

What is thine is mine, and all mine
is thine.
   PLAUTUS

Saul and Jonathan were lovely and
pleasant in their lives, and in their
death they were not divided.
   II SAMUEL. I. 23

Madam, I have been looking for a
person who disliked gravy all my
life; let us swear eternal friendship.
   SYDNEY SMITH—*Lady Holland's
   Memoir*

Be slow to fall into friendship; but
when thou art in continue firm and
constant.
   SOCRATES

True friendship is a plant of slow
growth, and must undergo and withstand the shocks of adversity before
it is entitled to the appellation.
   WASHINGTON—Letter, 1783

(See also ASSOCIATE, BROTHER-
HOOD, COMPANIONSHIP, FRIEND,
LOVE, SYMPATHY.)

FRUIT

By their fruits ye shall know them.
   MATTHEW. VII. 20

The ripest fruit first falls.
   SHAKESPEARE—*Richard II.* Act
   II. Sc. 1

FUN
See PLEASURE

FUTURE

Some day Love shall claim his own,
Some day Right ascend his throne,
Some day hidden Truth be known;
   Some day—some sweet day.
   LEWIS J. BATES—*Some Sweet
   Day*

When all else is lost, the future still remains.
BOVEE

'Tis the sunset of life gives me mystical lore,
And coming events cast their shadows before.
CAMPBELL—*Lochiel's Warning*

I never think of the future. It comes soon enough.
ALBERT EINSTEIN

I know of no way of judging the future but by the past.
PATRICK HENRY—Speech, 1775

The present is great with the future.
LEIBNITZ

Trust no Future, howe'er pleasant!
Let the dead Past bury its dead!
LONGFELLOW—*A Psalm of Life*

Go forth to meet the shadowy Future without fear and with a manly heart.
LONGFELLOW—*Hyperion*

Take therefore no thought for the morrow; for the morrow shall take thought for the things of itself. Sufficient unto the day is the evil thereof.
MATTHEW. VI. 34

There was a wise man in the East whose constant prayer was that he might see today with the eyes of tomorrow.
ALFRED MERCIER

There was the Door to which I found no key;
There was the Veil through which I might not see.
OMAR KHAYYÁM—*Rubaiyat*

I believe the future is only the past again, entered through another gate.
PINERO—*The Second Mrs. Tanqueray*

After us the deluge.
MME. DE POMPADOUR

Till the sun grows cold,
And the stars are old,
And the leaves of the Judgment Book unfold.
BAYARD TAYLOR—*Bedouin Song*

(See also DESTINY, ETERNITY, EXPECTATION, FATE, HEAVEN, HELL, IMMORTALITY, TIME, TOMORROW.)

GAIN
See BUSINESS

GAMBLING

The race is not always to the swift nor the battle to the strong—but that's the way to bet.
ANONYMOUS

There is but one good throw upon the dice, which is to throw them away.
CHATFIELD

By gaming we lose both our time and treasure—two things most precious to the life of man.
FELLTHAM

Keep flax from fire, youth from gaming.
FRANKLIN

Man is a gaming animal.
LAMB

It (gaming) is the child of avarice, the brother of iniquity, and the father of mischief.

WASHINGTON

(See also AMUSEMENT, CHANCE, FORTUNE, VICE.)

GARDEN

A garden is a lovesome thing—God
wot!
Rose plot,
Fringed pool,
Fern grot—
The veriest school
Of peace; and yet the fool
Contends that God is not.—
Not God in gardens! When the sun
is cool?
Nay, but I have a sign!
'Tis very sure God walks in mine.

THOMAS EDWARD BROWN—
My Garden

God the first garden made, and the first city Cain.

COWLEY—The Garden

The Lord God planted a garden eastward in Eden; and there he put the man whom he had formed.

GENESIS. II. 3

One is nearer God's heart in a garden
Than anywhere else on earth.

DOROTHY FRANCES GURNEY—
God's Garden

(See also AGRICULTURE, FLOWERS, NATURE, TREE.)

GENEROSITY
See LIBERALITY

GENIUS

There is no great genius without a mixture of madness.

ARISTOTLE

Genius is only great patience.

BUFFON

Genius is one per cent inspiration and ninety-nine per cent perspiration.

EDISON

Genius does what it must, and talent does what it can.

BULWER-LYTTON

Gift, like genius, I often think only means an infinite capacity for taking pains.

ELLICE HOPKINS—Work
amongst Working Men

Genius is a promontory jutting out into the infinite.

VICTOR HUGO—William
Shakespeare

Three-fifths of him genius and two-fifths sheer fudge.

LOWELL—Fable for Critics

The lamp of genius burns quicker than the lamp of life.

SCHILLER

The poets' scrolls will outlive the monuments of stone. Genius survives; all else is claimed by death.

SPENSER—Shepherd's Calendar

(See also ABILITY, CHARACTER, INTELLECT, MIND, TALENT.)

GENTLEMAN

A gentleman is a man who can disagree without being disagreeable.
ANONYMOUS

The gentleman is a Christian product.
GEORGE H. CALVERT

Once a gentleman, always a gentleman.
DICKENS—*Little Dorrit*

Propriety of manners and consideration for others are the two main characteristics of a gentleman.
DISRAELI

To make a fine gentleman, several trades are required, but chiefly a barber.
GOLDSMITH

(See also ANCESTRY, COURTESY, HEREDITY, MAN, MANNERS, NOBILITY.)

GENTLENESS
See KINDNESS

GERMANY

Let us put Germany, so to speak, in the saddle! you will see that she can ride.
BISMARCK—In Parliament of Confederation (1867)

We Germans will never produce another Goethe, but we may produce another Caesar.
OSWALD SPENGLER, 1925

(See also WAR.)

GIFT

It is more blessed to give than to receive.
ACTS. XX. 35

What is bought is cheaper than a gift.
CERVANTES

You give but little when you give of your possessions. It is when you give of yourself that you truly give.
KAHLIL GIBRAN—*The Prophet*

I make presents to the mother, but think of the daughter.
GOETHE

Give an inch, he'll take an ell.
HOBBES—*Liberty and Necessity*

He gives twice who gives quickly.
PUBLIUS MIMUS

Or what man is there of you, whom if his son ask bread, will he give him a stone?
MATTHEW. VII. 9

Rich gifts wax poor when givers prove unkind.
SHAKESPEARE—*Hamlet*. Act III. Sc. 1

I fear the Greeks, even when they bring gifts.
VERGIL—*Aeneid*

Behold, I do not give lectures or a little charity,
When I give I give myself.
WALT WHITMAN—*Song of Myself*

(See also CHARITY, GOODNESS, KINDNESS, LIBERALITY, PHILANTHROPY.)

GIRL
See DAUGHTER

GLORY

There is one glory of the sun, and another glory of the moon, and another glory of the stars: for one star differeth from another star in glory.

> I Corinthians. XV. 41

The paths of glory lead but to the grave.

> Gray—*Elegy in a Country Churchyard*

Mine eyes have seen the coming of the glory of the Lord.

> Julia Ward Howe—*Battle Hymn of the Republic*

O how quickly passes away the glory of the earth.

> Thomas à Kempis—*Imitation of Christ*

One crowded hour of glorious life
Is worth an age without a name.

> Scott—*Old Mortality*

(See also AMBITION, AMERICA, CONQUEST, FAME, HERO, HONOR, PRAISE, SOLDIER, WAR.)

GOD

Fear that man who fears not God.

> Abd-el-Kader

Nearer, my God, to Thee—
Nearer to Thee—
E'en though it be a cross
That raiseth me;
Still all my song shall be
Nearer, my God, to Thee,
Nearer to Thee!

> Sarah Flower Adams

God helps those who help themselves.

> Anonymous

Man proposes, and God disposes.

> Ariosto—*Orlando Furioso*

They that deny a God destroy man's nobility; for certainly man is of kin to the beasts by his body; and, if he be not of kin to God by his spirit, he is a base and ignoble creature.

> Bacon—*Essays*

God's in His Heaven—
All's right with the world!

> Browning—*Pippa Passes*

I took a day to search for God,
And found Him not. But as I trod
    By rocky ledge, through woods untamed,
    Just where one scarlet lily flamed,
I saw His foot print in the sod.

> Bliss Carman—*Vestigia*

A picket frozen on duty—
    A mother starved for her brood—
Socrates drinking the hemlock,
    And Jesus on the rood;
And millions who, humble and nameless,
    The straight, hard pathway trod—
Some call it Consecration,
    And others call it God.

> W. H. Carruth—*Evolution*

God hath chosen the foolish things of the world to confound the wise; and God hath chosen the weak things of the world to confound the things that are mighty.

> I Corinthians. I. 27

God moves in a mysterious way
  His wonders to perform;
He plants his footsteps in the sea
  And rides upon the storm.
  COWPER—*Hymn*

God is incorporeal, divine, supreme,
infinite Mind, Spirit, Soul, Principle,
Life, Truth, Love.
  MARY BAKER EDDY—*Science
  and Health*

An honest God is the noblest work
of man.
  INGERSOLL—*The Gods*

"We trust, Sir, that God is on our
side." "It is more important to know
that we are on God's side."
  LINCOLN—Reply to deputation
  during Civil War

A mighty fortress is our God,
  A bulwark never failing,
Our helper he amid the flood
  Of mortal ills prevailing.
  LUTHER

Everyone is in a small way the image
of God.
  MANILIUS

What is it: is man only a blunder
of God, or God only a blunder of
man?
  NIETZSCHE—*The Twilight of
  the Idols*

A God-intoxicated man.
  NOVALIS (of Spinoza)

There is a God within us, and we
glow when he stirs us.
  OVID

Fear God. Honour the King.
  I PETER. II. 17

God is truth and light his shadow.
  PLATO

He mounts the storm, and walks
upon the wind.
  POPE—*Essay on Man*

The heavens declare the glory of
God; and the firmament showeth his
handiwork.
  PSALMS. XIX. 1

He maketh me to lie down in green
pastures: he leadeth me beside the
still waters.
  PSALMS. XXIII. 2

God is our refuge and strength, a
very present help in trouble.
  PSALMS. XLVI. 1

There is no respect of persons with
God.
  ROMANS. II. 11

If God be for us, who can be against
us?
  ROMANS. VIII. 31

For the greater glory of God.
  Motto of the Society of Jesus

God tempers the wind to the shorn
lamb.
  LAURENCE STERNE

The divine essence itself is love and
wisdom.
  SWEDENBORG

God, the Great Giver, can open the
whole universe to our gaze in the
narrow space of a single lane.
  TAGORE

Rock of Ages, cleft for me,
  Let me hide myself in thee.
  AUGUSTUS TOPLADY—*Living
  and Dying Prayer*

If there were no God, it would be necessary to invent him.

VOLTAIRE

By night an atheist half believes a God.

YOUNG—*Night Thoughts*

(See also CHRIST, CHRISTIANITY, FAITH, HEAVEN, PRAYER, PROVIDENCE, RELIGION, WORSHIP.)

GODS

The Ethiop gods have Ethiop lips,
Bronze cheeks, and woolly hair;
The Grecian gods are like the Greeks,
As keen-eyed, cold and fair.

WALTER BAGEHOT—*Ignorance of Man*

Ye immortal gods! where in the world are we?

CICERO

There's a one-eyed yellow idol to the north of Khatmandu,
There's a little marble cross below the town,
There's a broken-hearted woman tends the grave of Mad Carew,
And the yellow god forever gazes down.

J. MILTON HAYES—*The Green Eye of the Yellow God*

Yet verily these issues lie on the lap of the gods.

HOMER—*Iliad*

The trident of Neptune is the sceptre of the world.

LEMIERRE

Man is certainly stark mad; he cannot make a flea, and yet he will be making gods by dozens.

MONTAIGNE

(See also DESTINY, FATE, GOD.)

GOLD

You shall not press down upon the brow of labor this crown of thorns—you shall not crucify mankind upon a cross of gold!

W. J. BRYAN, at Democratic National Convention, 1896

Gold begets in brethren hate;
Gold in families debate;
Gold does friendship separate;
Gold does civil wars create.

COWLEY—*Anacreontics*

Gold! Gold! Gold! Gold!
Bright and yellow, hard and cold.

HOOD—*Miss Kilmansegg*

Accursed thirst for gold! what dost thou not compel mortals to do?

VERGIL—*Aeneid.*

(See also MONEY, RICHES, WEALTH.)

GOLDEN RULE

My duty towards my neighbor is to love him as myself, and to do to all men as I would they should do unto me.

BOOK OF COMMON PRAYER, 1662

What you do not want others to do to you, do not do to others.

CONFUCIUS, c. 500 B.C.

Whatsoever thou wouldst that men should not do to thee, do not do that to them.

HILLEL HA-BABLI, c. 30 B.C.

Do not do to others what would anger you if done to you by others.
ISOCRATES, c. 375 B.C.

As ye would that men should do to you, do ye also to them likewise.
LUKE. VI. 31, c. 75 A. D.

This is the sum of all true righteousness: deal with others as thou wouldst thyself be dealt by. Do nothing to thy neighbor which thou wouldst not have him do to thee hereafter.
THE MAHABHARATA, c. 150 B.C.

We have committed the Golden Rule to memory; let us now commit it to life.
EDWIN MARKHAM

All things whatsoever ye would that men should do to you, do ye even so to them: for this is the law and the prophets.
MATTHEW. VII. 12, c. 75 A. D.

Do not do unto others as you would that they should do unto you. Their tastes may not be the same.
GEORGE BERNARD SHAW, 1903

What thou thyself hatest, do to no man.
TOBIT. IV. c. 180 B.C.

Do unto the other feller the way he'd like to do unto you an' do it fust.
EDWARD N. WESTCOTT—
David Harum

(See also BROTHERHOOD, CHRISTIANITY, HUMANITY, RELIGION, TOLERATION.)

GOOD-HUMOR

Good-humor makes all things tolerable.
HENRY WARD BEECHER

The sunshine of the mind.
BULWER-LYTTON

Good-humor is goodness and wisdom combined.
OWEN MEREDITH

(See also CHARACTER, CHEERFULNESS, MERRIMENT.)

GOODNESS

For the cause that lacks assistance,
The wrong that needs resistance,
For the future in the distance,
    And the good that I can do.
        GEORGE LINNAEUS BANKS—
        What I Live For

Happy were men if they but understood
There is no safety but in doing good.
JOHN FOUNTAIN

Can there any good thing come out of Nazareth?
JOHN. I. 46

Be good, sweet maid, and let who will be clever;
    Do noble things, not dream them all day long;
And so make life, death, and that vast forever
    One grand, sweet song.
        KINGSLEY—*Farewell*

The crest and crowning of all good,
Life's final star, is Brotherhood.
> EDWIN MARKHAM—*Brother-
> hood*

Since good, the more
Communicated, more abundant
grows.
> MILTON—*Paradise Lost*

A glass is good, and a lass is good,
    And a pipe to smoke in cold
        weather;
The world is good, and the people
    are good,
    And we're all good fellows to-
        gether.
> JOHN O'KEEFE—*Sprigs of
> Laurel*

He that does good for good's sake
seeks neither praise nor reward,
though sure of both at last.
> WILLIAM PENN

The fragrance of the flower is never
borne against the breeze; but the
fragrance of human virtues diffuses
itself everywhere.
> THE RAMAYANA

What is beautiful is good, and who
is good will soon also be beautiful.
> SAPPHO

There is some soul of goodness in
    things evil,
Would men observingly distil it out.
> SHAKESPEARE—*Henry V.* Act
> IV. Sc. 1

'Tis only noble to be good.
> TENNYSON—*Lady Clara Vere
> de Vere*

For the Lord Jesus Christ's sake,
Do all the good you can,
To all the people you can,
In all the ways you can,
As long as ever you can.
> Tombstone Inscription in
> Shrewsbury, England

(See also CHARACTER, CHARITY,
HUMANITY, KINDNESS, LIBERALITY,
MORALITY.)

GOOSE

What is sauce for the goose is sauce
for the gander.
> VARRO, quoting Gellius

The goose gabbles amid the melo-
dious swans.
> VERGIL—*Eclogues.* IX. 37

GOSPEL
See SCRIPTURE

GOSSIP

He that repeateth a matter separateth
very friends.
> PROVERBS. XVII. 9

Let the greater part of the news thou
hearest be the least part of what
thou believest.
> QUARLES

Foul whisperings are abroad.
> SHAKESPEARE—*Macbeth.* Act
> V. Sc. 1

I heard the little bird say so.
> SWIFT—*Letter to Stella*

Tattlers also and busybodies, speaking things which they ought not.
> I TIMOTHY. V. 13

There is only one thing in the world worse than being talked about, and that is not being talked about.

WILDE—*The Picture of Dorian Gray*

(See also CALUMNY, NEWS, RUMOR, SCANDAL, SLANDER, SNEER, TALK, TONGUE.)

GOVERNMENT

The declaration that our People are hostile to a government made by themselves, for themselves, and conducted by themselves, is an insult.

JOHN ADAMS—Address to the citizens of Westmoreland Co., Virginia

Experience teaches us to be most on our guard to protect liberty when the government's purposes are beneficent.

BRANDEIS—Olmstead vs. U. S., 1928

Government is a contrivance of human wisdom to provide for human wants.

BURKE

Government is a trust, and the officers of the government are trustees; and both the trust and the trustees are created for the benefit of the people.

HENRY CLAY—Speech, 1829

Though the people support the government the government should not support the people.

GROVER CLEVELAND

The best government is not that which renders men the happiest, but that which renders the greatest number happy.

DUCLOS

What government is the best? That which teaches us to govern ourselves.

GOETHE

I think we have more machinery of government than is necessary, too many parasites living on the labor of the industrious.

JEFFERSON—Letter to William Ludlow

The will of the people is the only legitimate foundation of any government, and to protect its free expression should be our first object.

JEFFERSON, 1801

The safety of the State is the highest law.

JUSTINIAN

Govern a great nation as you would cook a small fish. (Don't overdo it.)

LAO-TSZE

No man is good enough to govern another man without that other's consent.

LINCOLN—Speech, 1854

A house divided against itself cannot stand—I believe this government cannot endure permanently half-slave and half-free.

LINCOLN—Speech. June 17, 1858

The state!— it is I!

Attributed to LOUIS XIV of France

The principal foundation of all states are good laws and good arms.

MACHIAVELLI

Every nation has the government that it deserves.

> JOSEPH DE MAISTRE—Letter, 1811

The executive of the modern state is but a committee for managing the common affairs of the bourgeoisie.

> KARL MARX AND FRIEDRICH ENGELS—*Communist Manifesto*

Republics end through luxury; monarchies through poverty.

> MONTESQUIEU

When it shall be said in any country in the world, "My poor are happy; neither ignorance nor distress is to be found among them; my jails are empty of prisoners, my streets of beggars; the aged are not in want, the taxes are not oppressive . . ."—when these things can be said, then may that country boast of its constitution and its government.

> THOMAS PAINE

Democracy is direct self-government, over all the people, for all the people, by all the people.

> THEODORE PARKER—Music Hall, Boston, July 4, 1858

Governments exist to protect the rights of minorities. The loved and the rich need no protection,—they have many friends and few enemies.

> WENDELL PHILLIPS

Themistocles said, "The Athenians govern the Greeks; I govern the Athenians; you, my wife, govern me; your son governs you."

> PLUTARCH

The labor unions shall have a square deal, and the corporations shall have a square deal, and in addition, all private citizens shall have a square deal.

> THEODORE ROOSEVELT

No man undertakes a trade he has not learned, even the meanest; yet every one thinks himself sufficiently qualified for the hardest of all trades —that of government.

> SOCRATES

The basis of our political systems is the right of the people to make and to alter their constitutions of government.

> WASHINGTON—Farewell Address, 1796

(See also AMERICA, AUTHORITY, LAW, PARTY, PATRIOTISM, POLITICS, STATESMANSHIP.)

GRACE

An outward and visible sign of an inward and spiritual grace.

> BOOK OF COMMON PRAYER

There, but for the grace of God, goes John Bradford.

> JOHN BRADFORD, on seeing a condemned man

Ye are fallen from grace.

> GALATIANS. V. 4

He does it with a better grace, but I do it more natural.

> SHAKESPEARE—*Twelfth Night.* Act II. Sc. 3

(See also CHARACTER, COURTESY, MANNERS.)

GRAFT
See BRIBERY

GRASS
See NATURE

GRATITUDE

He who receives a good turn should never forget it; he who does one should never remember it.
CHARRON

Gratitude is the heart's memory.
FRENCH PROVERB

The gratitude of most men is but a secret desire of receiving greater benefits.
LA ROCHEFOUCAULD

Gratitude is a duty which ought to be paid, but which none have a right to expect.
ROUSSEAU

(See also INGRATITUDE, THANKFULNESS.)

GRAVE

I would rather sleep in the southern corner of a little country churchyard, than in the tombs of the Capulets.
BURKE—Letter to Matthew Smith

O death, where is thy sting? O grave, where is thy victory?
I CORINTHIANS. XV. 55

Some village Hampden, that, with dauntless breast,
 The little tyrant of his fields withstood,
Some mute inglorious Milton here may rest,
 Some Cromwell guiltless of his country's blood.
GRAY—Elegy in a Country Churchyard

The house appointed for all living.
JOB. XXX. 23

Teach me to live that I may dread
The grave as little as my bed.
BISHOP KEN—Evening Hymn

The temple of silence and reconciliation.
MACAULAY

Dust into dust, and under dust, to lie,
Sans wine, sans song, sans singer, and—sans end.
OMAR KHAYYÁM—Rubaiyat

Oh, how a small portion of earth will hold us when we are dead, who ambitiously seek after the whole world while we are living!
PHILIP, King of Macedon

Is but the threshold of eternity.
SOUTHEY—Vision of the Maid of Orleans

Under the wide and starry sky,
Dig the grave and let me lie.
STEVENSON—Requiem

Hark! from the tombs a doleful sound.
ISAAC WATTS—Hymns and Spiritual Songs

(See also DEATH, EPITAPH, ETERNITY, MONUMENT.)

GRAVITY
See DIGNITY

GREATNESS

Great warriors, like great earthquakes, are principally remembered for the mischief they have done.
BOVEE

Everything great is not always good, but all good things are great.
DEMOSTHENES

All great men come out of the middle classes.
EMERSON

No man ever yet became great by imitation.
SAMUEL JOHNSON

The nearer we come to great men the more clearly we see that they are only men. They rarely seem great to their valets.
LA BRUYÈRE

It is the prerogative of great men only to have great defects.
LA ROCHEFOUCAULD

The great are only great because we carry them on our shoulders; when we throw them off they sprawl on the ground.
MONTANDRÉ

Some are born great, some achieve greatness, and some have greatness thrust upon 'em.
SHAKESPEARE—*Twelfth Night.* Act II. Sc. 5

The great are great only because we are on our knees. Let us rise!
STIRNER—*The Ego and His Own*

(See also DIGNITY, FAME, HERO, HONOR, NOBILITY, POWER, REPUTATION, SUCCESS.)

GREECE

Fair Greece! sad relic of departed worth!
Immortal, though no more; though fallen great!
BYRON—*Childe Harold*

Beware of Greeks bearing gifts.
LATIN PROVERB

Athens, the eye of Greece, mother of arts
And eloquence.
MILTON—*Paradise Regained*

The glory that was Greece.
POE—*To Helen*

GRIEF

It is foolish to tear one's hair in grief, as though sorrow would be made less by baldness.
CICERO

There is no grief which time does not lessen and soften.
CICERO

The only cure for grief is action.
G. H. LEWES—*The Spanish Drama*

Heavy hearts, like heavy clouds in the sky, are best relieved by the letting of water.
RIVAROL

Every one can master a grief but he that has it.
SHAKESPEARE—*Much Ado about Nothing.* Act III. Sc. 2

What's gone and what's past help Should be past grief.
SHAKESPEARE—*Winter's Tale.* Act III. Sc. 2

(See also AFFLICTION, DEATH, MISERY, SADNESS, SORROW, SUFFERING, TEARS.)

GUEST

Every guest hates the others, and the host hates them all.
ALBANIAN PROVERB

Hail, guest, we ask not what thou
art;
If friend, we greet thee, hand and
heart;
If stranger, such no longer be;
If foe, our love shall conquer thee.
    Old Welsh door verse

No one can be so welcome a guest
that he will not annoy his host
after three days.
    PLAUTUS

                Unbidden guests
Are often welcomest when they are
gone.
    SHAKESPEARE—*Henry VI.* Pt.
    I. Act II. Sc. 2

(See also DRINKING, EATING, FES-
TIVITIES, FRIENDS, HOME, HOS-
PITALITY, TOASTS, WELCOME.)

GUILT

Let no guilty man escape, if it can
be avoided. No personal consideration should stand in the way of
performing a public duty.
    ULYSSES S. GRANT

It is base to filch a purse, daring to
embezzle a million, but it is great
beyond measure to steal a crown.
The sin lessens as the guilt increases.
    SCHILLER

Let wickedness escape as it may at
the bar, it never fails of doing justice
upon itself; for every guilty person
is his own hangman.
    SENECA

He who flees from trial confesses
his guilt.
    SYRUS

(See also BRIBERY, CONSCIENCE,
CRIME, EVIL, LAW, MURDER, PUN-
ISHMENT, SIN.)

HABIT

Habit, if not resisted, soon becomes
necessity.
    ST. AUGUSTINE

Sow an act and you reap a habit.
Sow a habit and you reap a character. Sow a character and you reap
a destiny.
    CHARLES READE

How use doth breed a habit in a
man!
    SHAKESPEARE—*Two Gentlemen
    of Verona.* Act V. Sc. 4

Habits are at first cobwebs, then
cables.
    SPANISH PROVERB

The fox changes his skin but not
his habits.
    SUETONIUS

(See also CUSTOM, FASHION,
MANNERS.)

HAIR

His hair stood upright like porcu-
pine quills.
    BOCCACCIO—*Decameron*

Bring down my gray hairs with sorrow to the grave.
    GENESIS. XLII. 38

Gray hair is a sign of age, not of
wisdom.
    GREEK PROVERB

One hair of a woman can draw more
than a hundred pair of oxen.
    JAMES HOWELL

The beauty of the heavens is the
stars; the beauty of women is their
hair.
    ITALIAN PROVERB

The very hairs of your head are all numbered.

MATTHEW. X. 30

The hoary beard is a crown of glory if it be found in the way of righteousness.

PROVERBS. XVI. 31

There was never a saint with red hair.

RUSSIAN PROVERB

(See also BEAUTY, WOMAN.)

HAND

For through the South the custom still commands
The gentleman to kiss the lady's hands.

BYRON—*Don Juan*

His hand will be against every man, and every man's hand against him.

GENESIS. XVI. 12

The voice is Jacob's voice, but the hands are the hands of Esau.

GENESIS. XXVII. 22

Let not thy left hand know what thy right hand doeth.

MATTHEW. VI. 3

They may seize
On the white wonder of dear Juliet's hand.

SHAKESPEARE—*Romeo and Juliet*. Act III. Sc. 3

(See also HELP, WOMAN.)

HANGING

As well be hanged for a sheep as a lamb.

ENGLISH PROVERB

So they hanged Haman on the gallows that he had prepared for Mordecai.

ESTHER. VII. 10

We must all hang together, else we shall all hang separately.

FRANKLIN, on signing the Declaration of Independence

They're hangin' Danny Deever in the morning!

KIPLING—*Danny Deever*

(See also CRIME, PRISON, PUNISHMENT.)

HAPPINESS

The greatest happiness of the greatest number.

BECCARIA

Happiness lies, first of all, in health.

GEORGE WILLIAM CURTIS

Our greatest happiness . . . does not depend on the condition of life in which chance has placed us, but is always the result of a good conscience, good health, occupation, and freedom in all just pursuits.

JEFFERSON—*Notes on Virginia*

Happiness grows at our own firesides, and is not to be picked in strangers' gardens.

DOUGLAS JERROLD

We are never so happy, nor so unhappy, as we suppose ourselves to be.

LA ROCHEFOUCAULD

I have learned to seek my happiness by limiting my desires, rather than in attempting to satisfy them.

JOHN STUART MILL

What happiness is there which is not purchased with more or less of pain?

MARGARET OLIPHANT

The secret of happiness is this: let your interests be as wide as possible, and let your reactions to the things and persons that interest you be as far as possible friendly rather than hostile.

BERTRAND RUSSELL—*The Conquest of Happiness*

Everyone speaks of it, few know it.

MME. JEANNE P. ROLAND

Man is the artificer of his own happiness.

THOREAU

(See also BLISS, CHEERFULNESS, JOY, MERRIMENT, PLEASURE.)

HARVEST

Whatsoever a man soweth, that shall he also reap.

GALATIANS. VI. 7

The harvest truly is plenteous, but the labourers are few.

MATTHEW. IX. 37

Dry August and warm,
Doth harvest no harm.

TUSSER

(See also AGRICULTURE, AUTUMN, SEASONS.)

HASTE

The more haste, ever the worst speed.

CHARLES CHURCHILL—*The Ghost*

Haste makes waste.

ENGLISH PROVERB

Take time for all things.

FRANKLIN

Haste is of the Devil.

THE KORAN

Make haste slowly.

LATIN PROVERB

Too great haste leads us to error.

MOLIÈRE

(See also PATIENCE, PROMPTNESS.)

HATE

To harbor hatred and animosity in the soul makes one irritable, gloomy, and prematurely old.

AUERBACH

Whosoever hateth his brother is a murderer.

I JOHN. III. 15

I like a good hater.

SAMUEL JOHNSON

But I do hate him as I hate the devil.

BEN JONSON—*Every Man out of His Humour*

The hatred we bear our enemies injures their happiness less than our own.

J. PETIT-SENN

People hate, as they love, unreasonably.

THACKERAY

HEAD

An old head upon young shoulders.

ENGLISH PHRASE

Two heads are better than one.
ENGLISH PROVERB

The head is always the dupe of the
heart.
LA ROCHEFOUCAULD

(See also INTELLECT, MIND,
REASON.)

HEALTH

He who has health has hope, and he
who has hope has everything.
ARABIAN PROVERB

Refuse to be ill. Never tell people
you are ill; never own it to yourself. Illness is one of those things
which a man should resist on principle at the onset.
BULWER-LYTTON

Health is not a condition of matter,
but of Mind.
MARY BAKER EDDY—*Science
and Health*

The first wealth is health.
EMERSON—*The Conduct of
Life*

Health lies in labor, and there is no
royal road to it but through toil.
WENDELL PHILLIPS

The fate of a nation has often depended on the good or bad digestion
of a prime minister.
VOLTAIRE

Look to your health; and if you have
it, praise God, and value it next to
a good conscience.
IZAAK WALTON

(See also DISEASE, LIFE, MEDICINE,
MIND, QUACK, STRENGTH.)

HEARING

None so deaf as those that will not
hear.
MATTHEW HENRY—*Commen-
taries.* Psalm LVIII

Little pitchers have wide ears.
GEORGE HERBERT—*Jacula
Prudentum*

Went in at the one ear and out at
the other.
JOHN HEYWOOD—*Proverbs*

We have two ears and only one
tongue in order that we may hear
more and speak less.
DIOGENES

He that hath ears to hear, let him
hear.
MARK. IV. 9

Where more is meant than meets the
ear.
MILTON—*Il Penseroso*

Friends, Romans, countrymen, lend
me your ears.
SHAKESPEARE—*Julius Caesar.*
Act III. Sc. 2

(See also LISTENING, SOUND,
VOICE.)

HEART

My heart's in the Highlands, my
heart is not here;
My heart's in the Highlands a-chas-
ing the deer.
ROBERT BURNS

Maid of Athens, ere we part,
Give, oh, give me back my heart!
BYRON—*Maid of Athens*

Soul of fibre and heart of oak.
CERVANTES—*Don Quixote*

Some people's hearts are shrunk in them, like dried nuts. You can hear 'em rattle as they walk.
DOUGLAS JERROLD

I caused the widow's heart to sing for joy.
JOB. XXIX. 13

Let not your heart be troubled.
JOHN. XIV. 1

Still stands thine ancient sacrifice—
An humble and a contrite heart.
KIPLING—*Recessional*

No one is so accursed by fate,
No one so utterly desolate,
    But some heart, though unknown,
    Responds unto his own.
LONGFELLOW—*Endymion*

Where your treasure is, there will your heart be also.
MATTHEW. VI. 21

But the beating of my own heart
Was all the sound I heard.
RICHARD MONCKTON MILNES—
The Brookside

Hearts are stronger than swords.
WENDELL PHILLIPS

The heart knoweth his own bitterness.
PROVERBS. XIV. 10

A merry heart maketh a cheerful countenance.
PROVERBS. XV. 13

But I will wear my heart upon my sleeve
For daws to peck at; I am not what I am.
SHAKESPEARE—*Othello.* Act I. Sc. 1

Tears may be dried up, but the heart never.
MARGUERITE DE VALOIS

(See also HAPPINESS, LOVE, MATRIMONY, WOMAN, WOOING.)

HEAVEN

Heaven will be inherited by every man who has heaven in his soul.
HENRY WARD BEECHER

The road to heaven lies as near by water as by land.
JEREMY COLLIER

Heaven means to be one with God.
CONFUCIUS

All this, and Heaven too!
PHILIP HENRY

There the wicked cease from troubling, and there the weary be at rest.
JOB. III. 17

In my father's house are many mansions.
JOHN. XIV. 2

        When Christ ascended
Triumphantly from star to star
He left the gates of Heaven ajar.
LONGFELLOW—*Golden Legend*

Lay up for yourselves treasures in heaven.
MATTHEW. VI. 20

A heaven on earth.
MILTON—*Paradise Lost*

Earth has no sorrow that heaven cannot heal.
MOORE

Heav'n but the Vision of fulfill'd
Desire.
And Hell the Shadow from a Soul on
fire.
OMAR KHAYYÁM—*Rubaiyat*

A day in thy courts is better than a
thousand. I had rather be a door-
keeper in the house of my God than
to dwell in the tents of wickedness.
PSALMS. LXXXIV. 10

In Heaven an angel is nobody in
particular.
GEORGE BERNARD SHAW

Worse than a bloody hand is a hard
heart.
SHELLEY—*The Cenci*

There is a land of pure delight,
 Where saints immortal reign;
Infinite day excludes the night,
 And pleasures banish pain.
  ISAAC WATTS—*Hymns and Spir-
  itual Songs*

(See also ETERNITY, FUTURE, GOD,
HAPPINESS, IMMORTALITY, PARA-
DISE, SKY, SOUL.)

HELL

Hell is truth seen too late.
 H. G. ADAMS

Hell is paved with good intentions.
Attributed to ST. BERNARD OF
CLAIRVAUX

Nor ear can hear nor tongue can tell
The tortures of that inward hell.
 BYRON—*The Giaour*

No hell will frighten men away from
sin; no dread of prospective misery;
only goodness can cast hell out of any
man, and set up the kingdom of
heaven within.
 HUGH R. HAWEIS

Hell from beneath is moved for thee
to meet thee at thy coming.
 ISAIAH. XIV. 9

All hell broke loose.
 MILTON—*Paradise Lost*

The cunning livery of hell.
 SHAKESPEARE — *Measure for
 Measure*. Act III. Sc. 1

If there is no Hell, a good many
preachers are obtaining money under
false pretenses.
 WILLIAM A. SUNDAY

Self-love and the love of the world
constitute hell.
 SWEDENBORG — *Apocalypse Ex-
 plained*

(See also DESPAIR, DEVIL, MISERY,
PAIN, PUNISHMENT.)

HELP

Light is the task when many share
the toil.
 HOMER—*Iliad*

Make two grins grow where there
was only a grouch before.
 ELBERT HUBBARD—*Pig-Pen
 Pete*

Art thou lonely, O my brother?
Share thy little with another!
Stretch a hand to one unfriended,
And thy loneliness is ended.
 JOHN OXENHAM—*Lonely
 Brother*

Help me, Cassius, or I sink!
 SHAKESPEARE—*Julius Caesar*.
 Act I. Sc. 2

HEREDITY

It runs in the blood like wooden legs.
CHESHIRE SAYING

The fathers have eaten sour grapes, and the children's teeth are set on edge.
EZEKIEL. XVII. 2

Noble fathers have noble children.
EURIPIDES

A good tree cannot bring forth evil fruit, neither can a corrupt tree bring forth good fruit.
MATTHEW. VII. 18

He's a chip o' th' old block.
WILLIAM ROWLEY—A Match at Midnight

Clever father, clever daughter; clever mother, clever son.
RUSSIAN PROVERB

(See also ANCESTRY, POSTERITY, ROYALTY.)

HERO

No man is a hero to his own wife; no woman is a wife to her own hero.
ANONYMOUS

Hero-worship exists, has existed, and will forever exist, universally among mankind.
CARLYLE—Sartor Resartus

No man is a hero to his valet.
MME. DE CORNUEL

Every hero becomes a bore at last.
EMERSON

The boy stood on the burning deck
Whence all but him had fled;
The flame that lit the battle's wreck,
Shone round him o'er the dead.
FELICIA D. HEMANS — Casabianca

Hail, ye heroes! heaven-born band!
Who fought and bled in Freedom's cause.
JOSEPH HOPKINSON—Hail, Columbia!

The idol of today pushes the hero of yesterday out of our recollection; and will, in turn, be supplanted by his successor of tomorrow.
WASHINGTON IRVING—The Sketch Book

See the conquering hero comes!
Sound the trumpets, beat the drums!
THOMAS MORELL

(See also BRAVERY, COURAGE, DARING, FAME, GLORY, HONOR, SOLDIER, VALOR, WAR.)

HILL
SEE NATURE

HISTORY

History is something that never happened, written by a man who wasn't there.
ANONYMOUS

The economic interpretation of history does not necessarily mean that all events are determined solely by economic forces. It simply means that economic facts are the ever recurring decisive forces, the chief points in the process of history.
EDWARD BERNSTEIN—Evolutionary Socialism

History, a distillation of rumor.
CARLYLE—*French Revolution*

Assassination has never changed the history of the world.
DISRAELI

There is properly no history, only biography.
EMERSON—*Essays*

History is indeed little more than the register of the crimes, follies, and misfortunes of mankind.
GIBBON—*Decline and Fall of the Roman Empire*

What is history but a fable agreed upon?
NAPOLEON

The historian is a prophet looking backwards.
SCHLEGEL

History is only a record of crimes and misfortunes.
VOLTAIRE

All history is a lie!
SIR ROBERT WALPOLE

Human history is in essence a history of ideas.
H. G. WELLS—*The Outline of History*

(See also BOOKS, CREATION, EVENTS, PAST, PEACE, READING, WAR.)

HOLINESS
See CHURCH

HOME

No outward doors of a man's house can in general be broken open to execute any civil process; though in criminal cases the public safety supersedes the private.
BLACKSTONE

For a man's house is his castle.
SIR EDWARD COKE

Many a man who thinks to found a home discovers that he has merely opened a tavern for his friends.
GEORGE NORMAN DOUGLAS—*South Wind*

Weep no more, my lady;
  Oh, weep no more today!
We will sing one song for the old Kentucky home,
For the old Kentucky home, far away.
FOSTER—*My Old Kentucky Home*

He is happiest, be he king or peasant who finds peace in his home.
GOETHE

To Adam Paradise was home. To the good among his descendants home is paradise.
HARE

Peace and rest at length have come,
  All the day's long toil is past;
And each heart is whispering,
  "Home,
Home at last!"
HOOD—*Home at Last*

The foxes have holes, and the birds of the air have nests; but the Son of Man hath not where to lay his head.
MATTHEW. VIII. 20

A man travels the world over in search of what he needs and returns home to find it.
>GEORGE MOORE—*The Brook Kerith*

'Mid pleasures and palaces though we may roam,
Be it ever so humble, there's no place like Home.
>J. HOWARD PAYNE—*Home Sweet Home*

Home is where the heart is.
>PLINY

(See also ABSENCE, ARCHITECTURE, CONTENTMENT, COUNTRY LIFE, GUEST, HAPPINESS, HOSPITALITY, HOUSE, PEACE, WELCOME, YUKON.)

HONESTY

Honesty is the best policy.
>CERVANTES—*Don Quixote*

When rogues fall out, honest men get into their own.
>SIR MATTHEW HALE

An honest man's the noblest work of God.
>POPE

Ay, sir; to be honest, as this world goes, is to be one man picked out of ten thousand.
>SHAKESPEARE—*Hamlet.* Act II. Sc. 2

I hope I shall always possess firmness and virtue enough to maintain what I consider the most enviable of all titles, the character of an "Honest Man."
>WASHINGTON—*Moral Maxims*

(See also CHARACTER, HONOR, SINCERITY, TRUTH.)

HONOR

Dead on the field of honour.
>Answer given in the roll-call of La Tour d'Auvergne's regiment after his death.

Honor lies in honest toil.
>GROVER CLEVELAND

These were honoured in their generations, and were the glory of the times.
>ECCLESIASTICUS. XLIV. 7

I could not love thee, dear, so much, Loved I not honor more.
>LOVELACE—*To Lucasta, on Going to the Wars.*

For Brutus is an honourable man;
So are they all, all honourable men.
>SHAKESPEARE—*Julius Caesar.* Act III. Sc. 2

The nation's honor is dearer than the nation's comfort; yes, than the nation's life itself.
>WOODROW WILSON

(See also DIGNITY, FAME, GLORY, GREATNESS, HERO, HONESTY, SHAME, SOLDIER, WAR.)

HOPE

To the sick, while there is life there is hope.
>CICERO

Abandon hope, all ye who enter here.
>DANTE—*Inferno*

A woman's hopes are woven of sunbeams; a shadow annihilates them.
>GEORGE ELIOT

Hope for the best, but prepare for the worst.
ENGLISH PROVERB

Youth fades; love droops, the leaves of friendship fall;
A mother's secret hope outlives them all.
HOLMES—*A Mother's Secret*

Hope, deceitful as it is, serves at least to lead us to the end of life along an agreeable road.
LA ROCHEFOUCAULD

Hope says to us constantly, "Go on, go on," and leads us thus to the grave.
MME. DE MAINTENON

The Worldly Hope men set their Hearts upon
Turns Ashes—or it prospers; and anon,
   Like Snow upon the Desert's dusty Face,
Lighting a little hour or two—is gone.
OMAR KHAYYÁM—*Rubaiyat*

Hope springs eternal in the human breast.
POPE—*Essay on Man*

Hope deferred maketh the heart sick.
PROVERBS. XIII. 12

Who against hope believed in hope.
ROMANS. IV. 18

The sickening pang of hope deferr'd.
SCOTT—*Lady of the Lake*

Hope is the poor man's bread.
THALES

Prisoners of hope.
ZECHARIAH. IX. 12

(See also BELIEF, DESIRE, FAITH, FUTURE, TRUST.)

HORSE

You may lead a horse to water but you can't make him drink.
ENGLISH PROVERB

One white foot—buy him;
Two white feet—try him;
Three white feet—look well about him;
Four white feet—go without him.
OLD ENGLISH RHYME

A horse! a horse! my kingdom for a horse!
SHAKESPEARE—*Richard III.* Act V. Sc. 4

(See also ANIMALS.)

HOSPITALITY

Let me live in my house by the side of the road,
   Where the race of men go by;
They are good, they are bad; they are weak, they are strong,
   Wise, foolish,—so am I;
Then why should I sit in the scorner's seat,
   Or hurl the cynic's ban?
Let me live in my house by the side of the road,
   And be a friend to man.
SAM WALTER FOSS—*House by the Side of the Road*

For 't is always fair weather
When good fellows get together
With a stein on the table and a good song ringing clear.
RICHARD HOVEY—*Spring*

Oh that I had in the wilderness a
lodging-place of wayfaring men!
JEREMIAH. IX. 2

I was an hungered, an ye gave me
meat: I was thirsty, and ye gave me
drink; I was a stranger, and ye took
me in.
MATTHEW. XXV. 35

For I, who hold sage Homer's rule
    the best,
Welcome the coming, speed the go-
    ing guest.
POPE

(See also DRINKING, EATING, FES-
TIVITIES, FRIENDSHIP, GUEST,
HOME, TOASTS, WELCOME.)

HOUSE

Houses are built to live in, and not
to look on.
BACON—*Essays*

Fools build houses, and wise men buy
them.
ENGLISH PROVERB

He that lives in a glass house must
not throw stones.
ENGLISH PROVERB

A foolish man . . . built his house
upon the sand.
MATTHEW. VII. 26

A comfortable house is a great source
of happiness. It ranks immediately
after health and a good conscience.
SYDNEY SMITH

(See also ARCHITECTURE, BUILDING,
HOME.)

HUMANITY

Our humanity were a poor thing but
for the divinity that stirs within us.
BACON

I love my country better than my
family; but I love humanity better
than my country.
FÉNELON

W'en you see a man in woe,
Walk right up and say "hullo."
Say "hullo" and "how d'ye do,"
"How's the world a-usin' you?"
SAM WALTER FOSS—*Hullo.*

He held his seat; a friend to human
race.
HOMER—*Iliad*

Oh, God! that bread should be so
    dear,
    And flesh and blood so cheap!
HOOD—*Song of a Shirt*

Every human heart is human.
LONGFELLOW—*Hiawatha*

The love of humanity is the whole
of morality. This is Goodness, this is
Humanism, this is the Social Conscience.
J. WILLIAM LLOYD

After all there is but one race—
humanity.
GEORGE MOORE—*The Bending
of the Bough*

The world is my country, all mankind are my brethren, and to do good
is my religion.
THOMAS PAINE—*Rights of Man*

Humanity is the Son of God.
THEODORE PARKER

I am not an Athenian, nor a Greek, but a citizen of the world.
SOCRATES

The age of chivalry has gone; the age of humanity has come.
CHARLES SUMNER

I am a man; I count nothing human foreign to me.
TERENCE

Our true nationality is mankind.
H. G. WELLS—*The Outline of History*

For the interesting and inspiring thing about America, gentlemen, is that she asks nothing for herself except what she has a right to ask for humanity itself.
WOODROW WILSON

(See also CHARITY, GOODNESS, KINDNESS, MAN, PHILANTHROPY, PITY, SYMPATHY, TOLERATION.)

HUMAN NATURE
See CHARACTER

HUMILITY

Humility is the solid foundation of all the virtues.
CONFUCIUS

'Umble we are, 'umble we have been, 'umble we shall ever be.
DICKENS—*David Copperfield*

After crosses and losses, men grow humbler and wiser.
FRANKLIN

In humility imitate Jesus and Socrates.
FRANKLIN

God hath sworn to lift on high
Who sinks himself by true humility.
KEBLE—*Miscellaneous Poems*

I believe the first test of a truly great man is his humility.
JOHN RUSKIN

(See also MODESTY, VIRTUE.)

HUMOR

Humor is the harmony of the heart.
DOUGLAS JERROLD

It is not humor to be malignant.
LATIN PROVERB

Whenever you find Humor, you find Pathos close by its side.
WHIPPLE

(See also JESTING, JOKE, LAUGHTER, SATIRE, WIT.)

HUNGER

Better cross an angry man than a hungry man.
DANISH PROVERB

Oliver Twist has asked for more.
DICKENS—*Oliver Twist*

An empty stomach is not a good political adviser.
ALBERT EINSTEIN—*Cosmic Religion*

If thine enemy be hungry, give him bread to eat.
PROVERBS

A hungry people listens not to reason, nor cares for justice, nor is bent by any prayers.
SENECA

Yond Cassius has a lean and hungry look.
SHAKESPEARE—*Julius Caesar*.
Act I. Sc. 2

(See also APPETITE, COOKING, EAT-
ING, POVERTY.)

HUSBAND

All husbands are alike, but they have different faces so you can tell them apart.
ANONYMOUS

A good husband is never the first to go to sleep at night or the last to awake in the morning.
BALZAC—*The Physiology of Marriage*

Husbands, love your wives, even as Christ also loved the church, and gave himself for it.
EPHESIANS. V. 24

A good husband should be deaf and a good wife blind.
FRENCH PROVERB

A man should be taller, older, heavier, uglier, and hoarser than his wife.
E. W. HOWE—*Country Town Sayings*

Men are April when they woo, De-
cember when they wed.
SHAKESPEARE—*As You Like It*.
Act IV. Sc. 1

(See also HOME, LOVE, MATRIMONY,
PARENT, WIFE.)

HYPOCRISY

Saint abroad, and a devil at home.
BUNYAN—*Pilgrim's Progress*

Every man is a hypocrite.
FREDERICK IV

Hypocrites do the devil's drudgery in Christ's livery.
MATTHEW HENRY

Hypocrisy is the homage which vice renders to virtue.
LA ROCHEFOUCAULD

Who stole the livery of the court of Heaven
To serve the Devil in.
POLLOK—*Course of Time*

When you see a man with a great deal of religion displayed in his shop window, you may depend upon it he keeps a very small stock of it within.
SPURGEON

I hope you have not been leading a double life, pretending to be wicked and being really good all the time. That would be hypocrisy.
WILDE—*Importance of Being Earnest*

(See also DECEPTION, FALSEHOOD,
FRAUD, LYING.)

IDEALS

Be true to your own highest convic-
tions.
WILLIAM ELLERY CHANNING

What we need most is not so much to realize the ideal as to idealize the real.
F. H. HEDGE

Every life has its actual blanks, which the ideal must fill up, or which else remain bare and profitless forever.
JULIA WARD HOWE

All men need something to poetize and idealize their life a little—something which they value for more than its use, and which is a symbol of their emancipation from the mere materialism and drudgery of daily life.

THEODORE PARKER

(See also CHARACTER, MAN, PROGRESS.)

IDEAS

The material universe exists only in the mind.

JONATHAN EDWARDS

Ideas must work through the brains and the arms of good and brave men, or they are no better than dreams.

EMERSON

No army can withstand the strength of an idea whose time has come.

VICTOR HUGO

An idea, to be suggestive, must come to the individual with the force of a revelation.

WILLIAM JAMES—*The Varieties of Religious Experience*

It is only liquid currents of thought that move men and the world.

WENDELL PHILLIPS

Ideas are like beards: men do not have them until they grow up.

VOLTAIRE

(See also CHARACTER, INTELLECT, MIND, THOUGHT.)

IDLENESS

Lost time is never found again.

AUGHEY

Idleness is the holiday of fools.

CHESTERFIELD

Some people have a perfect genius for doing nothing, and doing it assiduously.

HALIBURTON

He is not only idle who does nothing, but he is idle who might be better employed.

SOCRATES

For Satan finds some mischief still
For idle hands to do.

ISAAC WATTS—*Against Idleness*

(See also INDUSTRY, LABOR, LEISURE, NOTHINGNESS, WORK.)

IGNORANCE

I am not ashamed to confess that I am ignorant of what I do not know.

CICERO

Ignorance never settles a question.

DISRAELI

Where ignorance is bliss,
'Tis folly to be wise.

GRAY—*On a Distant Prospect of Eton College*

Ignorance is the mother of fear.

HENRY HOME

Ignorance, when voluntary, is criminal.

SAMUEL JOHNSON

The more we study, we the more discover our ignorance.

SHELLEY

(See also FOLLY, KNOWLEDGE, LEARNING, STUPIDITY, SUPERSTITION, WISDOM.)

ILLUSION

The loss of our illusions is the only loss from which we never recover.
OUIDA

Illusion is the first of all pleasures.
VOLTAIRE

(See also DREAMS, IMAGINATION, VISION.)

IMAGINATION

Imagination is more important than knowledge.
ALBERT EINSTEIN—*On Science*

He who has imagination without learning has wings but no feet.
JOUBERT

Imagination is the eye of the soul.
JOUBERT

The human race is governed by its imagination.
NAPOLEON

Imagination disposes of everything; it creates beauty, justice, and happiness, which is everything in this world.
PASCAL

(See also DREAMS, VISION.)

IMITATION

Imitation is the sincerest (form) of flattery.
COLTON

It is impossible to imitate Voltaire without being Voltaire.
FREDERICK THE GREAT

He who imitates what is evil always goes beyond the example that is set; on the contrary, he who imitates what is good always falls short.
GUICCIARDINI—*Storia d' Italia*

A good imitation is the most perfect originality.
VOLTAIRE

(See also EXAMPLE, FLATTERY, ORIGINALITY.)

IMMORTALITY

What is human is immortal!
BULWER-LYTTON

I have been dying for twenty years, now I am going to live.
JAMES DRUMMOND BURNS—*His Last Words*

A good man never dies.
CALLIMACHUS

Immortality is the glorious discovery of Christianity.
WILLIAM ELLERY CHANNING—*Immortality*

No one could ever meet death for his country without the hope of immortality.
CICERO

Then shall the dust return to the earth as it was; and the spirit shall return unto God who gave it.
ECCLESIASTES. XII. 7

Oh, may I join the choir invisible
Of those immortal dead who live again.
GEORGE ELIOT—*The Choir Invisible*

Life is the childhood of our immortality.
GOETHE

The nearer I approach the end, the plainer I hear around me the immortal symphonies of the worlds which invite me. It is marvelous, yet simple.
VICTOR HUGO

Our hope of immortality does not come from any religions, but nearly all religions come from that hope.
INGERSOLL, 1879

I wish to believe in immortality—I wish to live with you forever.
KEATS—Letter to Fanny Brawne

There is no death! the stars go down
To rise upon some fairer shore.
J. L. McCREERY—There Is No Death

For tho' from out our bourne of time and place
The flood may bear me far,
I hope to see my Pilot face to face
When I have crost the bar.
TENNYSON—Crossing the Bar

Never did Christ utter a single word attesting to a personal resurrection and a life beyond the grave.
TOLSTOY—What I Believe

(See also CHRISTIANITY, DEATH, ETERNITY, FAME, FUTURE, HEAVEN, LIFE, MORTALITY, RELIGION, SOUL, SPIRIT.)

IMPATIENCE
See HASTE

IMPERIALISM

The conquest of the earth, which mostly means the taking it away from those who have a different complexion or slightly flatter noses than ourselves, is not a pretty thing when you look into it.
JOSEPH CONRAD—Heart of Darkness

Take up the white man's burden—
Send forth the best ye breed—
Go bind your sons to exile
To serve your captives' need.
KIPLING—The White Man's Burden

Imperialism, in a sense, is the transition stage from capitalism to Socialism. . . . It is capitalism dying, not dead.
LENIN, 1917

The mission of the United States is one of benevolent assimilation.
WILLIAM McKINLEY—Letter, 1898

(See also CONQUEST, DICTATOR, GOVERNMENT, STATESMANSHIP, TYRANNY.)

IMPOSSIBILITY

You cannot make a crab walk straight.
ARISTOPHANES

You can't get blood out of a turnip.
ENGLISH PROVERB

You can't make a silk purse out of a sow's ear.
ENGLISH PROVERB

Few things are impossible to diligence and skill.
SAMUEL JOHNSON—*Rasselas*

Never let me hear that foolish word again.
MIRABEAU

Impossible is a word only to be found in the dictionary of fools.
NAPOLEON

To the timid and hesitating everything is impossible because it seems so.
SCOTT

(See also DIFFICULTY, TROUBLE.)

IMPROVEMENT

It is necessary to try to surpass one's self always; this occupation ought to last as long as life.
QUEEN CHRISTINA

People seldom improve when they have no other model but themselves to copy after.
GOLDSMITH

Slumber not in the tents of your fathers. The world is advancing. Advance with it!
MAZZINI

(See also AMBITION, EDUCATION, LEARNING, PROGRESS, REFORM.)

INCREDULITY

Nothing is so contemptible as that affectation of wisdom, which some display, by universal incredulity.
GOLDSMITH

Incredulity robs us of many pleasures, and gives us nothing in return.
LOWELL

Incredulity is the wisdom of a fool.
H. W. SHAW

(See also BELIEF, DISTRUST, DOUBT, SUSPICION.)

INDEPENDENCE

No one can build his security upon the nobleness of another person.
WILLA CATHER—*Alexander's Bridge*

I never thrust my nose into other men's porridge. It is no bread and butter of mine: Every man for himself and God for us all.
CERVANTES—*Don Quixote*

Can anything be so elegant as to have few wants, and to serve them one's self?
EMERSON

When in the course of human events, it becomes necessary for one people to dissolve the political bonds which have connected them with another, and to assume among the powers of the earth the separate and equal station to which the laws of nature and of nature's God entitle them, a decent respect to the opinions of mankind requires that they should declare the causes which impel them to the separation.
JEFFERSON—*Declaration of Independence*

Voyager upon life's sea:—
To yourself be true,
And whate'er your lot may be,
Paddle your own canoe.
EDWARD P. PHILPOTS—*Paddle Your Own Canoe*

I would rather sit on a pumpkin, and have it all to myself, than to be crowded on a velvet cushion.

THOREAU

(See also AMERICA, DEMOCRACY, FREEDOM, LIBERTY, REBELLION, RIGHTS.)

INDIVIDUALITY

An institution is the lengthened shadow of one man.

EMERSON

Every individual has a place to fill in the world, and is important in some respect, whether he chooses to be so or not.

HAWTHORNE

The epoch of individuality is concluded, and it is the duty of reformers to initiate the epoch of association. Collective man is omnipotent upon the earth he treads.

MAZZINI

The worth of a state, in the long run, is the worth of the individuals composing it.

JOHN STUART MILL

(See also EGOTISM, FREEDOM, MAN, SELF-RELIANCE, SOLITUDE.)

INDOLENCE
See IDLENESS

INDUSTRY

The bread earned by the sweat of the brow is thrice blessed bread, and it is far sweeter than the tasteless loaf of idleness.

CROWQUILL

Whatsoever thy hand findeth to do, do it with thy might.

ECCLESIASTES. IX. 10

The more we do, the more we can do; the more busy we are, the more leisure we have.

HAZLITT

In this theater of man's life, it is reserved only for God and angels to be lookers-on.

PYTHAGORAS

(See also IDLENESS, LABOR, WORK.)

INFAMY
See CRIME

INFLUENCE

The humblest individual exerts some influence, either for good or evil, upon others.

HENRY WARD BEECHER

A little leaven leaveneth the whole lump.

GALATIANS. V. 9

A woman is more influenced by what she divines than by what she is told.

NINON DE L'ENCLOS

If the nose of Cleopatra had been shorter, the whole face of the earth would have been changed.

PASCAL—*Thoughts*

Thou wert my guide, philosopher, and friend.

POPE—*Essay on Man*

I am a part of all that I have met.

TENNYSON—*Ulysses*

(See also POWER, SYMPATHY, TEACHING.)

INGRATITUDE

We set ourselves to bite the hand that feeds us.
BURKE

Brutes leave ingratitude to man.
COLTON

Do you know what is more hard to bear than the reverses of fortune? It is the baseness, the hideous ingratitude, of man.
NAPOLEON

This was the most unkindest cut of all;
For when the noble Caesar saw him stab,
Ingratitude, more strong than traitor's arm,
Quite vanquish'd him; then burst his mighty heart.
SHAKESPEARE—*Julius Caesar.*
Act III. Sc. 2

(See also DECEPTION, GRATITUDE, SELFISHNESS, THANKFULNESS.)

INJURY

The injury we do and the one we suffer are not weighed in the same scales.
AESOP—*Fables*

Recompense injury with justice, and recompense kindness with kindness.
CONFUCIUS

If the other person injures you, you may forget the injury; but if you injure him you will always remember.
KAHLIL GIBRAN—*Sand and Foam*

If an injury has to be done to a man it should be so severe that his vengeance need not be feared.
MACHIAVELLI—*The Prince*

There is no ghost so difficult to lay as the ghost of an injury.
ALEXANDER SMITH

(See also CRUELTY, HATE, INSULT, JUSTICE, SCANDAL, SLANDER, WOUND.)

INJUSTICE

There is but one blasphemy, and that is injustice.
INGERSOLL—Speech, 1880

He who commits injustice is ever made more wretched than he who suffers it.
PLATO

A kingdom founded on injustice never lasts.
SENECA

(See also CRUELTY, INJURY, JUSTICE, LAW, WOUND.)

INN

He who has not been at a tavern knows not what a paradise it is.
ARETINO

When you go to an inn let it not be with the feeling that you must have whatever you ask for.
CONFUCIUS

There is nothing which has yet been contrived by man, by which so much happiness is produced as by a good tavern or inn.
SAMUEL JOHNSON

A region of repose it seems,
A place of slumber and of dreams.
LONGFELLOW—*Tales of a Way-
side Inn*

(See also DRINKING, EATING, FES-
TIVITIES, HOSPITALITY, TOASTS,
WINE AND SPIRITS.)

INNOCENCE

It is better that ten guilty persons
escape than that one innocent suffer.
BLACKSTONE—*Commentaries*

As innocent as a new-laid egg.
W. S. GILBERT—*Engaged*

They that know no evil will suspect
none.
BEN JONSON

Innocence finds not near so much
protection as guilt.
LA ROCHEFOUCAULD

(See also CHARACTER, CHILDHOOD,
MODESTY, PURITY, VIRTUE.)

INQUISITIVENESS

Shun the inquisitive person, for he
is also a talker.
HORACE

In ancient days the most celebrated
precept was, "Know thyself"; in modern times it has been supplanted by
the more fashionable maxim, "Know
thy neighbor, and everything about
him."
JOHNSON

(See also CURIOSITY, SECRECY.)

INSANITY

No excellent soul is exempt from a
mixture of madness.
ARISTOTLE

Mad as a March hare.
HALLIWELL—*Archaic Diet*

I teach that all men are mad.
HORACE

Insanity in individuals is something
rare—but in groups, parties, nations,
and epochs it is the rule.
NIETZSCHE

That he is mad, 'tis true; 'tis true 'tis
pity;
And pity 'tis 'tis true.
SHAKESPEARE—*Hamlet.* Act II.
Sc. 2

Though this be madness, yet there is
method in 't.
SHAKESPEARE—*Hamlet.* Act II.
Sc. 2

Whom Jupiter would destroy he first
drives mad.
SOPHOCLES—*Antigone*

Insanity is not a distinct and separate
empire; our ordinary life borders
upon it, and we cross the frontier in
some part of our nature.
TAINE

(See also MELANCHOLY, MIND,
RUIN, THOUGHT.)

INSPIRATION

No man was ever great without a
touch of divine afflatus.
CICERO

A writer is rarely so well inspired as
when he talks about himself.
ANATOLE FRANCE

Inspiration and genius—one and the
same.
VICTOR HUGO

(See also GENIUS, MIND, TALENT.)

INSTINCT

Instinct is untaught ability.
BAIN—*Senses and Intellect*

Instinct is the nose of the mind.
MME. DE GIRARDIN

A goose flies by a chart which the
Royal Geographical Society could not
improve.
HOLMES

(See also ABILITY, MIND, TALENT.)

INSULT

The way to procure insults is to submit to them. A man meets with no
more respect than he exacts.
HAZLITT

Thou hast added insult to injury.
PHAEDRUS

It is often better not to see an insult
than to avenge it.
SENECA

(See also CRUELTY, INJURY, SCAN-
DAL, SLANDER, SNEER.)

INTEGRITY
See CHARACTER

INTELLECT

God has placed no limit to intellect.
BACON

Works of the intellect are great only
by comparison with each other.
EMERSON—*Literary Ethics*

In the scale of the destinies, brawn
will never weigh so much as brain.
LOWELL

(See also GENIUS, KNOWLEDGE,
MIND, TALENT, THOUGHT.)

INTEMPERANCE

All the crimes on earth do not destroy
so many of the human race, nor
alienate so much property, as drunkenness.
BACON

Bacchus has drowned more men than
Neptune.
GARIBALDI

Of all calamities this is the greatest.
JEFFERSON—Letter, 1798

The smaller the drink, the clearer the
head.
WILLIAM PENN

Drunkenness is nothing but voluntary madness.
SENECA

O God, that men should put an enemy in their mouths to steal away
their brains! that we should, with
joy, pleasance, revel, and applause,
transform ourselves into beasts!
SHAKESPEARE—*Othello*. Act II.
Sc. 3

He is certainly as guilty of suicide
who perishes by a slow, as he who
is despatched by an immediate,
poison.
STEELE

(See also DRINKING, HEALTH, TEM-
PERANCE, WINE AND SPIRITS.)

INTOLERANCE

The devil loves nothing better than
the intolerance of reformers.
LOWELL

It were better to be of no church, than to be bitter for any.

WILLIAM PENN

(See also GOLDEN RULE, HUMANITY, REFORM, TOLERATION.)

INVENTION

A tool is but the extension of a man's hand, and a machine is but a complex tool. And he that invents a machine augments the power of a man and the well-being of mankind.

HENRY WARD BEECHER

Want, the mistress of invention.

SUSANNA CENTLIVRE—*The Busy Body*

God hath made man upright; but they have sought out many inventions.

ECCLESIASTES. VII. 29

All our inventions have endowed material forces with intellectual life, and degraded human life into a material force.

KARL MARX—Speech, 1856

(See also GENIUS, NAVIGATION, NECESSITY, SCIENCE, WONDER.)

INVESTIGATION
See FACTS

IRELAND

When Erin first rose from the dark-swelling flood,
God blessed the green island, he saw it was good.
The Emerald of Europe, it sparkled and shone
In the ring of this world, the most precious stone.

WILLIAM DRENNAN—*Erin*

Ireland is a country in which the probable never happens and the impossible always does.

Attributed to J. P. MAHAFFY

Whether on the scaffold high
Or on the battle-field we die,
Oh, what matter, when for Erin dear we fall.

T. D. SULLIVAN—*God Save Ireland*

IRRESOLUTION

Nothing of worth or weight can be achieved with half a mind, with a faint heart, and with a lame endeavor.

BARROW

Don't stand shivering upon the bank; plunge in at once and have it over.

HALIBURTON

(See also DECISION, NEUTRALITY, RESOLUTION.)

ITALY

Open my heart and you will see
Graved inside of it, "Italy."

BROWNING—*Men and Women*

Beyond the Alps lies Italy.

ENGLISH SAYING

On desperate seas long wont to roam,
Thy hyacinth hair, thy classic face,
Thy naiad airs have brought me home
To the glory that was Greece
And the grandeur that was Rome.

POE—*Helen*

My soul today
Is far away
Sailing the Vesuvian Bay.

THOMAS B. READ—*Drifting*

You may have the universe if I may have Italy.

VERDI—*Attila*

(See also ROME.)

JEALOUSY

He that is not jealous is not in love.

ST. AUGUSTINE

In jealousy there is more self-love than love.

LA ROCHEFOUCAULD

Jealousy is an awkward homage which inferiority renders to merit.

MME. DE PUISIEUX

O jealousy! thou magnifier of trifles.

SCHILLER

(See also ENVY, HATE, SUSPICION.)

JESTING

A man who could make so vile a pun would not scruple to pick a pocket.

JOHN DENNIS—*The Gentleman's Magazine*

Many a true word is spoken in jest.

ENGLISH PROVERB

Alas, poor Yorick! I knew him, Horatio: a fellow of infinite jest, of most excellent fancy.

SHAKESPEARE—*Hamlet.* Act V. Sc. 1

Jesters do often prove prophets.

SHAKESPEARE—*King Lear.* Act V. Sc. 3

(See also HUMOR, JOKE, LAUGHTER, SATIRE, SMILE, WIT.)

JESUS
See CHRIST

JEW

The Jews were God's chosen people.

ST. CHRYSOSTOM

The Jews are among the aristocracy of every land; if a literature is called rich in the possession of a few classic tragedies, what shall we say to a national tragedy lasting for fifteen hundred years, in which the poets and the actors were also the heroes.

GEORGE ELIOT—*Daniel Deronda*

I will make of thee a great nation, and I will bless thee, and make thy name great.

GENESIS. XII. 2

The Jewish bourgeoisie are our enemies, not as Jews but as bourgeoisie. The Jewish worker is our brother.

LENIN—Speech, 1918

To undo a Jew is charity, and not sin.

MARLOWE—*The Jew of Malta*

It is not possible for Christians to take part in anti-Semitism. We are Semites spiritually.

POPE PIUS XI

I am a Jew: Hath not a Jew eyes? hath not a Jew hands, organs, dimensions, senses, affections, passions? fed with the same food, hurt with the same weapons, subject to the same diseases, healed by the same means, warmed and cooled by the same winter and summer, as a Christian is?

SHAKESPEARE—*Merchant of Venice.* Act III. Sc. 1

The world is divided into two groups of nations—those which want to expel the Jews and those which do not want to receive them.
> Attributed to CHAIM WEIZMANN

JEWEL

Neither cast ye your pearls before swine.
> MATTHEW. VII. 6

Pearl of great price.
> MATTHEW. XIII. 46

On her white breast a sparkling cross she wore,
Which Jews might kiss and Infidels adore.
> POPE—*Rape of the Lock*

(See also BIRTHDAY, GOLD, WOMAN.)

JOKE

Jokes are the cayenne of conversation, and the salt of life.
> CHATFIELD

A joke's a very serious thing.
> CHURCHILL—*Ghost*

Be not affronted at a joke. If one throw salt at thee, thou wilt receive no harm, unless thou art raw.
> JUNIUS

A joke loses everything when the joker laughs himself.
> SCHILLER

(See also HUMOR, JESTING, LAUGHTER, SATIRE, SMILE, WIT.)

JOURNALISM

Journalism has already come to be the first power in the land.
> SAMUEL BOWLES

Writing good editorials is chiefly telling the people what they think, not what you think.
> ARTHUR BRISBANE

Burke said there were Three Estates in Parliament; but, in the Reporters' gallery yonder, there sat a Fourth Estate more important far than they all.
> CARLYLE—*Heroes and Hero-Worship*

Get your facts first, and then you can distort 'em as much as you please.
> S. L. CLEMENS (MARK TWAIN)

The best use of a journal is to print the largest practical amount of important truth,—truth which tends to make mankind wiser, and thus happier.
> HORACE GREELEY

Every newspaper editor owes tribute to the devil.
> LA FONTAINE

I fear three newspapers more than a hundred thousand bayonets.
> NAPOLEON

We live under a government of men and morning newspapers.
> WENDELL PHILLIPS

The newspapers! Sir, they are the most villainous—licentious—abominable—infernal—not that I ever read them—no—I make it a rule never to look into a newspaper.
> R. B. SHERIDAN—*The Critic*

(See also AUTHORSHIP, CRITICISM, GOSSIP, NEWS, NEWSPAPER, RUMOR.)

JOY

The joyfulness of a man prolongeth his days.
ECCLESIASTICUS. XXX. 22

All human joys are swift of wing,
    For heaven doth so allot it;
That when you get an easy thing,
    You find you haven't got it.
EUGENE FIELD—*Ways of Life*

A thing of beauty is a joy forever.
KEATS

I wish you all the joy that you can wish.
SHAKESPEARE—*Merchant of Venice.* Act III. Sc. 2

Sweets with sweets war not, joy delights in joy.
SHAKESPEARE—*Sonnet*

I have drunken deep of joy,
And I will taste no other wine to-night.
SHELLEY—*The Cenci*

(See also BLISS, HAPPINESS, MERRIMENT, PLEASURE.)

JUDGE

The cold neutrality of an impartial judge.
BURKE

It is better that a judge should lean on the side of compassion than severity.
CERVANTES

Judges are but men, and are swayed like other men by vehement prejudices. This is corruption in reality, give it whatever other name you please.
DAVID DUDLEY FIELD

Judges are apt to be naïve, simple-minded men.
O. W. HOLMES II—Speech, 1913

Let the judges answer to the question of law, and the jurors to the matter of fact.
LAW MAXIM

Thieves for their robbery have authority
When judges steal themselves.
SHAKESPEARE—*Measure for Measure.* Act II. Sc. 2

A Daniel come to judgment! yea, a Daniel!
O wise young judge, how I do honor thee!
SHAKESPEARE—*The Merchant of Venice.* Act IV. Sc. 1

Four things belong to a judge: to hear courteously, to answer wisely, to consider soberly, and to decide impartially.
SOCRATES

(See also JUDGMENT, JUSTICE, LAW, LAWYER, OPINION.)

JUDGMENT

Thou art weighed in the balances, and art found wanting.
DANIEL. V. 27

One man's word is no man's word; we should quietly hear both sides.
GOETHE

I know of no way of judging the future but by the past.
PATRICK HENRY, 1775

We judge ourselves by what we feel capable of doing, while others judge us by what we have already done.
LONGFELLOW—*Kavanagh*

Give your decisions, never your reasons; your decisions may be right, your reasons are sure to be wrong.
LORD MANSFIELD

Judge not, that ye be not judged.
MATTHEW. VII. 1

Give every man thine ear, but few thy voice;
Take each man's censure, but reserve thy judgment.
SHAKESPEARE—*Hamlet*. Act I. Sc. 3

Forbear to judge, for we are sinners all.
SHAKESPEARE—*Henry VI*. Pt. II. Act III. Sc. 3

O judgment! thou art fled to brutish beasts,
And men have lost their reason!
SHAKESPEARE—*Julius Caesar*. Act III. Sc. 2

One cool judgment is worth a thousand hasty councils. The thing to do is to supply light and not heat.
WOODROW WILSON—Speech, 1916

(See also CRIME, CRUELTY, DECISION, DISCRETION, GUILT, INJUSTICE, JUDGE, JUSTICE, LAW, MERCY, OPINION, PRISON, PUNISHMENT, RIGHT.)

JURY

The jury system puts a ban upon intelligence and honesty, and a premium upon ignorance, stupidity and perjury.
S. L. CLEMENS (MARK TWAIN) —*Roughing It*

The trial of all crimes, except in cases of impeachment, shall be by jury.
CONSTITUTION OF THE UNITED STATES

The jury, passing on the prisoner's life,
May in the sworn twelve have a thief or two
Guiltier than him they try.
SHAKESPEARE—*Measure for Measure*. Act II. Sc. 4

Are you good men and true?
SHAKESPEARE—*Much Ado About Nothing*. Act III. Sc. 2

(See also CRIME, JUDGE, LAW, PUNISHMENT.)

JUSTICE

There is no virtue so truly great and godlike as justice.
ADDISON—*The Guardian*

Thrice is he armed that hath his quarrel just;
And four times he who gets his fist in fust.
Accredited to JOSH BILLINGS

It looks to me to be narrow and pedantic to supply the ordinary ideas of criminal justice to this great public contest. I do not know the method of drawing up an indictment against a whole people.
BURKE—Speech on Conciliation with America

There is no such thing as justice—
in or out of court.
CLARENCE DARROW, 1936

Pity and forbearance should characterize all acts of justice.
FRANKLIN

That which is unjust can really
profit no one; that which is just can
really harm no one.
HENRY GEORGE—*The Land
Question*

I have loved justice and hated iniquity; and therefore I die in exile.
POPE GREGORY VII

The spirits of just men made perfect.
HEBREWS. XII. 23

God's mill grinds slow, but sure.
GEORGE HERBERT

The sword of the law should never
fall but on those whose guilt is so
apparent as to be pronounced by
their friends as well as foes.
JEFFERSON—Letter, 1801

Delay of justice is injustice.
LANDOR

Justice with mercy, as may illustrate
most
Them fully satisfied, and thee ap-
pease.
MILTON—*Paradise Lost*

Justice is the insurance which we
have on our lives and property; to
which may be added, and obedience
is the premium which we pay for it.
WILLIAM PENN

The path of the just is as the shining
light, that shineth more and more
unto the perfect day.
PROVERBS. IV. 18

Render therefore to all their dues.
ROMANS. XIII. 7

He who decides a case without hearing the other side, though he decide
justly, cannot be considered just.
SENECA

Thrice is he arm'd that hath his
quarrel just,
And he but naked, though lock'd up
in steel,
Whose conscience with injustice is
corrupted.
SHAKESPEARE—*Henry VI*. Pt.
II. Act III. Sc. 2

This bond is forfeit;
And lawfully by this the Jew may
claim
A pound of flesh.
SHAKESPEARE—*Merchant of
Venice*. Act IV. Sc. 1

Let justice be done, though the heavens fall.
WILLIAM WATSON, 1602

(See also EQUALITY, JUDGE, JUDG-
MENT, LAW, MERCY, PUNISHMENT,
TRUTH.)

KINDNESS

Have you had a kindness shown?
Pass it on;
'Twas not given for thee alone,
Pass it on;
Let it travel down the years,
Let it wipe another's tears,
'Til in Heaven the deed appears—
Pass it on.
REV. HENRY BURTON—
Pass It On

Their cause I plead—plead it in heart
and mind;
A fellow-feeling makes one wondrous
kind.
DAVID GARRICK, 1776

Kindness is the golden chain by which society is bound together.
GOETHE

Wherever there is a human being there is an opportunity for a kindness.
SENECA

A little more than kin, and less than kind.
SHAKESPEARE—*Hamlet*, Act I. Sc. 2

           Yet do I fear thy nature;
It is too full o' the milk of human kindness.
SHAKESPEARE—*Macbeth*. Act I. Sc. 5

Kindness gives birth to kindness.
SOPHOCLES

(See also CHARITY, GOODNESS, HUMANITY, SYMPATHY.)

KISS

Some women blush when they are kissed; some call for the police, some swear; some bite. But the worst are those who laugh.
ANONYMOUS

Gin a body meet a body
  Comin' through the rye,
Gin a body kiss a body
  Need a body cry?
    BURNS

Come, lay thy head upon my breast,
And I will kiss thee into rest.
BYRON—*The Bride of Abydos*

A long, long kiss, a kiss of youth, and love.
BYRON—*Don Juan*

It was thy kiss, Love, that made me immortal.
MARGARET FULLER—*Dryad Song*

Give me a kisse, and to that kisse a
  score;
Then to that twenty, adde a hundred more;
A thousand to that hundred; so kisse
  on,
To make that thousand up a million;
Treble that million, and when that
  is done,
Let's kisse afresh, as when we first
  begun.
    HERRICK—*To Anthea*

Stolen kisses are always sweetest.
LEIGH HUNT

Jenny kissed me when we met,
  Jumping from the chair she sat in;
Time, you thief, who love to get
  Sweets into your list, put that in.
Say I'm weary, say I'm sad,
  Say that health and wealth have
    missed me;
Say I'm growing old, but add
  Jenny kissed me.
    LEIGH HUNT—*Jenny Kissed Me*

Drink to me only with thine eyes
  And I will pledge with mine;
Or leave a kiss but in the cup,
  And I'll not look for wine.
    BEN JONSON—*To Celia*

It is delightful to kiss the eyelashes of the beloved—is it not? But never so delightful as when fresh tears are on them.
LANDOR

This done, he took the bride about
the neck
And kiss'd her lips with such a
clamorous smack
That at the parting, all the church
did echo.
SHAKESPEARE—*Taming of the
Shrew*. Act III. Sc. 3

Soul meets soul on lovers' lips.
SHELLEY—*Prometheus Un-
bound*

See! the mountains kiss high heaven,
    And the waves clasp one another;
No sister flower would be forgiven
    If it disdained its brother;
And the sunlight clasps the earth,
    And the moonbeams kiss the sea:—
What are all these kissings worth,
    If thou kiss not me?
SHELLEY—*Love's Philosophy*

Lord! I wonder what fool it was
that first invented kissing.
SWIFT—*Polite Conversation*

(See also LOVE, WOMAN, WOOING.)

KNAVERY
See CRIME

KNOWLEDGE

Strange how much you've got to
know
Before you know how little you
know.
ANONYMOUS

I take all knowledge to be my prov-
ince.
BACON

For knowledge, too, is itself a power.
BACON

That jewel knowledge is great riches,
which is not plundered by kinsmen,
nor carried off by thieves, nor de-
creased by giving.
BHAVABHUTI

Men are four:
He who knows not and knows not
    he knows not, he is a fool—shun
    him;
He who knows not and knows he
    knows not, he is simple—teach
    him;
He who knows and knows not he
    knows, he is asleep—wake him;
He who knows and knows he knows,
    he is wise—follow him!
ARABIC APOTHEGM

When you know a thing, to hold
that you know it; and when you do
not know a thing, to allow that you
do not know it; this is knowledge.
CONFUCIUS—*Analects*

Many shall run to and fro, and
knowledge shall be increased.
DANIEL. XII. 4

The only good is knowledge, and
the only evil ignorance.
DIOGENES

To be conscious that you are ignorant is a great step to knowledge.
DISRAELI—*Sybil*

He that increaseth knowledge increaseth sorrow.
ECCLESIASTES. I. 18

Our knowledge is the amassed
thought and experience of innu-
merable minds.
EMERSON—*Letters and Social
Aims*

One cannot know everything.
HORACE

Knowledge is of two kinds. We know a subject ourselves, or we know where we can find information upon it.
SAMUEL JOHNSON—*Boswell's Life of Johnson*

He who knows others is learned;
  He who knows himself is wise.
LAO-TSZE

It ain't the things you don't know what gets you into trouble; it's the things you know for sure what ain't so.
NEGRO SAYING

Better know nothing than half-know many things.
NIETZSCHE—*Thus Spake Zarathustra*

He that hath knowledge spareth his words.
PROVERBS. XVII. 27

Then I began to think, that it is very true which is commonly said, that the one-half of the world knoweth not how the other half liveth.
RABELAIS

We know what we are, but know not what we may be.
SHAKESPEARE—*Hamlet*. Act IV. Sc. 5

And seeing ignorance is the curse of God,
Knowledge the wing wherewith we fly to heaven.
SHAKESPEARE—*Henry VI*. Pt. II. Act IV. Sc. 7

Know thyself.
SOCRATES

As for me, all I know is that I know nothing.
SOCRATES

Knowledge comes, but wisdom lingers.
TENNYSON—*Locksley Hall*

(See also EDUCATION, FACTS, INTELLECT, LEARNING, MIND, SCIENCE, STUDY, TEACHING.)

LABOR

He who prays and labours lifts his heart to God with his hands.
ST. BERNARD

Labor is life. From the inmost heart of the worker rises his God-given force—the sacred celestial life-essence breathed into him by Almighty God.
THOMAS CARLYLE

They can expect nothing but their labor for their pains.
CERVANTES—*Don Quixote*

The labor of a human being is not a commodity or article of commerce.
CLAYTON ANTITRUST ACT

A truly American sentiment recognises the dignity of labor and the fact that honor lies in honest toil.
CLEVELAND

For as labor cannot produce without the use of land, the denial of the equal right to use of land is necessarily the denial of the right of labor to its own produce.
HENRY GEORGE—*Progress and Poverty*

Shall you complain who feed the
world?
Who clothe the world?
Who house the world?
Shall you complain who are the
world,
Of what the world may do?
As from this hour
You use your power,
The world must follow you!
CHARLOTTE PERKINS GILMAN
—To Labor

The labor union is an elemental re-
sponse to the human instinct for
group action in dealing with group
problems.
WILLIAM GREEN—Speech,
1925

If little labour, little are our gaines:
Man's fortunes are according to his
paines.
HERRICK—Hesperides

Labor conquers all things.
HOMER

With fingers weary and worn,
With eyelids heavy and red,
A woman sat in unwomanly rags,
Plying her needle and thread.
HOOD—Song of the Shirt

Labor, if it were not necessary for
the existence, would be indispensable
for the happiness of man.
SAMUEL JOHNSON

Labor, like Israel, has many sorrows.
Its women weep for their fallen and
they lament for the future of the
children of the race.
JOHN L. LEWIS—Speech, 1937

If we rightly estimate things, what
in them is purely owing to nature,
and what to labour, we shall find
ninety-nine parts of a hundred are
wholly to be put on the account of
labour.
JOHN LOCKE

Bowed by the weight of centuries
he leans
Upon his hoe and gazes on the
ground,
The emptiness of ages in his face,
And on his back the burden of the
world.
EDWIN MARKHAM—The Man
with the Hoe

And all labor without any play, boys,
Makes Jack a dull boy in the end.
H. A. PAGE

The duty of labor is written on a
man's body: in the stout muscle of
the arm, and the delicate machinery
of the hand.
THEODORE PARKER

If you want knowledge, you must
toil for it; if food, you must toil for
it; and if pleasure, you must toil for
it: toil is the law.
RUSKIN

Many faint with toil,
That few may know the cares and
woe of sloth.
SHELLEY—Queen Mab

Labour was the first price, the original purchase money that was paid
for all things.
ADAM SMITH—Wealth of
Nations

The Russian Socialist Federated Soviet Republic declares labor the duty of all citizens of the republic.
SOVIET CONSTITUTION

Labour of love.
I THESSALONIANS. I. 3

The labourer is worthy of his reward.
I TIMOTHY. V. 18

(See also ACTION, CAPITAL AND LABOR, DEED, WORK.)

LAMB

God tempers the wind to the shorn lamb.
ENGLISH PROVERB

Mary had a little lamb
Its fleece was white as snow,
And everywhere that Mary went
The lamb was sure to go.
MRS. SARAH J. HALE—*Mary's Little Lamb*

Like lambs to the slaughter.
JEREMIAH. LI. 40

(See also ANIMALS, SHEEP.)

LAND

If a man own land, the land owns him.
EMERSON—*Wealth*

The small landholders are the most precious part of a state.
JEFFERSON—Letter, 1785

The land shall not be sold for ever: for the land is mine; for ye are strangers and sojourners with me.
LEVITICUS. XXV. 23

That which is built upon the land goes with the land.
LEGAL MAXIM

(See also AGRICULTURE, FARMING, HARVEST, POVERTY, PROGRESS, PROPERTY, WEALTH.)

LANGUAGE

I love the language, that soft bastard Latin,
Which melts like kisses from a female mouth.
BYRON—*Beppo*

He Greek and Latin speaks with greater ease
Than hogs eat acorns, and tame pigeons peas.
CRANFIELD—*Panegyric on Tom Coriate*

Language is a city to the building of which every human being brought a stone.
EMERSON—*Letters and Social Aims*

The whole earth was of one language, and of one speech.
GENESIS. XI. 1

Babel; because the Lord did there confound the language of all the earth.
GENESIS. XI. 9

But, for my own part, it was Greek to me.
SHAKESPEARE—*Julius Caesar.* Act I. Sc. 2

No man fully capable of his own language ever masters another.
> George Bernard Shaw—*Maxims for Revolutionists*

I am the King of Rome, and above grammar.
> Sigismund—At the Council of Constance

Language, as well as the faculty of speech, was the immediate gift of God.
> Noah Webster

Language is not an abstract construction of the learned, or of dictionary-makers, but is something arising out of the work, needs, ties, joys, affections, tastes, of long generations of humanity, and has its bases broad and low, close to the ground.
> Walt Whitman—*Slang in America*

(See also CONVERSATION, ORATORY, SPEECH, TALK, TONGUE, WIT, WORD.)

LARK

Rise with the lark, and with the lark to bed.
> James Hurdis—*The Village Curate*

Lo! here the gentle lark, weary of rest,
From his moist cabinet mounts up on high,
And wakes the morning, from whose silver breast
The sun ariseth in his majesty.
> Shakespeare—*Venus and Adonis*

Hail to thee, blithe Spirit!
  Bird thou never wert,
That from Heaven, or near it,
  Pourest thy full heart
In profuse strains of unpremeditated art.
> Shelley—*To a Skylark*

(See also BIRDS.)

LAUGHTER

To provoke laughter without joining in it greatly heightens the effect.
> Balzac

I hasten to laugh at everything, for fear of being obliged to weep.
> Beaumarchais

The man who cannot laugh is not only fit for treasons, stratagems, and spoils, but his whole life is already a treason and a stratagem.
> Carlyle

Nothing is more silly than silly laughter.
> Catullus

As the crackling of thorns under a pot, so is the laughter of a fool.
> Ecclesiastes. VII. 6

Man is the only creature endowed with the power of laughter.
> Greville

Man alone suffers so excruciatingly in the world that he was compelled to invent laughter.
> Nietzsche—*The Will to Power*

He laughs best who laughs last.
> Old English Proverb

Laugh and the world laughs with you,
Weep and you weep alone;
For the sad old earth must borrow its mirth,
But has trouble enough of its own.
ELLA WHEELER WILCOX—*Solitude*

People who do not know how to laugh, are always pompous and self-conceited.
THACKERAY

(See also HAPPINESS, JESTING, JOY, MERRIMENT, SMILE.)

LAW

Written laws are like spiders' webs, and will like them only entangle and hold the poor and weak, while the rich and powerful will easily break through them.
ANACHARSIS to Solon

Law is a bottomless pit.
J. ARBUTHNOT—Title of a Pamphlet. 1700

There is but one law for all; namely, that law which governs all law,—the law of our Creator, the law of humanity, justice, equity; the law of nature and of nations.
BURKE

'Tis easier to make certain things legal than to make them legitimate.
CHAMFORT

Possession is eleven points in the law.
COLLEY CIBBER

After an existence of nearly twenty years of almost innocuous desuetude these laws are brought forth.
GROVER CLEVELAND. 1886

Reason is the life of the law; nay, the common law itself is nothing else but reason. The law which is perfection of reason.
SIR EDWARD COKE—*First Institute*

"If the law supposes that," said Mr. Bumble, "the law is a ass, a idiot."
DICKENS—*Oliver Twist*

Laws too gentle are seldom obeyed; too severe, seldom executed.
FRANKLIN—*Poor Richard's Almanac*

Be you never so high, the law is above you.
THOMAS FULLER

The English laws punish vice; the Chinese laws do more, they reward virtue.
GOLDSMITH

Laws grind the poor, and rich men rule the law.
GOLDSMITH—*The Traveller*

I know no method to secure the repeal of bad or obnoxious laws so effective as their stringent execution.
ULYSSES S. GRANT—Address, 1869

If the law is upheld only by government officials, then all law is at an end.
HERBERT HOOVER—Message, 1929

The execution of the laws is more important than the making of them.
JEFFERSON—Letter, 1789

The laws sometimes sleep, but never die.
LAW MAXIM

All things obey fixed laws.
MANILIUS—*Astronomica*

Render therefore unto Caesar the things which are Caesar's.
MATTHEW. XXII. 21

There is no man so good, who, were he to submit all his thoughts and actions to the laws would not deserve hanging ten times in his life.
MONTAIGNE

Petty laws breed great crimes.
OUIDA—*Wisdom, Wit and Pathos*

Where law ends, there tyranny begins.
WILLIAM PITT

The law hath not been dead, though it hath slept.
SHAKESPEARE—*Measure for Measure*. Act II. Sc. 2

Do as adversaries do in law,
Strive mightily, but eat and drink as friends.
SHAKESPEARE—*Taming of the Shrew*. Act I. Sc. 2

(See also CRIME, GOVERNMENT, JUDGE, JUSTICE, PUNISHMENT.)

LAWYER

A lawyer must first get on, then get honor, and then get honest.
ANONYMOUS

A lawyer starts life giving $500 worth of law for $5, and ends giving $5 worth for $500.
Attributed to BENJAMIN H. BREWSTER

Our wrangling lawyers are so litigious and busy here on earth, that I think they will plead their clients' causes hereafter, some of them in hell.
BURTON

It is a secret worth knowing that lawyers rarely go to law.
MOSES CROWELL

A lawyer's opinion is worth nothing unless paid for.
ENGLISH PROVERB

The first thing we do, let's kill all the lawyers.
SHAKESPEARE—*Henry VI*. Pt. II. Act IV. Sc. 2

Most good lawyers live well, work hard, and die poor.
DANIEL WEBSTER

(See also JUDGE, JUSTICE, LAW.)

LAZY
See IDLENESS

LEADERSHIP

When we think we lead we most are led.
BYRON—*The Two Foscari*

An army of stags led by a lion would be better than an army of lions led by a stag.
LATIN PROVERB

If the blind lead the blind, both shall fall into the ditch.
MATTHEW. XV. 14

Reason and judgment are the qualities of a leader.
TACITUS

(See also CHARACTER, GOVERNMENT, QUALITY, SUCCESS, WORTH.)

LEARNING

Much learning doth make thee mad.
ACTS. XXVI. 24

It is always in season for old men to learn.
AESCHYLUS—*Agamemnon*

Reading maketh a full man; conference a ready man; and writing an exact man.
BACON—*Essays*

The three foundations of learning: Seeing much, suffering much, and studying much.
CATHERALL

Wear your learning like your watch, in a private pocket; and do not pull it out and strike it, merely to show that you have one.
CHESTERFIELD

I have learned silence from the talkative, toleration from the intolerant, and kindness from the unkind; yet strange, I am ungrateful to these teachers.
KAHLIL GIBRAN—*Sand and Foam*

And still they gazed, and still the wonder grew,
That one small head should carry all it knew.
GOLDSMITH—*The Deserted Village*

All wish to be learned, but no one is willing to pay the price.
JUVENAL

The great man learns only what he wants to learn; the mediocre man can learn what others think he should learn.
GEORGE MOORE

They have learned nothing, and forgotten nothing.
CHEVALIER DE PANAT

A little learning is a dangerous thing;
Drink deep, or taste not the Pierian spring;
Their shallow draughts intoxicate the brain,
And drinking largely sobers us again.
POPE—*Essay on Criticism*

Men learn while they teach.
SENECA

A learned man is an idler who kills time by study.
GEORGE BERNARD SHAW—
Maxims for Revolutionists

(See also ART, BOOKS, EDUCATION, FACTS, HISTORY, INTELLECT, KNOWLEDGE, LANGUAGE, LITERATURE, MIND, SCIENCE, STUDENT, STUDY.)

LEISURE

Increased means and increased leisure are the two civilizers of man.
DISRAELI—Speech, 1872

The wisdom of a learned man cometh by opportunity of leisure.
ECCLESIASTICUS. XXXVIII. 24

A life of leisure and a life of laziness are two things.

FRANKLIN—*Poor Richard's Almanac*

Leisure is the mother of philosophy.

THOMAS HOBBES—*Leviathan*

A workman ought to have leisure in proportion to the wear and tear of his strength.

POPE LEO XIII

(See also IDLENESS, REPOSE, REST.)

LENDING

If you lend you either lose the money or gain an enemy.

ALBANIAN PROVERB

Better give a shilling than lend and lose half a crown.

THOMAS FULLER

A good man showeth favor, and lendeth.

PSALMS. CXII. 5

If thou wilt lend this money, lend
   it not
As to thy friends; for when did
   friendship take
A breed of barren metal of his
   friend?
But lend it rather to thine enemy;
Who, if he break, thou mayst with
   better face
Exact the penalty.

SHAKESPEARE—*The Merchant of Venice*. Act I. Sc. 3

(See also BORROWING, CREDITOR, DEBT.)

LETTER

In a man's letters his soul lies naked.

SAMUEL JOHNSON

Every letter of declination ought to be written by a skilful man—a diplomatist who can write an unpleasant truth without offence.

WALTER HINES PAGE—*A Publisher's Confession*

I have made this letter longer than usual because I lack the time to make it shorter.

PASCAL

You say there is nothing to write about. Then write to me that there is nothing to write about.

PLINY THE YOUNGER

I have received no more than one or two letters in my life that were worth the postage.

THOREAU—*Walden*

(See also POST, WRITING.)

LIAR
See LYING

LIBERAL

One who has both feet firmly planted in the air.

ANONYMOUS

A gentleman . . . is liberal in his attainments, opinions, practices and concessions. He asks for himself no more than he is willing to concede to others.

COOPER—*The American Democrat*

Liberalism is trust of the people tempered by prudence; conservatism, distrust of the people tempered by fear.

GLADSTONE

A liberal is a man who is willing to spend somebody else's money.
CARTER GLASS, 1938

(See also CONSERVATISM, POLITICS.)

LIBERALITY

He that defers his charity until he is dead is, if a man weighs it rightly, rather liberal of another man's goods than his own.
BACON

Liberality consists less in giving much than in giving at the right moment.
LA BRUYÈRE

The liberal soul shall be made fat.
PROVERBS. XI. 25

What's mine is yours, and what is yours is mine.
SHAKESPEARE—*Measure for Measure*. Act V. Sc. 1

(See also CHARITY, GOODNESS, PHILANTHROPY.)

LIBERTY

The tree of liberty grows only when watered by the blood of tyrants.
BARÈRE

The people never give up their liberties but under some delusion.
BURKE

Liberty's in every blow!
Let us do or die.
BURNS—*Bruce to His Men at Bannockburn*

Where the spirit of the Lord is, there is Liberty.
II CORINTHIANS. III. 17

Eternal vigilance is the price of liberty.
JOHN PHILPOT CURRAN— Dublin, 1808

The love of liberty with life is given, And life itself the inferior gift of Heaven.
DRYDEN—*Palamon and Arcite*

Those who would give up essential liberty to purchase a little temporary safety deserve neither liberty nor safety.
FRANKLIN

Give me liberty, or give me death.
PATRICK HENRY

The God who gave us life, gave us liberty at the same time.
JEFFERSON

Proclaim liberty throughout all the land unto all the inhabitants thereof.
LEVITICUS. XXV. 10. Inscription on Liberty Bell at Philadelphia.

Give me the liberty to know, to think, to believe, and to utter freely according to conscience, above all other liberties.
MILTON

License they mean when they cry, Liberty!
For who loves that, must first be wise and good.
MILTON

O liberty! how many crimes are committed in thy name!
MME. JEANNE ROLAND

So every bondman in his own hand
  bears
The power to cancel his captivity.
  SHAKESPEARE—*Julius Caesar*
  Act I. Sc. 3

Give me your tired, your poor,
Your huddled masses, yearning to
  breathe free,
The wretched refuse of your teeming
  shore.
Send these, the homeless, tempest
  tossed, to me:
I lift my lamp beside the golden
  door.
  EMMA LAZARUS—Inscription on
  Statue of Liberty, New York
  Harbor

Liberty, when it begins to take root,
is a plant of rapid growth.
  WASHINGTON

Liberty *and* Union, now and for ever,
one and inseparable!
  WEBSTER—Speech, 1830

Liberty is the only thing you cannot
have unless you are willing to give it
to others.
  WILLIAM ALLEN WHITE, 1940

I have always in my own thought
summed up individual liberty, and
business liberty, and every other kind
of liberty, in the phrase that is common in the sporting world, "A free
field and no favor."
  WOODROW WILSON—Speech,
  1915

(See also AMERICA, EQUALITY, FREE-
  DOM, INDEPENDENCE, RIGHTS,
  SLAVERY, SOLDIER, WAR.)

LIBRARY
See BOOKS

LIFE

Ofttimes the test of courage becomes
rather to live than to die.
  ALFIERI—*Orestes*

Every man's life is a fairy-tale written
by God's fingers.
  HANS CHRISTIAN ANDERSEN

Life is a jig saw puzzle with most of
the pieces missing.
  ANONYMOUS

I expect to pass through this world
but once. Any good therefore that I
can do, or any kindness that I can
show to any fellow creature, let me
do it now. Let me not defer or neg-
lect it, for I shall not pass this way
again.
  ANONYMOUS

They live that they may eat, but he
himself (Socrates) eats that he may
live.
  ATHENAEUS

We come and we cry, and that is
life; we yawn and we depart, and that
is death!
  AUSONE DE CHANCEL—*Lines in
  an Album*

It matters not how long we live, but
how.
  BAILEY—*Festus*

Life is a long lesson in humility.
  BARRIE—*Little Minister*

It is a misery to be born, a pain to
live, a trouble to die.
  ST. BERNARD OF CLAIRVAUX

Life, believe, is not a dream,
  So dark as sages say;
Oft a little morning rain
  Foretells a pleasant day!
    CHARLOTTE BRONTË—*Life*

Life is but a day at most.
    BURNS—*Friars' Carse Hermitage*

Through life's road, so dim and dirty,
I have dragged to three and thirty;
What have these years left to me?
Nothing, except thirty-three.
    BYRON—*Diary*

One life—a little gleam of Time between two Eternities.
    CARLYLE

Hurried and worried until we're
    buried, and there's no curtain
    call,
Life's a very funny proposition, after
    all.
    GEORGE M. COHAN

For life in general, there is but one
decree: youth is a blunder, manhood
a struggle, old age a regret.
    DISRAELI

Out of sleeping a waking,
Out of waking a sleep.
    EMERSON—*The Sphinx*

No one is to be despaired of as long
as he breathes. (While there is life
there is hope.)
    ERASMUS

Dost thou love life? Then do not
squander time, for that is the stuff
life is made of.
    FRANKLIN—*Poor Richard*

A useless life is an early death.
    GOETHE

All that a man hath will he give for
his life.
    JOB. II. 4

Our whole life is like a play.
    BEN JONSON

Life is a tragedy for those who feel,
and a comedy for those who think.
    LA BRUYÈRE

Man is a torch, then ashes soon,
May and June, then dead December,
Dead December, then again June.
Who shall end my dream's confu-
    sion?
Life is a loom, weaving illusion.
    VACHEL LINDSAY—*The Chinese
    Nightingale*

Tell me not, in mournful numbers,
  Life is but an empty dream!
    LONGFELLOW—*A Psalm of Life*

Christian life consists in faith and
charity.
    LUTHER

Strait is the gate and narrow is the
way which leadeth unto life.
    MATTHEW. VII. 14

My candle burns at both ends;
  It will not last the night;
But, ah, my foes, and, oh, my
    friends—
  It gives a lovely light.
    EDNA ST. VINCENT MILLAY—
    Figs from Thistles

Life is but jest:
  A dream, a doom;
  A gleam, a gloom—
  And then—good rest!

Life is but play;
  A throb, a tear:
  A sob, a sneer;
  And then—good day.
    LEON DE MONTENAEKEN

Ah Love! could you and I with him
  conspire
  To grasp this sorry Scheme of
  Things entire
  Would we not shatter it to bits—
  and then
Re-mould it nearer to the Heart's
  Desire?
    OMAR KHAYYÁM—*Rubaiyat*

One awakens, one rises, one dresses,
  and one goes forth;
One returns, one dines, one sups, one
  retires and one sleeps.
    DE PIIS

Learn to live well, or fairly make
  your will;
You've play'd, and lov'd, and ate,
  and drank your fill:
Walk sober off, before a sprightlier
  age
Comes titt'ring on, and shoves you
  from the stage.
    POPE—*Second Book of Horace*

Lord, make me to know mine end,
and the measure of my days, what it
is; that I may know how frail I am.
    PSALMS. XXXIX. 4

As for man his days are as grass; as
a flower of the field so he flourisheth.
    PSALMS. CIII. 15

Only deeds give strength to life,
only moderation gives it charm.
    JEAN PAUL RICHTER—*Titan*

Life is the game that must be played:
  This truth at least, good friends,
  we know;
So live and laugh, nor be dismayed
  As one by one the phantoms go.
    EDWIN ARLINGTON ROBINSON
    —*Ballade by the Fire*

I wish to preach not the doctrine of
ignoble ease, but the doctrine of the
strenuous life.
    THEODORE ROOSEVELT

Say, what is life? 'Tis to be born,
  A helpless Babe, to greet the light
With a sharp wail, as if the morn
  Foretold a cloudy noon and night;
To weep, to sleep, and weep again,
  With sunny smiles between; and
  then?
    J. G. SAXE—*The Story of
    Life*

His saying was: live and let live.
    SCHILLER

As is a tale, so is life: not how long
it is, but how good it is, is what
matters.
    SENECA

       Out, out, brief candle!
Life's but a walking shadow.
    SHAKESPEARE—*Macbeth*. Act V.
    Sc. 5

To make good use of life, one should
have in youth the experience of ad-
vanced years, and in old age the
vigor of youth.
    STANISLAUS

Away with funeral music—set
  The pipe to powerful lips—
The cup of life's for him that drinks
  And not for him that sips.
    STEVENSON. Boulogne, 1872

May you live all the days of your life.

SWIFT

Let your life lightly dance on the edges of Time like dew on the tip of a leaf.

TAGORE—*Gardener*

The white flower of a blameless life.

TENNYSON—*Idylls of the King*

Life is a game of whist. From unseen sources
The cards are shuffled, and the hands are dealt.

. . . .

I do not like the way the cards are shuffled,
But yet I like the game and want to play.

EUGENE F. WARE—*Whist*

Our lives are albums written through
With good or ill, with false or true;
And as the blessed angels turn
The pages of our years,
God grant they read the good with smiles,
And blot the ill with tears!

WHITTIER—*Written in a Lady's Album*

Our lives are songs; God writes the words
And we set them to music at pleasure;
And the song grows glad, or sweet or sad,
As we choose to fashion the measure.

ELLA WHEELER WILCOX—*Our Lives*

Men know life too early, women know life too late.

WILDE—*A Woman of No Importance*

All the things I really like to do are either immoral, illegal or fattening.

ALEXANDER WOOLLCOTT

In masks outrageous and austere
The years go by in single file;
But none has merited my fear,
And none has quite escaped my smile.

ELINOR HOYT WYLIE—*Let No Charitable Hope*

(See also BIRTH, DEATH, DESTINY, EVOLUTION, FATE, IMMORTALITY, MAN, SOUL, WORLD.)

LIGHT

I shall light a candle of understanding in thine heart, which shall not be put out.

II ESDRAS. XIV. 25

And God said, Let there be light: and there was light.

GENESIS. I. 3

The true light, which lighteth every man that cometh into the world.

JOHN. I. 9

He was a burning and a shining light.

JOHN. V. 35

Lead, kindly Light, amid the encircling gloom,
Lead Thou me on!
The night is dark, and I am far from home—
Lead Thou me on!
Keep Thou my feet; I do not ask to see
The distant scene,—one step enough for me.

JOHN HENRY NEWMAN

And this I know; whether the one
     True Light
Kindle to Love, or Wrath consume
     me quite,
One flash of it within the Tavern
     caught
Better than in the temple lost out-
     right.
          OMAR KHAYYÁM—*Rubaiyat*

Nature and Nature's laws lay hid in
     night:
God said, "Let Newton be!" and all
     was light.
          POPE—Epitaph for Sir Isaac
          Newton

(See also DAY, EYE, MORNING, SUN,
SUNRISE, SUNSET, TWILIGHT.)

LIKE

Birds of a feather flock together.
          ENGLISH PROVERB

Like mother, like daughter
          ENGLISH PROVERB

One crow will not pick out another
crow's eyes.
          ENGLISH PROVERB

Like will to like, each creature loves
his kind.
          HERRICK—*Hesperides*

Like father, like son.
          LATIN PROVERB

I shall not look upon his like again.
          SHAKESPEARE—*Hamlet*. Act I.
          Sc. 2

(See also COMPARISON, JUDGMENT,
QUALITY, WORTH.)

LINCOLN

Honesty rare as a man without self-
     pity,
Kindness as large and plain as a
     prairie wind.
          STEPHEN VINCENT BENÉT—
          John Brown's Body

O, Uncommon Commoner! may
     your name
Forever lead like a living flame!
Unschooled scholar! how did you
     learn
The wisdom a lifetime may not earn?
Unsainted martyr! higher than saint!
You were a *man* with a man's con-
     straint.
          EDMUND VANCE COOKE—*The
          Uncommon Commoner*

His heart was as great as the world,
but there was no room in it to hold
the memory of a wrong.
          EMERSON—*Letters and Social
          Aims*

Nature, they say, doth dote,
And cannot make a man
Save on some worn-out plan
Repeating us by rote:
For him her Old World moulds
     aside she threw
And, choosing sweet clay from the
     breast
Of the unexhausted West,
With stuff untainted shaped a hero
     new.
          LOWELL—*A Hero New*

O captain! my captain! our fearful
     trip is done;
The ship has weather'd every rack;
     the prize we sought is won;
The port is near, the bells I hear,
     the people all exulting,

While follow eyes the steady keel, the
    vessel grim and daring;
But O heart! heart! heart!
    O the bleeding drops of red,
Where on the deck my captain lies,
    Fallen cold and dead.
> WALT WHITMAN— *O Captain!*
> *My Captain!*

(See also AMERICA, CAPITAL AND
LABOR, GOVERNMENT, RIGHTS,
SLAVERY.)

LION

The lion is not so fierce as they
paint him.
> HERBERT

Do not pluck the beard of a dead
lion.
> MARTIAL

A lion among ladies is a most dreadful thing.
> SHAKESPEARE—*A Midsummer
> Night's Dream*. Act III. Sc. 1

It is not good to wake a sleeping lion.
> PHILIP SIDNEY—*Arcadia*

(See also ANIMALS.)

LISTENING

From listening comes wisdom, and
from speaking repentance.
> ITALIAN PROVERB

A good listener is not only popular
everywhere, but after a while he
knows something.
> WILSON MIZNER

(See also HEARING, LEARNING,
SOUND, VOICE.)

LITERATURE

The great standard of literature as
to purity and exactness of style is
the Bible.
> HUGH BLAIR

Literature has her quacks no less
than medicine, and they are divided
into two classes; those who have
erudition without genius, and those
who have volubility without depth;
we shall get second-hand sense from
the one, and original nonsense from
the other.
> COLTON

Literature is my Utopia. Here I am
not disfranchised. No barrier of the
senses shuts me out from the sweet,
gracious discourse of my book-friends.
They talk to me without embarrass-
ment or awkwardness.
> HELEN KELLER—*The Story of
> My Life*

The classics are only primitive literature. They belong to the same class
as primitive machinery and primitive
music and primitive medicine.
> STEPHEN LEACOCK—*Homer
> and Humbug*

The republic of letters.
> MOLIÈRE

The man who writes about himself
and his own time is the only man
who writes about all people and
about all time.
> GEORGE BERNARD SHAW—*The
> Sanity of Art*

The difference between literature
and journalism is that journalism is
unreadable, and literature is not read.
> WILDE—*The Critic as Artist*

Literature always anticipates life. It does not copy it, but molds it to its purpose.

WILDE—*The Decay of Lying,* 1891

(See also AUTHORSHIP, BOOKS, CRITICISM, EDUCATION, JOURNALISM, POETRY, READING, WRITING.)

LOGIC

Men are apt to mistake the strength of their feeling for the strength of their argument. The heated mind resents the chill touch and relentless scrutiny of logic.

GLADSTONE

Logic is logic. That's all I say.

HOLMES—*The One-Hoss Shay*

Logic is neither a science nor an art, but a dodge.

BENJAMIN JOWETT

Grammar is the logic of speech, even as logic is the grammar of reason.

TRENCH

(See also ARGUMENT, PHILOSOPHY, REASON.)

LONDON

A mighty mass of brick, and smoke, and shipping,
    Dirty and dusty, but as wide as eye
Could reach, with here and there a sail just skipping
    In sight, then lost amidst the forestry
Of masts; a wilderness of steeples peeping
    On tiptoe through their sea-coal canopy;

A huge, dun cupola, like a foolscap crown
    On a fool's head—and there is London Town.

BYRON—*Don Juan*

London is a roost, for every bird.

DISRAELI—*Lothair*

(See also CITY, ENGLAND)

LORD
See GOD, NOBILITY

LOSS
See FAILURE

LOVE

Mysterious love, uncertain treasure,
Hast thou more of pain or pleasure!
Endless torments dwell about thee:
Yet who would live, and live without thee!

ADDISON—*Rosamond*

I seek for one as fair and gay,
    But find none to remind me,
How blest the hours pass'd away
    With the girl I left behind me.

ANONYMOUS

The sweetest joy, the wildest woe is love.

BAILEY—*Festus*

Man loves little and often, woman much and rarely.

BASTA

Love in France is a comedy; in England a tragedy; in Italy an opera seria; and in Germany a melodrama.

MARGUERITE BLESSINGTON

Our first and last love is—self-love.

BOVEE

The first sigh of love is the last of wisdom.
ANTOINE BRET

Oh my luve's like a red, red rose,
  That's newly sprung in June;
Oh my luve's like the melodie
  That's sweetly played in tune.
BURNS—*Red, Red Rose*

No cord nor cable can so forcibly draw, or hold so fast, as love can do with a twined thread.
BURTON—*Anatomy of Melancholy*

Oh Love! young Love! bound in thy
  rosy band,
Let sage or cynic prattle as he will,
These hours, and only these, redeem
  Life's years of ill.
BYRON—*Childe Harold*

Man's love is of man's life a thing
  apart,
  'Tis woman's whole existence.
BYRON—*Don Juan*

Yes, Love indeed is light from
  heaven;
A spark of that immortal fire
With angels shared, by Allah given
  To lift from earth our low desire.
BYRON—*The Giaour*

Of all the girls that are so smart
  There's none like pretty Sally;
She is the darling of my heart,
  And lives in our alley.
HENRY CAREY—*Sally in Our Alley*

There's no love lost between us.
CERVANTES—*Don Quixote*

All thoughts, all passions, all delights,
  Whatever stirs this mortal frame,
All are but ministers of Love,
  And feed his sacred flame.
COLERIDGE—*Love*

Heaven has no rage like love to hatred turned.
CONGREVE

How wise are they that are but fools in love!
JOSHUA COOKE

Love with men is not a sentiment, but an idea.
MME. DE GIRARDIN

Love is an ocean of emotions, entirely surrounded by expenses.
LORD DEWAR

We are all born for love. . . . It is the principle of existence and its only end.
DISRAELI—*Sybil*

I have found it impossible to carry the heavy burden of responsibility and to discharge my duties as King as I would wish to do without the help and support of the woman I love.
EDWARD VIII (later the Duke of Windsor) in his farewell address, 1936

All mankind love a lover.
EMERSON—*Essays*

But one always returns to one's first loves.
ÉTIENNE—*Joconde*

If you would be loved, love and be lovable.

FRANKLIN

It's love, it's love that makes the world go round.

FRENCH SONG

Young men wish: love, money and health. One day, they'll say: health, money and love.

PAUL GERALDY

Love possesses not nor would it be possessed;
For love is sufficient unto love.

KAHLIL GIBRAN—*The Prophet*

Girls we love for what they are;
Young men for what they promise to be.

GOETHE

Thus let me hold thee to my heart,
    And every care resign:
And we shall never, never part,
    My life—my all that's mine!

GOLDSMITH—*The Hermit*

Man begins by loving love and ends by loving a woman. Woman begins by loving a man and ends by loving love.

REMY DE GOURMONT

Whom the Lord loveth he chasteneth.

HEBREWS. XII. 6

You say to me-ward's your affection's strong;
Pray love me little, so you love me long.

HERRICK

Love is a conflict between reflexes and reflections.

MAGNUS HIRSCHFELD—*Sex in Human Relationship*

Pale hands I loved beside the Shalimar,
    Where are you now? Who lies beneath your spell?
Whom do you lead on Rapture's roadway, far,
    Before you agonize them in farewell?

LAURENCE HOPE—*Kashmiri Song*

Love's like the measles—all the worse when it comes late in life.

DOUGLAS JERROLD

Greater love hath no man than this, that a man lay down his life for his friends.

JOHN. XV. 13

There is no fear in love; but perfect love casteth out fear.

I JOHN. IV. 18

Love in a hut, with water and a crust,
Is—Love, forgive us!—cinders, ashes, dust.

KEATS—*Lamia*

Sing, for faith and hope are high—
    None so true as you and I—
Sing the Lovers' Litany:
    "Love like ours can never die!"

KIPLING—*Lovers' Litany*

The reason why lovers and their mistresses never tire of being together is that they are always talking of themselves.

LA ROCHEFOUCAULD

Do you know you have asked for
   the costliest thing
Ever made by the Hand above—
A woman's heart, and a woman's life,
And a woman's wonderful love?
   MARY T. LATHROP

I love a lassie, a bonnie, bonnie
   lassie,
She's as pure as the lily in the dell.
   She's as sweet as the heather,
   The bonnie, bloomin' heather,
Mary, ma Scotch Blue-bell.
   HARRY LAUDER AND GERALD
   GRAFTON

That was the first sound in the song
   of love!
Scarce more than silence is, and yet
   a sound.
Hands of invisible spirits touch the
   strings
Of that mysterious instrument, the
   soul,
And play the prelude of our fate.
   We hear
The voice prophetic, and are not
   alone.
   LONGFELLOW—Spanish Student

I could not love thee, dear, so much
   Loved I not honour more.
   LOVELACE—To Lucasta, on
   Going to the Wars

He who loves not wine, woman, and
   song,
Remains a fool his whole life long.
   Attributed to LUTHER

Come live with me, and be my love,
And we will all the pleasures prove,
That valleys, groves, or hills, or
   fields,
Or woods and steepy mountains,
   yield.
   MARLOWE—The Passionate
   Shepherd to His Love

He who for love hath undergone
   The worst that can befall,
Is happier thousandfold than one
   Who never loved at all.
   RICHARD MONCKTON MILNES
   —To Myrzha

So dear I love him, that with him
   all deaths
I could endure, without him live no
   life.
   MILTON—Paradise Lost

Love is often a fruit of marriage.
   MOLIÈRE

But there's nothing half so sweet in
   life
As love's young dream.
   MOORE

The only victory over love is flight.
   NAPOLEON

Love—a grave mental disease.
   PLATO

Of all affliction taught a lover yet,
'Tis true the hardest science to for-
   get.
   POPE—Eloisa to Abelard

Everybody in love is blind.
   PROPERTIUS

Better is a dinner of herbs where
love is, than a stalled ox and hatred
therewith.
   PROVERBS. XV. 17

Love can never more grow old,
Locks may lose their brown and
   gold,
Cheeks may fade and hollow grow,
But the hearts that love will know
Never winter's frost and chill,
Summer's warmth is in them still.
   EBEN E. REXFORD—Silver
   Threads Among the Gold

As one who cons at evening o'er an
   album all alone,
And muses on the faces of the friends
   that he has known,
So I turn the leaves of Fancy, till in
   shadowy design
I find the smiling features of an old
   sweetheart of mine.
   JAMES WHITCOMB RILEY—*An
   Old Sweetheart of Mine*

Love must have wings to fly away
   from love,
And to fly back again.
   EDWIN ARLINGTON ROBINSON
   —*Tristram*

The hours I spent with thee, dear
   heart,
   Are as a string of pearls to me;
I count them over, every one apart,
   My rosary, my rosary.
   ROBERT CAMERON ROGERS—
   My Rosary

Love is the fulfilling of the law.
   ROMANS. XIII. 10

Whither thou goest, I will go; and
where thou lodgest, I will lodge;
thy people shall be my people, and
thy God my God.
   RUTH. I. 16

And love is loveliest when embalm'd
in tears.
   SCOTT—*Lady of the Lake*

Men have died from time to time,
and worms have eaten them,—but
not for love.
   SHAKESPEARE—*As You Like It.*
   Act IV. Sc. 1

Ay me! for aught that I ever could
   read,
Could ever hear by tale or history,
The course of true love never did
   run smooth.
   SHAKESPEARE—*Midsummer
   Night's Dream.* Act I. Sc. 1

Friendship is constant in all other
   things
Save in the office and affairs of love:
Therefore, all hearts in love use
   their own tongues;
Let every eye negotiate for itself
And trust no agent.
   SHAKESPEARE—*Much Ado
   about Nothing.* Act II. Sc. 1

Give me my Romeo; and, when he
   shall die,
Take him, and cut him out in little
   stars,
And he will make the face of heaven
   so fine,
And all the world will be in love
   with night,
And pay no worship to the garish
   sun.
   SHAKESPEARE—*Romeo and
   Juliet.* Act III. Sc. 2

Love sought is good, but given un-
sought is better.
   SHAKESPEARE—*Twelfth Night.*
   Act III. Sc. 1

The fickleness of the woman I love
is only equalled by the infernal constancy of the women who love me.
   GEORGE BERNARD SHAW—*The
   Philanderer*

Love is strong as death; jealousy is
cruel as the grave.
   SONG OF SOLOMON. VIII. 6

Many waters cannot quench love,
neither can the floods drown it.
SONG OF SOLOMON. VIII. 7

Blue eyes say, "Love me or I die";
black eyes say, "Love me or I kill
thee."
SPANISH PROVERB

To love her was a liberal education.
STEELE—Of Lady Elizabeth
Hastings

Some pray to marry the man they
love,
My prayer will somewhat vary:
I humbly pray to Heaven above
That I love the man I marry.
ROSE PASTOR STOKES—My
Prayer

Love in its essence is spiritual fire.
SWEDENBORG—True Christian
Religion

I that have love and no more
Give you but love of you, sweet;
He that hath more, let him
give;
He that hath wings, let him soar;
Mine is the heart at your feet
Here, that must love you to live.
SWINBURNE—The Oblation

I love thee, I love but thee,
With a love that shall not die
Till the sun grows cold,
And the stars are old,
And the leaves of the Judgment
Book unfold!
BAYARD TAYLOR—Bedouin
Song

'Tis better to have loved and lost,
Than never to have loved at all.
TENNYSON—In Memoriam

Werther had a love for Charlotte,
Such as words could never utter;
Would you know how first he met
her?
She was cutting bread and butter.
THACKERAY—The Sorrows of
Werther

"I'm sorry that I spell'd the word;
I hate to go above you,
Because"—the brown eyes lower
fell,—
"Because, you see, I love you!"
WHITTIER—In School-Days

(See also BABYHOOD, CHILDHOOD,
FRIENDSHIP, HUSBAND, KISS, MATRI-
MONY, MOTHER, PARENT, PASSION,
PATRIOTISM, WOMAN, WOOING.)

LUCK

Good luck is a lazy man's estimate
of a worker's success.
ANONYMOUS

Throw a lucky man into the sea, and
he will come up with a fish in his
mouth.
ARAB PROVERB

As ill-luck would have it.
CERVANTES—Don Quixote

A pound of pluck is worth a ton of
luck.
JAMES A. GARFIELD

Behind bad luck comes good luck.
GIPSY PROVERB

He who is lucky in love should never
play cards.
ITALIAN PROVERB

A lucky man is rarer than a white crow.

JUVENAL

(See also CHANCE, DESTINY, FATE, FORTUNE, GAMBLING, SUCCESS.)

LULLABY

Rock-a-bye baby, on the tree top,
When the wind blows the cradle will
    rock;
When the bough breaks the cradle
    will fall;
Down will come baby, cradle and all.

ENGLISH NURSERY RHYME

Sweet and low, sweet and low,
    Wind of the western sea,
Low, low, breathe and blow,
    Wind of the western sea!
Over the rolling waters go,
Come from the dying moon, and
    blow,
    Blow him again to me;
While my little one, while my pretty
    one sleeps.

TENNYSON—*The Princess*

Hush, my dear, lie still and slumber,
    Holy angels guard thy bed!
Heavenly blessings without number
    Gently falling on thy head.

ISAAC WATTS

(See also BABYHOOD, MOTHER, POETRY, SLEEP, SONG.)

LUST
See PASSION

LUXURY
See RICHES

LYING

Peter said, Ananias, why hath Satan filled thine heart to lie to the Holy

Ghost? . . . And Ananias hearing these words fell down, and gave up the ghost.

ACTS. III. 3–5

Any fool can tell the truth, but it requires a man of some sense to know how to lie well.

SAMUEL BUTLER—*Note-Books*

And, after all, what is a lie? 'Tis but
The truth in masquerade.

BYRON—*Don Juan*

A liar is not believed even though he tell the truth.

CICERO

Terminological inexactitude.

WINSTON CHURCHILL—Speech, 1906

An experienced, industrious, ambitious, and often quite picturesque liar.

S. L. CLEMENS (MARK TWAIN) —*My Military Campaign*

A good memory is needed once we have lied.

CORNEILLE

Show me a liar, and I will show thee a thief.

HERBERT

Who dares think one thing, and another tell,
My heart detests him as the gates of hell.

HOMER—*Iliad*

The liar's punishment is not in the least that he is not believed, but that he cannot believe anyone else.

GEORGE BERNARD SHAW

That a lie which is half a truth is
ever the blackest of lies;
That a lie which is all a lie may be
met and fought with outright—
But a lie which is part a truth is a
harder matter to fight.
TENNYSON—*The Grandmother*

(See also CALUMNY, DECEPTION,
FALSEHOOD, FRAUD, SLANDER,
TRUTH.)

MACHINE

A tool is but the extension of a man's
hand, and a machine is but a complex
tool. He that invents a machine augments the power of a man and the
well-being of mankind.
HENRY WARD BEECHER

Man is a tool-using animal.
CARLYLE—*Sartor Resartus*

One machine can do the work of fifty
ordinary men. No machine can do
the work of one extraordinary man.
ELBERT HUBBARD

Men have become the tools of their
tools.
THOREAU—*Walden*

(See also CAPITAL AND LABOR, IN-
VENTION, PROGRESS, SCIENCE,
WEALTH.)

MADNESS
See INSANITY

MAJORITY

One with the law is a majority.
CALVIN COOLIDGE—Speech,
1920

A minority may be right; a majority
is always wrong.
IBSEN—*An Enemy of the People*

It is my principle that the will of the
majority should always prevail.
JEFFERSON—Letter, 1787

One, on God's side, is a majority.
WENDELL PHILLIPS

(See also DEMOCRACY, GOVERN-
MENT, PARTY, PEOPLE, POLITICS.)

MALICE
See CRUELTY

MAMMON

Cursed Mammon be, when he with
treasures
To restless action spurs our fate!
GOETHE—*Faust*

Ye cannot serve God and mammon.
MATTHEW. VI. 24

What treasures here do Mammon's
sons behold!
Yet know that all that which glitters
is not gold.
QUARLES

(See also GOLD, MONEY, POSSES-
SION, RICHES, WEALTH.)

MAN

There never was such beauty in another man.
Nature made him, and then broke
the mould.
ARIOSTO—*Orlando Furioso*

Let each man think himself an act of
God.
His mind a thought, his life a breath
of God.
BAILEY—*Festus*

A man's a man for a' that!
BURNS—*For A' That and A'
That*

Man's inhumanity to man
  Makes countless thousands mourn!
    BURNS—*Man Was Made to Mourn*

                          Man!
Thou pendulum betwixt a smile and
  tear.
    BYRON—*Childe Harold*

We are the miracle of miracles, the
great inscrutable mystery of God.
    CARLYLE

Every man is a volume, if you know
how to read him.
    WILLIAM ELLERY CHANNING

There are times when one would like
to hang the whole human race, and
finish the farce.
    S. L. CLEMENS (MARK TWAIN)
    —*A Connecticut Yankee at King Arthur's Court*

I am made all things to all men.
    I CORINTHIANS. IX. 22

The first man is of the earth, earthy.
    I CORINTHIANS. XV. 47

His tribe were God Almighty's gentlemen.
    DRYDEN—*Absalom and Achito-phel*

Man is a piece of the universe made
alive.
    EMERSON

Man wants but little here below,
Nor wants that little long.
    GOLDSMITH—*The Hermit*

Man is the only animal that laughs
and weeps; for he is the only animal
that is struck with the difference be-

tween what things are, and what they
ought to be.
    HAZLITT

God give us men. A time like this
  demands
Strong minds, great hearts, true faith
  and ready hands!
Men whom the lust of office does not
  kill,
Men whom the spoils of office cannot
  buy,
Men who possess opinions and a will,
Men who love honor, men who cannot lie.
    J. G. HOLLAND

Man passes away; his name perishes
from record and recollection; his history is as a tale that is told, and his
very monument becomes a ruin.
    WASHINGTON IRVING—*The Sketch Book*

Cease ye from man, whose breath is
in his nostrils.
    ISAIAH. II. 22

Man that is born of a woman is of
few days, and full of trouble.
    JOB. XIV. 1

Though I've belted you and flayed
  you,
By the livin' Gawd that made you,
You're a better man than I am,
  Gunga Din.
    KIPLING—*Gunga Din*

If you can keep your head when all
  about you
Are losing theirs and blaming it on
  you,
If you can trust yourself when all
  men doubt you,
But make allowance for their doubt
  ing too;

Yours is the Earth and everything
that's in it,
And—which is more—you'll be a man,
my son!
KIPLING—*If*

Make ye no truce with Adam-zad—
the Bear that walks like a man.
KIPLING—*The Truce of the
Bear*

It is easier to know mankind in general than man individually.
LA ROCHEFOUCAULD

Men, in general, are but great children.
NAPOLEON

We must laugh at man, to avoid crying for him.
NAPOLEON

I teach you beyond Man (superman). Man is something that shall be surpassed. What have you done to surpass him?
NIETZSCHE—*Thus Spake Zarathustra*

Man's the bad child of the universe.
JAMES OPPENHEIM—*Laughter*

Does man differ from the other animals? Only in posture. The rest are bent, but he is a wild beast who walks upright.
PHILEMON

Chaos of thought and passion, all
confused;
Still by himself abused and disabused;
Created half to rise, and half to fall;
Great lord of all things, yet a prey to
all;

Sole judge of truth, in endless error
hurled;
The glory, jest and riddle of the
world!
POPE—*Essay on Man*

Know then thyself, presume not God
to scan;
The proper study of mankind is man.
POPE—*Essay on Man*

Man is the measure of all things.
PROTAGORAS

Thou hast made him a little lower
than the angels.
PSALMS. VIII. 5

Mark the perfect man, and behold
the upright.
PSALMS. XXXVII. 37

Quit yourselves like men.
I SAMUEL. IV. 9

A man after his own heart.
I SAMUEL. XIII. 14

Thou art the man.
II SAMUEL. XII. 7

Man is a social animal.
SENECA

He was a man, take him for all in all,
I shall not look upon his like again.
SHAKESPEARE—*Hamlet*. Act I.
Sc. 2

What a piece of work is a man! how noble in reason! how infinite in faculty! in form and moving how express and admirable! in action how like an angel! in apprehension how like a god! the beauty of the world! the paragon of animals! And, yet, to me, what is this quintessence of dust? man delights not me: no, nor woman neither, though by your smiling, you seem to say so.

SHAKESPEARE—*Hamlet.* Act II. Sc. 2

His life was gentle, and the elements So mix'd in him that Nature might stand up,
And say to all the world, This was a man!

SHAKESPEARE—*Julius Caesar.* Act V. Sc. 5

Man is an animal that makes bargains; no other animal does this,—one dog does not change a bone with another.

ADAM SMITH

I am an acme of things accomplished, and I am encloser of things to be.

WALT WHITMAN—*Song of Myself*

When faith is lost, when honor dies, The man is dead!

WHITTIER—*Ichabod*

(See also CHARACTER, LIFE, LOVE, MATRIMONY, WOMAN, WORLD.)

MANNERS

He was the mildest manner'd man That ever scuttled ship or cut a throat.

BYRON—*Don Juan*

Now as to politeness . . . I would venture to call it benevolence in trifles.

LORD CHATHAM

Manners must adorn knowledge and smooth its way through the world.

CHESTERFIELD

A moral, sensible, and well-bred man Will not affront me, and no other can.

COWPER—*Conversation*

"What sort of a doctor is he?" "Well, I don't know much about his ability; but he's got a very good bedside manner."

Punch, March 15, 1884

They asked Lucman, the fabulist, From whom did you learn manners? He answered: From the unmannerly.

SADI

Men make laws; women make manners.

DE SEGUR

What once were vices are now manners.

SENECA

Politeness goes far, yet costs nothing.

SAMUEL SMILES

Good manners is the art of making those people easy with whom we converse. Whoever makes the fewest persons uneasy, is the best bred in the company.

SWIFT

Suit your manner to the man.

TERENCE—*Adelphi*

(See also COURTESY, CULTURE, EDUCATION, GENTLEMAN, HUMANITY, SOCIETY.)

MARRIAGE
See MATRIMONY

MARTYR

It is the cause, and not the death,
that makes the martyr.
NAPOLEON

The blood of the martyrs is the seed
of the Church.
TERTULLIAN

(See also BRAVERY, COURAGE,
FAITH, GLORY, HERO, HONOR,
RELIGION, SACRIFICE.)

MATRIMONY

Marriage is a romance in which the
hero dies in the first chapter.
ANONYMOUS

Marriage is that relation between
man and woman in which the independence is equal, the dependence
mutual, and the obligation reciprocal.
LOUIS K. ANSPACHER—Address,
1934

It is better for a woman to marry a
man who loves her than a man she
loves.
ARAB PROVERB

A man finds himself seven years older
the day after his marriage.
BACON

He that hath a wife and children
hath given hostages to fortune; for
they are impediments to great enterprises, either of virtue or mischief.
BACON—Essays.

A woman must be a genius to create
a good husband.
BALZAC

To have and to hold from this day
forward, for better, for worse, for
richer, for poorer, in sickness, and in
health, to love and to cherish, till
death us do part.
BOOK OF COMMON PRAYER

To love, cherish, and to obey.
BOOK OF COMMON PRAYER

With this ring I thee wed, with my
body I thee worship, and with all my
worldly goods I thee endow.
BOOK OF COMMON PRAYER

Thus grief still treads upon the heels
of pleasure,
Marry'd in haste, we may repent at
leisure.
CONGREVE—The Old Bachelor.

A deaf husband and a blind wife are
always a happy couple.
DANISH PROVERB

To marry once is a duty, twice a
folly, thrice is madness.
DUTCH PROVERB

It destroys one's nerves to be amiable
every day to the same human being.
DISRAELI

Every woman should marry—and no
man.
DISRAELI—Lothair

Is not marriage an open question,
when it is alleged, from the beginning of the world, that such as are
in the institution wish to get out, and
such as are out wish to get in.
EMERSON—Representative Men

There is a French saying: "Love is
the dawn of marriage, and marriage
is the sunset of love."
DE FINOD

Where there's marriage without love, there will be love without marriage.
FRANKLIN—*Poor Richard*

Keep thy eyes wide open before marriage; and half shut afterward.
THOMAS FULLER—*Introductio ad Prudentiam*

It is not good that the man should be alone.
GENESIS. II. 18

Bone of my bones, and flesh of my flesh.
GENESIS. II. 23

Weeping bride, laughing wife; laughing bride, weeping wife.
GERMAN PROVERB

Matrimony,—the high sea for which no compass has yet been invented.
HEINE

Marriage is something you have to give your whole mind to.
IBSEN—*The League of Youth*

Heaven will be no heaven to me if I do not meet my wife there.
ANDREW JACKSON

What therefore God hath joined together let not man put asunder.
MATTHEW. XIX. 6

Something old, something new,
Something borrowed, something blue.
OLD ENGLISH RHYME. (The wedding dress)

If thou wouldst marry wisely, marry thine equal.
OVID

The woman cries before the wedding; the man afterward.
POLISH PROVERB

A prudent wife is from the Lord.
PROVERBS. XIX. 14

Advice to persons about to marry—Don't.
Punch's Almanack, 1845

Marriage is a lottery in which men stake their liberty, and women their happiness.
MME. DE RIEUX

Men are April when they woo, December when they wed; maids are May when they are maids, but the sky changes when they are wives.
SHAKESPEARE—*As You Like It.* Act IV. Sc. 1

The whole world is strewn with snares, traps, gins and pitfalls for the capture of men by women.
GEORGE BERNARD SHAW—*Man and Superman*

Marriages are made in Heaven.
TENNYSON—*Aylmer's Field*

Remember, it is as easy to marry a rich woman as a poor woman.
THACKERAY—*Pendennis*

Marriage is the one subject on which all women agree and all men disagree.
WILDE

Men marry because they are tired, women because they are curious: both are disappointed.
WILDE

(See also BABYHOOD, CHILDHOOD, COURTSHIP, HUSBAND, LOVE, PARENT, WIFE, WOMAN, WOOING.)

MEDICINE

The physician heals, Nature makes well.
ARISTOTLE

I find the medicine worse than the malady.
BEAUMONT AND FLETCHER—
Love's Cure

Nature, time, and patience are the three great physicians.
H. G. BOHN

The best doctor is the one you run for and can't find.
DIDEROT

An apple a day keeps the doctor away.
ENGLISH PROVERB

God heals and the doctor takes the fee.
FRANKLIN—*Poor Richard's Almanac*

He's the best physician that knows the worthlessness of the most medicines.
FRANKLIN—*Poor Richard's Almanac*

I firmly believe that if the whole *materia medica* as now used, could be sunk to the bottom of the sea, it would be all the better for mankind and all the worse for the fishes.
HOLMES—Lecture, Medical Society

Who shall decide when doctors disagree,
And soundest casuists doubt, like you and me?
POPE—*Moral Essays*

A sound mind in a sound body is a thing to be prayed for.
JUVENAL

Physician, heal thyself.
LUKE. IV. 23

Doctors are men who prescribe medicines of which they know little, to cure diseases of which they know less, in human beings of whom they know nothing.
VOLTAIRE

But nothing is more estimable than a physician who, having studied nature from his youth, knows the properties of the human body, the diseases which assail it, the remedies which will benefit it, exercises his art with caution, and pays equal attention to the rich and the poor.
VOLTAIRE—*A Philosophical Dictionary*

(See also DISEASE, HEALTH, MIND, QUACK, SICKNESS, WOUND.)

MEDITATION
See THOUGHT

MELANCHOLY

Melancholy
Is not, as you conceive, indisposition
Of body, but the mind's disease.
JOHN FORD—*The Lover's Melancholy*

There's not a string attuned to mirth
But has its chord in melancholy.
HOOD—*Ode to Melancholy*

Melancholy is the pleasure of being sad.
VICTOR HUGO

Employment and hardships prevent melancholy.

SAMUEL JOHNSON

(See also INSANITY, MIND.)

MEMORY

Time whereof the memory of man runneth not to the contrary.

BLACKSTONE—*Commentaries*

To live in hearts we leave behind,
Is not to die.

CAMPBELL—*Hallowed Ground*

Vanity plays lurid tricks with our memory.

JOSEPH CONRAD—*Lord Jim*

Don't you remember sweet Alice, Ben Bolt?
Sweet Alice, whose hair was so brown;
Who wept with delight when you gave her a smile,
And trembl'd with fear at your frown!

THOMAS DUNN ENGLISH—*Ben Bolt*

I remember, I remember,
The house where I was born,
The little window where the sun
Came peeping in at morn;
He never came a wink too soon,
Nor brought too long a day,
But now, I often wish the night
Had borne my breath away!

HOOD—*I Remember, I Remember*

We must always have old memories and young hopes.

ARSÈNE HOUSSAYE

The true art of memory is the art of attention.

SAMUEL JOHNSON

And when he is out of sight, quickly also is he out of mind.

THOMAS À KEMPIS—*Imitation of Christ*

All to myself I think of you,
Think of the things we used to do,
Think of the things we used to say,
Think of each happy bygone day,
Sometimes I sigh, and sometimes I smile,
But I keep each olden, golden while
All to myself.

WILBUR D. NESBIT—*All to Myself*

Women and elephants never forget.

DOROTHY PARKER—*Ballade of Unfortunate Mammals*

If I do not remember thee, let my tongue cleave to the roof of my mouth.

PSALMS. CXXXVII. 6

I have a room whereinto no one enters
Save I myself alone:
There sits a blessed memory on a throne,
There my life centres.

CHRISTINA G. ROSSETTI—*Memory*

The Right Honorable gentleman is indebted to his memory for his jests and to his imagination for his facts.

R. B. SHERIDAN

O memory, thou bitter sweet,—both a joy and a scourge!

MME. DE STAËL

Ah! memories of sweet summer eves,
  Of moonlit wave and willowy way,
Of stars and flowers, and dewy leaves,
  And smiles and tones more dear
    than they!
    WHITTIER—*Memories*

(See also PAST, THOUGHT, TIME.)

MERCY

Among the attributes of God, although they are all equal, mercy shines with even more brilliancy than justice.
    CERVANTES

Being all fashioned of the self-same dust.
Let us be merciful as well as just.
    LONGFELLOW—*Tales of a Wayside Inn*

The mercy of the Lord is from everlasting to everlasting upon them that fear Him.
    PSALMS. CIII. 17

The quality of mercy is not strain'd,
It droppeth as the gentle rain from
    heaven
Upon the place beneath: it is twice
    blest;
It blesseth him that gives and him
    that takes;
'Tis mightiest in the mightiest; it
    becomes
The throned monarch better than his
    crown;
His sceptre shows the force of temporal power,
The attribute to awe and majesty,
Wherein doth sit the dread and fear
    of kings;
But mercy is above this sceptred
    sway;

It is enthroned in the hearts of kings,
It is an attribute to God himself;
And earthly power doth then show
    likest God's
When mercy seasons justice.
    SHAKESPEARE—*Merchant of Venice*. Act IV. Sc. 1

(See also CHARITY, JUDGMENT, JUSTICE, LAW, LOVE, PHILANTHROPY, PITY, PUNISHMENT.)

MERIT

True merit, like a river, the deeper it is, the less noise it makes.
    LORD HALIFAX

Nature makes merit, and fortune puts it to work.
    LA ROCHEFOUCAULD

The world rewards the appearance of merit oftener than merit itself.
    LA ROCHEFOUCAULD

(See also ABILITY, CHARACTER, SUCCESS, WORTH.)

MERRIMENT

A source of innocent merriment!
  Of innocent merriment.
    W. S. GILBERT—*The Mikado*

Merry have we met, and merry have
    we been;
Merry let us part, and merry meet
    again;
With our merry sing-song, happy
    gay, and free,
With a merry ding-dong, happy let
    us be!
    OLD ENGLISH RHYME

A merry heart doeth good like a medicine.
    PROVERBS. XVII. 22

Let us eat, and be merry.
LUKE. XV. 23

Nothing is more hopeless than a scheme of merriment.
SAMUEL JOHNSON—*The Idler*

(See also HAPPINESS, HUMOR, JESTING, JOY, LAUGHTER.)

MIDNIGHT

Midnight! the outpost of advancing day!
The frontier town and citadel of night!
LONGFELLOW—*Two Rivers*

Once upon a midnight dreary, while I pondered weak and weary,
Over many a quaint and curious volume of forgotten lore.
POE—*The Raven*

The dreadful dead of dark midnight.
SHAKESPEARE—*The Rape of Lucrece*

(See also DARKNESS, NIGHT, SHADOW, SLEEP.)

MIGHT
See POWER

MILITARY
See WAR

MIND

Measure your mind's height by the shade it casts.
BROWNING—*Paracelsus*

The march of the human mind is slow.
BURKE—Speech on the Conciliation of America

When Bishop Berkeley said "there was no matter,"
And proved it,—'twas no matter what he said.
BYRON—*Don Juan*

God is Mind, and God is infinite; hence all is Mind.
MARY BAKER EDDY—*Science and Health*

The true, strong, and sound mind is the mind that can embrace equally great things and small.
SAMUEL JOHNSON—*Boswell's Life of Johnson*

What is mind? No matter. What is matter? Never mind.
T. H. KEY

The mind is its own place, and in itself
Can make a heaven of hell, a hell of heaven.
MILTON—*Paradise Lost*

Let every man be fully persuaded in his own mind.
ROMANS. XIV. 5

A feeble body weakens the mind.
ROUSSEAU—*Émile*

'Tis but a base, ignoble mind
That mounts no higher than a bird can soar.
SHAKESPEARE—*Henry V*. Act IV. Sc. 1

(See also INTELLECT, KNOWLEDGE, LEARNING, PHILOSOPHY, SOUL, THOUGHT, WISDOM.)

MIRACLE
See RELIGION, SUPERSTITION

MISCHIEF

In life it is difficult to say who do you the most mischief, enemies with the worst intentions, or friends with the best.
BULWER-LYTTON

He that mischief hatcheth mischief catcheth.
CAMDEN

The opportunity to do mischief is found a hundred times a day, and that of doing good once a year.
VOLTAIRE

(See also DECEPTION, FOLLY.)

MISER
See AVARICE

MISERY

He that is down need fear no fall.
BUNYAN

Misery loves company.
ENGLISH PROVERB

Fire tries gold, misery tries brave men.
SENECA

Misery acquaints a man with strange bedfellows.
SHAKESPEARE—*Tempest*. Act II. Sc. 2

(See also ADVERSITY, AFFLICTION, DESPAIR, MISFORTUNE, PAIN, SORROW.)

MISFORTUNE

Misfortunes always come in by a door that has been left open for them.
CZECH PROVERB

Little minds are tamed and subdued by misfortune; but great minds rise above it.
WASHINGTON IRVING

We have all of us sufficient fortitude to bear the misfortunes of others.
LA ROCHEFOUCAULD

Let us be of good cheer, however, remembering that the misfortunes hardest to bear are those which never come.
LOWELL—*Democracy and Addresses*

When I was happy I thought I knew men, but it was fated that I should know them in misfortune only.
NAPOLEON

              The worst is not
So long as we can say "This is the worst."
SHAKESPEARE—*King Lear*. Act IV. Sc. 1

The wise man sees in the misfortunes of others what he should avoid.
SYRUS

(See also ADVERSITY, CALAMITY, EVIL, MISERY, RUIN, SUFFERING, TROUBLE.)

MISTAKE
See ERROR

MOB

The mob is man voluntarily descending to the nature of the beast.
EMERSON

The mob is a sort of bear; while your ring is through its nose, it will even dance under your cudgel; but should the ring slip, and you lose your hold, the brute will turn and rend you.
JANE PORTER

It has been very truly said that the mob has many heads, but no brains.
RIVAROL

(See also CRIME, GOVERNMENT, LAW, ORDER, PEOPLE, REVOLUTION.)

MODERATION

It is best to rise from life as from a banquet, neither thirsty nor drunken.
ARISTOTLE

To live long, it is necessary to live slowly.
CICERO

A thing moderately good is not so good as it ought to be. Moderation in temper is always a virtue; but moderation in principle is always a vice.
THOMAS PAINE

In everything the middle course is best: all things in excess bring trouble to men.
PLAUTUS

Give me neither poverty nor riches.
PROVERBS. XXX. 8

(See also CONTENTMENT, EXTREME, HAPPINESS.)

MODESTY

Modesty is the conscience of the body.
BALZAC

Modesty is the only sure bait when you angle for praise.
CHESTERFIELD

Modesty died when false modesty was born.
S. L. CLEMENS (MARK TWAIN)

Man is the only animal that blushes. Or needs to.
S. L. CLEMENS (MARK TWAIN)

A modest man never talks of himself.
LA BRUYÈRE

With people of only moderate ability modesty is mere honesty; but with those who possess great talent it is hypocrisy.
SCHOPENHAUER

(See also CHARACTER, HUMILITY, INNOCENCE, VIRTUE, WOMAN.)

MONEY

Money makes the man.
ARISTODEMUS

Money is a good servant but a bad master.
Quoted by BACON

A fool and his money are soon parted.
GEORGE BUCHANAN

Penny wise, pound foolish.
BURTON

Wine maketh merry: but money answereth all things.
ECCLESIASTES. X. 19

If you would know the value of money, go and try to borrow some.
FRANKLIN—*Poor Richard's Almanac*

Never ask of money spent
Where the spender thinks it went.
Nobody was ever meant
To remember or invent
What he did with every cent.
ROBERT FROST—*The Hardship of Accounting*

The almighty dollar, that great object of universal devotion throughout our land, seems to have no genuine devotees in these peculiar villages.
WASHINGTON IRVING—*Creole Village*

Take care of the pence, and the pounds will take care of themselves.
WILLIAM LOWNDES

Jesus went into the temple . . . overthrew the tables of the money changers, and the seats of them that sold doves.
MARK. XI. 15

Up and down the City Road,
    In and out the Eagle,
That's the way the money goes—
    Pop goes the weasel!
W. R. MANDALE

Ah, take the Cash, and let the Credit go,
Nor heed the rumble of a distant Drum!
OMAR KHAYYÁM—*Rubaiyat*

When I had money everyone called me brother.
POLISH PROVERB

When money speaks the truth is silent.
RUSSIAN PROVERB

Money is not required to buy one necessity of the soul.
THOREAU

Not greedy of filthy lucre.
I TIMOTHY. III. 3

The love of money is the root of all evil.
I TIMOTHY. VI. 10

Money is a new form of slavery, and distinguishable from the old simply by the fact that it is impersonal—that there is no human relation between master and slave.
TOLSTOY—*What Shall We Do?*

Make all you can, save all you can, give all you can.
JOHN WESLEY

(See also AVARICE, BUSINESS, ECONOMY, GOLD, MAMMON, RICHES, SUCCESS, THRIFT, WEALTH.)

MONTHS

October turned my maple's leaves to gold;
The most are gone now; here and there one lingers;
Soon these will slip from out the twig's weak hold,
Like coins between a dying miser's fingers.
T. B. ALDRICH—*Maple Leaves*

If cold December gave you birth,
The month of snow and ice and mirth,
Place on your hand a turquoise blue,
Success will bless whate'er you do.
ANONYMOUS

Thirty days hath September,
April, June, and November;
All the rest have thirty-one
Excepting February alone:
Which hath but twenty-eight, in fine,
Till leap year gives it twenty-nine.
ANONYMOUS

O sweet September, thy first breezes
bring
The dry leaf's rustle and the squir-
rel's laughter,
The cool fresh air whence health and
vigor spring
And promise of exceeding joy here-
after.
GEORGE ARNOLD—*September
Days*

Oh, to be in England
Now that April's there.
BROWNING—*Home Thoughts
from Abroad*

March comes in like a lion and goes
out like a lamb.
ENGLISH PROVERB

If February give much snow
A fine Summer it doth foreshow.
ENGLISH RHYME

Oh, the lovely fickleness of an April
day!
W. H. GIBSON—*Pastoral Days*

No park—no ring—no afternoon gen-
tility—
No company—no nobility—
No warmth, no cheerfulness, no
healthful ease.
No comfortable feel in any member—
No shade, no shine, no butterflies, no
bees,
No fruits, no flowers, no leaves, no
birds,
November!
HOOD—*November*

And what is so rare as a day in June?
Then, if ever, come perfect days;
Then Heaven tries earth if it be in
tune,
And over it softly her warm ear
lays.
LOWELL—*Vision of Sir Launfal*

As full of spirit as the month of May.
SHAKESPEARE—*King Henry IV*.
Pt. I. Act IV. Sc. 1

That blasts of January
Would blow you through and
through.
SHAKESPEARE—*Winter's Tale*.
Act IV. Sc. 4

The ides of March are come.
SHAKESPEARE—*Julius Caesar*.
Act III. Sc. 1

January grey is here,
Like a sexton by her grave;
February bears the bier,
March with grief doth howl and
rave,
And April weeps—but, O ye hours!
Follow with May's fairest flowers.
SHELLEY—*Dirge for the Year*

Among the changing months, May
stands confest
The sweetest, and in fairest colors
dressed.
JAMES THOMSON—*On May*

Sweet April showers
Do bring May flowers.
TUSSER—*Five Hundred Points
of Good Husbandry*

(See also BIRTHDAY, SEASONS.)

MONUMENT

Those only deserve a monument who
do not need one.
HAZLITT

Monuments! what are they? the very
pyramids have forgotten their build-
ers, or to whom they were dedicated.
Deeds, not stones, are the true monuments of the great.
MOTLEY

Soldiers, forty centuries are looking down upon you from these pyramids.
NAPOLEON

(See also DEATH, EPITAPH, GRAVE, LIFE, MEMORY.)

MOON

How like a queen comes forth the lonely Moon
From the slow opening curtains of the clouds
Walking in beauty to her midnight throne!
GEORGE CROLY—*Diana*

He should, as he list, be able to prove the moon is green cheese.
SIR THOMAS MORE—*English Works*

That orbed maiden, with white fire laden,
Whom mortals call the moon.
SHELLEY—*The Cloud*

And suddenly the moon withdraws
Her sickles from the lightening skies,
And to her sombre cavern flies,
Wrapped in a veil of yellow gauze.
WILDE

(See also NATURE, NIGHT, SKY, STAR.)

MORALITY

Morality is a private and costly luxury.
HENRY B. ADAMS—*The Education of Henry Adams*

"Tut, tut, child," said the Duchess. "Everything's got a moral if only you can find it."
LEWIS CARROLL—*Alice in Wonderland*

Dr. Johnson's morality was as English an article as a beefsteak.
HAWTHORNE—*Our Old Home*

I never did, or countenanced, in public life, a single act inconsistent with the strictest good faith; having never believed there was one code of morality for a public, and another for a private man.
JEFFERSON, 1809

Turning the other cheek is a kind of moral jiu-jitsu.
GERALD STANLEY LEE—*Crowds*

To give a man full knowledge of true morality, I would send him to no other book than the New Testament.
LOCKE

We know no spectacle so ridiculous as the British public in one of its periodical fits of morality.
MACAULAY—*On Moore's Life of Lord Byron*

Do you wish to see that which is really sublime? Repeat the Lord's Prayer.
NAPOLEON

Morality is the best of all devices for leading mankind by the nose.
NIETZSCHE—*The Antichrist*

Do not be too moral. You may cheat yourself out of much life so. Aim above morality. Be not simply good; be good for something.
THOREAU

All sects are different, because they come from men; morality is everywhere the same, because it comes from God.

VOLTAIRE

(See also CHARACTER, GOODNESS, PRINCIPLE, RELIGION, SIN, VICE, VIRTUE.)

MORNING

Sweet is the breath of morn, her rising sweet,
With charm of earliest birds.

MILTON—*Paradise Lost*

If I take the wings of the morning, and dwell in the uttermost parts of the sea.

PSALMS. CXXXIX. 9

The grey-ey'd morn smiles on the frowning night,
Chequering the eastern clouds with streaks of light.

SHAKESPEARE—*Romeo and Juliet.* Act I. Sc. 1

Now the frosty stars are gone:
I have watched them one by one,
Fading on the shores of Dawn.
Round and full the glorious sun
Walks with level step the spray,
Through his vestibule of Day.

BAYARD TAYLOR—*Ariel in the Cloven Pine.*

Lose an hour in the morning, and you will be all day hunting for it.

WHATELY

(See also DAY, LIGHT, SUNRISE.)

MORTALITY

All flesh shall perish together, and man shall turn again unto dust.

JOB. XXXIV. 15

Oh, why should the spirit of mortal be proud?
Like a fast-flitting meteor, a fast-flying cloud,
A flash of the lightning, a break of the wave,
He passes from life to his rest in the grave.

WILLIAM KNOX—*Mortality*

The lilies of the field whose bloom is brief;—
We are as they;
Like them we fade away
As doth a leaf.

CHRISTINA G. ROSSETTI—*Consider*

(See also DEATH, ETERNITY, GRAVE, IMMORTALITY, LIFE, SOUL.)

MOTHER

She's somebody's mother, boys, you know,
For all she's aged and poor and slow.

MARY DOW BRINE—*Somebody's Mother*

A mother is a mother still,
The holiest thing alive.

COLERIDGE—*The Three Graves*

Men are what their mothers made them.

EMERSON

The mother of all living.

GENESIS. III. 20

What is home without a mother?

ALICE HAWTHORNE. Title of a Poem

There is none,
In all this cold and hollow world, no
    fount
Of deep strong, deathless love, save
    that within
A mother's heart.
> FELICIA D. HEMANS—*Siege of
> Valencia*

I arose a mother in Israel.
> JUDGES. V. 7

If I were hanged on the highest hill,
Mother o' mine, O mother o' mine!
I know whose love would follow me
    still,
Mother o' mine, O mother o' mine!
> KIPLING—*Mother o' Mine*

All that I am or hope to be, I owe
to my angel mother.
> Attributed to LINCOLN

The bravest battle that ever was
    fought;
    Shall I tell you where and when?
On the maps of the world you will
    find it not;
    It was fought by the mothers of
    men.
> JOAQUIN MILLER—*The Bravest
> Battle*

Her children arise up and call her
blessed.
> PROVERBS. XXXI. 28

Who ran to help me when I fell,
And would some pretty story tell,
Or kiss the place to make it well?
    My Mother.
> ANNE TAYLOR—*My Mother*

For the hand that rocks the cradle
    Is the hand that rules the world.
> WILLIAM ROSS WALLACE—
> *What Rules the World*

Sure I love the dear silver that shines
    in your hair,
And the brow that's all furrowed, and
    wrinkled with care.
I kiss the dear fingers, so toil-worn
    for me,
Oh, God bless you and keep you,
    Mother Machree.
> RIDA JOHNSON YOUNG—*Mother
> Machree*

(See also BABYHOOD, CHILDHOOD,
DAUGHTER, FATHER, HUSBAND,
MATRIMONY, PARENT, WIFE,
WOMAN.)

MOTIVE
See REASON

MOUNTAIN

'Tis distance lends enchantment to
    the view,
And robes the mountain in its azure
    hue.
> CAMPBELL—*Pleasures of Hope*

To make a mountain of a mole-hill.
> HENRY ELLIS—*Original Letters*

If the mountain won't come to Mohammed, Mohammed must go to the
mountain.
> ENGLISH PROVERB

The mountain was in labour, and
Jove was afraid, but it brought forth
a mouse.
> TACHOS, King of Egypt

(See also NATURE.)

MOURNING

It is better to go to the house of
mourning than to go to the house of
feasting.
> ECCLESIASTES. VII. 2

Forever honour'd, and forever mourn'd.
> HOMER—*Iliad*

Blessèd are they that mourn: for they shall be comforted.
> MATTHEW. V. 4

By the waters of Babylon we sat down and wept,
Remembering thee.
> SWINBURNE—*Super Flumina Babylonis*

He mourns the dead who lives as they desire.
> YOUNG—*Night Thoughts*

(See also DEATH, EPITAPH, GRAVE, GRIEF, SORROW, TEARS.)

MOUSE

The mouse that hath but one hole is quickly taken.
> HERBERT

When a building is about to fall down all the mice desert it.
> PLINY THE ELDER

(See also ANIMALS.)

MOUSETRAP

If a man write a better book, preach a better sermon, or make a better mousetrap than his neighbor, though he build his house in the woods, the world will make a beaten path to his door.
> MRS. SARAH S. B. YULE credits the quotation to Emerson in her *Borrowings* (1889)

(See also BUSINESS, INVENTION, SUCCESS.)

MOUTH

A wise head makes a close mouth.
> ENGLISH PROVERB

Some asked me where the rubies grew,
And nothing I did say,
But with my finger pointed to
The lips of Julia.
> HERRICK

As a pomegranate, cut in twain,
White-seeded is her crimson mouth.
> WILDE

(See also FACE, SMILE.)

MULE
See ANIMALS

MURDER

Thou shalt not kill.
> EXODUS. XX. 13

Absolutism tempered by assassination.
> COUNT MUNSTER

Murder most foul, as in the best it is;
But this most foul, strange and unnatural.
> SHAKESPEARE—*Hamlet*. Act I. Sc. 5

For murder, though it have no tongue, will speak
With most miraculous organ.
> SHAKESPEARE—*Hamlet*. Act II. Sc. 2

(See also CRIME, DEATH, GUILT, LAW, PUNISHMENT, REVENGE, SUICIDE.)

MUSIC

All of heaven we have below.
ADDISON

Music should strike fire from the heart of man, and bring tears from the eyes of woman.
BEETHOVEN

Music hath charms to soothe the savage beast.
JAMES BRAMSTON—*Man of Taste*

Soprano, basso, even the contra-alto
Wished him five fathom under the Rialto.
BYRON—*Beppo*

There's music in the sighing of a reed;
  There's music in the gushing of a rill;
There's music in all things, if men had ears:
Their earth is but an echo of the spheres.
BYRON—*Don Juan*

Music is well said to be the speech of angels.
CARLYLE—*Essays*

Why should the devil have all the good tunes?
ROWLAND HILL—*Sermons*

The musician who always plays on the same string, is laughed at.
HORACE

When the morning stars sang together, and all the sons of God shouted for joy.
JOB. XXXVII. 7

Yea, music is the Prophet's art
Among the gifts that God hath sent,
One of the most magnificent!
LONGFELLOW—*Christus*

Music is the universal language of mankind.
LONGFELLOW—*Outre-Mer*

Such sweet compulsion doth in music lie.
MILTON—*Arcades*

Let me die to the sounds of delicious music.
Last words of MIRABEAU

The harp that once through Tara's halls
  The soul of music shed,
Now hangs as mute on Tara's walls,
  As if that soul were fled.
MOORE—*Harp That Once Through Tara's Halls*

Wagner's music is better than it sounds.
BILL NYE

Light quirks of music, broken and uneven,
Make the soul dance upon a jig to Heav'n.
POPE—*Moral Essays*

Seated one day at the organ,
  I was weary and ill at ease,
And my fingers wandered idly
  Over the noisy keys.

I do not know what I was playing,
  Or what I was dreaming then,
But I struck one chord of music
  Like the sound of a great Amen.
ADELAIDE A. PROCTER—*Lost Chord*

Above the pitch, out of tune, and
off the hinges.
RABELAIS—*Works*

Everything that heard him play,
Even the billows of the sea,
Hung their heads, and then lay by;
In sweet music is such art:
Killing care and grief of heart
Fall asleep, or, hearing, die.
SHAKESPEARE—*Henry VIII.*
Act III. Sc. 1

The man that hath no music in him-
self,
Nor is not moved with concord of
sweet sounds,
Is fit for treasons, stratagems and
spoils.
SHAKESPEARE—*Merchant of
Venice.* Act V. Sc. 1

Hell is full of musical amateurs.
GEORGE BERNARD SHAW—*Man
and Superman*

I can't sing. As a singist I am not a
success . . . I am saddest when I
sing. So are those who hear me.
They are sadder even than I am.
ARTEMUS WARD—Lecture

The music in my heart I bore,
Long after it was heard no more.
WORDSWORTH—*The Solitary
Reaper*

(See also ART, POETRY, SONG.)

MYSTERY

There was the door to which I found
no key,
There was the veil through which
I might not see.
OMAR KHAYYÁM—*Rubaiyat*

There be three things which are too
wonderful for me, yea, four which

I know not: the way of an eagle in
the air; the way of a serpent upon a
rock; the way of a ship in the midst
of the sea; and the way of a man
with a maid.
PROVERBS. XXX. 18–19

Mystery is the wisdom of block-
heads.
HORACE WALPOLE

(See also FUTURE, SECRECY,
SUPERSTITION, WISDOM.)

NAME

Ah! replied my gentle fair,
Beloved, what are names but air?
Choose thou whatever suits the
line:
Call me Sappho, call me Chloris,
Call me Lalage, or Doris,
Only, only, call me thine.
COLERIDGE—*What's in a Name*

Sticks and stones will break my
bones, but names will never hurt me.
ENGLISH PROVERB

Father calls me William, sister calls
me Will,
Mother calls me Willie, but the fel-
lers call me Bill!
EUGENE FIELD—*Jest 'Fore
Christmas*

Adam gave names to all cattle, and
to the fowl of the air, and to every
beast of the field.
GENESIS. II. 20

A nickname is the hardest stone that
the devil can throw at a man.
Quoted by HAZLITT

And, lo! Ben Adhem's name led all
the rest.
LEIGH HUNT—*Abou Ben Ad-
hem*

He left the name, at which the
world grew pale,
To point a moral, or adorn a tale.
SAMUEL JOHNSON—*Vanity of
Human Wishes*

My name is Legion.
MARK. V. 9

A good name is rather to be chosen
than great riches.
PROVERBS. XXII. 1

I cannot tell what the dickens his
name is.
SHAKESPEARE—*Merry Wives of
Windsor.* Act III. Sc. 2

Good name in man and woman, dear
my lord,
Is the immediate jewel of their souls:
Who steals my purse steals trash; 'tis
something, nothing;
'Twas mine, 'tis his, and has been
slave to thousands;
But he that filches from me my good
name
Robs me of that which not enriches
him,
And makes me poor indeed.
SHAKESPEARE—*Othello.* Act
III. Sc. 3

What's in a name? that which we
call a rose
By any other name would smell as
sweet.
SHAKESPEARE—*Romeo and
Juliet.* Act II. Sc. 1

(See also CHARACTER, GLORY,
HONOR, MEMORY, PRAISE,
REPUTATION, SCANDAL,
SLANDER.)

NATIONALISM

Nationalism is an infantile disease.
It is the measles of mankind.
ALBERT EINSTEIN

Born in iniquity and conceived in
sin, the spirit of nationalism has
never ceased to bend human institutions to the service of dissension and
distress.
VEBLEN—*Absentee Ownership*

(See also BROTHERHOOD,
HUMANITY, RACE.)

NATURE

All art, all education, can be merely
a supplement to nature.
ARISTOTLE

Nature is the most thrifty thing in
the world; she never wastes anything;
she undergoes change, but there's no
annihilation, the essence remains—
matter is eternal.
BINNEY

Earth's crammed with Heaven,
And every common bush afire with
God.
E. B. BROWNING—*Aurora
Leigh*

To him who in the love of Nature
holds
Communion with her visible forms,
she speaks
A various language.
BRYANT—*Thanatopsis*

I love not man the less, but nature
more.
BYRON—*Childe Harold*

For Art may err, but Nature cannot
miss.
DRYDEN—*Fables*

And see the rivers how they run
Through woods and meads, in shade
and sun,
Sometimes swift, sometimes slow,—
Wave succeeding wave, they go
A various journey to the deep
Like human life to endless sleep!
JOHN DYER—*Grongar Hill*

The woods were made for the hunter
of dreams,
The brooks for the fishers of song.
SAM WALTER FOSS—*Bloodless
Sportsman*

Nature is a volume of which God is
the author.
HARVEY

Nature, like a kind and smiling
mother, lends herself to our dreams
and cherishes our fancies.
VICTOR HUGO

Grass is the forgiveness of nature—
her constant benediction. . . . For-
ests decay, harvests perish, flowers
vanish, but grass is immortal.
INGALLS—Speech, 1874

Speak to the earth, and it shall teach
thee.
JOB. XII. 8

Everything in nature acts in con-
formity with law.
IMMANUEL KANT

Accuse not Nature, she hath done
her part;
Do thou but thine!
MILTON—*Paradise Lost*

Seas roll to waft me, suns to light
me rise;
My footstool Earth, my canopy the
skies.
POPE—*Essay on Man*

Nature abhors a vacuum.
RABELAIS—*Gargantua*

To hold, as 't were, the mirror up to
nature.
SHAKESPEARE—*Hamlet*. Act
III. Sc. 2

One touch of nature makes the whole
world kin.
SHAKESPEARE—*Troilus and
Cressida*. Act III. Sc. 3

I chatter, chatter, as I flow
To join the brimming river,
For men may come and men may go,
But I go on forever.
TENNYSON—*The Brook*

When I would recreate myself, I
seek the darkest wood, the thickest
and most interminable, and to the
citizen, most dismal swamp. I enter
a swamp as a sacred place—a *sanc-
tum sanctorum*. There is the
strength, the marrow of Nature.
THOREAU

Nature has always had more force
than education.
VOLTAIRE—*Life of Molière*

Nature never did betray
The heart that loved her.
WORDSWORTH—*Lines Com-
posed above Tintern Abbey*

(See also ANIMALS, BIRDS, DEW,
FLOWERS, MOUNTAIN, OCEAN,
RAIN, SEA, SNOW, STORM,
THUNDER, TREE.)

NAVIGATION

O pilot! 'tis a fearful night,
There's danger on the deep.
THOMAS HAYNES BAYLY—*The Pilot*

The winds and waves are always on the side of the ablest navigators.
GIBBON—*Decline and Fall of the Roman Empire*

Oh, I am a cook and a captain bold
  And the mate of the *Nancy* brig,
And a bo'sun tight and a midshipmite
  And the crew of the captain's gig.
W. S. GILBERT—*Yarn of the "Nancy Bell"*

Thus, I steer my bark, and sail
On even keel, with gentle gale.
MATTHEW GREEN—*Spleen*

(See also NAVY, OCEAN, SHIP, STORM.)

NAVY

Hearts of oak are our ships,
Hearts of oak are our men.
GARRICK

Now landsmen all, whoever you may be,
If you want to rise to the top of the tree,
If your soul isn't fettered to an office stool,
Be careful to be guided by this golden rule—
Stick close to your desks and *never go to sea*,
And you all may be Rulers of the Queen's Navee.
W. S. GILBERT—*H.M.S. Pinafore*

Tell that to the Marines—the sailors won't believe it.
Old saying quoted by SCOTT

(See also AMERICA, ENGLAND, PATRIOTISM, SHIP, VICTORY, WAR.)

NECESSITY

Necessity has no law.
ANONYMOUS

Necessity, the mother of invention.
ANONYMOUS

Necessity is often the spur to genius.
BALZAC

Necessity is the plea for every infringement of human freedom. It is the argument of tyrants; it is the creed of slaves.
WILLIAM PITT

Necessity makes even the timid brave.
SALLUST

(See also DESIRE, INVENTION, WISH.)

NEGLECT
See FAILURE

NEGRO

Not for myself I make this prayer,
  But for this race of mine
That stretches forth from shadowed places
  Dark hands for bread and wine.
COUNTEE CULLEN—*Pagan Prayer*

The image of God cut in ebony.
THOMAS FULLER

O black and unknown bards of long
ago,
How came your lips to touch the
sacred fire?
How, in your darkness, did you come
to know
The power and beauty of the min-
strel's lyre?
JAMES WELDON JOHNSON—*O
Black and Unknown Bards*

In the negro countenance you will
often meet with strong traits of be-
nignity. I have felt yearnings of
tenderness towards some of these
faces.
LAMB

The best way to uncolor the negro
is to give the white man a white
heart.
PANIN

The negro is an exotic of the most
gorgeous and superb countries of the
world, and he has deep in his heart
a passion for all that is splendid,
rich and fanciful.
HARRIET BEECHER STOWE

(See also HUMANITY, RACE.)

NEIGHBOR

Thou shalt not bear false witness
against thy neighbor.
EXODUS. XX. 16

We can live without our friends but
not without our neighbors.
THOMAS FULLER

When your neighbor's house is afire
your own property is at stake.
HORACE

Thou shalt love thy neighbor as thyself.
LEVITICUS. XIX. 18

The crop always seems better in our
neighbor's field, and our neighbor's
cow gives more milk.
OVID

In the field of world policy I would
dedicate this nation to the policy of
the good neighbor.
F. D. ROOSEVELT—Inaugural
Address, 1933

(See also BROTHERHOOD, CITY,
COUNTRY LIFE, FRIENDSHIP,
HOME.)

NEUTRALITY

The cold neutrality of an impartial
judge.
BURKE

Neutrality, as a lasting principle, is
an evidence of weakness.
KOSSUTH

The heart is never neutral.
SHAFTESBURY

A wise neuter joins with neither,
but uses both, as his honest interest
leads him.
WILLIAM PENN

A plague o' both your houses.
SHAKESPEARE—*Romeo and
Juliet.* Act III. Sc. 1

(See also DECISION, DIPLOMACY,
STATESMANSHIP, WAR.)

NEWNESS

There is nothing new except what
is forgotten.
MLLE. ROSE BERTIN (Milliner
to Marie Antoinette)

Spick and span new.
CERVANTES—*Don Quixote*

There is no new thing under the sun.
ECCLESIASTES. I. 9

Is there anything whereof it may be said, See, this is new? It hath been already of old time, which was before us.
ECCLESIASTES. I. 10

What is valuable is not new, and what is new is not valuable.
DANIEL WEBSTER

(See also AGE, CONSERVATISM, LIBERAL, PROGRESS.)

NEW YORK CITY

I like to visit New York, but I wouldn't live there if you gave it to me.
AMERICAN SAYING

If there ever was an aviary overstocked with jays it is that Yaptown-on-the-Hudson, called New York.
O. HENRY—*The Gentle Grafter*

Not like the brazen giant of Greek fame,
With conquering limbs astride from land to land;
Here at our sea-washed, sunset gates shall stand
A mighty woman with a torch, whose flame
Is the imprisoned lightning, and her name
Mother of exiles.
EMMA LAZARUS—*The New Colossus*

Shrill and high, newsboys cry
The worst of the city's infamy.
WILLIAM VAUGHN MOODY—*In New York*

Vulgar of manner, overfed,
Overdressed and underbred;
Heartless, Godless, hell's delight,
Rude by day and lewd by night;
Bedwarfed the man, o'ergrown the brute,
Ruled by boss and prostitute;
Purple-robed and pauper-clad,
Raving, rotting, money-mad;
A squirming herd in Mammon's mesh,
A wilderness of human flesh;
Crazed with avarice, lust and rum,
New York, thy name's Delirium.
BYRON R. NEWTON—*Owed to New York*

(See also CITY, COUNTRY LIFE.)

NEWS

If a man bites a dog, that is news.
JOHN BOGART

By evil report and good report.
II CORINTHIANS. VI. 8

It is good news, *worthy of all acceptation,* and yet not too good to be true.
MATTHEW HENRY—*Commentaries.* I Timothy. I. 15

As cold waters to a thirsty soul, so is good news from a far country.
PROVERBS. XXV. 25

There's villainous news abroad.
SHAKESPEARE—*Henry IV.* Pt. I. Act II. Sc. 4

When we hear news we should always wait for the sacrament of confirmation.
VOLTAIRE

(See also GOSSIP, JOURNALISM, NEWSPAPER, POST, PRESS, RUMOR.)

NEWSPAPER

Newspapers are the world's mirrors.
JAMES ELLIS

In the long, fierce struggle for freedom of opinion, the press, like the Church, counted its martyrs by thousands.
JAMES A. GARFIELD

Were it left to me to decide whether we should have a government without newspapers or newspapers without government, I should not hesitate a moment to prefer the latter.
JEFFERSON—Letter, 1787

Every editor of newspapers pays tribute to the devil.
LA FONTAINE

Four hostile newspapers are more to be feared than a thousand bayonets.
NAPOLEON

Let me make the newspapers, and I care not what is preached in the pulpit or what is enacted in Congress.
WENDELL PHILLIPS

All I know is what I see in the papers.
WILL ROGERS

The careful reader of a few good newspapers can learn more in a year than most scholars do in their great libraries.
F. B. SANBORN

(See also AUTHORSHIP, CRITICISM, GOSSIP, JOURNALISM, NEWS, PRESS, RUMOR.)

NIGHT

Night is a stealthy, evil Raven,
Wrapt to the eyes in his black wings.
T. B. ALDRICH—Day and Night

Most holy Night, that still dost keep
The keys of all the doors of sleep,
To me when my tired eyelids close
Give thou repose.
HILAIRE BELLOC—The Night

The Night has a thousand eyes,
The Day but one;
Yet the light of the bright world dies
With the dying sun.
F. W. BOURDILLON—Light

For the night
Shows stars and women in a better light.
BYRON—Don Juan

Night's black Mantle covers all alike.
DU BARTAS

Watchman, what of the night?
ISAIAH. XXI. 11

Night, when deep sleep falleth on men.
JOB. IV. 13

The night cometh when no man can work.
JOHN. IX. 4

And the night shall be filled with music
And the cares, that infest the day,
Shall fold their tents, like the Arabs,
And as silently steal away.
LONGFELLOW—The Day is Done

The nearer the dawn the darker the night.

> LONGFELLOW—*Tales of a Wayside Inn*

Night is the time for rest;
How sweet, when labours close,
To gather round an aching breast
The curtain of repose,
Stretch the tired limbs, and lay the head
Down on our own delightful bed!

> MONTGOMERY—*Night*

The night is dark, and I am far from home.

> JOHN HENRY NEWMAN—*Lead, Kindly Light*

To all, to each, a fair good night,
And pleasing dreams; and slumbers light.

> SCOTT—*Marmion*

Making night hideous.

> SHAKESPEARE—*Hamlet.* Act I. Sc. 4

Come, drink the mystic wine of Night,
Brimming with silence and the stars;
While earth, bathed in this holy light,
Is seen without its scars.

> LOUIS UNTERMEYER—*The Wine of Night*

(See also DARKNESS, EVENING, MIDNIGHT, NATURE, SKY, STAR, TWILIGHT.)

NIGHTINGALE

It is the hour when from the boughs
The nightingale's high note is heard;

It is the hour when lovers' vows
Seem sweet in every whisper'd word.

> BYRON

What bird so sings, yet does so wail?
O, 'tis the ravish'd nightingale—
Jug, jug, jug, jug—tereu—she cries,
And still her woes at midnight rise.

> LYLY—*The Songs of Birds*

Hark! that's the nightingale,
Telling the self-same tale
Her song told when this ancient earth was young:
So echoes answered when her song was sung
In the first wooded vale.

> CHRISTINA G. ROSSETTI—*Twilight Calm*

The angel of spring, the mellow-throated nightingale.

> SAPPHO

(See also BIRDS.)

NOBILITY

Send your noble blood to market
and see what it will bring.

> THOMAS FULLER

Noble blood is an accident of fortune;
noble actions characterize the great.

> GOLDONI—*Pamela*

Be noble in every thought
And in every deed!

> LONGFELLOW—*Christus*

This was the noblest Roman of them all.

> SHAKESPEARE—*Julius Caesar.* Act V. Sc. 5

(See also ANCESTRY, CHARACTER, GREATNESS, ROYALTY, WORTH.)

NONSENSE

A little nonsense now and then
Is relished by the wisest men.
ANONYMOUS

The Owl and the Pussy-Cat went to
  sea
  In a beautiful pea-green boat.
    EDWARD LEAR—*The Owl and
    the Pussy-Cat*

No one is exempt from talking nonsense; the misfortune is to do it
solemnly.
  MONTAIGNE

(See also JESTING, LAUGHTER,
  NOTHINGNESS.)

NOSE

Give me a man with a good allowance of nose, . . . when I want any
good head-work done I choose a
man—provided his education has
been suitable—with a long nose.
  NAPOLEON—Related in *Notes
  on Noses*

If the nose of Cleopatra had been a
little shorter the whole face of the
world would have been changed.
  PASCAL

Plain as a nose in a man's face.
  RABELAIS

(See also FACE.)

NOTHINGNESS

Nothing to do but work,
  Nothing to eat but food,
Nothing to wear but clothes,
  To keep one from going nude.
    BEN KING—*The Pessimist*

Nothing's new, and nothing's true,
and nothing matters.
  Attributed to LADY MORGAN

Blessed be he who expects nothing,
for he shall never be disappointed.
  POPE—Letter

They laboriously do nothing.
  SENECA

A life of nothing's nothing worth,
From that first nothing ere his birth,
To that last nothing under earth.
  TENNYSON—*Two Voices*

(See also IDLENESS, NONSENSE.)

OATH

You can have no oath registered in
heaven to destroy the Government;
while I shall have the most solemn
one to "preserve, protect, and defend" it.
  LINCOLN—First Inaugural Address

'Tis not the many oaths that makes
  the truth,
But the plain single vow that is vow'd
  true.
    SHAKESPEARE—*All's Well That
    End Well*. Act IV. Sc. 2

I'll take thy word for faith, not ask
  thine oath;
Who shuns not to break one will
  sure crack both.
    SHAKESPEARE—*Pericles*. Act I.
    Sc. 2

(See also DECISION, PROFANITY,
  PROMISE.)

OBEDIENCE

Obedience alone gives the right to
command.
  EMERSON

Let thy child's first lesson be obedience, and the second will be what thou wilt.
FRANKLIN

Women are perfectly well aware that the more they seem to obey the more they rule.
MICHELET

The eye that mocketh at his father, and despiseth to obey his mother, the ravens of the valley shall pick it out, and the young eagles shall eat it.
PROVERBS. XXX. 17

Let them obey that know not how to rule.
SHAKESPEARE—*Henry VI*. Pt. II. Act V. Sc. 1

(See also AUTHORITY, CHARACTER, GOVERNMENT, LAW.)

OBSCURITY

I give the fight up; let there be an end,
A privacy, an obscure nook for me,
I want to be forgotten even by God.
BROWNING—*Paracelsus*.

Full many a flower is born to blush unseen,
And waste its sweetness on the desert air.
GRAY—*Elegy in a Country Churchyard*

How happy is the blameless vestal's lot!
The world forgetting, by the world forgot.
POPE—*Eloisa to Abélard*

Thus let me live, unseen, unknown,
Thus unlamented let me die;
Steal from the world, and not a stone
Tell where I lie.
POPE—*Ode on Solitude*

How many a rustic Milton has passed by,
Stifling the speechless longings of his heart
In unremitting drudgery and care!
How many a vulgar Cato has compelled
His energies, no longer tameless then,
To mold a pin, or fabricate a nail!
SHELLEY—*Queen Mab*

(See also DARKNESS, SHADOW, SOLITUDE.)

OBSTINACY

Obstinacy and vehemency in opinion are the surest proofs of stupidity.
BERNARD BARTON

An obstinate man does not hold opinions, but they hold him.
POPE

(See also DECISION, FIRMNESS, OPINION.)

OCCUPATION

I hold every man a debtor to his profession; from the which as men of course do seek to receive countenance and profit, so ought they of duty to endeavor themselves, by way of amends, to be a help and ornament thereunto.
BACON—*Maxims of the Law*

The crowning fortune of a man is to be born to some pursuit which finds him employment and happiness, whether it be to make baskets, or broadswords, or canals, or statues, or songs.
EMERSON

The ugliest of trades have their moments of pleasure. Now, if I were a grave-digger, or even a hangman, there are some people I could work for with a great deal of enjoyment.
DOUGLAS JERROLD—*Ugly Trades*

(See also ACTING, AGRICULTURE, AUTHORSHIP, BUSINESS, CLERGYMAN, COOKING, JOURNALISM, LABOR, LAW, MEDICINE, NAVIGATION, NAVY, NEWSPAPER, PAINTING, SHOEMAKING, SOLDIER, TEACHING, WORK.)

OCEAN

What are the wild waves saying,
　Sister, the whole day long,
That ever amid our playing
　I hear but their low, lone song?
　JOSEPH E. CARPENTER

Full many a gem of purest ray serene,
　The dark unfathomed caves of ocean bear.
　GRAY—*Elegy in a Country Churchyard*

The breaking waves dashed high
　On a stern and rock-bound coast,
And the woods against a stormy sky,
　Their giant branches toss'd.
　FELICIA D. HEMANS—*The Landing of the Pilgrim Fathers in New England*

Praise the sea, but keep on land.
　GEORGE HERBERT

Love the sea? I dote upon it—from the beach.
　DOUGLAS JERROLD—*Love of the Sea*

Rocked in the cradle of the deep,
I lay me down in peace to sleep.
　EMMA WILLARD—*The Cradle of the Deep*

(See also FISH, NATURE, NAVIGATION, NAVY, SEA, SHIP, STORM.)

OFFICE

The very essence of a free government consists in considering offices as public trusts, bestowed for the good of the country, and not for the benefit of an individual or a party.
　CALHOUN—Speech, 1835

If a due participation of office is a matter of right, how are vacancies to be obtained? Those by death are few: by resignation, none.
　JEFFERSON—Letter, 1801

This struggle and scramble for office, for a way to live without work, will finally test the strength of our institutions.
　LINCOLN, 1861

Every time I fill a vacant place I make a hundred malcontents and one ingrate.
　Attributed to LOUIS XIV of France

Public office is the last refuge of the incompetent.
　Attributed to BOISE PENROSE

The insolence of office.
SHAKESPEARE—*Hamlet.* Act
III. Sc. 1

(See also ECONOMY, GOVERNMENT,
PARTY, POLITICS, TAXES.)

OPINION

Private opinion is weak, but public
opinion is almost omnipotent.
HENRY WARD BEECHER

Popular opinion is the greatest lie
in the world.
CARLYLE

It were not best that we should all
think alike; it is difference of opinion that makes horseraces.
S. L. CLEMENS (MARK TWAIN)
—*Pudd'nhead Wilson*

Stiff in opinion, always in the wrong.
DRYDEN—*Absalom and Achit-
ophel*

It is rare that the public sentiment
decides immorally or unwisely, and
the individual who differs from it
ought to distrust and examine well
his own opinion.
JEFFERSON—Letter, 1801

Those who never retract their opinions love themselves more than they
love truth.
JOUBERT

Public opinion, though often formed
upon a wrong basis, yet generally
has a strong underlying sense of
justice.
LINCOLN

The foolish and the dead alone never
change their opinion.
LOWELL

Opinions cannot survive if one has
no chance to fight for them.
THOMAS MANN—*The Magic
Mountain*

Force and not opinion is the queen
of the world; but it is opinion that
uses the force.
PASCAL

Public opinion is a compound of
folly, weakness, prejudice, wrong
feeling, right feeling, obstinacy, and
newspaper paragraphs.
ROBERT PEEL

The feeble tremble before opinion,
the foolish defy it, the wise judge it,
the skillful direct it.
MME. JEANNE ROLAND

I know where there is more wisdom
than is found in Napoleon, Voltaire,
or all the ministers present and to
come—in public opinion.
TALLEYRAND—In the Chamber
of Peers

(See also ARGUMENT, BELIEF,
CRITICISM, FAITH, INTELLECT,
JUDGMENT, MIND.)

OPPORTUNITY

There is an hour in each man's life
appointed
To make his happiness, if then he
seize it.
BEAUMONT AND FLETCHER

Do not suppose opportunity will
knock twice at your door.
CHAMFORT

Make hay while the sun shines.
ENGLISH PROVERB

Plough deep while sluggards sleep.
BENJAMIN FRANKLIN

To improve the golden moment of opportunity, and catch the good that is within our reach, is the great art of life.
SAMUEL JOHNSON

There's place and means for every man alive.
SHAKESPEARE—*All's Well That Ends Well.* Act IV. Sc. 3

There is a tide in the affairs of men, Which, taken at the flood, leads on to fortune.
SHAKESPEARE—*Julius Caesar.* Act IV. Sc. 3

The opportunity for doing mischief is found a hundred times a day, and of doing good once in a year.
VOLTAIRE—*Zadig*

(See also ACCIDENT, CHANCE, CIR- CUMSTANCE, DECISION, DESTINY, FATE, LIFE, LUCK, SUCCESS.)

OPPOSITION

No government can be long secure without a formidable opposition.
DISRAELI—*Coningsby*

To make a young couple love each other, it is only necessary to oppose and separate them.
GOETHE

Opposition always inflames the enthusiast, never converts him.
SCHILLER

(See also ARGUMENT, CONTRO- VERSY, COURTSHIP, GOVERN- MENT, LIFE, LOGIC, POLITICS, WOOING.)

OPPRESSION
See PERSECUTION

OPTIMISM

Optimism: A cheerful frame of mind that enables a tea kettle to sing though in hot water up to its nose.
ANONYMOUS

An optimist sees an opportunity in every calamity; a pessimist sees a calamity in every opportunity.
ANONYMOUS

To look up and not down,
To look forward and not back,
To look out and not in, and
To lend a hand.
EDWARD EVERETT HALE

Keep your face to the sunshine and you cannot see the shadow.
HELEN KELLER

Two men look out through the same bars:
One sees the mud, and one the stars.
FREDERICK LANGBRIDGE

(See also CHEERFULNESS, ENTHU- SIASM, PESSIMISM.)

ORATORY

Oratory is the power to talk people out of their sober and natural opinions.
CHATFIELD

Glittering generalities! They are blazing ubiquities.
EMERSON—Remark on Choate's words

I am not fond of uttering platitudes
In stained-glass attitudes.
> W. S. GILBERT—*Patience.* Bun-
> thorne's Song

The object of oratory is not truth,
but persuasion.
> MACAULAY—*The Athenian
> Orators*

What the orators want in depth,
they give you in length.
> MONTESQUIEU

(See also ACTING, ARGUMENT, ELO-
QUENCE, LANGUAGE, LOGIC,
SPEECH, TALK, TONGUE,
WORD.)

ORDER

Have a place for everything and
have everything in its place.
> ANONYMOUS

Let all things be done decently and
in order.
> I CORINTHIANS. XIV. 40

Set thine house in order.
> ISAIAH. XXXVIII. 1

Order is Heaven's first law.
> POPE—*An Essay on Man*

The heavens themselves, the planets
and this centre
Observe degree, priority and place,
Insisture, course, proportion, season,
form,
Office and custom, in all line of
order.
> SHAKESPEARE—*Troilus and
> Cressida.* Act I. Sc. 3

(See also DISCIPLINE, GOVERN-
MENT, LAW, NATURE.)

ORIGINALITY

Great men are more distinguished by
range and extent than by originality.
> EMERSON

Originality does not consist in saying what no one has ever said before,
but in saying exactly what you think
yourself.
> JAMES FITZ-JAMES STEPHEN

Originality is nothing but judicious
imitation.
> VOLTAIRE

(See also BEGINNING, CREATION,
IMITATION.)

OSTENTATION
See VANITY

OYSTER

It is unseasonable and unwholesome
in all months that have not an R in
their names to eat an oyster.
> WILLIAM BUTLER

The world's mine oyster,
Which I with sword will open.
> SHAKESPEARE—*The Merry
> Wives of Windsor.* Act II. Sc. 2

He was a bold man that first ate an
oyster.
> SWIFT—*Polite Conversation*

PAIN

Man endures pain as an undeserved
punishment; woman accepts it as a
natural heritage.
> ANONYMOUS

Pain and pleasure, like light and
darkness, succeed each other.
> LAURENCE STERNE

The pain of the mind is worse than the pain of the body.
SYRUS

Nothing begins, and nothing ends,
    That is not paid with moan;
For we are born in others' pain,
    And perish in our own.
FRANCIS THOMPSON—*Daisy*

The mark of rank in nature is capacity for pain,
And the anguish of the singer marks the sweetness of the strain.
SARAH WILLIAMS—*Twilight Hours*

(See also AFFLICTION, CRUELTY, GRIEF, MISERY, SICKNESS, SORROW, SUFFERING, TEARS.)

PAINTING

If we could but paint with the hand as we see with the eye!
BALZAC

Pictures must not be too picturesque.
EMERSON—*Essays*

The fellow mixes blood with his colors.
GUIDO RENI (about Rubens)

A picture is a poem without words.
HORACE

I mix them with my brains, sir.
JOHN OPIE, when asked with what he mixed his colors

                        But who can paint
Like nature? Can imagination boast,
Amid its gay creation, hues like hers?
JAMES THOMSON—*Seasons*

(See also ART, CRITICISM.)

PARADISE

In this fool's paradise, he drank delight.
CRABBE—*The Borough Players*

Unto you is paradise opened.
II ESDRAS. VIII. 52

A book of Verses underneath the Bough,
A Jug of Wine, a Loaf of Bread—and Thou
    Beside me singing in the Wilderness—
Oh, Wilderness were Paradise enow!
OMAR KHAYYÁM—*Rubaiyat*

The loves that meet in Paradise shall cast out fear,
And Paradise hath room for you and me and all.
CHRISTINA G. ROSSETTI—*Saints and Angels*

(See also FUTURE, GLORY, HAPPINESS, HEAVEN, IMMORTALITY.)

PARDON

Nothing in this low and ruined world bears the meek impress of the Son of God so surely as forgiveness.
ALICE CARY

As we grow in wisdom, we pardon more freely.
MME. DE STAËL

Patience is a necessary ingredient of genius.
DISRAELI

God will pardon me. It is His trade.
HEINE—On his deathbed

Pardon others often, thyself never.
SYRUS

(See also FORGIVENESS, LAW,
PRISON, PUNISHMENT.)

PARENT

There is no friendship, no love, like
that of the parent for the child.
HENRY WARD BEECHER

The first half of our lives is ruined
by our parents and the second half
by our children.
CLARENCE S. DARROW

Next to God, thy parents.
WILLIAM PENN

(See also BABYHOOD, BOY, CHILD-
HOOD, DAUGHTER, FATHER,
MOTHER.)

PARTING

Fare thee well! and if for ever,
Still for ever, fare thee well.
BYRON—Fare Thee Well

Oh hast thou forgotten how soon we
must sever?
Oh hast thou forgotten this day
we must part?
It may be for years and it may be
forever;
Oh why art thou silent, thou
voice of my heart?
JULIA CRAWFORD—Kathleen
Mavourneen

Departure should be sudden.
DISRAELI

Excuse me, then! you know my heart;
But dearest friends, alas! must part.
GAY—The Hare and Many
Friends

The sweetest flower that blows,
I give you as we part.
For you it is a rose
For me it is my heart.
FREDERICK PETERSON—At
Parting

Good-night, good-night! parting is
such sweet sorrow,
That I shall say good-night till it be
morrow.
SHAKESPEARE—Romeo and
Juliet. Act II. Sc. 2

(See also ABSENCE, DEATH,
FAREWELL, LIFE.)

PARTY

Political parties serve to keep each
other in check, one keenly watching
the other.
HENRY CLAY

Party honesty is party expediency.
GROVER CLEVELAND, 1889

I always voted at my party's call,
And I never thought of thinking for
myself at all.
W. S. GILBERT—H.M.S. Pinafore

He serves his party best who serves
the country best.
R. B. HAYES—Inaugural Ad-
dress, 1877

Now is the time for all good men
to come to the aid of the party.
CHARLES E. WELLER, 1867.
(Originated as a typing exercise.)

If I could not go to Heaven but with
a party I would not go there at all.
JEFFERSON, 1789

(See also DEMOCRACY, GOVERN-
MENT, POLITICS.)

PASSION

Passion is universal humanity. Without it religion, history, romance and art would be useless.
BALZAC

Knowledge of mankind is a knowledge of their passions.
DISRAELI—*The Young Duke*

Passions unguided are for the most part mere madness.
THOMAS HOBBES—*Leviathan*

Take heed lest passion sway
Thy judgment to do aught, which else free will
Would not admit.
MILTON—*Paradise Lost*

The ruling passion, be it what it will,
The ruling passion conquers reason still.
POPE—*Moral Essays*

Give me that man
That is not passion's slave.
SHAKESPEARE—*Hamlet*. Act III. Sc. 2

(See also ANGER, DESIRE, HATE, LOVE, REVENGE.)

PAST

The present contains nothing more than the past, and what is found in the effect was already in the cause.
HENRI BERGSON—*Creative Evolution*

Gone—glimmering through the dream of things that were.
BYRON—*Childe Harold*

O God! Put back Thy universe and give me yesterday.
HENRY ARTHUR JONES—*Silver King*

Weep no more, lady, weep no more,
Thy sorrow is in vain,
For violets plucked, the sweetest showers
Will ne'er make grow again.
THOMAS PERCY

I tell you the past is a bucket of ashes.
CARL SANDBURG—*Prairie*

The best prophet of the future is the past.
JOHN SHERMAN—Speech, 1890

(See also CHILDHOOD, MEMORY, TIME, YOUTH.)

PATIENCE

A handful of patience is worth more than a bushel of brains.
DUTCH PROVERB

Adopt the pace of nature: her secret is patience.
EMERSON

He that can have patience can have what he will.
FRANKLIN

By time and toil we sever
What strength and rage could never.
LA FONTAINE

All things come round to him who will but wait.
LONGFELLOW—*Tales of a Wayside Inn*

And makes us rather bear those ills we have
Than fly to others that we know not of?
SHAKESPEARE—*Hamlet*. Act III. Sc. 1

How poor are they that have not patience!
What wound did ever heal but by degrees?
SHAKESPEARE—*Othello*. Act II. Sc. 3

Patience is the art of hoping.
VAUVENARGUES

(See also DECISION, PERSEVERANCE, SUCCESS.)

PATRIOTISM

Swim or sink, live or die, survive or perish with my country was my unalterable determination.
JOHN ADAMS—*Works*

No man can be a patriot on an empty stomach.
W. C. BRANN—*Old Glory*

I have already given two cousins to the war, & I stand reddy to sacrifiss my wife's brother ruther'n not see the rebelyin krusht.
ARTEMUS WARD

I realize that patriotism is not enough. I must have no hatred toward any one.
EDITH CAVELL

I have heard something said about allegiance to the South: I know no South, no North, no East, no West, to which I owe any allegiance.
HENRY CLAY

Our country! In her intercourse with foreign nations, may she always be in the right; but our country, right or wrong.
STEPHEN DECATUR

Den I wish I was in Dixie, Hooray! Hooray!
In Dixie Land I'll take my stand
To lib and die in Dixie.
DANIEL D. EMMETT—*Dixie Land*

I only regret that I have but one life to lose for my country.
NATHAN HALE—Last Words, 1776

Strike—for your altars and your fires;
Strike—for the green graves of your sires;
God—and your native land!
FITZ-GREENE HALLECK—*Marco Bozzaris*

And have they fixed the where, and when?
And shall Trelawny die?
Here's thirty thousand Cornish men
Will know the reason why!
ROBERT STEPHEN HAWKER—*Song of the Western Men*

He serves his party best who serves the country best.
R. B. HAYES—Inaugural Address

The world is my country, all mankind are my brethren, and to do good is my religion.
THOMAS PAINE—*Rights of Man*

I am not a Virginian but an American.
PATRICK HENRY

Patriotism is the last refuge of a scoundrel.
SAMUEL JOHNSON

Millions for defence, but not one cent for tribute.
CHARLES C. PINCKNEY

Breathes there the man with soul so dead,
Who never to himself hath said,
This is my own, my native land!
SCOTT—*Lay of the Last Minstrel*

(See also AMERICA, DEMOCRACY, FLAG, FREEDOM, GOVERNMENT, HERO, INDEPENDENCE, NAVY, POLITICS, RIGHTS, SOLDIER, VICTORY, WAR.)

PEACE

I prefer the most unfair peace to the most righteous war.
CICERO

Peace rules the day, where reason rules the mind.
WILLIAM COLLINS—*Eclogue II*

Even peace may be purchased at too high a price.
FRANKLIN

Peace be with you.
GENESIS. XLIII. 23

I have never advocated war, except as a means of peace.
ULYSSES S. GRANT

They shall beat their swords into ploughshares, and their spears into pruninghooks: nation shall not lift up sword against nation neither shall they learn war any more.
ISAIAH. II. 4

The wolf also shall dwell with the lamb, and the leopard shall lie down with the kid.
ISAIAH. XI. 6

I am a man of peace. God knows how I love peace; but I hope I shall never be such a coward as to mistake oppression for peace.
KOSSUTH

Peace at any price.
LAMARTINE

Glory to God in the highest, and on earth peace, good will toward men.
LUKE. II. 14

Peace be to this house.
LUKE. X. 5

Peace hath her victories,
No less renowned than war.
MILTON

If they want peace, nations should avoid the pin-pricks that precede cannon-shots.
NAPOLEON

The peace of God, which passeth all understanding.
PHILIPPIANS. IV. 7

Her ways are ways of pleasantness, and all her paths are peace.
PROVERBS. III. 17

Mercy and truth are met together: righteousness and peace have kissed each other.
PSALMS. LXXXV. 10

Peace be within thy walls, and prosperity within thy palaces.
PSALMS. CXXII. 7

If peace cannot be maintained with honor, it is no longer peace.
LORD RUSSELL

Peace won by compromise is usually a short-lived achievement.
WINFIELD SCOTT

The war-drum throbb'd no longer, and the battle-flags were furl'd
In the parliament of man, the federation of the world.
TENNYSON—*Locksley Hall*

To be prepared for war is one of the most effectual means of preserving peace.
WASHINGTON

There is such a thing as a man being too proud to fight. There is such a thing as a nation being so right that it does not need to convince others by force that it is right.
WOODROW WILSON. May 10, 1915

It must be a peace without victory. Only a peace between equals can last: only a peace, the very principle of which is equality, and a common participation in a common benefit.
WOODROW WILSON. January 22, 1917

(See also BROTHERHOOD, CONTENTMENT, HUMANITY, REPOSE, REST, SOLDIER, STATESMANSHIP, WAR.)

PEN

The pen is mightier than the sword.
BULWER-LYTTON

If you give me six lines written by the hand of the most honest of men, I will find something in them which will hang him.
RICHELIEU

(See also AUTHORSHIP, JOURNALISM, LITERATURE, NEWSPAPER, WRITING.)

PEOPLE

The voice of the people is the voice of God.
ALCUIN—*Epistles*

The will of the people is the best law.
ULYSSES S. GRANT

The people are the only sure reliance for the preservation of our liberty.
JEFFERSON, 1787

We here highly resolve that these dead shall not have died in vain; that this nation, under God, shall have a new birth of freedom, and that government of the people, by the people, and for the people, shall not perish from the earth.
LINCOLN—Gettysburg Address

God must have loved the plain people: He made so many of them.
LINCOLN

You can fool some of the people all of the time, and all of the people some of the time, but you cannot fool all of the people all the time.
LINCOLN

The second, sober thought of the people is seldom wrong, and always efficient.
MARTIN VAN BUREN

The two kinds of people on earth
that I mean
Are the people who lift and the peo-
ple who lean.
ELLA WHEELER WILCOX—*To
Lift or to Lean*

(See also DEMOCRACY, HUMANITY,
PUBLIC.)

PERFECTION

The very pink of perfection.
GOLDSMITH—*She Stoops to
Conquer*

There are many lovely women, but
no perfect ones.
VICTOR HUGO

Trifles make perfection, and perfection is no trifle.
MICHELANGELO

Whoever thinks a faultless piece to
see,
Thinks what ne'er was, nor is, nor
e'er shall be.
POPE—*Essay on Criticism*

(See also BEAUTY, CHARACTER,
SUCCESS.)

PERJURY
See OATH, LYING

PERSECUTION

A religion which requires persecution to sustain it is of the devil's
propagation.
HOSEA BALLOU

The way of this world is, to praise
dead saints, and persecute living
ones.
NATHANIEL HOWE

Galileo probably would have escaped
persecution if his discoveries could
have been disproved.
WHATELY

(See also CRUELTY, LAW, OPINION,
WRONG.)

PERSEVERANCE

There is no royal road to anything.
One thing at a time, all things in
succession. That which grows fast
withers as rapidly; that which grows
slowly endures.
J. G. HOLLAND

The waters wear the stones.
JOB. XIV. 19

Victory belongs to the most persever-
ing.
NAPOLEON

Many strokes, though with a little
axe,
Hew down and fell the hardest-
timber'd oak.
SHAKESPEARE—*Henry VI*. Pt.
III. Act II. Sc. 1

Do what you love. Know your own
bone; gnaw at it, bury it, unearth
it, and gnaw it still.
THOREAU

(See also ABILITY, DECISION,
PATIENCE, SUCCESS.)

PERSONALITY
See CHARACTER

PESSIMISM

Pessimist: An optimist who endeav
ored to practice what he preached.
ANONYMOUS

A pessimist is one who feels bad when he feels good for fear he'll feel worse when he feels better.

ANONYMOUS

How happy are the pessimists! What joy is theirs when they have proved there is no joy.

MARIE EBNER-ESCHENBACH

A pessimist? A man who thinks everybody as nasty as himself, and hates them for it.

GEORGE BERNARD SHAW

(See also CONSERVATISM, OPTIMISM.)

PHILANTHROPY

Philanthropies and charities have a certain air of quackery.

EMERSON—*The Transcendentalist*

Steal the hog, and give the feet for alms.

HERBERT

I was eyes to the blind, and feet was I to the lame.

JOB. XXIX. 15

To pity distress is but human; to relieve it is Godlike.

HORACE MANN—*Lectures on Education*

Take heed that ye do not your alms before men, to be seen of them.

MATTHEW. VI. 1

When thou doest alms, let not thy left hand know what thy right hand doeth.

MATTHEW. VI. 3

The organized charity, scrimped and iced,
In the name of a cautious, statistical Christ.

JOHN BOYLE O'REILLY—*In Bohemia*

(See also CHARITY, GIFT, HUMANITY, SYMPATHY.)

PHILOSOPHY

A little philosophy inclineth man's mind to atheism; but depth in philosophy bringeth men's minds about to religion.

BACON—*Essays*

The philosophy of one century is the common sense of the next.

HENRY WARD BEECHER

Philosophy: A route of many roads leading from nowhere to nothing.

BIERCE—*The Devil's Dictionary*

Queen of arts, and daughter of heaven.

BURKE

In philosophy, it is not the attainment of the goal that matters, it is the things that are met with by the way.

HAVELOCK ELLIS—*The Dance of Life*

Philosophy goes no further than probabilities, and in every assertion keeps a doubt in reserve.

FROUDE

Whence? whither? why? how?—these questions cover all philosophy.

JOUBERT

There are more things in heaven and earth, Horatio,
Than are dreamt of in your philosophy.
SHAKESPEARE—*Hamlet*. Act I. Sc. 5

There was never yet philosopher
That could endure the toothache patiently.
SHAKESPEARE — *Much Ado About Nothing*. Act V. Sc. 1

The philosopher is Nature's pilot. And there you have our difference: to be in hell is to drift: to be in heaven is to steer.
GEORGE BERNARD SHAW—*Man and Superman*

The discovery of what is true and the practice of that which is good are the two most important objects of philosophy.
VOLTAIRE

When he to whom one speaks does not understand, and he who speaks himself does not understand, this is metaphysics.
VOLTAIRE

(See also ARGUMENT, INTELLECT, LOGIC, MIND, REASON, SCIENCE.)

PHYSICIAN
See MEDICINE

PIETY

If your neighbor has made one pilgrimage to Mecca, watch him; if two, avoid him; if three, move to another street.
ARAB PROVERB

I lie, I cheat, do anything for pelf,
But who on earth can say I am not pious?
HOOD—*Blanca's Dream*

Young Obadias,
David, Josias,
All were pious.
NEW ENGLAND PRIMER

Thou villain, thou art full of piety.
SHAKESPEARE — *Much Ado About Nothing*. Act IV. Sc. 2

Let them learn first to show piety at home.
I TIMOTHY. V. 4

(See also HYPOCRISY, RELIGION, VIRTUE.)

PITY

More helpful than all wisdom is one draught of simple human pity that will not forsake us.
GEORGE ELIOT—*The Mill on the Floss*

Pity is the feeling which arrests the mind in the presence of whatsoever is grave and constant in human sufferings and unites it with the human sufferer.
JAMES JOYCE—*A Portrait of the Artist as a Young Man*

He that hath pity upon the poor lendeth unto the Lord; and that which he hath given will he pay him again.
PROVERBS. XIX. 17

We pity in others only those evils which we have ourselves experienced.
ROUSSEAU

There are two sorts of pity: one is a balm and the other a poison; the first is realized by our friends, the last by our enemies.

CHARLES SUMNER

A book or poem which has no pity in it had better not be written.

WILDE

(See also CHARITY, HUMANITY, KINDNESS, MERCY, SYMPATHY.)

PLAGIARISM

They lard their lean books with the fat of others' works.

BURTON—*Anatomy of Melancholy*

Most plagiarists, like the drone, have neither taste to select, industry to acquire, nor skill to improve, but impudently pilfer the honey ready prepared, from the hive.

COLTON

Goethe said there would be little left of him if he were to discard what he owed to others.

CHARLOTTE CUSHMAN

When Shakespeare is charged with debts to his authors, Landor replies, "Yet he was more original than his originals. He breathed upon dead bodies and brought them into life."

EMERSON—*Letters and Social Aims*

Take the whole range of imaginative literature, and we are all wholesale borrowers. In every matter that relates to invention, to use, or beauty or form, we are borrowers.

WENDELL PHILLIPS—*The Lost Arts*

(See also AUTHORSHIP, BOOKS, BORROWING, IMITATION, JOURNALISM, LITERATURE, NEWSPAPER, POETRY, THIEVING, WRITING.)

PLEASURE

The great pleasure in life is doing what people say you cannot do.

WALTER BAGEHOT—*Literary Studies*

The rule of my life is to make business a pleasure, and pleasure my business.

AARON BURR—Letter to Pichon

There is no pleasure without a tincture of bitterness.

HAFIZ

Fly the pleasure that bites tomorrow.

HERBERT

Follow pleasure, and then will pleasure flee,
Flee pleasure, and pleasure will follow thee.

HEYWOOD—*Proverbs*

We tire of those pleasures we take, but never of those we give.

J. PETIT-SENN

He that loveth pleasure shall be a poor man.

PROVERBS. XXI. 17

(See also AMUSEMENT, BLISS, CONTENTMENT, DELIGHT, HAPPINESS, JOY, LAUGHTER, MERRIMENT, SMILE.)

A majority is always better than the best repartee.
DISRAELI

Damned Neuters, in their Middle way of Steering,
Are neither Fish, nor Flesh, nor good Red Herring.
DRYDEN—*Duke of Guise*

I always voted at my party's call,
And I never thought of thinking for myself at all.
W. S. GILBERT—*H.M.S. Pinafore*

The purification of politics is an iridescent dream.
INGALLS—*Epigram*

Like an armed warrior, like a plumed knight, James G. Blaine marched down the halls of the American Congress and threw his shining lance full and fair against the brazen foreheads of the defamers of his country, and the maligners of his honor.
INGERSOLL, in nomination of Blaine for President, 1876

If a due participation of office is a matter of right, how are vacancies to be obtained? Those by death are few; by resignation, none.
JEFFERSON, 1801

Nothing is politically right which is morally wrong.
DANIEL O'CONNELL

The statesman shears the sheep, the politician skins them.
AUSTIN O'MALLEY

Every time I fill a vacant office I make ten malcontents and one ingrate.
LOUIS XIV

Politics is but the common pulse-beat, of which revolution is the fever-spasm.
WENDELL PHILLIPS—Speech, 1853

The Republicans have their splits right after election and Democrats have theirs just before an election.
WILL ROGERS

There is a homely old adage which runs: "Speak softly and carry a big stick; you will go far." If the American nation will speak softly and yet build and keep at a pitch of the highest training a thoroughly efficient navy, the Monroe Doctrine will go far.
THEODORE ROOSEVELT, 1901

My hat's in the ring. The fight is on and I'm stripped to the buff.
THEODORE ROOSEVELT, 1912

Something is rotten in the state of Denmark.
SHAKESPEARE—*Hamlet*. Act I. Sc. 4

If nominated I will not accept; if elected I will not serve.
WILLIAM TECUMSEH SHERMAN, 1884

Who is the dark horse he has in his stable?
THACKERAY—*Adventures of Philip*

As long as I count the votes what are you going to do about it? Say.
WILLIAM M. TWEED

(See also DEMOCRACY, GOVERNMENT, INDEPENDENCE, LAW, LIBERTY, POLICY, STATESMANSHIP.)

POOR
See POVERTY

POPULARITY

Popular applause veers with the wind.
JOHN BRIGHT

The actor's popularity is evanescent; applauded today, forgotten tomorrow.
EDWIN FORREST

There was ease in Casey's manner as he stept into his place,
There was pride in Casey's bearing and a smile on Casey's face,
And when responding to the cheers he lightly doft his hat,
No stranger in the crowd could doubt, 't was Casey at the bat.
ERNEST L. THAYER—*Casey at the Bat*

(See also ADMIRATION, APPLAUSE, FAME, HERO, PRAISE, REPUTATION, SUCCESS.)

POSSESSION

When we have not what we love, we must love what we have.
BUSSY-RABUTIN, 1667

They who have nothing have little to fear,
Nothing to lose or to gain.
MADISON CAWEIN—*The Bellman*

As having nothing, and yet possessing all things.
II CORINTHIANS. VI. 10

Of a rich man who was mean and niggardly, he said, "That man does not possess his estate, but his estate possesses him."
DIOGENES

Property has its duties as well as its rights.
DRUMMOND

Wouldst thou both eat thy cake and have it?
HERBERT

Unto every one that hath shall be given, and he shall have abundance; but from him that hath not shall be taken away even that which he hath.
MATTHEW. XXV. 29

What is yours is mine, and all mine is yours.
PLAUTUS

Possession, they say, is eleven points of the law.
SWIFT

(See also GOLD, LAW, MONEY, POVERTY, PROPERTY, RICHES, WEALTH.)

POST

Neither snow, nor rain, nor heat, nor night stays these couriers from the swift completion of their appointed rounds.
HERODOTUS — Inscription on Postoffice, New York City

A strange volume of real life in the daily packet of the postman. Eternal love and instant payment!
DOUGLAS JERROLD—*The Postman's Budget*

A woman seldom writes her Mind,
but in her Postscript.
   STEELE—*Spectator*

Go, little letter, apace, apace,
   Fly;
Fly to the light in the valley below—
   Tell my wish to her dewy blue
   eye.
      TENNYSON—*The Letter*

(See also ABSENCE, GOSSIP, LETTER,
NEWS, PEN.)

POSTERITY

Think of your forefathers! Think of
your posterity!
   JOHN QUINCY ADAMS, 1802

People will not look forward to posterity who never look backward to
their ancestors.
   EDMUND BURKE

As to posterity, I may ask what has
it ever done to oblige me?
   GRAY—Letter to Dr. Wharton

(See also ANCESTRY, BOY, DAUGH-
TER, HEREDITY, PARENTS.)

POTTERY

All this of Pot and Potter—Tell me
then,
Who is the Potter, pray, and who the
Pot?
   OMAR KHAYYÁM—*Rubaiyat*

Hath not the potter power over the
clay, of the same lump to make one
vessel unto honour, and another unto
dishonour?
   ROMANS. IX. 21

(See also CREATION.)

POVERTY

Over the hill to the poor-house I'm
trudgin' my weary way.
   WILL CARLETON—*Over the
   Hill to the Poor-House*

He is now fast rising from affluence
to poverty.
   S. L. CLEMENS (MARK TWAIN)

The greatest man in history was the
poorest.
   EMERSON—*Domestic Life*

As poor as a church mouse.
   ENGLISH PHRASE

That amid our highest civilization
men faint and die with want is not
due to the niggardliness of nature,
but to the injustice of man.
   HENRY GEORGE—*Progress and
   Poverty*

Poverty is no sin.
   HERBERT

O God! that bread should be so dear,
   And flesh and blood so cheap!
      HOOD—*The Song of the Shirt*

What mean ye that ye beat my people to pieces, and grind the faces of
the poor? saith the Lord God of
Hosts.
   ISAIAH. III. 15

The poor always ye have with you.
   JOHN. XII. 8

Poverty is a soft pedal upon all
branches of human activity, not excepting the spiritual.
   H. L. MENCKEN—*A Book of
   Prefaces*

He that hath pity upon the poor lendeth unto the Lord.
PROVERBS. XIX. 17

Blessed is he that considereth the poor.
PSALMS. XLI. 1

I am as poor as Job, my lord, but not so patient.
SHAKESPEARE—*Henry IV*. Pt. II. Act I. Sc. 2

It is life near the bone, where it is sweetest.
THOREAU—*Walden*

(See also BEGGING, CHARITY, ECONOMY, HUMANITY, HUNGER, POSSESSION, SUFFERING, WEALTH.)

POWER

Give me a lever long enough
And a prop strong enough,
I can single-handed move the world.
ARCHIMEDES

Iron hand in a velvet glove.
CHARLES V

Power will intoxicate the best hearts, as wine the strongest heads. No man is wise enough, nor good enough to be trusted with unlimited power.
COLTON

The imbecility of men is always inviting the impudence of power.
EMERSON—*Representative Men*

Patience and gentleness is power.
LEIGH HUNT

I have never been able to conceive how any rational being could propose happiness to himself from the exercise of power over others.
JEFFERSON—Letter, 1811

Wherever I found a living creature, there I found the will to power.
NIETZSCHE—*Thus Spake Zarathustra*

Power is ever stealing from the many to the few.
WENDELL PHILLIPS

Unlimited power corrupts the possessor.
WILLIAM PITT, 1770

The powers that be are ordained of God.
ROMANS. XIII. 1

He who has great power should use it lightly.
SENECA

Lust of power is the most flagrant of all the passions.
TACITUS

(See also AUTHORITY, GOVERNMENT, INFLUENCE, KNOWLEDGE, LAW, MIND, STRENGTH, SUCCESS.)

PRAISE

I praise loudly; I blame softly.
CATHERINE II OF RUSSIA

A refusal of praise is a desire to be praised twice.
LA ROCHEFOUCAULD

I would have praised you more had you praised me less.
LOUIS XIV

Approbation from Sir Hubert Stanley is praise indeed.
THOMAS MORTON—*Cure for the Heartache*

Praise the wise man behind his back, but a woman to her face.
WELSH PROVERB

As the Greek said, "Many men know how to flatter, few men know how to praise."
WENDELL PHILLIPS

With faint praises one another damn.
WYCHERLEY—*Plain Dealer*

The sweetest of all sounds is praise.
XENOPHON

(See also ADMIRATION, APPLAUSE, FLATTERY, GLORY, POPULARITY, WORSHIP.)

PRAYER

I pray the prayer the Easterners do, May the peace of Allah abide with you.
ANONYMOUS

Between the humble and contrite heart and the majesty of heaven there are no barriers; the only password is prayer.
HOSEA BALLOU

A prayer, in its simplest definition, is merely a wish turned heavenward.
PHILLIPS BROOKS

They never sought in vain that sought the Lord aright!
BURNS—*The Cotter's Saturday Night*

Prayer is not to be used as a confessional, to cancel sin. Such an error would impede true religion. Sin is forgiven only as it is destroyed by Christ—Truth and Life.
MARY BAKER EDDY—*Science and Health*

You pray in your distress and in your need; would that you might pray also in the fullness of your joy and in your days of abundance.
KAHLIL GIBRAN—*The Prophet*

At church, with meek and unaffected grace,
His looks adorn'd the venerable place;
Truth from his lips prevailed with double sway,
And fools, who came to scoff, remain'd to pray.
GOLDSMITH—*The Deserted Village*

He that will learn to pray, let him go to Sea.
HERBERT

Prayer is the voice of faith.
HORNE

O God, if in the day of battle I forget Thee, do not Thou forget me.
WILLIAM KING

Our Father, which art in heaven, Hallowed be thy Name. Thy kingdom come. Thy will be done in earth as it is in heaven. Give us this day our daily bread. And forgive us our debts, as we forgive our debtors. And lead us not into temptation, but deliver us from evil: For thine is the kingdom and the power and the glory, for ever. Amen.
MATTHEW VI. 9–13 (The Lord's Prayer)

God warms his hands at man's heart when he prays.

> MASEFIELD—*Widow in the Bye Street*

Ask, and it shall be given you; seek, and ye shall find; knock, and it shall be opened unto you.

> MATTHEW. VII. 7

Every one that asketh receiveth; and he that seeketh findeth.

> MATTHEW. VII. 8

Now I lay me down to take my sleep,
I pray thee, Lord, my soul to keep;
If I should die before I wake,
I pray thee, Lord, my soul to take.

> NEW ENGLAND PRIMER, 1814

If I am right, Thy grace impart,
    Still in the right to stay;
If I am wrong, O teach my heart
    To find that better way!

> POPE—*Universal Prayer*

Our prayers should be for blessings in general, for God knows best what is good for us.

> SOCRATES

Pray as if everything depended on God, and work as if everything depended upon man.

> ARCHBISHOP FRANCIS J. SPELLMAN

Holy Father, in Thy mercy,
    Hear our anxious prayer.
Keep our loved ones, now far absent,
    'Neath Thy care.

> ISABELLA S. STEPHENSON— Hymn

Give us the strength to encounter that which is to come, that we may be brave in peril, constant in tribulation, temperate in wrath, and in all changes of fortune, and down to the gates of death, loyal and loving one to another.

> ROBERT LOUIS STEVENSON

From compromise and things half done,
    Keep me with stern and stubborn pride;
And when at last the fight is won,
    God, keep me still unsatisfied.

> LOUIS UNTERMEYER—Prayer

I have never made but one prayer to God, a very short one: "Oh Lord, make my enemies ridiculous." And God granted it.

> VOLTAIRE—Letter, 1767

The Lord's Prayer contains the sum total of religion and morals.

> DUKE OF WELLINGTON

(See also CHRISTIANITY, CHURCH, FAITH, GOD, INFLUENCE, RELIGION, WORSHIP.)

PREACHING

Do as we say, and not as we do.

> BOCCACCIO—*Decameron*

Alas for the unhappy man that is called to stand in the pulpit, and *not* give the bread of life.

> EMERSON

I would have every minister of the gospel address his audience with the zeal of a friend, with the generous energy of a father, and with the exuberant affection of a mother.

> FÉNELON

The test of a preacher is that his congregation goes away saying, not What a lovely sermon, but, I will do something!

St. Francis de Sales

But in his duty prompt at every call, He watch'd and wept, he pray'd and felt for all.

Goldsmith—*Deserted Village*

Sir, a woman preaching is like a dog's walking on his hind legs. It is not done well: but you are surprised to find it done at all.

Samuel Johnson

Some plague the people with too long sermons; for the faculty of listening is a tender thing, and soon becomes weary and satiated.

Luther

The Christian ministry is the worst of all trades, but the best of all professions.

Newton

I have taught you, my dear flock, for above thirty years how to live; and I will show you in a very short time how to die.

Sandys

Sermons in stones and good in every thing.

Shakespeare—*As You Like It.*
Act II. Sc. 1

Preach the word; be instant in season, out of season; reprove, rebuke, exhort with all long suffering and doctrine.

II Timothy. IV. 2

The minister's brain is often the "poor-box" of the church.

Whipple

(See also CHURCH, CLERGYMAN, ELOQUENCE, ORATORY, PRAYER, RELIGION.)

PREJUDICE

He hears but half who hears one party only.

Aeschylus

A fox should not be of the jury at a goose's trial.

Thomas Fuller

He who never leaves his country is full of prejudices.

Goldoni—*Pamela*

Prejudice is the child of ignorance.

Hazlitt

Opinions founded on prejudice are always sustained with the greatest violence.

Jeffrey

(See also CRITICISM, JUDGMENT, OPINION, SNEER.)

PREPAREDNESS

To lead an untrained people to war is to throw them away.

Confucius

In fair weather prepare for foul.

Thomas Fuller

Keep the munition, watch the way, make thy loins strong, fortify thy power mightily.

Nahum. II. 1

We should lay up in peace what we shall need in war.
SYRUS

To be prepared for war is one of the most effectual means of preserving peace.
WASHINGTON—Address, 1790

(See also GOVERNMENT, PEACE, WAR.)

PRESIDENCY

If you are as happy, my dear sir, on entering this house as I am in leaving it and returning home, you are the happiest man in this country.
BUCHANAN—To Lincoln, 1861

I would rather that the people should wonder why I wasn't President than why I am.
SALMON P. CHASE

I would rather be right than President.
HENRY CLAY—Speech, 1850

No man will ever bring out of the Presidency the reputation which carries him into it.
JEFFERSON—Letter, 1796

If forced to choose between the penitentiary and the White House for four years, I would say the penitentiary, thank you.
WILLIAM TECUMSEH SHERMAN

My movements to the chair of government will be accompanied by feelings not unlike those of a culprit who is going to the place of his execution.
WASHINGTON—Letter, 1789

(See also AMERICA, GOVERNMENT, POLITICS, STATESMANSHIP.)

PRESS

The liberty of the press is indeed essential to the nature of a free state, but this consists in laying no previous restraints upon publications, and not in freedom from censure for criminal matter when published.
BLACKSTONE—*Commentaries*

Congress shall make no law abridging the freedom of speech or of the press.
CONSTITUTION OF THE UNITED STATES

Our liberty depends on the freedom of the press, and that cannot be limited without being lost.
JEFFERSON—Letter, 1786

The freedom of the press is one of the great bulwarks of liberty and can never be restrained but by despotic governments.
GEORGE MASON—*Virginia Declaration of Rights*

Freedom of conscience, of education, of speech, of assembly are among the very fundamentals of democracy and all of them would be nullified should freedom of the press ever be successfully challenged.
F. D. ROOSEVELT

Freedom of the press is the staff of life for any vital democracy.
WENDELL L. WILLKIE

(See also JOURNALISM, NEWSPAPER.)

PRETENSION
See HYPROCRISY

PRIDE

They are proud in humility, proud in that they are not proud.
> BURTON—*Anatomy of Melancholy*

Pride ruined the angels.
> EMERSON—*The Sphinx*

Pride that dines on vanity, sups on contempt.
> FRANKLIN

The proud hate pride—in others.
> FRANKLIN—*Poor Richard's Almanac*

Oh! Why should the spirit of mortal be proud?
Like a swift-fleeting meteor, a fast flying cloud,
A flash of the lightning, a break of the wave,
Man passes from life to his rest in the grave.
> WILLIAM KNOX—*Mortality*

Pride and weakness are Siamese twins.
> LOWELL

In pride, in reas'ning pride, our error lies;
All quit their sphere and rush into the skies.
Pride still is aiming at the bless'd abodes,
Men would be angels, angels would be gods.
> POPE—*Essay on Man*

What the weak head with strongest bias rules,
Is pride, the never-failing vice of fools.
> POPE—*Essay on Criticism*

Pride goeth before destruction, and an haughty spirit before a fall.
> PROVERBS. XVI. 18

The infinitely little have a pride infinitely great.
> VOLTAIRE

(See also CONCEIT, DIGNITY, EGOTISM, SELFISHNESS, SELF-LOVE, VANITY.)

PRINCIPLE

Principles become modified in practise by facts.
> COOPER—*The American Democrat*

If principle is good for anything, it is worth living up to.
> FRANKLIN

Important principles may and must be flexible.
> LINCOLN—Speech, 1865

I *don't* believe in princerple,
But, oh, I *du* in interest.
> LOWELL—*The Biglow Papers*

Let us cling to our principles as the mariner clings to his last plank when night and tempest close around him.
> ADAM WOOLEVER

(See also CHARACTER, HONESTY, HONOR, MORALITY, TRUTH.)

PRINTING
See BOOKS, NEWSPAPERS

PRISON

In durance vile here must I wake and weep,
And all my frowsy couch in sorrow steep.
> BURNS

Stone walls do not a prison make,
    Nor iron bars a cage,
Minds innocent and quiet take
    That for an hermitage.
      LOVELACE—*To Althea, from
      Prison*

While we have prisons it matters
little which of us occupy the cells.
      GEORGE BERNARD SHAW—
      Maxims for Revolutionists

Under a government which im-
prisons any unjustly, the true place
for a just man is also a prison.
      THOREAU

I know not whether laws be right,
Or whether laws be wrong;
All that we know who lie in gaol
Is that the wall is strong;
And that each day is like a year,
A year whose days are long.
      WILDE—*The Ballad of Reading
      Gaol*

(See also CRIME, GUILT, JUSTICE,
    LAW, PUNISHMENT, VICE
    WICKEDNESS.)

PRIVACY
See SOLITUDE

PROCRASTINATION

By the street of "By and By" one
arrives at the house of "Never."
      CERVANTES

Never leave that till tomorrow which
you can do today.
      FRANKLIN

(See also DELAY, IDLENESS.)

PROFANITY

Bad language or abuse
I never, never use,
Whatever the emergency;
Though "Bother it" I may
Occasionally say,
I never never use a big, big D.
      W. S. GILBERT—*H.M.S. Pina-
      fore*

To swear is neither brave, polite, nor
wise.
      POPE

The foolish and wicked practice of
profane cursing and swearing is a
vice so mean and low that every
person of sense and character detests
and despises it.
      WASHINGTON

(See also OATH.)

PROFIT
See BUSINESS, MONEY

PROGRESS

Westward the star of empire takes
its way.
      JOHN QUINCY ADAMS, 1802

Modern invention has banished the
spinning-wheel, and the same law of
progress makes the woman of today
a different woman from her grandmother.
      SUSAN B. ANTHONY

                Progress is
The law of life, man is not
    Man as yet.
      BROWNING—*Paracelsus*

What we call progress is the exchange of one Nuisance for another
Nuisance.
      HAVELOCK ELLIS

So long as all the increased wealth which modern progress brings, goes but to build up great fortunes, to increase luxury, and make sharper the contest between the House of Have and the House of Want, progress is not real and cannot be permanent.

HENRY GEORGE—*Progress and Poverty*

Progress,—the stride of God!
VICTOR HUGO

New occasions teach new duties,
    time makes ancient good un-
    couth;
They must upward still and onward,
    who would keep abreast of
    truth.
LOWELL—*Present Crisis*

Every step of progress which the world has made has been from scaffold to scaffold, and from stake to stake.
WENDELL PHILLIPS

If you strike a thorn or rose,
             Keep a-goin!
If it hails or if it snows,
             Keep a-goin!
'Tain't no use to sit and whine
'Cause the fish ain't on your line;
Bait your hook an' keep on tryin'.
             Keep a-goin!
FRANK L. STANTON—*Keep a-goin'*.

He who has not the spirit of his age, has all the misery of it.
VOLTAIRE

(See also AMBITION, EVOLUTION, SUCCESS.)

PROMISE

An acre of performance is worth the whole world of promise.
JAMES HOWELL

He who is the most slow in making a promise is the most faithful in the performance of it.
ROUSSEAU

Promises and pie-crust are made to be broken.
SWIFT—*Polite Conversation*

Undertake not what you cannot perform but be careful to keep your promise.
WASHINGTON

(See also FUTURE, HOPE, OATH, WORD.)

PROMPTNESS

Know the true value of time; snatch, seize, and enjoy every moment of it. No idleness, no laziness, no procrastination; never put off till tomorrow what you can do today.
CHESTERFIELD

Timely service, like timely gifts, is doubled in value.
GEORGE MacDONALD

(See also HASTE, PUNCTUALITY, TIME.)

PROOF

You may prove anything by figures.
Quoted by CARLYLE

The burden of proof lies on the plaintiff.
LEGAL MAXIM

You cannot demonstrate an emotion or prove an aspiration.
JOHN MORLEY—*Rousseau*

Prove all things; hold fast that which is good.
I THESSALONIANS. V. 21

I come from a State that raises corn and cotton and cockleburs and Democrats, and frothy eloquence neither convinces nor satisfies me. I am from Missouri. You have got to show me.
WILLARD D. VANDIVER—Speech, 1899

(See also EVIDENCE, FACTS.)

PROPERTY

Property is at once the consequence and the basis of the state.
BAKUNIN

Mine is better than ours.
FRANKLIN—*Poor Richard's Almanac*

There can be to the ownership of anything no rightful title which is not derived from the title of the producer and does not rest upon the natural right of the man to himself.
HENRY GEORGE—*Progress and Poverty*

The instinct of ownership is fundamental in man's nature.
WILLIAM JAMES

Whenever there is, in any country, uncultivated land and unemployed poor, it is clear that the laws of property have been so far extended as to violate natural right.
JEFFERSON—Letter, 1785

Property is desirable, is a positive good in the world. Let not him who is houseless pull down the house of another, but let him work diligently and build one for himself, thus by example assuring that his own shall be safe from violence when built.
LINCOLN

The reason why men enter into society is the preservation of their property.
LOCKE—*Treatise on Government*

Is it not lawful for me to do what I will with mine own?
MATTHEW. XX. 15

Property is theft.
PROUDHON

Property exists by grace of the law. It is not a fact, but a legal fiction.
STIRNER—*The Ego and His Own*

The highest law gives a thing to him who can use it.
THOREAU

(See also CAPITAL AND LABOR, LAND, POSSESSION, RICHES, WEALTH.)

PROPHECY

Of all the horrid, hideous notes of woe,
Sadder than owl-songs or the midnight blast;
Is that portentous phrase, "I told you so."
BYRON—*Don Juan*

I shall always consider the best guesser the best prophet.
CICERO

We know in part, and we prophesy in part.
I CORINTHIANS. XIII. 9

A prophet is not without honour, save in his own country, and in his own house.
MATTHEW. XIII. 57

(See also FUTURE, REVELATION, VISION.)

PROSPERITY

It requires a strong constitution to withstand repeated attacks of prosperity.
J. L. BASFORD

The desert shall rejoice, and blossom as the rose.
ISAIAH. XXXV. 1

They shall sit every man under his vine and under his fig-tree.
MICAH. IV. 4

Length of days is in her right hand; and in her left hand riches and honour.
PROVERBS. III. 16

Prosperity makes some friends and many enemies.
VAUVENARGUES

(See also FORTUNE, MONEY, RICHES, SUCCESS, WEALTH.)

PROVERBS

Mind your P's and Q's.
ANONYMOUS

Better late than never.
ANONYMOUS

One foot in the grave.
BEAUMONT AND FLETCHER

I find the medicine worse than the malady.
BEAUMONT AND FLETCHER

From the crown of our head to the sole of our foot.
BEAUMONT AND FLETCHER

First come, first served.
BEAUMONT AND FLETCHER

One good turn deserves another.
BEAUMONT AND FLETCHER—
Little French Lawyer

Hit the nail on the head.
BEAUMONT AND FLETCHER—
Love's Cure

I'll have a fling.
BEAUMONT AND FLETCHER—
Rule a Wife and Have a Wife

Oil on troubled waters.
BEDE

What is sauce for the goose is sauce for the gander.
TOM BROWN—*New Maxims*

Curses are like young chickens,
And still come home to roost!
BULWER-LYTTON

Every man for himself, his own ends, the devil for all.
BURTON

Build castles in the air.
BURTON

As clear and as manifest as the nose in a man's face.
BURTON

Set a beggar on horseback, and he will ride a gallop.
BURTON

No rule is so general, which admits not some exception.
BURTON

Matches are made in heaven.
BURTON

Comparisons are odious.
BURTON

He that has two strings t' his bow.
SAMUEL BUTLER

Look before you ere you leap.
SAMUEL BUTLER

He that is down can fall no lower.
SAMUEL BUTLER

As you sow, y' are like to reap.
SAMUEL BUTLER

I'll make the fur
Fly 'bout the ears of the old cur.
SAMUEL BUTLER—*Hudibras*

Put himself upon his good behaviour.
BYRON—*Don Juan*

Better a bad excuse, than none at all.
CAMDEN—*Remains*

Better halfe a loafe than no bread.
CAMDEN

No man is a hero to his valet-de-chambre.
Attributed to MARSHAL CATINAT

All that glisters is not gold.
CERVANTES

Can one desire too much of a good thing?
CERVANTES

Here is the devil-and-all to pay.
CERVANTES

I can tell where my own shoe pinches me.
CERVANTES

Leap out of the frying pan into the fire.
CERVANTES—*Don Quixote*

Let the worst come to the worst.
CERVANTES—*Don Quixote*

Within a stone's throw of it.
CERVANTES—*Don Quixote*

Let pride go afore, shame will follow after.
GEORGE CHAPMAN

Make ducks and drakes with shillings.
GEORGE CHAPMAN—*Eastward Ho*

The more haste, ever the worst speed.
CHARLES CHURCHILL

Fortune befriends the bold.
CICERO

The fat's all in the fire.
COBBE—*Prophecies*

Imitation is the sincerest (form) of flattery.
COLTON

A thorn in the flesh.
II CORINTHIANS. XII. **7**

He that runs may read.
COWPER

Turn over a new leaf.
THOMAS DEKKER

Barkis is willin'.
DICKENS—*David Copperfield*

The mill cannot grind
With water that has past.
SARAH DOUDNEY

The coast was clear.
MICHAEL DRAYTON—
Nymphidia

Give the devil his due.
DRYDEN

He's a sure card.
DRYDEN

Living from hand to mouth.
DU BARTAS

With tooth and nail.
DU BARTAS—*Divine Weekes
and Workes*

Why, then, do you walk as if you
had swallowed a ramrod?
EPICTETUS—*Discourses*

Life is short, yet sweet.
EURIPIDES

Tall oaks from little acorns grow.
DAVID EVERETT

She is no better than she should be.
FIELDING

Faint heart ne'er won fair lady.
PHINEAS FLETCHER

If you would be loved, love and be
lovable.
FRANKLIN

Never leave that till tomorrow which
you can do today.
FRANKLIN

Three may keep a secret if two of
them are dead.
FRANKLIN

Where there's marriage without love
there will be love without marriage.
FRANKLIN

Silence gives consent.
THOMAS FULLER

Handsome is that handsome does.
GOLDSMITH

The very pink of perfection.
GOLDSMITH

Out of sight, out of mind.
GOOGE

Go West, young man, and grow up
with the country.
HORACE GREELEY

Oft times many things fall out between the cup and the lip.
ROBERT GREENE

Not lost, but gone before.
MATTHEW HENRY

Wouldst thou both eat thy cake and
have it?
HERBERT

God's mills grind slow but sure.
HERBERT

Half the world knows not how the
other half lives.
HERBERT

It is a poor sport that is not worth the candle.
HERBERT

Those that God loves, do not live long.
HERBERT

Thursday come, and the week is gone.
HERBERT

Whose house is of glass, must not throw stones at another.
HERBERT

His bark is worse than his bite.
HERBERT—*Country Parson*

Robbe Peter and pay Paule.
JOHN HEYWOOD

Set the cart before the horse.
JOHN HEYWOOD

Tell tales out of schoole.
JOHN HEYWOOD

Two heads are better than one.
JOHN HEYWOOD

Went in at the one eare and out at the other.
JOHN HEYWOOD

By hook or crook.
JOHN HEYWOOD

Give an inch, he'll take an ell.
THOMAS HOBBES

Bag and baggage.
RICHARD HULOET, 1552

Rise with the lark and with the lark to bed.
JAMES HURDIS

Greatest happiness of the greatest number.
HUTCHESON

Fitted him to a T.
SAMUEL JOHNSON—*Boswell's Life of Johnson*

The burnt child dreads the fire.
BEN JONSON

Man proposes, but God disposes.
THOMAS À KEMPIS

A proverb and a byword among all people.
I KINGS. IX. 7

Half as sober as a judge.
LAMB

Neat, not gaudy.
LAMB

Though this may be play to you, 'Tis death to us.
ROGER L'ESTRANGE

Facts are stubborn things.
LE SAGE—*Gil Blas*

There can no great smoke arise, but there must be some fire.
LYLY

A new broom sweepeth clean.
LYLY—*Euphues*

Every tub must stand upon its bottom.
MACKLIN—*Man of the World*

Where McGregor sits, there is the head of the table.
Attributed to THE McGREGOR, a Highland Chief

Have you summoned your wits from wool-gathering?
THOMAS MIDDLETON

Hold their noses to the grindstone.
THOMAS MIDDLETON—*Blurt, Master Constable*

On his last legs.
THOMAS MIDDLETON—*The Old Law*

Present company excepted.
JOHN O'KEEFE—*London Hermit*

Ossa on Pelion.
OVID

Of two evils I have chose the least.
PRIOR

The end must justify the means.
PRIOR

He always looked a given horse in the mouth.
RABELAIS

He did not care a button for it.
RABELAIS

How well I feathered my nest.
RABELAIS

I am just going to leap into the dark.
RABELAIS

Strike the iron whilst it is hot.
RABELAIS

You shall never want rope enough.
RABELAIS

Every man is the architect of his own fortunes.
SALLUST

Wickedness proceedeth from the wicked.
I SAMUEL. XXIV. 13

Blood is thicker than water.
SCOTT

Fat, fair and forty.
SCOTT

Scared out of his seven senses.
SCOTT—*Rob Roy*

A little more than kin, and less than kind.
SHAKESPEARE

All's well that ends well.
SHAKESPEARE

Although the last, not least.
SHAKESPEARE

Brevity is the soul of wit.
SHAKESPEARE

Every why hath a wherefore.
SHAKESPEARE

God save the mark!
SHAKESPEARE

Harp not on that string.
SHAKESPEARE

I have you on the hip.
SHAKESPEARE

Ill blows the wind that profits nobody.
SHAKESPEARE

It is a wise father that knows his own child.
SHAKESPEARE

Lord, what fools these mortals be.
SHAKESPEARE

My man's as true as steel.
SHAKESPEARE

That was laid on with a trowel.
SHAKESPEARE

The game is up.
SHAKESPEARE

The short and the long of it.
SHAKESPEARE

The time is out of joint.
SHAKESPEARE

There's a time for all things.
SHAKESPEARE

They that touch pitch will be defiled.
SHAKESPEARE

'Tis neither here nor there.
SHAKESPEARE

We have scotch'd the snake, not killed it.
SHAKESPEARE

Westward-ho!
SHAKESPEARE

He knew what is what.
SKELTON

Go West, young man! Go West.
JOHN L. B. SOULE

Pity's akin to love.
THOMAS SOUTHERNE

There, though last, not least.
SPENSER

A happy accident.
MME. DE STAËL

Snug as a bug in a rug.
The Stratford Jubilee

A carpenter's known by his chips.
SWIFT

Bread is the staff of life.
SWIFT

I won't quarrel with my bread and butter.
SWIFT

She watches him as a cat would watch a mouse.
SWIFT

Big-endians and small-endians.
SWIFT—*Gulliver's Travels*

Hail, fellow, well met.
SWIFT—*My Lady's Lamentation*

Walls have tongues, and hedges ears.
SWIFT—*Pastoral Dialogue*

A rolling stone gathers no moss.
SYRUS

Familiarity breeds contempt.
SYRUS

There are some remedies worse than the disease.
SYRUS

Cut off your nose to spite your face.
TALLEMENT DES REAUX

A cat may look at a king.
Title of a Pamphlet, 1652

That which is everybody's business
is nobody's business.
  Izaak Walton

What is the matter with Kansas!
  William Allen White

I will die in the last ditch.
  William of Orange

PROVIDENCE

And pleas'd th' Almighty's orders to
  perform,
Rides in the whirlwind and directs
  the storm.
  Addison—*The Campaign*

Fear not, but trust in Providence,
Wherever thou may'st be.
  Thomas Haynes Bayly—
  The Pilot

He that doth the ravens feed,
Yea, providently caters for the spar-
  row,
Be comfort to my age!
  Shakespeare—*As You Like It.*
  Act II. Sc. 3

There is a divinity that shapes our
  ends,
Rough-hew them how we will.
  Shakespeare—*Hamlet.* Act V.
  Sc. 2

I firmly believe in Divine Providence.
Without belief in Providence I
think I should go crazy. Without
God the world would be a maze
without a clue.
  Woodrow Wilson—Speech,
  1919

(See also CHANCE, CHRIST, DES-
  TINY, FATE, GOD, GODS.)

PRUDENCE

Put your trust in God, my boys, and
keep your powder dry.
  Col. Valentine Blacker

And it is a common saying that it is
best first to catch the stag, and afterwards, when he has been caught, to
skin him.
  Bracton

Dine on little, and sup on less.
  Cervantes

I recommend you to take care of the
minutes, for the hours will take care
of themselves.
  Chesterfield

Men are born with two eyes, but
with one tongue, in order that they
should see twice as much as they
say.
  Colton

People who live in glass houses
should not throw stones.
  English Proverb

The first years of man must make
provision for the last.
  Samuel Johnson

He that fights and runs away
Will live to fight another day.
  Old English Rhyme

I won't quarrel with my bread and
butter.
  Swift—*Polite Conversation*

(See also ADVICE, CARE, CAUTION,
  SAFETY, WISDOM.)

PRUDERY
See MODESTY, SECRECY

PUBLIC

We would not listen to those who were wont to say the voice of the people is the voice of God, for the voice of the mob is near akin to madness.

ALCUIN

The public! why, the public's nothing better than a great baby.

THOMAS CHALMERS

The public! the public! How many fools does it take to make up a public?

CHAMFORT

The public have neither shame nor gratitude.

HAZLITT

It is to the middle class we must look for the safety of England.

THACKERAY—*Four Georges*

The public be damned.

W. H. VANDERBILT

In a free and republican government, you cannot restrain the voice of the multitude. Every man will speak as he thinks, or, more properly, without thinking, and consequently will judge of effects without attending to their causes.

WASHINGTON

(See also DEMOCRACY, HUMANITY, PEOPLE.)

PUN

I never knew an enemy to puns who was not an ill-natured man.

LAMB

Of puns it has been said that those most dislike who are least able to utter them.

POE—*Marginalia*

He that would pun would pick a pocket.

POPE

(See also HUMOR, LAUGHTER.)

PUNCTUALITY

Unfaithfulness in the keeping of an appointment is an act of clear dishonesty. You may as well borrow a person's money as his time.

HORACE MANN

I have always been a quarter of an hour before my time, and it has made a man of me.

NELSON

(See also HASTE, PROMPTNESS, TIME.)

PUNISHMENT

Let them stew in their own grease (or juice).

BISMARCK

Eye for eye, tooth for tooth, hand for hand, foot for foot.

DEUTERONOMY. XIX. 21

My punishment is greater than I can bear.

GENESIS. IV. 13

Whoso sheddeth man's blood, by man shall his blood be shed.

GENESIS. IX. 6

My object all sublime
I shall achieve in time—
To let the punishment fit the crime.

W. S. GILBERT—*Mikado*

It is more dangerous that even a guilty person should be punished without the forms of law than that he should escape.
JEFFERSON, 1788

One man meets an infamous punishment for that crime which confers a diadem upon another.
JUVENAL

No one should be twice punished for one crime.
LEGAL MAXIM

It were better for him that a millstone were hanged about his neck, and he cast into the sea.
LUKE. XVII. 2

The object of punishment is, prevention from evil; it never can be made impulsive to good.
HORACE MANN

He that spareth his rod hateth his son.
PROVERBS. XIII. 24

The punishment of criminals should be of use; when a man is hanged he is good for nothing.
VOLTAIRE

(See also CRIME, JUDGMENT, JUSTICE, LAW, PAIN, PRISON.)

PURITY

Only the heart without a stain knows perfect ease.
GOETHE

The stream is always purer at its source.
PASCAL—Lettres Provinciales

Unto the pure all things are pure.
TITUS. I. 15

(See also CLEANLINESS, MODESTY, WOMAN.)

QUACK

Quacks pretend to cure other men's disorders, but fail to find a remedy for their own.
CICERO

Take the humbug out of this world, and you haven't much left to do business with.
H. W. SHAW

(See also DISEASE, HEALTH, HYPOCRISY, MEDICINE, SICKNESS.)

QUALITY

The best is the cheapest.
FRANKLIN

Quality, not quantity, is my measure.
DOUGLAS JERROLD

Many individuals have, like uncut diamonds, shining qualities beneath a rough exterior.
JUVENAL

Ye are the salt of the earth: but if the salt have lost his savour, wherewith shall it be salted?
MATTHEW. V. 13

Nothing endures but personal qualities.
WALT WHITMAN—Leaves of Grass

(See also CHARACTER, NOBILITY, WORTH.)

QUARRELING

He that blows the coals in quarrels
he has nothing to do with has no
right to complain if the sparks fly in
his face.
FRANKLIN

Those who in quarrels interpose,
Must often wipe a bloody nose.
GAY—*Fables*

A quarrel is quickly settled when
deserted by one party: there is no
battle unless there be two.
SENECA

In quarreling the truth is always lost.
SYRUS

(See also ANGER, ARGUMENT, CON-
TROVERSY, REBELLION, WAR.)

QUESTION

A fool may ask more questions in an
hour than a wise man can answer in
seven years.
ENGLISH PROVERB

Ask me no questions, and I'll tell
you no fibs.
GOLDSMITH—*She Stoops to
Conquer*

Questioning is not the mode of conversation among gentlemen.
SAMUEL JOHNSON

It is not every question that deserves
an answer.
SYRUS

(See also CONVERSATION, LEARN-
ING, LOGIC, SCIENCE, WISDOM.)

RACE

God hath made of one blood all nations of men.
ACTS XVII. 26

The race to which we belong is the
most arrogant and rapacious, the
most exclusive and indomitable in
history. All other races have been its
enemies or its victims.
INGALLS—Speech, 1890

Race is precisely of as much consequence in man as it is in any other
animal.
RUSKIN—*Modern Painters*

(See also BROTHERHOOD, HUMAN-
ITY, NATIONALISM.)

RAIN

After the rain cometh the fair
weather.
AESOP—*Fables*

Nature, like man, sometimes weeps
for gladness.
DISRAELI

It never rains but it pours.
ENGLISH PROVERB

The rain cometh down, and the
snow from heaven, and returneth
not thither, but watereth the earth,
and maketh it bring forth and bud,
that it may give seed to the sower,
and bread to the eater.
ISAIAH. LV. 10

Be still, sad heart, and cease repin-
ing;
Behind the clouds is the sun still
shining;
Thy fate is the common fate of all,
Into each life some rain must fall,
Some days must be dark and dreary.
LONGFELLOW—*The Rainy Day*

He shall come down like rain upon the mown grass.
PSALMS. LXXII. 6

I know Sir John will go, though he was sure it would rain cats and dogs.
SWIFT—*Polite Conversation*

Vexed sailors curse the rain for which poor shepherds prayed in vain.
EDMUND WALLER

(See also NATURE, SKY, STORM, SUNSHINE.)

RAINBOW

Triumphal arch, that fill'st the sky
When storms prepare to part,
I ask not proud Philosophy
To teach me what thou art.
CAMPBELL—*To the Rainbow*

Look upon the rainbow, and praise him that made it.
ECCLESIASTICUS. XLIII. 11

O beautiful rainbow;—all woven of light!
There's not in thy tissue one shadow of night;
Heaven surely is open when thou dost appear,
And, bending above thee, the angels draw near,
And sing,—"The rainbow! the rainbow!
The smile of God is here."
MRS. SARAH J. HALE—*Poems*

A rainbow in the morning
Is the Shepherd's warning;
But a rainbow at night
Is the Shepherd's delight.
OLD WEATHER RHYME

(See also NATURE, RAIN, SKY, STORM, SUNSHINE.)

READING

Reading is to the mind, what exercise is to the body.
ADDISON—*The Tatler*

Reading maketh a full man.
BACON—*Of Studies*

Read, mark, learn, and inwardly digest.
BOOK OF COMMON PRAYER

In science, read, by preference, the newest works; in literature, the oldest. The classic literature is always modern.
BULWER-LYTTON

My early and invincible love of reading, I would not exchange for the treasures of India.
GIBBON—*Memoirs*

When I am reading a book, whether wise or silly, it seems to me to be alive and talking to me.
SWIFT

He that runs may read.
TENNYSON—*The Flower*

Read the best books first, or you may not have a chance to read them at all.
THOREAU

(See also AUTHORSHIP, BOOKS, EDUCATION, JOURNALISM, LEARNING, NEWSPAPER, POETRY, STUDY.)

REASON

Reason is the mistress and queen of all things.
CICERO

He who will not reason, is a bigot; he who cannot is a fool; and he who dares not, is a slave.
WILLIAM DRUMMOND

Reasons are not like garments, the worse for wearing.
EARL OF ESSEX, 1598

Reason can in general do more than blind force.
GALLUS

If I go to heaven I want to take my reason with me.
INGERSOLL

Come now, and let us reason together.
ISAIAH. I. 18

Error of opinion may be tolerated where reason is left free to combat it.
JEFFERSON—Inaugural Address, 1801

Human reason is like a drunken man on horseback; set it up on one side, and it tumbles over on the other.
LUTHER

You know, my friends, with what a brave carouse
I made a second marriage in my house;
  Divorced old barren reason from my bed,
And took the daughter of the vine to spouse.
OMAR KHAYYÁM—Rubaiyat

The feast of reason and the flow of soul.
POPE

Every why hath a wherefore.
SHAKESPEARE—Comedy of Errors. Act II. Sc. 2

I have no other but a woman's reason.
I think him so because I think him so.
SHAKESPEARE—Two Gentlemen of Verona. Act I. Sc. 2

Many are destined to reason wrongly; others, not to reason at all; and others, to persecute those who do reason.
VOLTAIRE

Reason is the wise man's guide, example the fool's.
WELSH PROVERB

(See also ARGUMENT, INTELLECT, LOGIC, MIND, PHILOSOPHY, SCIENCE.)

REBELLION

Men seldom, or rather never for a length of time and deliberately, rebel against anything that does not deserve rebelling against.
CARLYLE—Essays

Rebellion to tyrants is obedience to God.
Motto on JEFFERSON's seal

A little rebellion now and then . . . is a medicine necessary for the sound health of government.
JEFFERSON—Letter to Madison

The only justification of rebellion is success.
THOMAS B. REED. Speech, 1878

(See also GOVERNMENT, OPPOSITION, REVOLUTION, SOLDIER, WAR.)

RECKLESSNESS
See CARELESSNESS

REDEMPTION
See RELIGION

REFLECTION
See THOUGHT

REFORM

Reforms should begin at home and stay there.
ANONYMOUS

At twenty a man is full of fight and hope. He wants to reform the world. When he's seventy he still wants to reform the world, but he knows he can't.
CLARENCE S. DARROW

But 'tis the talent of our English nation,
Still to be plotting some new reformation.
DRYDEN

We are reformers in Spring and Summer; in Autumn and Winter we stand by the old; reformers in the morning, conservers at night.
EMERSON—*The Conservative*

Reform must come from within, not from without. You cannot legislate for virtue.
JAMES CARDINAL GIBBONS

The hole and the patch should be commensurate.
JEFFERSON—Letter, 1787

To make a crooked stick straight, we bend it the contrary way.
MONTAIGNE

An indefinable something is to be done, in a way nobody knows how, at a time nobody knows when, that will accomplish nobody knows what.
THOMAS B. REED

(See also CHANGE, IMPROVEMENT, PROGRESS, REPENTANCE, REVOLUTION.)

REGRET
See REPENTANCE

RELATIVE

Dreadful indeed are the feuds of relatives, and difficult the reconciliation.
EURIPIDES

Visit your aunt, but not every day; and call at your brother's, but not every night.
FRANKLIN—*Poor Richard's Almanac*

And so do his sisters and his cousins and his aunts!
His sisters and his cousins
Whom he reckons up by dozens,
And his aunts!
W. S. GILBERT—*H.M.S. Pinafore*

No man will be respected by others who is despised by his own relatives.
PLAUTUS

The worst hatred is that of relatives.
TACITUS

Relations are simply a tedious pack of people who haven't got the remotest knowledge of how to live, nor the smallest instinct about when to die.
WILDE—*The Importance of Being Earnest*

(See also DAUGHTER, FATHER, HOME, MOTHER, PARENT.)

RELIGION

There was never law, or sect, or opinion did so much magnify goodness, as the Christian religion doth.
BACON—*Essays*

One religion is as true as another.
BURTON—*The Anatomy of Melancholy*

His religion at best is an anxious wish,—like that of Rabelais, a great Perhaps.
CARLYLE—*Burns*

Men will wrangle for religion; write for it; fight for it; die for it; anything but—live for it.
COLTON—*Lacon*

Religion, if in heavenly truths attired, Needs only to be seen to be admired.
COWPER—*Expostulation.*

If men are so wicked with religion, what would they be without it?
FRANKLIN

A good life is the only religion.
THOMAS FULLER

The best religion is the most tolerant.
MME. DE GIRARDIN

I don't go much on religion,
  I never ain't had no show;
But I've got a middlin' tight grip, sir,
  On the handful o' things I know.
I don't pan out on the prophets
  And free-will, and that sort of thing,—
But I b'lieve in God and the angels
  Ever sence one night last spring.
JOHN HAY—*Little Breeches*

I am for religion against religions.
VICTOR HUGO—*Les Misérables*

My creed is this:
  Happiness is the only good.
  The place to be happy is here.
  The time to be happy is now.
  The way to be happy is to help make others so.
INGERSOLL

To be of no Church is dangerous.
SAMUEL JOHNSON—*Life of Milton*

Religion is the opium of the people.
KARL MARX—*A Criticism of Hegelian Philosophy*

The world is my country, all mankind are my brethren, and to do good is my religion.
THOMAS PAINE—*The Age of Reason*

Religion is nothing else but love to God and man.
WILLIAM PENN

He that hath no cross deserves no crown.
QUARLES—*Esther*

So many gods, so many creeds—
  So many paths that wind and wind
  While just the art of being kind
Is all the sad world needs.
ELLA WHEELER WILCOX—*The World's Need*

(See also BELIEF, BIBLE, CHRISTIANITY, CHURCH, DOCTRINE, FAITH, GOD, HEAVEN, HELL, IMMORTALITY, PRAYER, PREACHING, RESURRECTION, RIGHTEOUSNESS, SABBATH, SCRIPTURE, SOUL, WORSHIP.)

REMORSE
See CONSCIENCE

REPENTANCE

To err is human, but the contrition felt for the crime distinguishes the virtuous from the wicked.

ALFIERI

If you would be good, first believe that you are bad.

EPICTETUS

Repentance is not so much remorse for what we have done as the fear of consequences.

LA ROCHEFOUCAULD

And while the lamp holds out to burn,
The vilest sinner may return.

ISAAC WATTS—*Hymns and Spiritual Songs*

(See also CHRISTIANITY, CON-SCIENCE, PRAYER, REFORM, SIN, SORROW.)

REPOSE

What sweet delight a quiet life affords.

DRUMMOND

Vulgar people can't be still.

HOLMES

Too much rest itself becomes a pain.

HOMER

(See also CONTENTMENT, PEACE, REST, SLEEP.)

REPUBLIC

Republics are ungrateful.

ANONYMOUS

A monarchy is a merchantman which sails well, but will sometimes strike on a rock, and go to the bottom; a republic is a raft which will never sink, but then your feet are always in water.

FISHER AMES—Speech, 1795

It is of great importance in a republic not only to guard against the oppression of its rulers, but to guard one part of society against the injustice of the other part.

ALEXANDER HAMILTON—*The Federalist*

A republican government is slow to move, yet when once in motion, its momentum becomes irresistible.

JEFFERSON—Letter, 1815

Republics are brought to their ends by luxury; monarchies by poverty.

MONTESQUIEU—*The Spirit of the Laws*

Republics exist only on tenure of being agitated.

WENDELL PHILLIPS, 1852

(See also DEMOCRACY, FREEDOM, GOVERNMENT, LIBERTY, PARTY, POLITICS.)

REPUTATION

How many people live on the reputation of the reputation they might have made!

HOLMES

When I did well, I heard it never;
When I did ill, I heard it ever.

OLD ENGLISH RHYME

The purest treasure mortal times afford
Is spotless reputation; that away,
Men are but gilded loam or painted clay.
>   SHAKESPEARE—*Richard II*. Act
>   I. Sc. 1

The reputation of a man is like his shadow,—gigantic when it precedes him, and pygmy in its proportions when it follows.
>   TALLEYRAND

Associate with men of good quality, if you esteem your own reputation; for it is better to be alone than in bad company.
>   WASHINGTON

(See also CHARACTER, FAME, GLORY, GOSSIP, HONOR, NAME, SCANDAL SLANDER.)

RESIGNATION

Welcome death, quoth the rat, when the trap fell.
>   THOMAS FULLER

A wise man cares not for what he cannot have.
>   HERBERT

The Lord gave, and the Lord hath taken away; blessed be the name of the Lord.
>   JOB. I. 21

That's best
Which God sends. 'Twas His will: it is mine.
>   OWEN MEREDITH—*Lucile*

Job feels the rod,
Yet blesses God.
>   NEW ENGLAND PRIMER

(See also HUMILITY, PATIENCE, RELIGION.)

RESOLUTION

I will sit down now, but the time will come when you will hear me.
>   DISRAELI—Maiden Speech in
>   the House of Commons

I am in earnest—I will not equivocate—I will not excuse—I will not retreat a single inch *and I will be heard*.
>   WILLIAM LLOYD GARRISON—
>   Salutatory of the Liberator,
>   1831

I propose to fight it out on this line if it takes all Summer.
>   ULYSSES S. GRANT—Dispatch
>   to Lincoln

Tell your master that if there were as many devils at Worms as tiles on its roofs, I would enter.
>   LUTHER

Never tell your resolution beforehand.
>   JOHN SELDEN—*Table Talk*

(See also ACTION, CHARACTER, COURAGE, DECISION, DEED, POWER, STRENGTH.)

RESPECTABILITY
See CHARACTER

REST

He that can take rest is greater than he that can take cities.
>   FRANKLIN—*Poor Richard's Almanac*

On the seventh day God ended his
work which he had made; and he
rested on the seventh day.
GENESIS. II. 2

Calm on the bosom of thy God,
Fair spirit! rest thee now!
FELICIA D. HEMANS—*Siege of
Valencia*

Come unto me, all ye that labor and
are heavy laden, and I will give you
rest.
MATTHEW. XI. 28

Take rest; a field that has rested gives
a bountiful crop.
OVID

Life's race well run,
Life's work well done,
Life's victory won,
  Now cometh rest.
DR. EDWARD H. PARKER

(See also DEATH, PEACE, REPOSE,
SILENCE, SLEEP.)

RESULT

They have sown the wind, and they
shall reap the whirlwind.
HOSEA. VIII. 7

By their fruits ye shall know them.
MATTHEW. VII. 20

Whoso diggeth a pit shall fall therein.
PROVERBS. XXVI. 27

(See also CAUSE, CIRCUMSTANCE.)

RESURRECTION

Earth to earth, ashes to ashes, dust
to dust, in sure and certain hope of
the resurrection.
BOOK OF COMMON PRAYER—
Burial of the Dead

For as in Adam all die, even so in
Christ shall all be made alive.
I CORINTHIANS. XV. 22

Many of them that sleep in the dust
of the earth shall awake, some to
everlasting life, and some to shame
and everlasting contempt.
DANIEL. XII. 2

The last loud trumpet's wondrous
  sound,
Shall thro' the rending tombs re-
  bound,
And wake the nations under ground.
WENTWORTH DILLON—*On the
Day of Judgment*

Shall man alone, for whom all else
  revives,
No resurrection know? Shall man
  alone,
Imperial man! be sown in barren
  ground,
Less privileged than grain, on which
  he feeds?
YOUNG—*Night Thoughts*

(See also CHRIST, DEATH, EASTER,
ETERNITY, FUTURE, GRAVE, IM-
MORTALITY, MORTALITY, RELI-
GION, SOUL.)

RETALIATION

I am accustomed to pay men back in
their own coin.
BISMARCK

And would'st thou evil for good re-
pay?
HOMER—*Odyssey*

(See also CRUELTY, PUNISHMENT,
RETRIBUTION, REVENGE.)

RETRIBUTION

The mills of the gods grind slowly,
but they grind exceedingly fine.
ENGLISH PROVERB

The way of transgressors is hard.
PROVERBS. XIII. 15

(See also COMPENSATION, CRIME,
PUNISHMENT, RETALIATION,
REVENGE.)

REVELATION

'Tis Revelation satisfies all doubts,
Explains all mysteries except her own.
COWPER—*The Task*

Nature is a revelation of God;
Art a revelation of man.
LONGFELLOW—*Hyperion*

(See also BIBLE, DOCTRINE, FUTURE,
GOD, PROPHECY, RELIGION,
SCRIPTURE, VISION.)

REVENGE

In taking revenge a man is but equal
to his enemy, but in passing it over
he is his superior.
BACON

Vengeance is a dish that should be
eaten cold.
ENGLISH PROVERB

Revenge is sweeter than life itself. So
think fools.
JUVENAL

Vengeance is sweet.
WILLIAM PAINTER—*The Palace
of Pleasure*

Not to be provoked is best; but if
moved, never correct till the fume is
spent; for every stroke our fury
strikes is sure to hit ourselves at last.
WILLIAM PENN

Revenge is an inhuman word.
SENECA

(See also ANGER, HATE, PASSION,
PUNISHMENT, RETALIATION,
RETRIBUTION.)

REVERENCE
See HONOR

REVOLUTION

Revolutions are not about trifles, but
spring from trifles.
ARISTOTLE—*Politics*

A reform is a correction of abuses; a
revolution is a transfer of power.
BULWER-LYTTON

Do you think then that revolutions
are made with rose water?
CHAMFORT to Marmontel, on
the excesses of the Revolution

At last I perceive that in revolutions
the supreme power finally rests with
the most abandoned.
DANTON

It is impossible to predict the time
and progress of revolution. It is governed by its own more or less mysterious laws. But when it comes it
moves irresistibly.
LENIN, 1918

It is not a revolt, it is a revolution.
DUC DE LIANCOURT to Louis
XVI, July 14, 1789

This country, with its institutions, belongs to the people who inhabit it. Whenever they shall grow weary of the existing government they can exercise their constitutional right of amending it, or their revolutionary right to dismember or overthrow it.

LINCOLN—Inaugural Address, 1861

Let the ruling classes tremble at a Communist revolution. The proletarians have nothing to lose but their chains. They have a world to win. Working men of all countries, unite!

KARL MARX AND FRIEDRICH ENGELS—*The Communist Manifesto*

Revolutions are not made; they come.

WENDELL PHILLIPS

If I were an American, as I am an Englishman, while a foreign troop was landed in my country I never would lay down my arms,—never! never! never!

WILLIAM PITT—Speech, 1777

Arise, ye prisoners of starvation,
Arise, ye wretched of the earth,
For justice thunders condemnation,
A better world's in birth.
No more tradition's chain shall bind us
Arise, ye slaves! no more in thrall!
The earth shall rise on new foundations,
We have been naught; we shall be all.

EUGENE POTTIER—*The Internationale*

(See also CHANGE, DEMOCRACY, FORCE, FREEDOM, GOVERNMENT, LIBERTY, MOB, POWER, REFORM, RIGHTS, ROYALTY, TYRANNY, WAR.)

REWARD
See COMPENSATION

RICHES

A little house well filled, a little land well tilled, and a little wife well willed, are great riches.

ANONYMOUS

Ah, if the rich were rich as the poor fancy riches!

EMERSON

The pleasures of the rich are bought with the tears of the poor.

THOMAS FULLER

Lay not up for yourselves treasures upon earth, where moth and rust doth corrupt, and where thieves break through and steal.

MATTHEW. VI. 19

A man's true wealth is the good he does in this world.

MOHAMMED

I am rich beyond the dreams of avarice.

EDWARD MOORE—*The Gamester*

It is the wretchedness of being rich that you have to live with rich people.

LOGAN PEARSALL SMITH

Nothing is so hard for those who abound in riches as to conceive how others can be in want.

SWIFT

That man is the richest whose pleasures are the cheapest.

THOREAU

(See also GOLD, MONEY, POVERTY, PROPERTY, PROSPERITY, WEALTH.)

RIDICULE

Cervantes smiled Spain's chivalry away.
BYRON

He will laugh thee to scorn.
ECCLESIASTICUS. XIII. 7

Resort is had to ridicule only when reason is against us.
JEFFERSON—Letter, 1813

There is only one step from the sublime to the ridiculous.
NAPOLEON

I have never made but one prayer to God, a very short one: "Oh Lord, make my enemies ridiculous." And God granted it.
VOLTAIRE—Letter, 1767

(See also CRITICISM, JESTING, LAUGHTER, SATIRE, SCANDAL, SNEER, WIT.)

RIGHT

The glittering and sounding generalities of natural right which make up the Declaration of Independence.
RUFUS CHOATE

Sir, I would rather be right than be President.
HENRY CLAY—Speech, 1850

He will hew to the line of right, let the chips fly where they may.
ROSCOE CONKLING—Speech, 1880

Be sure you are right, then go ahead.
DAVID CROCKETT

Two wrongs can never make a right.
ENGLISH PROVERB

Let us have faith that Right makes Might, and in that faith let us to the end dare to do our duty as we understand it.
LINCOLN—Second Inaugural Address

Right is the eternal sun; the world cannot delay its coming.
WENDELL PHILLIPS

One truth is clear, Whatever is is right.
POPE—Essay on Man

Heaven itself has ordained the right.
WASHINGTON

No question is ever settled
Until it is settled right.
ELLA WHEELER WILCOX

(See also JUSTICE, MORALITY, RIGHTS.)

RIGHTEOUSNESS

Be not righteous overmuch.
ECCLESIASTES. VII. 16

Righteousness exalteth a nation.
PROVERBS. XIV. 34

The righteous shall flourish like the palm-tree: he shall grow like a cedar in Lebanon.
PSALMS. XCII. 12

(See also CHARACTER, HUMANITY, MORALITY, RELIGION, RIGHT.)

RIGHTS

Among the natural rights of the colonists are these: First a right to life, secondly to liberty, thirdly to property; together with the right to defend them in the best manner they can.
SAMUEL ADAMS

We hold these truths to be self-evident,—that all men are created equal; that they are endowed by their Creator with certain unalienable rights; that among these are Life, Liberty, and the pursuit of happiness.

DECLARATION OF INDEPENDENCE

Wherever there is a human being, I see God-given rights inherent in that being, whatever may be the sex or complexion.

WILLIAM LLOYD GARRISON

The equal right of all men to the use of land is as clear as their equal right to breathe the air—it is a right proclaimed by the fact of their existence. For we cannot suppose that some men have a right to be in this world, and others no right.

HENRY GEORGE—*Progress and Poverty*

Equal rights for all, special privileges for none.

JEFFERSON

The constitution of Soviet Russia must insure equal rights for all citizens regardless of sex, creed, race, or nationality.

LENIN, 1917

(See also DEMOCRACY, EQUALITY, FREEDOM, GOVERNMENT, POLITICS.)

RIVER
See NATURE

ROMANCE
See LOVE

ROME

If you are at Rome live in the Roman style; if you are elsewhere live as they live elsewhere.

ST. AMBROSE TO ST. AUGUSTINE

Rome was not built in a day.

ANONYMOUS

All roads lead to Rome; but our antagonists think we should choose different paths.

LA FONTAINE

The grandeur that was Rome.

POE—*To Helen*

Would that the Roman people had but one neck!

SUETONIUS

(See also ITALY.)

ROYALTY

The king reigns but does not govern.

BISMARCK

That the king can do no wrong is a necessary and fundamental principle of the English constitution.

BLACKSTONE

Every noble crown is, and on Earth will forever be, a crown of thorns.

CARLYLE—*Past and Present*

Who made thee a prince and a judge over us?

EXODUS. II. 14

The trappings of a monarchy would set up an ordinary commonwealth.

SAMUEL JOHNSON—*Life of Milton*

Ah! vainest of all things
Is the gratitude of kings.
LONGFELLOW—*Belisarius*

I am the State.
LOUIS XIV of France

The King is dead! Long live the King!
PARDOE—*Life of Louis XIV*

Put not your trust in princes.
PSALMS. CXLVI. 3

Here lies our sovereign lord, the king,
Whose word no man relies on,
Who never said a foolish thing,
And never did a wise one.
EARL OF ROCHESTER—*To Charles II*

Uneasy lies the head that wears a crown.
SHAKESPEARE—*Henry IV*. Pt. II. Act III. Sc. 1

Ay, every inch a king.
SHAKESPEARE—*King Lear*. Act IV. Sc. 6

(See also GOVERNMENT, NOBILITY, POLITICS, POWER, STATESMAN-SHIP, WAR.)

RUIN

While in the progress of their long decay,
Thrones sink to dust, and nations pass away.
EARL OF CARLISLE—*On the Ruins of Paestum*

The ruins of himself! now worn away
With age, yet still majestic in decay.
HOMER—*Odyssey*

Babylon is fallen, is fallen.
ISAIAH. XXI. 9

Red ruin and the breaking-up of all.
TENNYSON—*Idylls of the King*

(See also MISFORTUNE.)

RUMOR

"They say so" is half a lie.
THOMAS FULLER

I cannot tell how the truth may be;
I say the tale as 'twas said to me.
SCOTT—*Lay of the Last Minstrel*

What some invent the rest enlarge.
SWIFT

Tattlers also and busybodies, speaking things which they ought not.
I TIMOTHY. V. 13

(See also GOSSIP, NEWS, SCANDAL, SLANDER.)

SABBATH

Of all the days that's in the week,
I dearly love but one day,
And that's the day that comes betwixt
A Saturday and Monday.
HENRY CAREY—*Sally in Our Alley*

Some keep the Sabbath going to church;
I keep it staying at home,
With a bobolink for a chorister,
And an orchard for a dome.
EMILY DICKINSON—*A Service of Song*

Remember the sabbath day, to keep it holy. Six days shalt thou labor, and do all thy work: but the seventh day is the sabbath of the Lord thy God.
EXODUS. XX. 8–11

God blessed the seventh day, and sanctified it: because that in it he had rested from all his work which God created and made.
GENESIS. II. 3

Day of the Lord, as all our days should be!
LONGFELLOW—*Christus*

The Sabbath was made for man, and not man for the Sabbath.
MARK. II. 27

(See also CHRISTIANITY, CHURCH, RELIGION, REST.)

SACRIFICE

What millions died—that Caesar might be great!
CAMPBELL—*Pleasures of Hope*

He is brought as a lamb to the slaughter.
ISAIAH. LIII. 7

It is easier to sacrifice great than little things.
MONTAIGNE

(See also MARTYR, RELIGION.)

SADNESS
See SORROW

SAFETY

It is better to be safe than sorry.
AMERICAN PROVERB

The trodden path is the safest.
LEGAL MAXIM

The desire for safety stands against every great and noble enterprise.
TACITUS

(See also CARE, CAUTION, PRUDENCE.)

SAILOR

The wonder is always new that any sane man can be a sailor.
EMERSON—*English Traits*

The wind that blows, the ship that goes
And the lass that loves a sailor.
OLD ENGLISH TOAST

They that go down to the sea in ships, that do business in great waters; these see the works of the Lord, and his wonders in the deep.
PSALMS. XVII. 23–24

Sailors get money like horses and spend it like asses.
SMOLLETT

(See also NAVY, OCEAN, SHIP.)

SARCASM
See SATIRE

SATAN
See DEVIL

SATIRE

It has been my constant aim in all my writings to lash vice, but to spare persons.
MARTIAL

Satire will always be unpleasant to those that deserve it.

THOMAS SHADWELL

Satire lies about literary men while they live and eulogy lies about them when they die.

VOLTAIRE

In my youth I thought of writing a satire on mankind; but now in my age I think I should write an apology for them.

HORACE WALPOLE

(See also CRITICISM, EPITAPH, HUMOR, JESTING, JOKE, LAUGHTER, SNEER, SPEECH, WIT.)

SATISFACTION

If the crow had been satisfied to eat his prey in silence, he would have had more meat and less quarreling and envy.

HORACE

My cup runneth over.

PSALMS. XXIII. 5

Enough is as good as a feast.

JOSHUA SYLVESTER—*Works*

(See also CONTENTMENT, HAPPINESS.)

SAVING
See THRIFT

SCANDAL

There is so much good in the worst of us,
And so much bad in the best of us,
That it hardly becomes any one of us
To talk about the rest of us.

ANONYMOUS

Scandal is what one-half the world takes pleasure in inventing, and the other half in believing.

CHATFIELD

(See also GOSSIP, NAME, RUMOR, SLANDER, TALK.)

SCHOOL
See TEACHING

SCIENCE

Art is I; science is we.

CLAUDE BERNARD

Every great advance in science has issued from a new audacity of imagination.

JOHN DEWEY—*The Quest for Certainty*

Steam is no stronger now than it was a hundred years ago, but it is put to better use.

EMERSON

Science and art belong to the whole world, and before them vanish the barriers of nationality.

GOETHE

Science is a first-rate piece of furniture for a man's upper chamber, if he has common sense on the ground floor.

HOLMES

Science is simply common sense at its best—that is, rigidly accurate in observation, and merciless to fallacy in logic.

T. H. HUXLEY

Science is the systematic classification of experience.

GEORGE HENRY LEWES

Science is nothing but perception.
PLATO

Science is nothing but developed perception, interpreted intent, common sense rounded out and minutely articulated.
SANTAYANA—*The Life of Reason*

Science is organized knowledge.
SPENCER—*Education*

Science falsely so called.
I TIMOTHY. VI. 20

(See also FACTS, INTELLECT, INVENTION, KNOWLEDGE, LEARNING, MIND, NATURE, PHILOSOPHY, STUDY.)

SCORN
See SNEER

SCOTLAND

Give me but one hour of Scotland,
Let me see it ere I die.
WILLIAM E. AYTOUN

Long may thy hardy sons of rustic toil
 Be blest with health, and peace, and sweet content.
BURNS—*Cotter's Saturday Night*

O Caledonia! stern and wild,
Meet nurse for a poetic child!
Land of brown heath and shaggy wood,
Land of the mountain and the flood,
Land of my sires! what mortal hand
Can e'er untie the filial band,
That knits me to thy rugged strand!
SCOTT—*Lay of the Last Minstrel*

SCRIPTURE

A glory gilds the sacred page,
 Majestic like the sun,
It gives a light to every age,
 It gives, but borrows none.
COWPER—*Olney Hymns*

Thy word is a lamp unto my feet and a light unto my path.
PSALMS. CXIX. 105

We search the world for truth; we cull
The good, the pure, the beautiful,
From all old flower fields of the soul;
And, weary seekers of the best,
We come back laden from our quest,
To find that all the sages said
Is in the Book our mothers read.
WHITTIER—*Miriam*

(See also BIBLE, CHRISTIANITY, RELIGION, REVELATION.)

SCULPTURE

Madame de Staël pronounced architecture to be frozen music; so is statuary crystallized spirituality.
ALCOTT

It was Dante who called this noble art God's grandchild.
WASHINGTON ALLSTON

Then marble, soften'd into life, grew warm.
POPE—*Second Book of Horace*

(See also ART, CULTURE.)

SEA

All the rivers run into the sea, yet the sea is not full.
ECCLESIASTES. I. 7

I never saw the use of the sea. Many a sad heart it has caused, and many a sick stomach has it occasioned. The boldest sailor climbs on board with a heavy soul, and leaps on land with a light spirit.
DISRAELI—*Vivian Grey*

Praise the sea; on shore remain.
JOHN FLORIO

He that will learn to pray, let him go to sea.
HERBERT

I must go down to the seas again, to the lonely sea and the sky,
And all I ask is a tall ship and a star to steer her by.
MASEFIELD—*Sea-Fever*

The sea hath no king but God alone.
ROSSETTI—*The White Ship*

Break, break, break,
On thy cold gray stones, O sea!
And I would that my tongue could utter
The thoughts that arise in me.
TENNYSON

(See also NAVIGATION, NAVY, OCEAN, SHIP.)

SEASONS

Autumn to winter, winter into spring,
Spring into summer, summer into fall,—
So rolls the changing year, and so we change;
Motion so swift, we know not that we move.
DINAH MULOCK CRAIK—*Immutable*

Spring is a virgin, Summer a mother, Autumn a widow, and Winter a stepmother.
POLISH PROVERB

(See also AUTUMN, NATURE, SPRING, SUMMER, WINTER.)

SECRECY

There is a skeleton in every house.
ANONYMOUS

A man can hide all things, excepting twain—
That he is drunk, and that he is in love.
ANTIPHANES

The secret things belong unto the Lord our God.
DEUTERONOMY. XXIX. 29

Nothing is secret which shall not be made manifest.
LUKE. VIII. 17

Tell it not in Gath; publish it not in the streets of Askelon.
II SAMUEL. I. 20

If you would wish another to keep your secret, first keep it yourself.
SENECA

(See also CURIOSITY, INQUISITIVENESS, SOLITUDE, STRATEGY.)

SELFISHNESS

The force of selfishness is as inevitable and as calculable as the force of gravitation.
HAILLIARD

The same people who can deny others everything are famous for refusing themselves nothing.
LEIGH HUNT

That man who lives for self alone
Lives for the meanest mortal known.
JOAQUIN MILLER—*Walker in Nicaragua*

Despite those titles, power, and pelf,
The wretch, concentred all in self,
Living, shall forfeit fair renown,
And, doubly dying, shall go down
'To the vile dust from whence he sprung,
Unwept, unhonour'd and unsung.
SCOTT—*Lay of the Last Minstrel*

Selfishness is the only real atheism; aspiration, unselfishness, the only real religion.
ZANGWILL—*Children of the Ghetto*

(See also CONCEIT, POSSESSION, PRIDE, SELF-LOVE, VANITY.)

SELF-KNOWLEDGE

He who knows himself best esteems himself least.
H. G. BOHN

Oh, wad some power the giftie gie us
To see oursels as ithers see us!
It wad frae monie a blunder free us,
And foolish notion.
ROBERT BURNS—*To a Louse*

Thales was asked what was most difficult to man; he answered: "To know one's self."
DIOGENES

We know what we are, but know not what we may be.
SHAKESPEARE—*Hamlet.* Act IV. Sc. 5

Know thyself.
Attributed to SOCRATES

(See also CHARACTER, EDUCATION, INDIVIDUALITY, QUALITY, SUCCESS.)

SELF-LOVE

He was like a cock who thought the sun had risen to hear him crow.
GEORGE ELIOT—*Adam Bede*

He that falls in love with himself will have no rivals.
FRANKLIN

Self-love is the greatest of all flatterers.
LA ROCHEFOUCAULD

All men love themselves.
PLAUTUS

I to myself am dearer than a friend.
SHAKESPEARE—*Two Gentlemen of Verona.* Act II. Sc. 6

To love one's self is the beginning of a life-long romance.
WILDE

(See also CONCEIT, EGOTISM, PRIDE, SELFISHNESS, VANITY.)

SELF-MADE

He is a self-made man, and worships his creator.
JOHN BRIGHT, referring tc Disraeli.

Every man is the architect of his own fortune.
ENGLISH PROVERB

Our self-made men are the glory of our institutions.
WENDELL PHILLIPS

(See also ACTION, AMBITION, CHARACTER, DEED, DECISION, EDUCATION, PROGRESS, SUCCESS.)

SELF-PRAISE

God hates those who praise themselves.
ST. CLEMENT

If you wish in this world to advance
Your merits you're bound to enhance;
  You must stir it and stump it,
  And blow your own trumpet,
Or, trust me, you haven't a chance.
W. S. GILBERT—*Ruddigore*

Let another man praise thee, and not thine own mouth.
PROVERBS. XXVII. 2

(See also EGOTISM, VANITY.)

SELF-RELIANCE

Doubt whom you will, but never yourself.
BOVEE

No man should part with his own individuality and become that of another.
CHANNING

Think wrongly, if you please, but in all cases think for yourself.
LESSING

I have ever held it as a maxim never to do that through another which it was possible for me to execute myself.
MONTESQUIEU

A man is a lion in his own cause.
SCOTTISH PROVERB

For they can conquer who believe they can.
VERGIL

(See also CHARACTER, DECISION, INDIVIDUALITY, RESOLUTION, STRENGTH, SUCCESS.)

SELF-SACRIFICE

Whether on the scaffold high,
  Or in the battle's van,
The fittest place where man can die
  Is where he dies for man.
MICHAEL JOSEPH BARRY—*The Place to Die*

Greater love hath no man than this, that a man lay down his life for his friends.
JOHN. XV. 13

Then out spake brave Horatius,
  The captain of the gate:
"To every man upon this earth
  Death cometh soon or late.
And how can man die better
  Than facing fearful odds,
For the ashes of his fathers
  And the temples of his gods?"
MACAULAY—*Lays of Ancient Rome*

(See also CHARACTER, HUMANITY, MARTYR.)

SENSE
See COMMON SENSE

SERVICE

They also serve who only stand and wait.
MILTON—*On His Blindness*

Servant of God, well done.
MILTON—*Paradise Lost*

They serve God well,
Who serve his creatures.
CAROLINE NORTON—*The Lady of La Garaye*

My heart is ever at your service.
SHAKESPEARE—*Timon of Athens.* Act I. Sc. 2

He profits most who serves best.
ARTHUR F. SHELDON—Motto for Rotary International

(See also DUTY, HELP, KINDNESS, PHILANTHROPY.)

SEX
See LOVE

SHADOW

What shadows we are, what shadows we pursue!
BURKE—Speech, 1775

Coming events cast their shadows before.
CAMPBELL—*Lochiel's Warning*

Shadows are in reality, when the sun is shining, the most conspicuous thing in a landscape, next to the highest lights.
RUSKIN—*Painting*

(See also DARKNESS, EVENING, NIGHT, OBSCURITY.)

SHAKESPEARE

No man is too busy to read Shakespeare.
CHARLES BUXTON

Now you who rhyme, and I who rhyme,
Have not we sworn it, many a time,
That we no more our verse would scrawl,
For Shakespeare he had said it all!
R. W. GILDER—*The Modern Rhymer*

Whatever can be known of the heart of man may be found in Shakespeare's plays.
GOETHE

If we wish to know the force of human genius we should read Shakespeare. If we wish to see the insignificance of human learning we may study his commentators.
HAZLITT—*On the Ignorance of the Learned*

He was not of an age, but for all time!
BEN JONSON—*Line to the Memory of Shakespeare*

Shakespeare has had neither equal nor second.
MACAULAY

SHAME

Shame is an ornament to the young; a disgrace to the old.
ARISTOTLE

I count him lost, who is lost to shame.
PLAUTUS

We live in an atmosphere of shame. We are ashamed of everything that is real about us; ashamed of ourselves, of our relatives, of our incomes, of our accents, of our opinion, of our experience, just as we are ashamed of our naked skins.

> GEORGE BERNARD SHAW—*Man and Superman*

O shame! Where is thy blush?

> SHAKESPEARE—*Hamlet.* Act III. Sc. 4

(See also CONSCIENCE, DISGRACE, GUILT, HONOR.)

SHEEP

Baa, baa, black sheep,
  Have you any wool?
Yes, marry, have I
  Three bags full:
One for the master,
  And one for my dame,
And one for the little boy
  Who lives in the lane.

> NURSERY RHYME

A leap year
Is never a good sheep year.

> OLD ENGLISH SAYING

(See also ANIMALS, LAMB.)

SHIP

She walks the waters like a thing of life,
And seems to dare the elements to strife.

> BYRON—*The Corsair*

For she *is* such a smart little craft,
Such a neat little, sweet little craft—
  Such a bright little,
  Tight little,
  Slight little,
  Light little,
Trim little, slim little craft!

> W. S. GILBERT—*Ruddigore*

Being in a ship is being in a jail, with the chance of being drowned.

> SAMUEL JOHNSON—*Boswell's Life of Johnson*

Don't give up the ship!

> JAMES LAWRENCE, commander of the *Chesapeake,* 1813

Ships that pass in the night.

> LONGFELLOW—*Tales of a Wayside Inn,* 1893

They that go down to the sea in ships, that do business in great waters.

> PSALMS. CVII. 23

Ships are but boards, sailors but men.

> SHAKESPEARE—*The Merchant of Venice.* Act I. Sc. 3

Every drunken skipper trusts to Providence. But one of the ways of Providence with drunken skippers is to run them on the rocks.

> GEORGE BERNARD SHAW— *Heartbreak House*

There breaks in every Gloucester wave
A widowed woman's heart.

> ELIZABETH WARD—*Gloucester Harbor*

If all the ships I have at sea
Should come a-sailing home to me,
  Ah, well! the harbor would not hold
So many ships as there would be
If all my ships came home from sea.

> ELLA WHEELER WILCOX—*My Ships*

(See also NAVIGATION, NAVY, OCEAN, SEA.)

SHIPWRECK
See SHIP

SHOEMAKING

Him that makes shoes go barefoot
himself.
> BURTON—*Anatomy of Melan-
> choly*

I can tell where my own shoe pinches
me.
> CERVANTES—*Don Quixote*

Shoemaker, stick to your last.
> Proverb quoted by PLINY THE
> ELDER

(See also CLOTHES, DRESS.)

SICKNESS

Be not slow to visit the sick.
> ECCLESIASTICUS. VII. 35

Sickness is a belief, which must be
annihilated by the divine Mind.
> MARY BAKER EDDY—*Science
> and Health*

Prevention is better than cure.
> ERASMUS—*Adagia*

Some maladies are rich and precious
and only to be acquired by the right
of inheritance or purchased with
gold.
> HAWTHORNE—*The Old Manse*

The whole head is sick, and the
whole heart faint.
> ISAIAH. I. 5

(See also DISEASE, HEALTH, MEDI-
CINE, MIND, QUACK, WOUND.)

SIGHT
See EYE

SILENCE

Silence gives consent.
> POPE BONIFACE VIII

Silence is more eloquent than words.
> CARLYLE—*Heroes and Hero-
> Worship*

Silence is the unbearable repartee.
> CHESTERTON

Still waters run deep.
> ENGLISH PROVERB

Speech is silver; silence is golden.
> GERMAN PROVERB

Vessels never give so great a sound
as when they are empty.
> BISHOP JOHN JEWELL

It is a great misfortune neither to
have enough wit to talk well nor
enough judgment to be silent.
> LA BRUYÈRE

Keep quiet and people will think you
a philosopher.
> LATIN PROVERB

Blessed are they who have nothing to
say, and who cannot be persuaded to
say it.
> LOWELL

Be silent and safe—silence never betrays you.
> JOHN BOYLE O'REILLY—*Rules
> of the Road*

He that keepeth his mouth keepeth
his life; but he that openeth wide his
lips shall have destruction.
> PROVERBS. XIII. 3

Bekker is silent in seven languages.
SCHLEIERMACHER

The rest is silence.
SHAKESPEARE—*Hamlet.* Act V.
Sc. 2

Smooth runs the water where the
brook is deep.
SHAKESPEARE—*Henry VI.* Pt.
II. Act III. Sc. 1

I regret often that I have spoken;
never that I have been silent.
SYRUS

(See also PEACE, REPOSE, REST,
SOLITUDE, SOUND, SPEECH.)

SIMPLICITY

Nothing is more simple than greatness; indeed, to be simple is to be
great.
EMERSON—*Literary Ethics*

Simplicity of character is the natural
result of profound thought.
HAZLITT

Affected simplicity is refined impos-
ture.
LA ROCHEFOUCAULD

The fewer our wants, the nearer we
resemble the gods.
SOCRATES

A man is simple when his chief care
is the wish to be what he ought to be,
that is, honestly and naturally human.
CHARLES WAGNER—*Simple
Life*

(See also APPEARANCE, BABYHOOD,
CHARACTER, CHILDHOOD, INNO-
CENCE, MANNERS, YOUTH.)

SIN

O sin, what hast thou done to this
fair earth!
R. H. DANA

He that falls into sin is a man; that
grieves at it, is a saint; that boasteth
of it, is a devil.
THOMAS FULLER—*Holy State*

Poverty and wealth are comparative
sins.
VICTOR HUGO

He that is without sin among you,
let him cast the first stone.
JOHN. VIII. 7

Jesus said unto her, Neither do I
condemn thee: go, and sin no more.
JOHN. VIII. 11

The sin they do by two and two they
must pay for one by one.
KIPLING—*Tomlinson*

So many laws argue so many sins.
MILTON—*Paradise Lost*

It is not alone what we do, but also
what we do not do, for which we are
accountable.
MOLIÈRE

In Adam's Fall
We sinned all.
NEW ENGLAND PRIMER

O thou, who didst with pitfall and
with gin
Beset the road I was to wander in,
Thou wilt not with predestin'd evil
round
Enmesh, and then impute my fall to
sin.
OMAR KHAYYÁM—*Rubaiyat*

My son, if sinners entice thee, consent thou not.
PROVERBS. I. 10

The way of transgressors is hard.
PROVERBS. XIII. 15

The wages of sin is death.
ROMANS. VI. 23

I am a man
More sinn'd against than sinning.
SHAKESPEARE—*King Lear*. Act
III. Sc. 2

There is no sin. There are only stages
of development.
TIBETAN PROVERB

But he who never sins can little boast
Compared to him who goes and
sins no more!
N. P. WILLIS—*The Lady Jane*

(See also CRIME, EVIL, FAULT, FOR-
GIVENESS, GUILT, VICE, WICKED-
NESS.)

SINCERITY

Of all the evil spirits abroad at this
hour in the world, insincerity is the
most dangerous.
FROUDE—*Short Studies on
Great Subjects*

There is no greater delight than to
be conscious of sincerity on self-
examination.
MENCIUS

A little sincerity is a dangerous thing,
and a great deal of it is absolutely
fatal.
WILDE—*The Critic as Artist*

(See also CHARACTER, HONESTY,
TRUTH.)

SINGING
See SONG

SKEPTICISM

Skepticism means, not intellectual
doubt alone, but moral doubt.
CARLYLE—*Heroes and Hero-
Worship*

Skeptics are never deceived.
FRENCH PROVERB

I am ready to reject all belief and
reasoning, and can look upon no
opinion even as more probable or
likely than another.
HUME—*A Treatise on Human
Nature*

Believe nothing and be on your guard
against everything.
LATIN PROVERB

With most people, doubt about one
thing is simply blind belief in another.
G. C. LICHTENBERG

Great intellects are skeptical.
NIETZSCHE

(See also DOUBT, INTELLECT, LOGIC,
SCIENCE, THOUGHT.)

SKY

And that inverted Bowl they call the
Sky,
Whereunder crawling coop'd we live
and die,
Lift not your hands to it for help—
for it
As impotently moves as you or I.
OMAR KHAYYÁM—*Rubaiyat*

Sometimes gentle, sometimes capricious, sometimes awful, never the same for two moments together; almost human in its passions, almost spiritual in its tenderness, almost Divine in its infinity.

RUSKIN—*The Sky*

(See also HEAVEN, MOON, NATURE, RAIN, SUNRISE, SUNSET, THUNDER, TWILIGHT.)

SLANDER

I hate the man who builds his name
On ruins of another's fame.

GAY—*The Poet and the Rose*

If slander be a snake, it is a winged one—it flies as well as creeps.

DOUGLAS JERROLD—*Slander*

Never throw mud. You may miss your mark, but you must have dirty hands.

JOSEPH PARKER

I am disgrac'd, impeach'd and baffled here,—
Pierc'd to the soul with slander's venom'd spear.

SHAKESPEARE—*Richard II.* Act I. Sc. 1

A slander is like a hornet; if you cannot kill it dead the first blow, better not strike at it.

H. W. SHAW

(See also CALUMNY, GOSSIP, LYING, RUMOR, SCANDAL, SPEECH, TALK, TONGUE, WORD.)

SLAVERY

If you put a chain around the neck of a slave, the other end fastens itself around your own.

EMERSON—*Compensation*

Corrupted freemen are the worst slaves.

DAVID GARRICK

The compact which exists between the North and the South is a covenant with death and an agreement with hell; involving both parties in atrocious criminality, and should be immediately annulled.

WILLIAM LLOYD GARRISON

The man who gives me employment, which I must have or suffer, that man is my master, let me call him what I will.

HENRY GEORGE—*Social Problems*

I believe this government cannot endure permanently half slave and half free.

LINCOLN—Speech, 1858

They are slaves who fear to speak
For the fallen and the weak;

. . .

They are slaves who dare not be
In the right with two or three.

LOWELL—*Stanzas on Freedom*

They (the blacks) had no right which the white man was bound to respect.

ROGER B. TANEY—*The Dred Scott Case*

Englishmen never will be slaves; they are free to do whatever the Government and public opinion allow them to do.

GEORGE BERNARD SHAW—*Man and Superman*

That execrable sum of all villainies
commonly called the Slave-trade.
JOHN WESLEY—*Journal*

(See also EQUALITY, FREEDOM,
HUMANITY, INDEPENDENCE,
LABOR, LIBERTY, RIGHTS.)

SLEEP

Over my slumber your loving watch
   keep—
Rock me to sleep, mother; rock me to
   sleep.
ELIZABETH AKERS ALLEN

Sleep is the best cure for waking
troubles.
CERVANTES

The sleep of a labouring man is
sweet.
ECCLESIASTES. V. 12

Fatigue is the best pillow.
FRANKLIN

Great eaters and great sleepers are
incapable of anything else that is
great.
HENRY IV of France

One hour's sleep before midnight is
worth three after.
GEORGE HERBERT

       Soft closer of our eyes!
Low murmurer of tender lullabies!
KEATS—*Sleep and Poetry*

Sleep, rest of nature, O sleep, most
gentle of the divinities, peace of the
soul, thou at whose presence care
disappears, who soothest hearts
wearied with daily employments,
and makest them strong again for
labour!
OVID—*Metamorphoses*

I will both lay me down in peace,
and sleep: for thou, Lord, only
makest me dwell in safety.
PSALMS. IV. 8

He giveth His beloved sleep.
PSALMS. CXXVII. 2

I never sleep comfortably except
when I am at sermon or when I pray
to God.
RABELAIS—*Gargantua*

She slept the sleep of the just.
RACINE

To all, to each, a fair good-night,
And pleasing dreams, and slumbers
   light.
SCOTT—*Marmion*

To sleep! perchance to dream; ay,
   there's the rub;
For in that sleep of death what
   dreams may come,
When we have shuffled off this
   mortal coil,
Must give us pause.
SHAKESPEARE—*Hamlet*. Act
III. Sc. 1

O sleep, O gentle sleep,
Nature's soft nurse.
SHAKESPEARE—*Henry IV*. Part
II. Act III. Sc. 1

Hush, my dear, lie still and slumber!
   Holy angels guard thy bed!
Heavenly blessings without number
   Gently falling on thy head.
ISAAC WATTS—*Cradle Hymn*

(See also DEATH, DREAMS, NIGHT,
REPOSE, REST.)

SMILE

What's the use of worrying?
  It never was worth while, so
Pack up your troubles in your old
    kit-bag,
  And smile, smile, smile.
    GEORGE ASAF—*Smile, Smile,
    Smile.*

Smiles form the channels of a future
tear.
    BYRON—*Childe Harold*

The thing that goes the farthest to-
    wards making life worth while,
That costs the least, and does the
    most, is just a pleasant smile.

· · ·

It's full of worth and goodness too,
    with manly kindness blent,
It's worth a million dollars and it
    doesn't cost a cent.
    WILBUR D. NESBIT—*Let Us
    Smile*

There is a snake in thy smile, my
dear,
And bitter poison within thy tear.
    SHELLEY—*Beatrice Cenci*

'Tis easy enough to be pleasant,
  When life flows along like a
    song;
But the man worth while is the one
    who will smile
  When everything goes dead wrong.
    ELLA WHEELER WILCOX—
    Worth While

(See also FACE, HAPPINESS, JOY,
    LAUGHTER, MERRIMENT.)

SNEER

Who can refute a sneer?
    WILLIAM PALEY

It is just as hard to do your duty
when men are sneering at you as
when they are shooting at you.
    WOODROW WILSON—Speech,
    1914

(See also SATIRE.)

SNOW

Year of snow
Fruit will grow.
    OLD ENGLISH RHYME

But where are the snows of yester-
year?
    VILLON

O the snow, the beautiful snow,
Filling the sky and earth below;
Over the house-tops, over the street,
Over the heads of the people you
    meet,
  Dancing, flirting, skimming along.
    JAMES W. WATSON—*Beautiful
    Snow*

(See also NATURE, WINTER.)

SOCIALISM

Socialism is that contemplated system
of industrial society which proposes
the abolition of private property in
the great material instruments of
production, and the substitution
therefor of collective property; and
advocates the collective management
of production, together with the dis-
tribution of social income by society,
and private property in the larger
proportion of this social income.
    RICHARD T. ELY—*Socialism
    and Social Reform*

The ideal of Socialism is grand and noble; and it is, I am convinced, possible of realization; but such a state of society cannot be manufactured—it must grow. Society is an organism, not a machine.
HENRY GEORGE—*Progress and Poverty*

These monstrous views, . . . these venomous teachings.
POPE LEO XIII

Socialism is not at all the enemy of civilization. It only wants to extend civilization to all humanity; under capitalism, civilization is the monopoly of a privileged minority.
WILLIAM LIEBKNECHT

What is characteristic of socialism is the joint ownership by all members of the community of the instruments and means of production, which carries with it the consequence that the division of all the produce among the body of owners must be a public act performed according to the rules laid down by the community.
JOHN STUART MILL—*The Principles of Political Economy*

All Socialism involves slavery.
SPENCER—*The Coming Slavery*

(See also CAPITAL AND LABOR, COMMUNISM, DEMOCRACY, INDUSTRY, PROGRESS, POVERTY, WEALTH.)

SOCIETY

Society would be a charming affair if we were only interested in one another.
CHAMFORT

These families, you know, are our upper crust, not upper ten thousand.
COOPER—*The Ways of the Hour*

He might have proved a useful adjunct, if not an ornament to society.
LAMB—*Captain Starkey*

Man is a social animal.
SENECA

It is impossible, in our condition of Society, not to be sometimes a Snob.
THACKERAY—*Book of Snobs*

To get into the best society nowadays, one has either to feed people, amuse people, or shock people.
WILDE—*A Woman of No Importance*

Other people are quite dreadful. The only possible society is oneself.
WILDE—*An Ideal Husband*

There is
One great society alone on earth:
The noble Living and noble Dead.
WORDSWORTH—*The Prelude*

(See also ANCESTRY, CONVERSATION, FASHION, GOSSIP, LIFE, MANNERS.)

SOLDIER

The king of France with twenty thousand men
Went up the hill, and then came down again:
The king of Spain with twenty thousand more
Climbed the same hill the French had climbed before.
ANONYMOUS

God and a soldier all people adore
In time of war, but not before;
And when war is over and all things
    are righted,
God is neglected and an old soldier
    slighted.
    ANONYMOUS

See! There is Jackson standing like a
stone wall.
    BERNARD E. BEE—Battle of
    Manassas

How sleep the brave, who sink to
    rest,
By all their country's wishes blest!
    WILLIAM COLLINS—Ode

We are coming, Father Abraham,
three hundred thousand more.
    J. S. GIBBONS

Every citizen should be a soldier.
This was the case with the Greeks
and Romans, and must be that of
every free state.
    JEFFERSON—Letter, 1813

Let not him that girdeth on his har-
ness boast himself as he that putteth
it off.
    I KINGS. XX. 11

For it's Tommy this an' Tommy
    that, and "Chuck 'im out, the
    brute."
But it's "Savior of 'is country," when
    the guns begin to shoot.
    KIPLING—Tommy

It is not the guns or armament
    Or the money they can pay,
It's the close co-operation
    That makes them win the day.
It is not the individual
    Or the army as a whole,
But the everlastin' teamwork
    Of every bloomin' soul.
    J. MASON KNOX

But in a larger sense we cannot
dedicate, we cannot consecrate, we
cannot hallow this ground. The brave
men, living and dead, who struggled
here, have consecrated it far above
our poor power to add or detract.
    LINCOLN—Gettysburg Address

The muffled drum's sad roll has beat
    The soldier's last tattoo;
No more on Life's parade shall meet
    The brave and fallen few.
On Fame's eternal camping-ground
    Their silent tents are spread,
And Glory guards, with solemn
    round
    The bivouac of the dead.
    THEODORE O'HARA—The
    Bivouac of the Dead

I want to see you shoot the way
you shout.
    THEODORE ROOSEVELT

A soldier is an anachronism of which
we must get rid.
    GEORGE BERNARD SHAW—
    Devil's Disciple

Home they brought her warrior dead.
    TENNYSON—The Princess

(See also AUDACITY, BRAVERY,
COURAGE, DARING, HERO,
NAVY, PATRIOTISM, VALOR,
WAR, YOUTH.)

SOLITUDE

In solitude, when we are least alone.
    BYRON—Childe Harold

Alone, alone, all, all alone,
    Alone on a wide, wide sea.
    COLERIDGE—Ancient Mariner

I praise the Frenchman; his remark
    was shrewd,—
"How sweet, how passing sweet is
    solitude."
But grant me still a friend in my re-
    treat,
Whom I may whisper—Solitude is
    sweet.
        Cowper—*Retirement*

Oh, for a lodge in some vast wilder-
    ness,
Some boundless contiguity of shade,
Where rumour of oppression and
    deceit,
Of unsuccessful or successful war,
Might never reach me more!
        Cowper—*Task*

We enter the world alone, we leave
it alone.
        Froude

Far from the madding crowd's ignoble strife.
        Gray—*Elegy in a Country
        Churchyard*

The strongest man is the one who
stands most alone.
        Ibsen—*An Enemy of the People*

Solitude is as needful to the imagination as society is wholesome for
the character.
        Lowell—*Among My Books*

The thoughtful Soul to Solitude retires.
        Omar Khayyám—*Rubaiyat*

I never found the companion that
was so companionable as solitude.
        Thoreau—*Solitude*

(See also COMPANIONSHIP, EGO-
    TISM, INDIVIDUALITY, NATURE,
    PEACE, REST, SELF-RELIANCE,
    SILENCE.)

SONG

Swans sing before they die—'twere
    no bad thing
Should certain persons die before
    they sing.
        Coleridge—*On a Bad Singer*

A song will outlive all sermons in
the memory.
        Henry Giles

The morning stars sang together,
and all the sons of God shouted for
joy.
        Job. XXXVIII. 7

And so make life, death and that
    vast forever
One grand, sweet song.
        Kingsley—*A Farewell*

Such songs have power to quiet
    The restless pulse of care,
And come like the benediction
    That follows after prayer.
        Longfellow—*The Day Is
        Done*

God sent his Singers upon earth
With songs of sadness and of mirth,
That they might touch the hearts of
    men,
And bring them back to heaven
    again.
        Longfellow—*The Singers*

Sing again, with your dear voice re-
    vealing
        A tone
Of some world far from ours,
Where music and moonlight and
    feeling
        Are one.
        Shelley—*To Jane*

Our sweetest songs are those that
tell of saddest thought.
        Shelley—*To a Skylark*

They sang of love and not of fame;
  Forgot was Britain's glory;
Each heart recalled a different name,
  But all sang "Annie Laurie."
      BAYARD TAYLOR—*A Song of
      the Camp*

A careless song, with a little nonsense in it now and then, does not
misbecome a monarch.
      HORACE WALPOLE

(See also ART, MUSIC, POETRY.)

SORROW

The busy have no time for tears.
      BYRON—*The Two Foscari*

Every noble crown is, and on earth
will ever be, a crown of thorns.
      CARLYLE

All sorrows are bearable, if there is
bread.
      CERVANTES

I walked a mile with Sorrow
  And ne'er a word said she;
But, oh, the things I learned from
    her
  When Sorrow walked with me.
      ROBERT BROWNING HAMILTON
      —*Along the Road*

Hang sorrow, care'll kill a cat.
      BEN JONSON—*Every Man in
      His Humour*

To Sorrow
  I bade good-morrow,
And thought to leave her far away
    behind;
  But cheerly, cheerly,
  She loves me dearly:
She is so constant to me, and so kind.
      KEATS—*Endymion*

Sorrows are like thunderclouds—in
the distance they look black, over
our heads scarcely gray.
      JEAN PAUL RICHTER—*Hesperus*

More in sorrow than in anger.
      SHAKESPEARE—*Hamlet.* Act I.
      Sc. 2

The deeper the sorrow, the less
tongue hath it.
      THE TALMUD

Joy was a flame in me
  Too steady to destroy.
Lithe as a bending reed,
Loving the storm that sways her—
I found more joy in sorrow
  Than you could find in joy.
      SARA TEASDALE—*The Answer*

There can be no rainbow without a
cloud and a storm.
      J. H. VINCENT

**(See also AFFLICTION, GRIEF,
MELANCHOLY, PAIN, TEARS.)**

SOUL

John Brown's body lies a-mould'ring
  in the grave,
His soul goes marching on.
      THOMAS BRIGHAM BISHOP—
      John Brown's Body

The one thing in the world, of value,
is the active soul.
      EMERSON—*American Scholar*

It matters not how strait the gate,
  How charged with punishments
    the scroll,
I am the master of my fate:
  I am the captain of my soul.
      W. E. HENLEY—*Invictus*

Out of the night that covers me,
  Black as the Pit from pole to pole,
I thank whatever gods may be
  For my unconquerable soul.
    W. E. HENLEY—*Invictus*

Soul, thou hast much goods laid up
for many years; take thine ease, eat,
drink and be merry.
    LUKE. XII. 19

What is a man profited, if he shall
gain the whole world, and lose his
own soul?
    MATTHEW. XVI. 26

I sent my Soul through the Invisible,
Some letter of that After-life to spell,
And by and by my Soul returned to
    me,
And answered "I Myself am Heav'n
    and Hell."
    OMAR KHAYYÁM—*Rubaiyat*

The iron entered into his soul.
    PSALMS. CV. 18

Self is the only prison that can ever
bind the soul.
    HENRY VAN DYKE—*The Prison
    and the Angel.*

A charge to keep I have,
  A God to glorify:
A never-dying soul to save,
  And fit it for the sky.
    CHARLES WESLEY—*Hymns*

I loafe and invite my soul,
I lean and loafe at my ease, observ-
    ing a spear of summer grass.
    WALT WHITMAN—*Song of
    Myself*

The windows of my soul I throw
Wide open to the sun.
    WHITTIER—*My Psalm*

(See also HEART, IMMORTALITY,
LIFE, MIND, MORTALITY,
RELIGION, SPIRIT.)

SOUND

The murmur that springs
From the growing of grass.
    POE—*Al Aaraaf*

The empty vessel makes the greatest sound.
    SHAKESPEARE—*Henry V*. Act
    IV. Sc. 4

Hark! from the tombs a doleful
sound.
    ISAAC WATTS—*Hymns and
    Spiritual Songs*

(See also HEARING, MUSIC, SILENCE,
THUNDER, VOICE.)

SPEECH

Hear much; speak little.
    BIAS

That which is repeated too often becomes insipid and tedious.
    BOILEAU

Let him now speak, or else hereafter
for ever hold his peace.
    BOOK OF COMMON PRAYER

His speech was a fine sample, on
    the whole,
Of rhetoric, which the learn'd call
    "rigmarole."
    BYRON—*Don Juan*

Speech is silvern, silence is golden.
    CARLYLE—*A Swiss Inscription*

He mouths a sentence as curs mouth a bone.

> CHARLES CHURCHILL—*The Rosciad*

Let your speech be alway with grace, seasoned with salt.

> COLOSSIANS. IV. 6

Congress shall make no law . . . abridging the freedom of speech or of the press.

> CONSTITUTION OF THE UNITED STATES. Amendment I

Seeing then that we have such hope, we use great plainness of speech.

> II CORINTHIANS. III. 12

But though I be rude in speech, yet not in knowledge.

> II CORINTHIANS. XI. 6

I realize that there are certain limitations placed upon the right of free speech. I may not be able to say all I think, but I am not going to say anything I do not think.

> EUGENE V. DEBS—Speech, 1918

A vessel is known by the sound, whether it be cracked or not; so men are proved, by their speech, whether they be wise or foolish.

> DEMOSTHENES

A sophistical rhetorician, inebriated with the exuberance of his own verbosity.

> DISRAELI—Speech, 1878

I will sit down now, but the time will come when you will hear me.

> DISRAELI—Maiden Speech in the House of Commons

The hare-brained chatter of irresponsible frivolity.

> DISRAELI—Speech, 1878

Miss not the discourse of the elders.

> ECCLESIASTICUS. VIII. 9

Blessed is the man who having nothing to say, abstains from giving us wordy evidence of the fact.

> GEORGE ELIOT—*Impressions of Theophrastus*

Speech is power: speech is to persuade, to convert, to compel.

> EMERSON

I love to hear thine earnest voice,
  Wherever thou art hid . . .
Thou say'st an undisputed thing
  In such a solemn way.

> HOLMES—*To an Insect*

For that man is detested by me as the gates of hell, whose outward words conceal his inmost thoughts.

> HOMER—*Iliad*

His speech flowed from his tongue sweeter than honey.

> HOMER—*Iliad*

For God's sake, let us freely hear both sides!

> JEFFERSON—Letter, 1814

Every man has a right to utter what he thinks truth, and every other man has a right to knock him down for it.

> SAMUEL JOHNSON

Woe unto you, when all men shall speak well of you!

> LUKE. VI. 26

They think that they shall be heard for their much speaking.

> MATTHEW. VI. 7

Out of the abundance of the heart the mouth speaketh.
MATTHEW. XII. 34

If you your lips would keep from slips,
Five things observe with care;
To whom you speak, of whom you speak,
And how, and when, and where.
W. E. NORRIS—*Thirlby Hall.*

Rhetoric is the art of ruling the minds of men.
PLATO

It is a tiresome way of speaking, when you should despatch the business, to beat about the bush.
PLAUTUS

Let no one be willing to speak ill of the absent.
PROPERTIUS

A soft answer turneth away wrath.
PROVERBS. XV. 1

He replies nothing but monosyllables. I believe he would make three bites of a cherry.
RABELAIS—*Pantagruel*

Speak after the manner of men.
ROMANS. VI. 19

Speech is the index of the mind.
SENECA

I disapprove of what you say, but I will defend to the death your right to say it.
Attributed to VOLTAIRE

(See also ELOQUENCE, LANGUAGE, ORATORY, SILENCE, TALK, TONGUE, VOICE, WORD.)

SPIRIT

Not of the letter, but of the spirit; for the letter killeth, but the spirit giveth life.
II CORINTHIANS. III. 6

The spirit indeed is willing, but the flesh is weak.
MATTHEW. XXVI. 41

He that is slow to anger is better than the mighty; and he that ruleth his spirit than he that taketh a city.
PROVERBS. XVI. 32

(See also FAIRIES, IMAGINATION, SOUL, VISION.)

SPORT

I have never been able to understand why pigeon-shooting at Hurlingham should be refined and polite, while a rat-killing match in Whitechapel is low.
T. H. HUXLEY

When I play with my cat, who knows whether I do not make her more sport, than she makes me?
MONTAIGNE

If all the year were playing holidays,
To sport would be as tedious as to work.
SHAKESPEARE—*Henry IV.* Pt. I. Act I. Sc. 2

When a man wants to murder a tiger he calls it sport: when the tiger wants to murder him he calls it ferocity.
GEORGE BERNARD SHAW—
Maxims for Revolutionists

(See also AMUSEMENT, FISHING, GAMBLING.)

SPRING

Spring hangs her infant blossoms
    on the trees,
Rock'd in the cradle of the western
    breeze.
> COWPER—*Tirocinium*

If there comes a little thaw,
Still the air is chill and raw,
Here and there a patch of snow,
Dirtier than the ground below,
Dribbles down a marshy flood;
Ankle-deep you stick in mud
In the meadows while you sing,
    "This is Spring."
> C. P. CRANCH—*A Spring Growl*

Daughter of heaven and earth, coy
    Spring,
With sudden passion languishing,
Teaching barren moors to smile,
Painting pictures mile on mile,
Holds a cup of cowslip wreaths
Whence a smokeless incense
    breathes.
> EMERSON—*May Day*

Came the Spring with all its splen-
    dor,
All its birds and all its blossoms,
All its flowers, and leaves, and
    grasses.
> LONGFELLOW—*Hiawatha*

Yet Ah, that Spring should vanish
    with the Rose.
  That Youth's sweetscented manu-
    script should close!
The Nightingale that in the branches
    sang
Ah whence and whither flown again,
    who knows?
> OMAR KHAYYÁM—*Rubaiyat*

For, lo! The winter is past, the rain
is over and gone; the flowers appear
on the earth; the time of the singing of birds is come, and the voice
of the turtle is heard in our land.
> THE SONG OF SOLOMON. II.
> 11, 12

In the Spring a livelier iris changes
    on the burnish'd dove;
In the Spring a young man's fancy
    lightly turns to thoughts of
    love.
> TENNYSON—*Locksley Hall*

'Tis spring-time on the eastern hills!
Like torrents gush the summer rills;
Through winter's moss and dry dead
    leaves
The bladed grass revives and lives,
Pushes the mouldering waste away,
And glimpses to the April day.
> WHITTIER—*Mogg Megone*

(See also NATURE, SEASONS.)

STAGE
See ACTING

STAR

                What are ye orbs?
The words of God? the Scriptures
    of the skies?
> BAILEY—*Festus*

And the sentinel stars set their watch
in the sky.
> CAMPBELL—*The Soldier's
> Dream*

No one sees what is before his feet:
we all gaze at the stars.
> CICERO

Hitch your wagon to a star.
> EMERSON—*Society and Solitude*

The morning stars sang together, and all the sons of God shouted for joy.
JOB XXXVIII. 7

When sunset flows into golden glows,
And the breath of the night is new,
Love finds afar eve's eager star—
That is my thought of you.
ROBERT UNDERWOOD JOHNSON
—Star Song

Who falls for love of God shall rise a star.
BEN JONSON—Underwoods

The stars in their courses fought against Sisera.
JUDGES. V. 21

Silently, one by one, in the infinite meadows of heaven,
Blossomed the lovely stars, the forget-me-nots of the angels.
LONGFELLOW—Evangeline

Stars of the summer night!
Far in yon azure deeps
Hide, hide your golden light!
She sleeps!
My lady sleeps!
Sleeps.
LONGFELLOW—Spanish Student

Stars are the daisies that begem
The blue fields of the sky.
D. M. MOIR—Dublin University Magazine

No star is ever lost we once have seen,
We always may be what we might have been.
ADELAIDE A. PROCTER—Legend of Provence

Her blue eyes sought the west afar,
For lovers love the western star.
SCOTT—Lay of the Last Minstrel

These blessed candles of the night.
SHAKESPEARE—Merchant of Venice. Act V. Sc. 1

Twinkle, twinkle, little star!
How I wonder what you are,
Up above the world so high,
Like a diamond in the sky!
ANNE TAYLOR—Rhymes for the Nursery

(See also EVENING, NIGHT, SKY, SUNSET, TWILIGHT.)

STATE

States are great engines moving slowly.
BACON

A thousand years scarce serve to form a state;
An hour may lay it in the dust.
BYRON—Childe Harold

The state is no more than a machine for the oppression of one class by another; this is true of a democracy as well as of a monarchy.
FRIEDRICH ENGELS

A state is a perfect body of free men, united together to enjoy common rights and advantages.
HUGO GROTIUS

The origin of the state, and its reason for existence, lie in the fact that it works in favor of the propertied minority and against the propertyless.
PETER KROPOTKIN

A state from which religion is banished can never be well governed.
POPE LEO XIII

I am the state.
LOUIS XIV of France

States are as the men are; they grow out of human characters.
PLATO—*The Republic*

The state calls its own violence law, but that of the individual crime.
STIRNER—*The Ego and His Own*

(See also DEMOCRACY, DICTATOR, GOVERNMENT, LAW, POLITICS, ROYALTY, STATESMANSHIP.)

STATESMANSHIP

I have the courage of my opinions, but I have not the temerity to give a political blank cheque to Lord Salisbury.
GOSCHEN. In Parliament, 1884

Ambassadors are the eye and ear of states.
GUICCIARDINI—*Storia d'Italia*

Learn to think continentally.
ALEXANDER HAMILTON

Peace, commerce, and honest friendship with all nations—entangling alliances with none.
JEFFERSON—First Inaugural Address

The politician says: "I will give you what you want." The statesman says: "What you think you want is this. What it is possible for you to get is

that. What you really want, therefore, is the following."
WALTER LIPPMANN—*A Preface to Morals*

You can always get the truth from an American statesman after he has turned seventy, or given up all hope of the Presidency.
WENDELL PHILLIPS

Why don't you show us a statesman who can rise up to the emergency, and cave in the emergency's head?
ARTEMUS WARD—*Things in New York*

'Tis our true policy to steer clear of permanent alliances, with any portion of the foreign world—as far, I mean, as we are now at liberty to do it.
WASHINGTON—Farewell Address, 1796

An ambassador is an honest man sent to lie abroad for the commonwealth.
SIR HENRY WOTTON

(See also DIPLOMACY, GOVERNMENT, PARTY, PEACE, POLITICS, POLICY, ROYALTY, STRATEGY, WAR.)

STEALING
See THIEVING

STORM

Rides in the whirlwind, and directs the storm.
ADDISON—*The Campaign*

He used to raise a storm in a teapot.
CICERO

The winds grow high;
Impending tempests charge the sky;
The lightning flies, the thunder roars;
And big waves lash the frightened shores.
PRIOR—*The Lady's Looking-Glass*

His rash fierce blaze of riot cannot last,
For violent fires soon burn out themselves;
Small showers last long, but sudden storms are short.
SHAKESPEARE—*Richard II*. Act II. Sc. 1

For many years I was self-appointed inspector of snow-storms and rain-storms and did my duty faithfully.
THOREAU—*Walden*

(See also NATURE, NAVIGATION, OCEAN, RAIN, RAINBOW, SHIP, THUNDER, WIND.)

STORY-TELLING

A schoolboy's tale, the wonder of an hour!
BYRON—*Childe Harold*

This story will never go down.
FIELDING—*Tumble-Down Dick*

And what so tedious as a twice-told tale.
HOMER—*Odyssey*

But that is another story.
KIPLING—*Plain Tales from the Hills*

It is a sign of a poor intellect to be always telling anecdotes.
LA BRUYÈRE

It is a foolish thing to make a long prologue, and to be short in the story itself.
II MACCABEES. II. 32

An' all us other children, when the supper things is done,
We set around the kitchen fire an' has the mostest fun
A-list'nin' to the witch tales 'at Annie tells about
An' the gobble-uns 'at gits you
  Ef you
    Don't
      Watch
        Out!
JAMES WHITCOMB RILEY—*Little Orphant Annie*

I cannot tell how the truth may be;
I say the tale as 'twas said to me.
SCOTT—*Lay of the Last Minstrel*

And thereby hangs a tale.
SHAKESPEARE—*Taming of the Shrew*. Act IV. Sc. 1

For seldom shall she hear a tale
So sad, so tender, yet so true.
SHENSTONE—*Jemmy Dawson*

(See also BOOKS, LITERATURE, POETRY.)

STRANGER

A stranger in a strange land.
EXODUS. II. 22

I was a stranger, and ye took me in.
MATTHEW. XXV. 35

A stranger's eyes see clearest.
 READE—*The Cloister and the Hearth*

(See also HOME, HOSPITALITY, KINDNESS, TRAVELING.)

STRATEGY

There webs were spread of more
 than common size,
And half-starved spiders preyed on
 half-starved flies.
 CHARLES CHURCHILL—*The Prophecy of Famine*

Strategy is a system of makeshifts.
 HELMUTH VON MOLTKE— *Essay on Strategy*

(See also DECEPTION, POLITICS, POLICY, STATESMANSHIP, WAR.)

STRENGTH

My strength is made perfect in
weakness.
 II CORINTHIANS. XII. 9

As thy days, so shall thy strength be.
 DEUTERONOMY. XXXIII. 25

A threefold cord is not quickly
broken.
 ECCLESIASTES. IV. 12

They go from strength to strength.
 PSALMS. LXXXIV. 7

I feel like a Bull Moose.
 THEODORE ROOSEVELT. On returning from the Spanish War

 O, it is excellent
To have a giant's strength, but it is
 tyrannous
To use it like a giant.
 SHAKESPEARE—*Measure for Measure.* Act II. Sc. 2

Three things give hardy strength:
sleeping on hairy mattresses, breath-
ing cold air, and eating dry food.
 WELSH PROVERB

(See also ABILITY, CHARACTER, DE-
CISION, POWER, RESOLUTION.)

STUDY

Histories make men wise; poets,
witty; the mathematics, subtile; natural philosophy, deep; morals, grave;
logic and rhetoric, able to contend.
 BACON—*Of Studies*

There are more men ennobled by
study than by nature.
 CICERO

Much study is a weariness of the
flesh.
 ECCLESIASTES. XII. 12

The world's great men have not
commonly been great scholars, nor
its great scholars great men.
 HOLMES—*Autocrat of the Breakfast-Table*

As turning the logs will make a dull
fire burn, so change of studies a dull
brain.
 LONGFELLOW—*Drift-Wood*

You are in some brown study.
 LYLY—*Euphues*

Iron sharpens iron; scholar, the
scholar.
 THE TALMUD

(See also ART, BOOKS, EDUCATION,
HISTORY, LEARNING, STUDY,
TEACHING.)

STUPIDITY

We are growing serious, and, let me
tell you, that's a very next step to
being dull.
ADDISON—*The Drummer*

The bookful blockhead, ignorantly
read,
With loads of learned lumber in his
head.
POPE—*Essay on Criticism*

Against stupidity the very gods
Themselves contend in vain.
SCHILLER—*Maid of Orleans*

Peter was dull; he was at first
Dull,—Oh, so dull—so very dull!
Whether he talked, wrote, or re-
hearsed—
Still with his dulness was he cursed—
Dull—beyond all conception—dull.
SHELLEY—*Peter Bell the Third*

(See also EDUCATION, LEARNING,
STUDENT.)

STYLE

One who uses many periods is a
philosopher; many interrogations, a
student; many exclamations, a fanatic.
J. L. BASFORD

Style is the dress of thoughts.
CHESTERFIELD—Letter to His
Son

Montesquieu had the style of a gen-
ius;
Buffon, the genius of style.
BARON GRIMM

Neat, not gaudy.
LAMB—Letter to Wordsworth

Long sentences in a short composi-
tion are like large rooms in a little
house.
SHENSTONE

Clearness ornaments profound
thoughts.
VAUVENARGUES

(See also ART, AUTHORSHIP, BOOKS,
CRITICISM, LITERATURE, POETRY,
TASTE.)

SUCCESS

Successful minds work like a gimlet,
—to a single point.
BOVEE

Be it jewel or toy,
Not the prize gives the joy,
But the striving to win the prize.
PISISTRATUS CAXTON—*The
Boatman*

All you need in this life is ignorance
and confidence, and then Success is
sure.
S. L. CLEMENS (MARK
TWAIN), 1887

Success is counted sweetest
By those who ne'er succeed
EMILY DICKINSON—*Success*

Nothing succeeds like success.
DUMAS—*Ange Pitou*

The race is not to the swift, nor the
battle to the strong.
ECCLESIASTES. IX. 11

If a man has good corn, or wood, or
boards, or pigs to sell, or can make
better chairs or knives, crucibles, or
church organs, than anybody else,

you will find a broad, hard-beaten road to his house, tho it be in the woods.
EMERSON—In his Journal (1855)

If you wish in this world to advance,
Your merits you're bound to enhance;
  You must stir it and stump it,
  And blow your own trumpet,
Or trust me, you haven't a chance.
W. S. GILBERT—*Ruddigore*

Somebody said that it couldn't be done,
But he with a chuckle replied
That "maybe it couldn't," but he would be one
Who wouldn't say so till he'd tried.

So he buckled right in with the trace of a grin
  On his face. If he worried he hid it.
He started to sing as he tackled the thing
  That couldn't be done, and he did it.
EDGAR A. GUEST—*It Couldn't Be Done*

There are but two ways of rising in the world: either by one's own industry or profiting by the foolishness of others.
LA BRUYÈRE

I have always observed that to succeed in the world one should appear like a fool but be wise.
MONTESQUIEU

Either do not attempt at all, or go through with it.
OVID

To climb steep hills
Requires slow pace at first.
SHAKESPEARE—*Henry VIII.*
Act I. Sc. 1

And he gave it for his opinion, that whoever could make two ears of corn, or two blades of grass, to grow upon a spot of ground where only one grew before, would deserve better of mankind and do more essential service to his country, than the whole race of politicians put together.
SWIFT—*Gulliver's Travels*

Faith, mighty faith, the promise sees,
  And looks to that alone;
Laughs at impossibilities,
  And cries it shall be done.
CHARLES WESLEY—*Hymns*

If a man write a better book, preach a better sermon, or make a better mouse-trap than his neighbor, though he build his house in the woods, the world will make a beaten path to his door.
MRS. SARAH S. B. YULE credits the quotation to Emerson in her Borrowings (1889)

(See also AMBITION, CHARACTER, DESTINY, FAME, FATE, FORTUNE, HAPPINESS, HONOR, LUCK, POSSESSION, VICTORY, WEALTH.)

SUFFERING

I have trodden the wine-press alone.
ISAIAH. LXIII. 3

It requires more courage to suffer than to die.
NAPOLEON

No pain, no palm; no thorns, no
throne; no gall, no glory; no cross,
no crown.
WILLIAM PENN

We are healed of a suffering only by
experiencing it to the full.
MARCEL PROUST—*The Sweet
Cheat Gone*

I reckon that the sufferings of this
present time are not worthy to be
compared with the glory which shall
be revealed in us.
ROMANS. VIII. 18

Is it so, O Christ in heaven, that the
highest suffer most,
That the strongest wander furthest,
and more hopelessly are lost?
SARAH WILLIAMS—*In Twilight
Hours*

(See also AFFLICTION, MISERY, MIS-
FORTUNE, PAIN, SICKNESS,
SORROW, TRIAL.)

SUICIDE

I have a hundred times wished that
one could resign life as an officer
resigns a commission.
ROBERT BURNS—Letter, 1788

It is cowardice to commit suicide.
NAPOLEON, 1817

The relatives of a suicide always
take it in bad part that he did not
remain alive out of consideration for
the family dignity.
NIETZSCHE—*Human All-too-
Human*

There is no refuge from confession
but suicide; and suicide is confession.
DANIEL WEBSTER

(See also CRIME, DEATH, LIFE,
MURDER.)

SUMMER

One swallow alone does not make
the summer.
CERVANTES—*Don Quixote*

I question not if thrushes sing,
If roses load the air;
Beyond my heart I need not reach
When all is summer there.
JOHN VANCE CHENEY—*Love's
World*

Oh, the summer night
Has a smile of light
And she sits on a sapphire throne.
B. W. PROCTER—*The Nights*

Before green apples blush,
Before green nuts embrown,
Why, one day in the country
Is worth a month in town.
CHRISTINA G. ROSSETTI—
Summer

(See also NATURE, SEASONS.)

SUN

The sun, centre and sire of light,
The keystone of the world-built arch
of heaven.
BAILEY—*Festus*

Make hay while the sun shines.
CERVANTES—*Don Quixote*

Truly the light is sweet, and a pleasant thing it is for the eyes to behold
the sun.
ECCLESIASTES. XI. 7

Whence are thy beams, O sun! thy
everlasting light? Thou comest forth,
in thy awful beauty; the stars hide
themselves in the sky; the moon, cold
and pale, sinks in the western wave.
But thou, thyself, movest alone.
MACPHERSON—*Ossian*

The sun shines even on the wicked.
SENECA

Fairest of all the lights above,
Thou sun, whose beams adorn the
spheres,
And with unwearied swiftness move,
To form the circles of our years.
ISAAC WATTS

(See also DAY, LIGHT, MORNING,
SKY, SUNRISE, SUNSET.)

SUN DIAL MOTTOES

Let not the sun go down upon your
wrath.
EPHESIANS. IV. 26

    Time is
Too Slow for those who Wait,
Too Swift for those who Fear,
Too Long for those who Grieve,
Too Short for those who Rejoice,
    But for those who Love
    Time is not.
HENRY VAN DYKE—Motto for
the Sun Dial in the Garden of
Yaddo, Saratoga Springs, N. Y.

Let others tell of storms and showers,
I'll only mark your sunny hours.
On a Sun Dial at Pittsfield,
Mass.

SUNRISE

Wake! For the sun who scatter'd into
flight
The stars before him from the field
of night,
    Drives night along with them from
heav'n and strikes
The sultan's turret with a shaft of
light.
OMAR KHAYYÁM—Rubaiyat

But yonder comes the powerful King
of Day,
Rejoicing in the East.
JAMES THOMSON—Seasons

(See also DAY, LIGHT, MORNING,
SKY, SUN.)

SUNSET

The death-bed of a day, how beautiful!
BAILEY—Festus

The night cometh when no man can
work.
JOHN. IX. 9

Now in his Palace of the West,
    Sinking to slumber, the bright
Day,
Like a tired monarch fann'd to rest,
    'Mid the cool airs of Evening lay;
While round his couch's golden rim
    The gaudy clouds, like courtiers,
crept—
Struggling each other's light to dim,
    And catch his last smile ere he
slept.
MOORE—The Summer Fête

Sunset and evening star
    And one clear call for me!
And may there be no moaning of the
bar,
    When I put out to sea.
TENNYSON—Crossing the Bar

(See also DARKNESS, EVENING,
NIGHT, SHADOW, STAR,
TWILIGHT.)

SUPERIORITY

There are three marks of a superior
man: being virtuous, he is free from
anxiety; being wise, he is free from

perplexity; being brave, he is free from fear.

CONFUCIUS

We can all perceive the difference between ourselves and our inferiors, but when it comes to a question of the difference between us and our superiors we fail to appreciate merits of which we have no proper conceptions.

COOPER—*The American Democrat*

There are men too superior to be seen except by the few, as there are notes too high for the scale of most ears.

EMERSON—Lecture, 1864

Superiority is always detested.

BALTASAR GRACIÁN

(See also CHARACTER, COMPARISON, CONCEIT, EGOTISM, INDIVIDUALITY, LEADERSHIP, QUALITY, VIRTUE.)

SUPERSTITION

The general root of superstition is that men observe when things hit, and not when they miss; and commit to memory the one, and forget and pass over the other.

BACON

Superstition is the religion of feeble minds.

BURKE

Religion is not removed by removing superstition.

CICERO

There is in superstition a senseless fear of God.

CICERO

I die adoring God, loving my friends, not hating my enemies, and detesting superstition.

VOLTAIRE

(See also FAIRIES, FAITH, GODS, IGNORANCE, RELIGION, WONDER.)

SURRENDER
See WAR

SUSPICION

Suspicion is far more apt to be wrong than right; oftener unjust than just. It is no friend to virtue, and always an enemy to happiness.

HOSEA BALLOU

As to Caesar, when he was called upon, he gave no testimony against Clodius, nor did he affirm that he was certain of any injury done to his bed. He only said, "He had divorced Pompeia because the wife of Caesar ought not only to be clear of such a crime, but of the very suspicion of it."

PLUTARCH—*Life of Cicero*

Suspicion always haunts the guilty mind;
The thief doth fear each bush an officer.

SHAKESPEARE—*Henry VI.* Pt. III. Act V. Sc. 6

The less we know the more we suspect.

H. W. SHAW

A woman of honor should not suspect another of things she would not do herself.

MARGUERITE DE VALOIS

(See also DOUBT, INCREDULITY, JEALOUSY.)

SWAN

All our geese are swans.
> BURTON—*Anatomy of Melancholy*

Place me on Sunium's marbled steep,
  Where nothing save the waves
    and I
May hear our mutual murmurs
    sweep;
  There, swan-like, let me sing and
    die.
> BYRON—*Don Juan*

You think that upon the score of
fore-knowledge and divining I am
infinitely inferior to the swans. When
they perceive approaching death they
sing more merrily than before, because of the joy they have in going
to the God they serve.
> SOCRATES

(See also ANTICIPATION, BIRDS, DEATH, FUTURE.)

SWEARING
See PROFANITY

SWEETNESS

The pursuit of the perfect, then, is
the pursuit of sweetness and light.
> MATTHEW ARNOLD—*Culture and Anarchy*

Every sweet hath its sour, every evil
its good.
> EMERSON—*Compensation*

Sweet meat must have sour sauce.
> BEN JONSON—*Poetaster*

Sweets to the sweet.
> SHAKESPEARE—*Hamlet*. Act V. Sc. 1

(See also GOODNESS, HAPPINESS, KINDNESS.)

SYMPATHY

Of a truth, men are mystically
united: a mystic bond of brotherhood makes all men one.
> CARLYLE—*Essays*

                    The man who melts
With social sympathy, though not
    allied,
Is of more worth than a thousand
    kinsmen.
> EURIPIDES

He watch'd and wept, he pray'd and
felt for all.
> GOLDSMITH—*The Deserted Village*

Never elated while one man's op-
    press'd;
Never dejected while another's
    bless'd.
> POPE—*Essay on Man*

Rejoice with them that do rejoice,
and weep with them that weep.
> ROMANS. XII. 15

No one really understands the grief
or joy of another.
> FRANZ SCHUBERT

(See also COMPANIONSHIP, FRIEND-SHIP, KINDNESS, PITY, SORROW, SUFFERING, TEARS.)

TACT

Women and foxes, being weak, are
distinguished by superior tact.
> BIERCE

Without tact you can learn nothing.
> DISRAELI—*Endymion*

To have the reputation of possessing the most perfect social tact, talk to every woman as if you loved her, and to every man as if he bored you.
WILDE—*A Woman of No Importance*

(See also DIPLOMACY, DISCRETION, JUDGMENT, POLICY, WISDOM.)

TALE

Beware of him that telleth tales.
ANONYMOUS

A schoolboy's tale, the wonder of an hour.
BYRON—*Childe Harold*

Tush! These are trifles, and mere old wives' tales.
MARLOWE—*Dr. Faustus*

What so tedious as a twice-told tale?
POPE

I cannot tell how the truth may be;
I say the tale as 'twas said to me.
SCOTT—*The Lay of the Last Minstrel*

A tale never loses in the telling.
SCOTTISH PROVERB

And thereby hangs a tale.
SHAKESPEARE—*As You Like It.* Act II. Sc. 7

I will a round unvarnish'd tale deliver.
SHAKESPEARE—*Othello.* Act I. Sc. 3

(See also GOSSIP, RUMOR, SCANDAL, STORY-TELLING, TONGUE.)

TALENT

Every man hath his proper gift of God, one after this manner, and another after that.
I CORINTHIANS. V. 7

Concealed talent brings no reputation.
ERASMUS

The world is always ready to receive talent with open arms.
HOLMES

(See also ABILITY, ART, CHARACTER, GENIUS, INTELLECT, MIND.)

TALK

"The time has come," the Walrus said,
  "To talk of many things:
Of shoes—and ships—and sealing-wax—
  Of cabbages—and kings—
And why the sea is boiling hot—
  And whether pigs have wings."
LEWIS CARROLL—*Through the Looking Glass*

But far more numerous was the herd of such,
Who think too little, and who talk too much.
DRYDEN—*Absalom and Achitophel*

Talk is cheap.
ENGLISH PROVERB

In much of your talking, thinking is half murdered.
KAHLIL GIBRAN—*The Prophet*

In general those who nothing have
to say
Contrive to spend the longest time
in doing it.
LOWELL—*An Oriental Apologue*

Those who have few things to attend
to are great babblers; for the less
men think, the more they talk.
MONTESQUIEU

They never taste who always drink;
They always talk who never think.
PRIOR

Talkers are no good doers.
SHAKESPEARE—*Richard III.* Act
I. Sc. 3

He who talks too much commits a
sin.
THE TALMUD

The secret of being tiresome is in telling everything.
VOLTAIRE

(See also CONVERSATION, ELO-
QUENCE, GOSSIP, ORATORY,
SPEECH, TONGUE, WORD.)

TASTE

Taste is nothing but a delicate good
sense.
M. J. DE CHENIER

Everyone to his taste.
FRENCH PROVERB

Every man as he loveth, quoth the
good man when he kissed the cow.
JOHN HEYWOOD

My tastes are aristocratic; my actions
democratic.
VICTOR HUGO

A man's palate can, in time, become
accustomed to anything.
NAPOLEON

Good taste is the flower of good sense.
POINCELOT

The finer impulse of our nature.
SCHILLER

(See also CHOICE, MANNERS, STYLE,
VARIETY.)

TAXES

The art of taxation consists in so
plucking the goose as to obtain the
largest amount of feathers with the
least possible amount of hissing.
Attributed to J. B. COLBERT

The tax upon land values (Single
Tax) is the most just and equal of all
taxes. It is the taking by the community, for the use of the community, of that value which is the
creation of the community.
HENRY GEORGE—*Progress and
Poverty*

Death and taxes are inevitable.
HALIBURTON

The power to tax carries with it the
power to embarrass and destroy.
Supreme Court of the United
States—Evans vs. Gore, 1920

(See also ECONOMY, GOVERNMENT,
PARTY, POLITICS.)

TEACHING

You cannot teach old dogs new tricks.
ANONYMOUS

A man should first direct himself in the way he should go. Only then should he instruct others.

BUDDHA

You cannot teach a man anything; you can only help him to find it within himself.

GALILEO

A teacher who is attempting to teach without inspiring the pupil with a desire to learn is hammering on cold iron.

HORACE MANN

Speak to the earth, and it shall teach thee.

JOB. XII. 8

Public instruction should be the first object of government.

NAPOLEON

The teacher is like the candle which lights others in consuming itself.

RUFFINI

I am not a teacher: only a fellow-traveller of whom you asked the way. I pointed ahead—ahead of myself as well as of you.

GEORGE BERNARD SHAW—*Getting Married*

Everybody who is incapable of learning has taken to teaching.

WILDE—*The Decay of Lying*

(See also EDUCATION, LEARNING, STUDENT, STUDY.)

TEARS

Tears are Summer showers to the soul.

ALFRED AUSTIN—*Savonarola*

There is a tear for all who die,
A mourner o'er the humblest grave.

BYRON—*Elegiac Stanzas*

For Beauty's tears are lovelier than her smile.

CAMPBELL—*Pleasures of Hope*

Words that weep and tears that speak.

COWLEY—*The Prophet*

Never a tear bedims the eye
That time and patience will not dry.

BRET HARTE—*Lost Galleon*

Oh! would I were dead now,
Or up in my bed now,
To cover my head now
    And have a good cry!

HOOD—*A Table of Errata*

Jesus wept.

JOHN. XI. 35 (Shortest verse in the Bible)

If the man who turnips cries,
Cry not when his father dies,
'Tis proof that he had rather
Have a turnip than his father.

SAMUEL JOHNSON

There shall be weeping and gnashing of teeth.

MATTHEW. VIII. 12

It is some relief to weep; grief is satisfied and carried off by tears.

OVID

If you have tears, prepare to shed them now.

SHAKESPEARE—*Julius Caesar.*
Act III. Sc. 2

Tears are the silent language of grief.
> VOLTAIRE—*A Philosophical Dictionary*

When summoned hence to thine
eternal sleep,
Oh, may'st thou smile while all
around thee weep.
> CHARLES WESLEY—*On an Infant*

(See also DEATH, GRIEF, PITY,
SORROW, SYMPATHY.)

TEMPERANCE

The first draught serveth for health,
the second for pleasure, the third for
shame, and the fourth for madness.
> ANACHARSIS

Temperate in all things.
> I CORINTHIANS. IX. 25

Every moderate drinker could abandon the intoxicating cup if he would;
every inebriate would if he could.
> J. B. GOUGH

Drinking water neither makes a man
sick, nor in debt, nor his wife a
widow.
> JOHN NEALE

The smaller the drink, the clearer
the head, and the cooler the blood.
> WILLIAM PENN

Use, do not abuse; neither abstinence
nor excess ever renders man happy.
> VOLTAIRE

(See also DRINKING, EATING, FESTIVITIES, INTEMPERANCE, MODERATION, WINE AND
SPIRITS.)

TEMPTATION

So you tell yourself you are pretty
fine clay
To have tricked temptation and
turned it away,
But wait, my friend, for a different
day;
Wait till you want to want to!
> EDMUND VANCE COOKE—*Desire*

Thou shalt abstain,
Renounce, refrain.
> GOETHE—*Faust*

Blessed is the man that endureth
temptation; for when he is tried, he
shall receive the crown of life.
> JAMES. I. 12

Honest bread is very well—it's the
butter that makes the temptation.
> DOUGLAS JERROLD—*The Catspaw*

Get thee behind me, Satan.
> MATTHEW. XVI. 23

Never resist temptation: prove all
things: hold fast that which is good.
> GEORGE BERNARD SHAW—*Maxims for Revolutionists*

I can resist everything except temptation.
> WILDE—*Lady Windermere's Fan*

(See also CRIME, DEVIL, GUILT, RELIGION, SIN, VICE, WICKEDNESS.)

THANKFULNESS

O give thanks unto the Lord, for he
is good: for his mercy endureth forever.
> PSALMS. CVII. 1

Beggar that I am, I am even poor in thanks.
> SHAKESPEARE—*Hamlet.* Act II. Sc. 2

How sharper than a serpent's tooth it is
To have a thankless child.
> SHAKESPEARE—*King Lear.* Act I. Sc. 4

From too much love of living,
  From hope and fear set free,
We thank with brief thanksgiving
  Whatever gods may be,
That no life lives forever,
That dead men rise up never;
That even the weariest river
  Winds somewhere safe to sea.
> SWINBURNE—*The Garden of Proserpine*

(See also GIFT, GRATITUDE, INGRATITUDE.)

THANKSGIVING DAY

Heap high the board with plenteous
  cheer, and gather to the feast,
And toast the sturdy Pilgrim band
  whose courage never ceased.
Give praise to that All-Gracious One
  by whom their steps were led,
And thanks unto the harvest's Lord
  who sends our "daily bread."
> ALICE WILLIAMS BROTHERTON
> —*The First Thanksgiving Day*

So once in every year we throng
  Upon a day apart,
To praise the Lord with feast and
  song
  In thankfulness of heart.
> ARTHUR GUITERMAN—*The First Thanksgiving*

Ah! on Thanksgiving day, when from East and from West,
From North and South, come the pilgrim and guest,
When the gray-haired New Englander sees round his board
The old broken links of affection restored,
When the care-wearied man seeks his mother once more,
And the worn matron smiles where the girl smiled before.
What moistens the lips and what brightens the eye?
What calls back the past, like the rich pumpkin pie?
> WHITTIER—*The Pumpkin*

(See also AUTUMN, HARVEST, MONTH, NATURE, THANKFULNESS.)

THEATER
See ACTING

THEOLOGY
See CHURCH

THIEVING

Thou shalt not steal.
> EXODUS. XX. 15

In vain we call old notions fudge
  And bend our conscience to our
    dealing.
The Ten Commandments will not
  budge
  And stealing will continue stealing.
> Motto of AMERICAN COPYRIGHT LEAGUE. Written 1885

There is honor among thieves.
> ENGLISH PROVERB

Set a thief to catch a thief.
ENGLISH PROVERB

When thieves fall out, honest men
come by their own.
ENGLISH PROVERB

Stolen waters are sweet, and bread
eaten in secret is pleasant.
PROVERBS. IX. 17

Stolen sweets are always sweeter:
Stolen kisses much completer;
Stolen looks are nice in chapels:
Stolen, stolen be your apples.
THOMAS RANDOLPH—*Song of
Fairies*

A plague upon it when thieves can-
not be true one to another!
SHAKESPEARE—*Henry IV*. Pt. I.
Act II. Sc. 2

(See also CRIME, JUSTICE, LAW,
PRISON, PUNISHMENT, VICE.)

THOUGHT

The power of Thought,—the magic
of the Mind!
BYRON—*Corsair*

My thoughts ran a wool-gathering.
CERVANTES—*Don Quixote*

Any man may make a mistake; none
but a fool will stick to it. Second
thoughts are best as the proverb says.
CICERO

Learning without thought is labor
lost.
CONFUCIUS

I think, therefore I am.
DESCARTES

Thoughts that breathe and words
that burn.
GRAY—*Progress of Poesy*

Great thoughts reduced to practice
become great acts.
HAZLITT

The mind grows by what it feeds on.
J. G. HOLLAND

Why can't somebody give us a list
of things that everybody thinks and
nobody says, and another list of
things that everybody says and nobody thinks?
HOLMES—*Professor at the
Breakfast Table*

That fellow seems to me to possess
but one idea, and that is a wrong
one.
SAMUEL JOHNSON

A penny for your thought.
LYLY

Which of you by taking thought can
add one cubit unto his stature?
MATTHEW. VI. 27

As he thinketh in his heart, so is he.
PROVERBS. XXIII. 7

There is nothing either good or bad,
but thinking makes it so.
SHAKESPEARE—*Hamlet*. Act II.
Sc. 2

Yond Cassius has a lean and hungry
    look;
He thinks too much: such men are
    dangerous.
SHAKESPEARE—*Julius Caesar*.
Act I. Sc. 2

A thought by thought is piled, till
    some great truth
Is loosened, and the nations echo
    round,
Shaken to their roots, as do the moun-
    tains now.
    SHELLEY—*Prometheus Un-
    bound*

They are never alone that are accompanied with noble thoughts.
    SIR PHILIP SIDNEY—*Arcadia*

Great thoughts come from the heart.
    VAUVENARGUES

**(See also INTELLECT, MEMORY,
MIND, REASON, WISDOM.)**

THRIFT

It's no use filling your pocket with
money if you have got a hole in the
corner.
    GEORGE ELIOT

A penny saved is a penny earned.
    ENGLISH PROVERB

He that will not stoop for a pin will
never be worth a pound.
    ENGLISH PROVERB

It is better to have a hen tomorrow
than an egg today.
    THOMAS FULLER

A man who both spends and saves
money is the happiest man, because
he has both enjoyments.
    SAMUEL JOHNSON

**(See also AVARICE, ECONOMY,
MONEY, PRUDENCE, WEALTH.)**

THUNDER

Loud roared the dreadful thunder,
The rain a deluge showers.
    ANDREW CHERRY—*Bay of Bis-
    cay*

The Lord thundered from heaven,
and the Most High uttered his voice.
    II SAMUEL. XXII. 14

That great artillery of God Almighty.
    WILLIAM TEMPLE

(See also RAIN, SKY, STORM.)

TIDE
See NATURE, SEA

TIME

Backward, turn backward, O Time in
    your flight;
Make me a child again just for to-
    night.
    ELIZABETH AKERS ALLEN—
    Rock Me to Sleep

In time take time while time doth
    last, for time
Is no time when time is past.
    ANONYMOUS

Time whereof the memory of man
runneth not to the contrary.
    BLACKSTONE—*Commentaries*

Time was made for slaves.
    JOHN B. BUCKSTONE—*Billy Tay-
    lor*

Time is money.
    BULWER-LYTTON—*Money*

I recommend you to take care of the
minutes, for the hours will take care
of themselves.
    CHESTERFIELD

Know the true value of time; snatch, seize, and enjoy every moment of it. No idleness, no laziness, no procrastination: never put off till tomorrow what you can do today.

CHESTERFIELD—*Letters to His Son*

O temporal! O mores!
O what times! what morals!
CICERO

Now is the accepted time.
II CORINTHIANS. VI. 2

See Time has touched me gently in his race,
And left no odious furrows in my face.
CRABBE—*Tales of the Hall*

To everything there is a season, and a time to every purpose under the heaven.
ECCLESIASTES. III. 1

A stitch in time saves nine.
ENGLISH PROVERB

Time and tide wait for no man.
ENGLISH PROVERB

Do not squander time, for that is the stuff life is made of.
FRANKLIN

Gather ye rose-buds while ye may,
Old Time is still aflying,
And this same flower that smiles today,
Tomorrow will be dying.
HERRICK—*Hesperides*

Enjoy the present day, trusting very little to the morrow.
HORACE—*Carmina*

My days are swifter than a weaver's shuttle.
JOB. VII. 6

My time is not yet come.
JOHN. VII. 6

Better late than never.
LIVY

The signs of the times.
MATTHEW—XVI. 3

The bird of time has but a little way
To flutter—and the bird is on the wing.
OMAR KHAYYÁM—*Rubaiyat*

Time is a great legalizer, even in the field of morals.
H. L. MENCKEN—*A Book of Prefaces*

When time is flown, how it fled
It is better neither to ask nor tell,
Leave the dead moments to bury their dead.
OWEN MEREDITH—*Wanderer*

These are the times that try men's souls.
THOMAS PAINE—*The American Crisis*

Time is the wisest counsellor.
PERICLES

Seize time by the forelock.
PITTACUS OF MITYLENE

A thousand years in thy sight are but as yesterday when it is past, and as a watch in the night.
PSALMS. XC. 4

We spend our years as a tale that is told.
PSALMS. XC. 9

An age builds up cities: an hour destroys them.

>   SENECA

There's a time for all things.

>   SHAKESPEARE—*Comedy of Errors*. Act II. Sc. 2

The time is out of joint.

>   SHAKESPEARE—*Hamlet*, Act I. Sc. 5

O, call back yesterday, bid time return.

>   SHAKESPEARE—*Richard II*. Act III. Sc. 2

Make use of time, let not advantage slip.

>   SHAKESPEARE—*Venus and Adonis*

A wonderful stream is the River Time,
>   As it runs through the realms of Tears,
With a faultless rhythm, and a musical rhyme,
>   As it blends with the ocean of Years.

>   BENJAMIN F. TAYLOR—*The Long Ago*

Once in Persia reigned a king
Who upon his signet ring
Graved a maxim true and wise,
Which if held before the eyes
Gave him counsel at a glance
Fit for every change and chance.
Solemn words, and these are they:
"Even this shall pass away."

>   THEODORE TILTON—*The King's Ring*

(See also DELAY, ETERNITY, FUTURE, HASTE, IDLENESS, LEISURE, PAST, PROCRASTINATION, TODAY, TOMORROW.)

TOASTS

Some hae meat, and canna eat,
>   And some wad eat that want it;
But we hae meat, and we can eat,
>   And sae the Lord be thankit.

>   BURNS—*The Selkirk Grace*

Here's a sigh to those who love me,
And a smile to those who hate;
And whatever sky's above me,
Here's a heart for every fate.

>   BYRON—Letter to Thomas Moore

Ho! stand to your glasses steady!
>   'Tis all we have left to prize.
A cup to the dead already,—
>   Hurrah for the next that dies.

>   BARTHOLOMEW DOWLING—*Revelry in India*

Here's to your good health, and your family's good health, and may you all live long and prosper.

>   IRVING—*Rip Van Winkle*

Drink to me only with thine eyes,
>   And I will pledge with mine;
Or leave a kiss but in the cup,
>   And I'll not look for wine.

>   BEN JONSON—*To Celia*

A glass is good, and a lass is good,
>   And a pipe to smoke in cold weather;
The world is good and the people are good,
>   And we're all good fellows together.

>   JOHN O'KEEFE—*Sprigs of Laurel*

Here's to you, as good as you are,
And here's to me, as bad as I am;

But as good as you are, and as bad as
I am,
I am as good as you are, as bad as I
am.
    OLD SCOTCH TOAST

May you live all the days of your life.
    SWIFT—*Polite Conversation*

Here is a toast that I want to give
  To a fellow I'll never know;
To the fellow who's going to take my
  place
  When it's time for me to go.
    LOUIS E. THAYER—*To My Suc-
cessor*

May all your labors be in vein.
    YORKSHIRE MINERS' TOAST

(See also DRINKING, WINE AND
SPIRITS.)

TOBACCO

Little tube of mighty pow'r,
Charmer of an idle hour,
  Object of my warm desire.
    ISAAC HAWKINS BROWNE—*A
Pipe of Tobacco*

A woman is only a woman, but a
good cigar is a smoke.
    KIPLING—*The Betrothed*

For thy sake, tobacco, I
Would do anything but die.
    LAMB—*A Farewell to Tobacco*

What this country needs is a good
five-cent cigar.
    THOMAS R. MARSHALL—Re-
mark to John Crockett, Chief
Clerk of the United States Senate

Yes, social friend, I love thee well,
  In learned doctors' spite;
Thy clouds all other clouds dispel
  And lap me in delight.
    CHARLES SPRAGUE—*To My
Cigar*

A cigarette is the perfect type of a
perfect pleasure. It is exquisite, and
it leaves one unsatisfied. What more
can you want?
    WILDE—*Picture of Dorian Gray*

TODAY

We are here today and gone tomorrow.
    ANONYMOUS

Out of Eternity
The new Day is born;
  Into Eternity
At night will return.
    CARLYLE—*Today*

Happy the man, and happy he alone,
He, who can call today his own:
He who, secure within, can say,
Tomorrow, do thy worst, for I have
  liv'd today.
    DRYDEN—*Imitation of Horace*

One today is worth two tomorrows.
    FRANKLIN

Tomorrow life is too late: live today.
    MARTIAL

We shall do so much in the years to
  come,
  But what have we done today?
We shall give our gold in a princely
  sum,
  But what did we give today?
    NIXON WATERMAN—*What
Have We Done Today?*

(See also PAST, TIME, TOMORROW.)

TOLERATION

Every man must get to heaven his
own way.
FREDERICK THE GREAT

Tolerance is the only real test of civilization.
ARTHUR HELPS

Toleration is the best religion.
VICTOR HUGO

It is intolerance to speak of toleration. Away with the word from the
dictionary!
MIRABEAU

Live and let live.
SCOTTISH PROVERB

I disapprove of what you say, but I
will defend to the death your right
to say it.
Attributed to VOLTAIRE

(See also FREEDOM, GOLDEN RULE,
HUMANITY, INTOLERANCE,
KINDNESS.)

TOMORROW

Never leave that till tomorrow which
you can do today.
FRANKLIN—*Poor Richard's Almanac*

There is a budding morrow in midnight.
KEATS

Tomorrow!—Why, tomorrow I may
be
Myself with yesterday's sev'n thousand years.
OMAR KHAYYÁM—*Rubaiyat*

Tomorrow never yet
On any human being rose or set.
WILLIAM MARSDEN—*What Is
Time?*

Boast not thyself of tomorrow; for
thou knowest not what a day may
bring forth.
PROVERBS. XXVII. 1

Tomorrow, tomorrow, not today,
Hear the lazy people say.
WEISSE

(See also FUTURE, TIME, TODAY.)

TONGUE

The magic of the tongue is the most
dangerous of all spells.
BULWER-LYTTON—*Eugene
Aram*

The stroke of the tongue breaketh
the bones. Many have fallen by the
edge of the sword; but not so many
as have fallen by the tongue.
ECCLESIASTICUS. XXVIII. 17,
18

Birds are entangled by their feet and
men by their tongues.
THOMAS FULLER

The tongue can no man tame; it is
an unruly evil.
JAMES. III. 8

Keep thy tongue from evil, and thy
lips from speaking guile.
PSALMS. XXXIV. 13

Many a man's tongue shakes out his
master's undoing.
SHAKESPEARE—*All's Well That
Ends Well*. Act II. Sc. 4

(See also CONVERSATION, ELO-
QUENCE, GOSSIP, ORATORY,
SPEECH, TALK, WORD.)

TRAGEDY
See AFFLICTION

TRAVELING

The traveled mind is the catholic mind educated from exclusiveness and egotism.
ALCOTT—*Table-Talk*

Travel teaches toleration.
DISRAELI

I have been a stranger in a strange land.
EXODUS. II. 22

I am fevered with the sunset,
I am fretful with the bay,
For the wander-thirst is on me
And my soul is in Cathay.
RICHARD HOVEY—*A Sea Gypsy*

A wise traveler never despises his own country.
GOLDONI—*Pamela*

As the Spanish proverb says, "He who would bring home the wealth of the Indies must carry the wealth of the Indies with him." So it is in travelling: a man must carry knowledge with him, if he would bring home knowledge.
SAMUEL JOHNSON—*Boswell's Life of Johnson*

Down to Gehenna or up to the throne,
He travels the fastest who travels alone.
KIPLING—*The Winners*

The little Road says, Go;
The little House says, Stay;
And oh, it's bonny here at home,
But I must go away.
JOSEPHINE P. PEABODY—*The House and the Road*

The more I see of other countries the more I love my own.
MME. DE STAËL

Good company in a journey makes the way to seem the shorter.
IZAAK WALTON—*The Compleat Angler*

(See also FAREWELL, HOME, NAVIGATION, PARTING, SHIP.)

TREACHERY

There is treachery, O Ahaziah.
II KINGS. IX. 23

Treachery, though at first very cautious, in the end betrays itself.
LIVY

Et tu Brute! (You too, Brutus!)
SHAKESPEARE—*Julius Caesar.* Act III. Sc. 1

(See also DECEPTION, FALSEHOOD, LYING, WAR.)

TREASON
See TREACHERY

TREE

I think that I shall never scan
A tree as lovely as a man.
. . .
A tree depicts divinest plan,
But God himself lives in a man.
ANONYMOUS

No tree in all the grove but has its charms,
Though each its hue peculiar.
COWPER—*The Task*

In the place where the tree falleth, there it shall be.
ECCLESIASTES. XI. 3

Tall oaks from little acorns grow.
DAVID EVERETT

The tree of knowledge of good and
evil.
GENESIS. II. 9

I think that I shall never see
A poem lovely as a tree.

. . .

Poems are made by fools like me,
But only God can make a tree.
JOYCE KILMER—*Trees*

This is the forest primeval.
LONGFELLOW—*Evangeline*

The tree is known by his fruit.
MATTHEW. XII. 33

Woodman, spare that tree!
Touch not a single bough!
In youth it sheltered me,
And I'll protect it now.
GEORGE P. MORRIS—*Wood-
man, Spare That Tree*

Welcome, ye shades! ye bowery
Thickets hail!
Ye lofty Pines! ye venerable Oaks!
Ye Ashes wild, resounding o'er the
steep!
Delicious is your shelter to the soul.
JAMES THOMSON—*Seasons.
Summer*

(See also NATURE.)

TRIAL

'Tis a lesson you should heed,
Try, try, try again
If at first you don't succeed,
Try, try, try again.
W. E. HICKSON—*Try and Try
Again*

There are no crown-bearers in heaven
who were not cross-bearers here below.
SPURGEON—*Gleaning among
the Sheaves*

(See also AFFLICTION, EXPERIENCE,
SORROW, SUFFERING, TROUBLE.)

TRIFLE

Little deeds of kindness, little words
of love,
Help to make earth happy, like the
heaven above.
JULIA F. CARNEY—*Little
Things*

For precept must be upon precept,
precept upon precept; line upon line,
line upon line; here a little, and there
a little.
ISAIAH. XXVIII. 10

A little one shall become a thousand,
and a small one a strong nation.
ISAIAH. IX. 22

Events of great consequence often
spring from trifling circumstances.
LIVY

Trifles make perfection—and perfection is no trifle.
Attributed to MICHELANGELO

For the maintenance of peace, nations should avoid the pin-pricks
which forerun cannon-shots.
NAPOLEON to the Czar Alexander

(See also DEEDS, EVENTS, LIFE,
PERFECTION.)

TRIUMPH
See VICTORY

TROUBLE

Never trouble trouble till trouble troubles you.
AMERICAN PROVERB

He that seeks trouble always finds it.
ENGLISH PROVERB

Troubles, like babies, grow larger by nursing.
LADY HOLLAND

Man is born unto trouble, as the sparks fly upward.
JOB. V. 7

The true way to soften one's troubles is to solace those of others.
MME. DE MAINTENON

To take arms against a sea of troubles.
SHAKESPEARE—*Hamlet*. Act III. Sc. 1

Though life is made up of mere bubbles,
'Tis better than many aver,
For while we've a whole lot of troubles,
The most of them never occur.
NIXON WATERMAN—*Why Worry?*

(See also AFFLICTION, GRIEF, MISERY, MISFORTUNE, SORROW, TRIAL.)

TRUST

Government is a trust, and the officers of the government are trustees; and both the trust and the trustees are created for the benefit of the people.
HENRY CLAY—Speech

Trust in God, and keep your powder dry.
CROMWELL

Thou trustest in the staff of this broken reed.
ISAIAH. XXXVI. 6

When a man assumes a public trust, he should consider himself as public property.
JEFFERSON

Public office is a public trust.
DAN S. LAMONT

To be trusted is a greater compliment than to be loved.
GEORGE MACDONALD—*The Marquis of Lossie*

In God have I put my trust: I will not be afraid what man can do unto me.
PSALMS. LVI. 11

(See also BELIEF, CONFIDENCE, EXPECTATION, FAITH, HOPE.)

TRUTH

Truth is mighty and will prevail.
THOMAS BROOKS, 1662

If it is not true it is very well invented.
GIORDANO BRUNO

Truth crushed to earth shall rise again:
Th' eternal years of God are hers;
But Error, wounded, writhes in pain,
And dies among his worshippers.
BRYANT—*The Battle Field*

'Tis strange—but true; for truth is
always strange,
Stranger than fiction.
BYRON—*Don Juan*

Truth ever lovely—since the world
began,
The foe of tyrants, and the friend of
man.
CAMPBELL

"It was as true," said Mr. Barkis,
. . . "as taxes is. And nothing's truer
than them."
DICKENS—*David Copperfield*

Time is precious, but truth is more
precious than time.
DISRAELI

For truth has such a face and such a
mien,
As to be lov'd needs only to be seen.
DRYDEN—*The Hind and the
Panther*

Truth is immortal; error is mortal.
MARY BAKER EDDY—*Science
and Health*

The greater the truth the greater the
libel.
LORD ELLENBOROUGH

Great is truth, and mighty above all
things.
I ESDRAS. IV. 41

And ye shall know the truth, and the
truth shall make you free.
JOHN. VIII. 32

There is no truth in him.
JOHN. VIII. 44

The truth, the whole truth, and nothing but the truth.
LEGAL OATH

Truth forever on the scaffold. Wrong
forever on the throne.
LOWELL—*The Present Crisis*

Peace, if possible, but the truth at
any rate.
LUTHER

He who keeps back the truth, or
withholds it from men, from motives
of expediency, is either a coward or
a criminal, or both.
MAX MÜLLER

We know the truth, not only by the
reason, but also by the heart.
PASCAL—*Thoughts*

        To thine own self be true,
And it must follow, as the night the
day,
Thou canst not then be false to any
man.
SHAKESPEARE—*Hamlet.* Act I.
Sc. 3

'Tis true, 'tis pity;
And pity 'tis 'tis true.
SHAKESPEARE—*Hamlet.* Act II.
Sc. 2

My man's as true as steel.
SHAKESPEARE—*Romeo and Juliet.* Act II. Sc. 4

All great truths begin as blasphemies.
GEORGE BERNARD SHAW—
Annajanska

My way of joking is to tell the
truth.
It's the funniest joke in the world.
GEORGE BERNARD SHAW—*John
Bull's Other Island*

It takes two to speak the truth—one to speak, and another to hear.
THOREAU

(See also BELIEF, ERROR, HONOR, SINCERITY, THOUGHT, WISDOM.)

TWILIGHT

The summer day is closed, the sun is set:
Well they have done their office, those bright hours,
The latest of whose train goes softly out
In the red west.
BRYANT—*An Evening Reverie*

                              Parting day
Dies like the dolphin, whom each pang imbues
With a new colour as it gasps away,
The last still loveliest, till—'tis gone—and all is gray.
BYRON—*Childe Harold*

How lovely are the portals of the night,
    When stars come out to watch the daylight die.
THOMAS COLE—*Twilight*

The west is broken into bars
    Of orange, gold, and gray,
Gone is the sun, come are the stars,
    And night infolds the day.
GEORGE MACDONALD—*Songs of the Summer*

Twilight and evening bell
And after that the dark.
TENNYSON—*Crossing the Bar*

(See also EVENING, NIGHT, SKY, STAR, SUNSET.)

TYRANNY

Bad laws are the worst sort of tyranny.
BURKE

Unlimited power corrupts the possessor; and this I know, that, where law ends, there tyranny begins.
LORD CHATHAM

He who strikes terror into others is himself in continual fear.
CLAUDIAN

Tyrants have not yet discovered any chains that can fetter the mind.
COLTON

Resistance to tyrants is obedience to God.
JEFFERSON

'Tis time to fear when tyrants seem to kiss.
SHAKESPEARE—*Pericles*. Act I. Sc. 2

Arbitrary power is most easily established on the ruins of liberty abused to licentiousness.
WASHINGTON

(See also CRUELTY, DICTATOR, GOVERNMENT, LAW, POLITICS, REVOLUTION, ROYALTY, WAR.)

UGLINESS

Better an ugly face than an ugly mind.
JAMES ELLIS

Absolute and entire ugliness is rare.
RUSKIN

Nobody's sweetheart is ugly.
J. J. VADÉ

(See also APPEARANCE, BEAUTY.)

UNION

When bad men combine, the good must associate; else they will fall, one by one, an unpitied sacrifice in a contemptible struggle.
BURKE

Then join in hand, brave Americans all!
By uniting we stand, by dividing we fall.
JOHN DICKINSON—*Liberty Song*, 1768

All for one; one for all.
DUMAS—*The Three Musketeers*

We must all hang together or assuredly we shall hang separately.
FRANKLIN

The union of lakes—the union of lands—
The union of States none can sever—
The union of hearts—the union of hands—
And the flag of our union for ever!
GEORGE P. MORRIS—*The Flag of Our Union*

United we stand; divided we fall.
Motto of Kentucky

Behold how good and how pleasant it is for brethren to dwell together in unity.
PSALMS. CXXXIII. 1

By union the smallest states thrive, by discord the greatest are destroyed.
SALLUST

Liberty and Union, now and forever, one and inseparable.
DANIEL WEBSTER. 1830

(See also AMERICA, BROTHERHOOD, EQUALITY, FRIENDSHIP.)

UNITED STATES
See AMERICA

UNITY
See UNION

UNIVERSE
See WORLD

USEFULNESS
See SERVICE

VALOR

Discretion, the best part of valor.
BEAUMONT AND FLETCHER

The mean of true valor lies between the extremes of cowardice and rashness.
CERVANTES

(See also AUDACITY, BRAVERY, COURAGE, DARING, HERO, SOLDIER, WAR.)

VALUE
See WORTH

VANITY

The vain being is the really solitary being.
AUERBACH

It beareth the name of Vanity Fair, because the town where it is kept is "lighter than vanity."
BUNYAN—*Pilgrim's Progress*

Oh, wad some power the giftie gie us
To see oursel's as ithers see us!
It wad frae monie a blunder free us,
And foolish notion.
BURNS—*To a Louse*

Vanity of vanities; all is vanity.
ECCLESIASTES. I. 2

All is vanity and vexation of spirit.
ECCLESIASTES. I. 14

Vanity makes men ridiculous, pride
odious, and ambition terrible.
STEELE

It is difficult to esteem a man as
highly as he would wish.
VAUVENARGUES

(See also APPEARANCE, CONCEIT,
EGOTISM, PRIDE, SELF-LOVE.)

VARIETY

Variety's the very spice of life,
That gives it all its flavour.
COWPER—*The Task*

It takes all sorts to make a world.
ENGLISH PROVERB

When our old Pleasures die,
Some new One still is nigh;
Oh! fair Variety!
NICHOLAS ROWE

Age cannot wither her, nor custom
stale
Her infinite variety.
SHAKESPEARE—*Antony and
Cleopatra*. Act II. Sc. 2

(See also CHANGE, CHOICE,
TASTE.)

VENGEANCE
See REVENGE

VICE

What's vice today may be virtue tomorrow.
FIELDING

What maintains one vice would bring
up two children.
FRANKLIN—*Poor Richard's Almanac*

When our vices leave us we flatter
ourselves with the idea that we have
left them.
LA ROCHEFOUCAULD

Saint Augustine! well hast thou said,
That of our vices we can frame
A ladder, if we will but tread
Beneath our feet each deed of
shame.
LONGFELLOW—*The Ladder of
St. Augustine*

Human nature is not of itself vicious.
THOMAS PAINE

There will be vices as long as there
are men.
TACITUS

Vice lives and thrives best by conceal-
ment.
VERGIL

(See also BRIBERY, CORRUPTION,
CRIME, EVIL, GUILT, SIN,
WICKEDNESS.)

VICTORY

Victories that are cheap are cheap.
Those only are worth having which
come as the result of hard fighting.
HENRY WARD BEECHER

How beautiful is victory, but how dear!

BOUFFLERS

The race is not to the swift, nor the battle to the strong.

ECCLESIASTES. IX. 11

To the victors belong the spoils.

ANDREW JACKSON

Who overcomes
By force, hath overcome but half his foe.

MILTON—*Paradise Lost*

There are some defeats more triumphant than victories.

MONTAIGNE

We have met the enemy and they are ours.

OLIVER HAZARD PERRY

Hannibal knew how to gain a victory, but not how to use it.

PLUTARCH

But if
We have such another victory, we are undone.

Attributed to PYRRHUS by BACON—*Apothegms*

There is nothing so dreadful as a great victory—except a great defeat.

Attributed to WELLINGTON

(See also CONQUEST, GLORY, HERO, SOLDIER, SUCCESS, WAR.)

VILLAINY
See CRIME

VIOLENCE
See FORCE

VIRTUE

One's outlook is a part of his virtue.

ALCOTT—*Concord Days*

Virtue is like a rich stone, best plain set.

BACON—*Essays*

Recommend to your children virtue; that alone can make them happy, not gold.

BEETHOVEN

Honor is the reward of virtue.

CICERO

I believe that Virtue shows quite as well in rags and patches as she does in purple and fine linen.

DICKENS

There are those who have nothing chaste but their ears, and nothing virtuous but their tongues.

DE FINOD

The only reward of virtue is virtue.

EMERSON—*Essays*

Most men admire
Virtue, who follow not her lore.

MILTON—*Paradise Regained*

Our virtues are most frequently but vices disguised.

LA ROCHEFOUCAULD

Virtue is an angel, but she is a blind one, and must ask of Knowledge to show her the pathway that leads to her goal.

HORACE MANN

I prefer an accommodation vice to an obstinate virtue.

MOLIÈRE

Virtue is health, vice is sickness.
PETRARCH

Virtue consists, not in abstaining from vice, but in not desiring it.
GEORGE BERNARD SHAW

Virtue often trips and falls on the sharp-edged rock of poverty.
EUGÈNE SUE

(See also CHARACTER, GOODNESS, INNOCENCE, MORALITY, TRUTH, WISDOM, WORTH.)

VISION

Abou Ben Adhem (may his tribe increase!)
Awoke one night from a deep dream of peace,
And saw, within the moonlight in his room,
Making it rich, and like a lily in bloom,
An angel, writing in a book of gold;
Exceeding peace had made Ben Adhem bold,
And to the presence in the room he said—
"What writest thou?" The Vision raised its head,
And, with a look made all of sweet accord,
Answered, "The names of those who love the Lord."
LEIGH HUNT—*Abou Ben Adhem and the Angel*

And it shall come to pass afterward, that I will pour out my Spirit upon all flesh; and your sons and your daughters shall prophesy, your old men shall dream dreams, your young men shall see visions.
JOEL. II. 28

My thoughts by night are often filled
With visions false as fair:
For in the past alone, I build
My castles in the air.
THOMAS LOVE PEACOCK— *Castles in the Air*

Where there is no vision, the people perish.
PROVERBS. XXIX. 18

(See also DREAMS, IMAGINATION, SPIRIT, WONDER.)

VOICE

The voice of the people is the voice of God.
HESIOD

A still, small voice.
I KINGS. XIX. 12

The voice of one crying in the wilderness.
MATTHEW. III. 3

Her voice was ever soft,
Gentle and low, an excellent thing in woman.
SHAKESPEARE—*King Lear*. Act V. Sc. 3

(See also CONVERSATION, ELOQUENCE, LANGUAGE, ORATORY, MUSIC, SONG, SOUND, SPEECH, TALK, TONGUE, WORD.)

VOWS
See OATH

WAGES

A fair day's wages for a fair day's work: it is as just a demand as governed men ever made of governing.
CARLYLE—*Past and Present*

It is but a truism that labor is most productive where its wages are largest. Poorly paid labor is inefficient labor, the world over.

> HENRY GEORGE—*Progress and Poverty*

The laborer is worthy of his hire.

> LUKE. X. 7

Be content with your wages.

> MARK. III. 14

If a business be unprofitable on account of bad management, want of enterprise, or out-worn methods, that is not a just reason for reducing the wages of its workers.

> POPE PIUS XI

The iron law of wages.

> A. R. J. TURGOT

(See also CAPITAL AND LABOR, COMMUNISM, INDUSTRY, POVERTY, SOCIALISM, WEALTH.)

WANT

Man wants but little here below, Nor wants that little long.

> GOLDSMITH—*The Hermit*

Constantly choose rather to want less, than to have more.

> THOMAS À KEMPIS

How few our real wants, and how vast our imaginary ones!

> LAVATER

The stoical scheme of supplying our wants by lopping off our desires is like cutting off our feet when we want shoes.

> SWIFT

(See also AMBITION, DESIRE, POVERTY.)

WAR

War is the science of destruction.

> JOHN S. C. ABBOTT

War cannot be put on a certain allowance.

> ARCHIDAMUS III

The inevitableness, the idealism, and the blessing of war, as an indispensable and stimulating law of development, must be repeatedly emphasized.

> BERNHARDI—*Germany and the Next War*

Just for a word—"neutrality," a word which in war-time had so often been disregarded—just for a scrap of paper, Great Britain was going to make war on a kindred nation who desired nothing better than to be friends with her.

> BETHMANN-HOLLWEG, German Chancellor, 1914

Better pointed bullets than pointed speeches.

> BISMARCK—Speech, 1850

(The great questions of the day) are not decided by speeches and majority votes, but by blood and iron.

> BISMARCK—To the Prussian House of Delegates

War never leaves, where it found a nation.

> BURKE

Veni, vidi, vici.
I came, I saw, I conquered.

> JULIUS CAESAR

What millions died—that Caesar might be great!
CAMPBELL

What distinguishes war is, not that man is slain, but that he is slain, spoiled, crushed by the cruelty, the injustice, the treachery, the murderous hand of man.
WILLIAM ELLERY CHANNING

General Taylor never surrenders.
THOMAS L. CRITTENDEN—
Reply to Gen. Santa

We give up the fort when there's not a man left to defend it.
GENERAL CROGHAN. At Fort Stevenson. (1812)

War, he sung, is toil and trouble;
Honour but an empty bubble.
DRYDEN—*Alexander's Feast*

By the rude bridge that arched the flood,
Their flag to April's breeze unfurl'd;
Here once the embattl'd farmers stood,
And fired the shot heard round the world.
EMERSON—Hymn sung at the completion of the Concord Monument

The essence of war is violence. Moderation in war is imbecility.
Attributed to LORD FISHER

My right has been rolled up. My left has been driven back. My center has been smashed. I have ordered an advance from all directions.
Attributed to GENERAL FOCH, World War I

There never was a good war or a bad peace.
FRANKLIN—Letter to Quincy

I . . . propose to fight it out on this line if it takes all summer.
U. S. GRANT—Despatch from Spotsylvania

Hang yourself, brave Crillon. We fought at Arques, and you were not there.
HENRY IV, to Crillon after a great victory

It is not right to exult over slain men.
HOMER—*Odyssey*

Mine eyes have seen the glory of the coming of the Lord:
He is trampling out the vintage where the grapes of wrath are stored:
He hath loosed the fateful lightning of his terrible swift sword:
His truth is marching on.
JULIA WARD HOWE—*Battle Hymn of the Republic*

We don't want to fight, but by jingo if we do,
We've got the ships, we've got the men, we've got the money too.
We've fought the Bear before and while we're Britons true,
The Russians shall not have Constantinople.
G. W. HUNT

War is as much a punishment to the punisher as to the sufferer.
JEFFERSON—Letter, 1794

I have prayed in her fields of poppies,
I have laughed with the men who died—

But in all my ways and through all
   my days
   Like a friend He walked beside.
I have seen a sight under Heaven
   That only God understands,
In the battle's glare I have seen
   Christ there
     With the Sword of God in His
     hand.
     GORDON JOHNSTONE—*On
     Fields of Flanders*

Modern warfare is an intricate business about which no one knows
everything and few know very much.
     FRANK KNOX—Speech, 1942

There is no such thing as an inevitable war. If war comes it will be
from failure of human wisdom.
     BONAR LAW—Speech before
     World War I

O God assist our side: at least, avoid
assisting the enemy and leave the
rest to me.
     PRINCE LEOPOLD of Anhalt-
     Dessau.

The ballot is stronger than the bullet.
     LINCOLN. (1856)

To arms! to arms! ye brave!
   The avenging sword unsheathe,
March on! march on! all hearts re-
   solved
     On victory or death!
     ROUGET DE LISLE—*The
     Marseillaise*

Ez for war, I call it murder,—
   There you hev it plain and flat;
I don't want to go no furder
   Than my Testyment for that.
     LOWELL—*The Biglow Papers*

War is the greatest plague that can
afflict humanity; it destroys religion,
it destroys states, it destroys families.
Any scourge is preferable to it.
     MARTIN LUTHER

I beg that the small steamers . . .
be spared if possible, or else sunk
without a trace being left. (Spurlos
versenkt.)
     COUNT KARL VON LUXBURG,
     Chargé d'Affaires at Buenos
     Aires to his Berlin Foreign
     Office, 1917

The warpipes are pealing, "The
   Campbells are coming."
They are charging and cheering.
   O dinna ye hear it?
     ALEXANDER MACLAGAN—
     Jennie's Dream

Wars and rumours of wars.
     MATTHEW. XXIV. 6

Take up our quarrel with the foe!
To you from failing hands we throw
   The torch; be yours to hold it
   high.
   If ye break faith with us who die
We shall not sleep, though poppies
   grow
   In Flanders' fields.
     JOHN McCRAE—*In Flanders'
     Fields*

And this I hate—not men, nor flag
   nor race,
But only War with its wild, grinning
   face.
     JOSEPH DANA MILLER—*The
     Hymn of Hate*

The brazen throat of war.
     MILTON—*Paradise Lost*

War hath no fury like a non-combatant.
> C. E. MONTAGUE—*Disenchantment*

When after many battles past,
Both tir'd with blows, make peace at last,
What is it, after all, the people get?
Why! taxes, widows, wooden legs, and debt.
> FRANCIS MOORE—*Almanac*

Providence is always on the side of the last reserve.
> Attributed to NAPOLEON

England expects every officer and man to do his duty this day.
> NELSON—Before the battle of Trafalgar

God how the dead men
  Grin by the wall,
Watching the fun
  Of the Victory Ball.
> ALFRED NOYES—*The Highwayman*

These are the times that try men's souls. The Summer soldier and the sunshine patriot will, in this crisis, shrink from the service of their country, but he that stands it *now* deserves the love and thanks of man and woman. Tyranny, like Hell, is not easily conquered; yet we have this consolation with us, that the harder the conflict the more glorious the triumph. What we obtain too cheaply we esteem too lightly; it is dearness only that gives everything its value. Heaven knows how to put a proper price upon its goods; and it would be strange indeed if so celestial an article as *freedom* should not be highly rated.
> THOMAS PAINE—*The Crisis*

Hell, Heaven or Hoboken by Christmas.
> Attributed to GENERAL JOHN JOSEPH PERSHING. (1918)

War its thousands slays,
Peace its ten thousands.
> PORTEUS—*Death*

O war! thou son of Hell!
> SHAKESPEARE—*Henry VI.* Pt. II. Act V. Sc. 2

A bad peace is even worse than war.
> TACITUS

As long as war is regarded as wicked, it will always have its fascination. When it is looked upon as vulgar, it will cease to be popular.
> WILDE

(See also AMERICA, ENGLAND, GLORY, GOVERNMENT, HERO, NAVY, PEACE, SOLDIER, STATESMANSHIP, VICTORY.)

WASHINGTON

The father of his country.
> FRANCIS BAILEY

Every countenance seeked to say, "Long live George Washington, the Father of the People."
> *Pennsylvania Packet,* April 21, 1789

WATER
See NATURE

WEAKNESS
See FEAR, FRAILTY

WEALTH

I have mental joys and mental health,
Mental friends and mental wealth,
I've a wife that I love and that loves
me;
I've all but riches bodily.
WILLIAM BLAKE—*Mammon*

Surplus wealth is a sacred trust
which its possessor is bound to ad-
minister in his lifetime for the good
of the community.
ANDREW CARNEGIE—*Gospel
of Wealth*

If you would be wealthy, think of
saving as well as of getting.
FRANKLIN

The ideal social state is not that in
which each gets an equal amount of
wealth, but in which each gets in
proportion to his contribution to the
general stock.
HENRY GEORGE—*Social
Problems*

Ill fares the land, to hastening ills a
prey,
Where wealth accumulates, and men
decay;
Princes and Lords may flourish, or
may fade—
A breath can make them, as a breath
has made—
But a bold peasantry, their country's
pride,
When once destroy'd can never be
supplied.
GOLDSMITH—*Deserted Village*

Riches either serve or govern the
possessor.
HORACE

The wealth of nations is men, not
silk and cotton and gold.
RICHARD HOVEY—*Peace*

Life is short. The sooner that a man
begins to enjoy his wealth the better.
SAMUEL JOHNSON

All wealth is the product of labor.
LOCKE

Our Lord commonly giveth Riches
to such gross asses, to whom he
affordeth nothing else that is good.
LUTHER—*Colloquies*

It is easier for a camel to go through
the eye of a needle, than for a rich
man to enter into the kingdom of
God.
MATTHEW. XIX. 24

I am rich beyond the dreams of
avarice.
EDWARD MOORE—*The Game-
ster*

Get place and wealth, if possible,
with grace;
If not, by any means get wealth and
place.
POPE—*Epistles of Horace*

Riches certainly make themselves
wings.
PROVERBS. XXIII. 5

He that maketh haste to be rich
shall not be innocent.
PROVERBS. XXVIII. 20

He heapeth up riches, and knoweth
not who shall gather them.
PSALMS. XXXIX. 6

No good man ever became suddenly
rich.
SYRUS

Rich in good works.
I Timothy. VI. 18

(See also AVARICE, FORTUNE, GOLD,
JEWEL, MAMMON, MONEY,
POSSESSION, RICHES.)

WEATHER

As a rule man is a fool,
When it's hot he wants it cool,
When it's cool he wants it hot,
Always wanting what is not.
Anonymous

I was born with a chronic anxiety
about the weather.
John Burroughs—*Is It Going
to Rain?*

Everybody talks about the weather
but nobody does anything about it.
Attributed to S. L. Clemens
(Mark Twain)

Change of weather is the discourse
of fools.
Thomas Fuller

Fair weather cometh out of the north.
Job. XXXVII. 22

Oh, what a blamed uncertain thing
This pesky weather is;
It blew and snew and then it thew,
And now, by jing, it's friz.
Philander Johnson

When two Englishmen meet, their
first talk is of the weather.
Samuel Johnson

(See also GOSSIP, PROPHECY,
NATURE, TALK.)

WEDDING
See MATRIMONY

WEDLOCK
See MATRIMONY

WEEPING
See TEARS

WELCOME

'Tis sweet to hear the watch-dog's
honest bark
Bay deep-mouth'd welcome as we
draw near home.
Byron—*Don Juan*

Come in the evening, come in the
morning,
Come when expected, come without
warning;
Thousands of welcomes you'll find
here before you,
And the oftener you come, the more
we'll adore you.
Irish Rhyme

Welcome as the flowers in May.
Scott—*Rob Roy*

(See also GUEST, HOME, HOS-
PITALITY, TOASTS.)

WEST

Westward the course of empire takes
its way.
Bishop Berkeley

Out where the handclasp's a little
stronger,
Out where the smile dwells a little
longer,
That's where the West begins.
Arthur Chapman

Go West, young man, and grow up with the country.
HORACE GREELEY

Westward, Ho!
GEORGE PEELE

(See also AMBITION, AMERICA, TRAVELING.)

WICKEDNESS

God bears with the wicked, but not forever.
CERVANTES—*Don Quixote*

No man ever became very wicked all at once.
JUVENAL

The world loves a spice of wickedness.
LONGFELLOW—*Hyperion*

Wickedness is weakness.
MILTON—*Samson Agonistes*

The wicked flee when no man pursueth; but the righteous are bold as a lion.
PROVERBS. XXVIII. 1

As saith the proverb of the Ancients, Wickedness proceedeth from the wicked.
I SAMUEL. XXIV. 13

The sun also shines on the wicked.
SENECA

'Cause I's wicked,—I is. I's mighty wicked, anyhow, I can't help it.
HARRIET BEECHER STOWE—*Uncle Tom's Cabin*

(See also BRIBERY, CORRUPTION, CRIME, PRISON, SIN, VICE.)

WIFE

Wives are young men's mistresses; companions for middle age; and old men's nurses.
BACON—*Of Marriage and Single Life*

She is a winsome wee thing,
She is a handsome wee thing,
She is a bonny wee thing,
   This sweet wee wife o' mine.
BURNS—*My Wife's a Winsome Wee Thing*

Think you, if Laura had been Petrarch's wife,
He would have written sonnets all his life?
BYRON—*Don Juan*

The wife of thy bosom.
DEUTERONOMY. XIII. 6

In every mess I find a friend,
In every port a wife.
CHARLES DIBDIN—*Jack in His Element*

An undutiful Daughter will prove an unmanageable Wife.
FRANKLIN—*Poor Richard*

He knows little who will tell his wife all he knows.
THOMAS FULLER—*Holy and Profane State*

Alas! another instance of the triumph of hope over experience.
SAMUEL JOHNSON, referring to the second marriage of a friend

All other goods by fortune's hand are given:
A wife is the peculiar gift of Heav'n.
POPE

She looketh well to the ways of her household, and eateth not the bread of idleness.
PROVERBS. XXXI. 27

It is a woman's business to get married as soon as possible, and a man's to keep unmarried as long as he can.
GEORGE BERNARD SHAW—*Man and Superman*

My dear, my better half.
PHILIP SIDNEY—*Arcadia*

Teacher, tender comrade, wife,
A fellow-farer true through life.
STEVENSON—*My Wife*

The world well tried—the sweetest thing in life
Is the unclouded welcome of a wife.
N. P. WILLIS—*Lady Jane*

(See also BABYHOOD, CHILDHOOD, HOME, HUSBAND, LOVE, MATRIMONY, MOTHER, PARENT, WOMAN, WOOING.)

WILL

He that will not when he may,
When he will he shall have nay.
BURTON—*Anatomy of Melancholy*

Barkis is willin'!
DICKENS—*David Copperfield*

Where there's a will there's a way.
ENGLISH PROVERB

There is nothing good or evil save in the will.
EPICTETUS

He who is firm in will molds the world to himself.
GOETHE

People do not lack strength; they lack will.
VICTOR HUGO

Man can do everything with himself, but he must not attempt to do too much with others.
WILHELM VON HUMBOLDT

Not my will, but thine, be done.
LUKE. XXII. 42

(See also DECISION, DEED, FORCE, MIND, RESOLUTION, STRENGTH.)

WIND

The wind moans, like a long wail from some despairing soul shut out in the awful storm!
W. H. GIBSON—*Pastoral Days*

An ill wind that bloweth no man good—
The blower of which blast is she.
JOHN HEYWOOD—*Idleness*

I hear the wind among the trees
Playing the celestial symphonies;
I see the branches downward bent,
Like keys of some great instrument.
LONGFELLOW—*A Day of Sunshine*

Who walketh upon the wings of the wind.
PSALMS. CIV. 3

Blow, wind, and crack your cheeks. Rage! Blow!
SHAKESPEARE—*King Lear*. Act III. Sc. 1

O wind,
If Winter comes, can Spring be far
behind?
SHELLEY—*Ode to the West
Wind*

Sweet and low, sweet and low,
Wind of the western sea,
Low, low, breathe and blow,
Wind of the western sea!
TENNYSON—*The Princess*

(See also STORM.)

WINE AND SPIRITS

John Barleycorn was a hero bold,
Of noble enterprise,
For if you do but taste his blood,
'Twill make your courage rise,
'Twill make a man forget his woe;
'Twill heighten all his joy.
BURNS—*John Barleycorn*

Few things surpass old wine; and
they may preach
Who please, the more because they
preach in vain,—
Let us have wine and women, mirth
and laughter,
Sermons and soda-water the day
after.
BYRON—*Don Juan*

Call things by their right names
. . . Glass of brandy and water!
That is the current, but not the
appropriate name; ask for *a glass of
liquid fire and distilled damnation.*
ROBERT HALL

No nation is drunken where wine
is cheap; and none sober where the
dearness of wine substitutes ardent
spirits as the common beverage. It
is, in truth, the only antidote to the
bane of whiskey.
JEFFERSON, 1818

Claret is the liquor for boys; port
for men; but he who aspires to be a
hero must drink brandy.
SAMUEL JOHNSON

There is a devil in every berry of the
grape.
THE KORAN

If with water you fill up your glasses,
You'll never write anything wise;
For wine is the horse of Parnassus,
Which hurries a bard to the skies.
MOORE

The Grape that can with Logic absolute
The Two-and-Seventy jarring Sects
confute:
The sovereign Alchemist that in a
trice
Life's leaden metal into Gold trans-
mute.
OMAR KHAYYÁM—*Rubaiyat*

Wine is the most healthful and most
hygienic of beverages.
LOUIS PASTEUR

Look not thou upon the wine when
it is red, when it giveth his colour in
the cup; . . . at the last it biteth
like a serpent, and stingeth like an
adder.
PROVERBS. XXIII. 31

Wine that maketh glad the heart of
man.
PSALMS. CIV. 15

Drink no longer water, but use a
little wine for thy stomach's sake.
I TIMOTHY. V. 23

(See also DRINKING, INTEMPERANCE,
MODERATION, TEMPERANCE,
TOASTS.)

WINTER

I crown thee king of intimate de-
    lights,
Fireside enjoyments, home-born
    happiness,
And all the comforts that the lowly
    roof
Of undisturb'd Retirement, and the
    hours
Of long uninterrupted evening,
    know.
        COWPER—*The Task*

Oh, the long and dreary Winter!
Oh, the cold and cruel Winter!
        LONGFELLOW—*Hiawatha*

If Winter comes, can Spring be far
behind?
        SHELLEY—*Ode to the West
        Wind*

Make we here our camp of winter;
    And, through sleet and snow,
Pitchy knot and beechen splinter
    On our hearth shall glow.
Here, with mirth to lighten duty,
    We shall lack alone
Woman's smile and girlhood's beauty,
    Childhood's lisping tone.
        WHITTIER—*Lumbermen*

(See also NATURE, SEASONS.)

WISDOM

The wisdom of our ancestors.
    BURKE

Wise men learn more from fools than
fools from the wise.
    CATO THE CENSOR

In much wisdom is much grief.
    ECCLESIASTES. I. 18

The words of the wise are as goads.
    ECCLESIASTES. XII. 11

It is easy to be wise after the event.
    ENGLISH PROVERB

No one could be so wise as Thurlow
looked.
    CHARLES JAMES FOX

Some are weather-wise, some are
otherwise.
    FRANKLIN—*Poor Richard*

Wisdom is only found in truth.
    GOETHE

The heart is wiser than the intellect.
    J. G. HOLLAND—*Katrina*

In youth and beauty wisdom is but
rare!
    HOMER—*Odyssey*

The price of wisdom is above rubies.
    JOB. XXVIII. 18

Days should speak, and multitude
of years should teach wisdom.
    JOB. XXXII. 7

Great men are not always wise.
    JOB. XXXII. 7

It is easier to be wise for others than
for ourselves.
    LA ROCHEFOUCAULD

Be ye therefore wise as serpents,
and harmless as doves.
    MATTHEW. X. 16

It is good to rub and polish our brain
against that of others.
    MONTAIGNE

He gains wisdom in a happy way, who gains it by another's experience.
PLAUTUS

No one is wise at all times.
PLINY THE ELDER

Wisdom crieth without; she uttereth her voice in the street.
PROVERBS. I. 20

Go to the ant, thou sluggard; consider her ways, and be wise.
PROVERBS. VI. 6

Wisdom is the principal thing; therefore get wisdom; and with all thy getting get understanding.
PROVERBS. VIII. 11

The fear of the Lord is the beginning of wisdom.
PSALMS. CXI. 10

Nine-tenths of wisdom consists in being wise in time.
THEODORE ROOSEVELT—Speech, 1917

I never knew so young a body with so old a head.
SHAKESPEARE—Merchant of Venice. Act IV. Sc. 1

As for me, all I know is that I know nothing.
SOCRATES

The doorstep to the temple of wisdom is a knowledge of our own ignorance.
SPURGEON—Gleanings among the Sheaves

The children of this world are in their generation wiser than the children of light.
I TIMOTHY. XVI. 8

Wisdom is the gray hair unto men, and an unspotted life is old age.
WISDOM OF SOLOMON. IV. 8

(See also DISCRETION, EDUCATION, FOLLY, GOLDEN RULE, JUDGMENT, KNOWLEDGE, LEARNING, MIND, MORALITY, TRUTH.)

WISH

"Man wants but little here below
  Nor wants that little long,"
'Tis not with me exactly so;
  But 'tis so in the song.
My wants are many, and, if told,
  Would muster many a score;
And were each wish a mint of gold,
  I still should long for more.
JOHN QUINCY ADAMS—The Wants of Man

If wishes were horses beggars might ride.
ENGLISH PROVERB

If a man could half his wishes he would double his Troubles.
FRANKLIN—Poor Richard

I wish I knew the good of wishing.
HENRY S. LEIGH—Wishing

O, that I were where I would be,
  Then would I be where I am not;
For where I am I would not be,
  And where I would be I can not.
A. QUILLER-COUCH

Thy wish was father to that thought.
SHAKESPEARE—Henry IV. Pt. II. Act IV. Sc. 5

As you cannot do what you wish, you should wish what you can do.
TERENCE

(See also ANTICIPATION, DESIRE, IMAGINATION.)

WIT

Sharp wits, like sharp knives, do
often cut their owner's fingers.
ARROWSMITH

Wit is the salt of conversation, not
the food.
HAZLITT

This man (Chesterfield) I thought
had been a lord among wits; but I
find he is only a wit among lords.
SAMUEL JOHNSON—*Boswell's
Life of Johnson*

A man does not please long when he
has only one species of wit.
LA ROCHEFOUCAULD

Avoid witticisms at the expense of
others.
HORACE MANN

True wit is nature to advantage
dress'd
What oft was thought, but ne'er so
well expressed.
POPE—*Essay on Criticism*

At their wit's end.
PSALMS. CVII. 27

Great men may jest with saints; 'tis
wit in them;
But, in the less foul profanation.
SHAKESPEARE—*Measure for
Measure*. Act II. Sc. 2

Wit consists in knowing the resemblance of things which differ, and
the difference of things which are
alike.
MME. DE STAËL

(See also CONVERSATION, EPITAPH,
HUMOR, JESTING, JOKE,
SATIRE, TOASTS.)

WOE
See MISERY

WOMAN

Oh, the shrewdness of their shrewdness when they're shrewd.
And the rudeness of their rudeness
when they're rude;
But the shrewdness of their shrewdness and the rudeness of their
rudeness,
Are nothing to their goodness when
they're good.
ANONYMOUS

You see, dear, it is not true that
woman was made from man's rib;
she was really made from his funny
bone.
BARRIE—*What Every Woman
Knows*

In her first passion woman loves her
lover;
In all the others, all she loves is love.
BYRON—*Don Juan*

Suffer women once to arrive at an
equality with you, and they will
from that moment become your superiors.
CATO THE CENSOR

A woman is like your shadow; follow her, she flies; fly from her, she
follows.
CHAMFORT

Heaven has no rage like love to ha-
tred turned,
Nor hell a fury like a woman
scorned.
CONGREVE—*The Mourning
Bride*

But what is woman? Only one of nature's agreeable blunders.
  COWLEY

Men *say* of women what pleases them; women *do* with men what pleases them.
  DE SEGUR

Women always have some mental reservation.
  DESTOUCHES

Cherchez la femme.
  Find the woman.
  DUMAS—*Les Mohicans de Paris*

There is no worse evil than a bad woman; and nothing has ever been produced better than a good one.
  EURIPIDES

Where is the man who has the power and skill
To stem the torrent of a woman's will?
For if she will, she will, you may depend on't;
And if she won't, she won't; so there's an end on't.
  From the Pillar Erected in Dane John Field, Canterbury

The society of women is the foundation of good manners.
  GOETHE

Most men who run down women are running down one woman only.
  REMY DE GOURMONT

Women forgive injuries, but never forget slights.
  HALIBURTON

The crown of creation.
  HERDER

Man has his will,—but woman has her way.
  HOLMES—*Autocrat of the Breakfast Table*

It is God who makes woman beautiful, it is the devil who makes her pretty.
  VICTOR HUGO

A woman's guess is much more accurate than a man's certainty.
  KIPLING—*Plain Tales*

An' I learned about women from 'er.
  KIPLING—*The Ladies*

The colonel's lady and Judy O'Grady
Are sisters under their skins.
  KIPLING—*The Ladies*

The silliest woman can manage a clever man; but it needs a very clever woman to manage a fool!
  KIPLING—*Plain Tales*

For the female of the species is more deadly than the male.
  KIPLING—*The Female of the Species*

A rag and a bone and a hank of hair.
  KIPLING—*The Vampire*

Those who always speak well of women do not know them sufficiently; those who always speak ill of them do not know them at all.
  GUILLAUME PIGAULT LEBRUN

There are no ugly women; there are only women who do not know how to look pretty.
  LA BRUYÈRE

Earth's noblest thing, a Woman perfected.
LOWELL—*Irene*

The great fault in women is to desire to be like men.
DE MAISTRE

Too fair to worship, too divine to love.
MILMAN—*Apollo Belvedere*

Grace was in all her steps, heaven in her eye,
In every gesture dignity and love.
MILTON—*Paradise Lost*

The weaker vessel.
I PETER. III. 7

Offend her, and she knows not to forgive;
Oblige her, and she'll hate you while you live.
POPE—*Moral Essays*

Woman's at best a contradiction still.
POPE—*Moral Essays*

It is better to dwell in a corner of the housetop than with a brawling woman in a wide house.
PROVERBS. XXI. 9

O wild, dark flower of woman,
Deep rose of my desire,
An Eastern wizard made you
Of earth and stars and fire.
C. G. D. ROBERTS—*The Rose of My Desire*

It is easier for a woman to defend her virtue against men than her reputation against women.
ROCHEBRUNE

Men who flatter women do not know them; men who abuse them know them still less.
MME. DE SALM

Such, Polly, are your sex—part truth, part fiction;
Some thought, much whim, and all contradiction.
RICHARD SAVAGE—*To a Young Lady*

Honor women! they entwine and weave heavenly roses in our earthly life.
SCHILLER

The weakness of their reasoning faculty also explains why women show more sympathy for the unfortunate than men; . . . and why, on the contrary, they are inferior to men as regards justice, and less honourable and conscientious.
SCHOPENHAUER—*On Women*

O Woman! in our hours of ease,
Uncertain, coy, and hard to please,
And variable as the shade
By the light quivering aspen made;
When pain and anguish wring the brow,
A ministering angel thou!
SCOTT—*Marmion*

Age cannot wither her, nor custom stale
Her infinite variety.
SHAKESPEARE—*Antony and Cleopatra*. Act II. Sc. 2

Frailty, thy name is woman!
SHAKESPEARE—*Hamlet*. Act I. Sc. 2

You are pictures out of doors,
Bells in your parlours, wild-cats in
your kitchens,
Saints in your injuries, devils being
offended,
Players in your housewifery, and
housewives in your beds.
SHAKESPEARE—*Othello*. Act II.
Sc. 1

In the beginning, said a Persian poet
—Allah took a rose, a lily, a dove,
a serpent, a little honey, a Dead
Sea apple, and a handful of clay.
When he looked at the amalgam—
it was a woman.
WILLIAM SHARP

The fickleness of the woman I love
is only equalled by the infernal constancy of the women who love me.
GEORGE BERNARD SHAW—
Philanderer

Woman's dearest delight is to wound
Man's self-conceit, though Man's
dearest delight is to gratify hers.
GEORGE BERNARD SHAW—
Unsocial Socialist

A man may brave opinion; a woman
must submit to it.
MME. DE STAËL

I am glad that I am not a man, for
then I should have to marry a
woman.
MME. DE STAËL

A woman either loves or hates: she
knows no medium.
SYRUS

Regard the society of women as a
necessary unpleasantness of social
life, and avoid it as much as possible.
TOLSTOY—*Diary*

There is no such thing as romance
in our day, women have become too
brilliant; nothing spoils a romance
so much as a sense of humor in the
woman.
WILDE—*A Woman of No
Importance*

She was a Phantom of delight
When first she gleamed upon my
sight;
A lovely Apparition, sent
To be a moment's ornament.
WORDSWORTH—*She Was a
Phantom of Delight*

(See also BABYHOOD, BEAUTY,
CHILDHOOD, FLIRTATION, FRAILTY,
HUSBAND, KISS, LOVE, MATRIMONY,
MODESTY, MOTHER, PARENT, VIR-
TUE, WIFE, WOOING.)

WONDER

A schoolboy's tale, the wonder of an
hour!
BYRON—*Childe Harold*

Wonder is the basis of worship.
CARLYLE

Men love to wonder and that is the
seed of our science.
EMERSON—*Works and Days*

No wonder can last more than three
days.
ITALIAN PROVERB

(See also IMAGINATION, INVENTION,
SUPERSTITION, THOUGHT.)

WOODS
See TREE

WOOING

Thrice happy's the wooing that's not
    long a-doing,
So much time is saved in the billing
    and cooing.
      R. H. BARHAM—*Sir Rupert the
      Fearless*

"Yes," I answered you last night;
    "No," this morning, sir, I say:
Colors seen by candle-light
    Will not look the same by day.
      E. B. BROWNING—*The Lady's
      "Yes."*

And let us mind, faint heart ne'er
    wan
A lady fair.
      BURNS—*To Dr. Blacklock*

There is a tide in the affairs of
    women
Which, taken at the flood, leads—
    God knows where.
      BYRON—*Don Juan*

                'Tis enough—
Who listens once will listen twice;
    Her heart be sure is not of ice,
And one refusal no rebuff.
      BYRON—*Mazeppa*

Never wedding, ever wooing,
Still a lovelorn heart pursuing,
Read you not the wrong you're do-
    ing
In my cheek's pale hue?
All my life with sorrow strewing;
    Wed or cease to woo.
      CAMPBELL—*The Maid's
      Remonstrance*

Perhaps if you address the lady
    Most politely, most politely,

Flatter and impress the lady
    Most politely, most politely,
Humbly beg and humbly sue,
She may deign to look on you.
      W. S. GILBERT—*Princess Ida*

A fool there was and he made his
    prayer
    (Even as you and I!)
To a rag and a bone and a hank of
    hair
(We called her the woman who did
    not care)
But the fool he called her his lady
    fair—
    (Even as you or I!)
      KIPLING—*The Vampire*

If I am not worth the wooing, I
surely am not worth the winning.
      LONGFELLOW—*Courtship of
      Miles Standish*

Why don't you speak for yourself,
John?
      LONGFELLOW—*Courtship of
      Miles Standish*

Come live in my heart and pay no
rent.
      SAMUEL LOVER

The time I've lost in wooing,
In watching and pursuing
    The light that lies
    In woman's eyes,
Has been my heart's undoing.
      MOORE—*The Time I've Lost in
      Wooing*

Ye shall know my breach of promise.
      NUMBERS. XIV. 34

They dream in courtship, but in
wedlock wake.
      POPE—*Wife of Bath*

The way of an eagle in the air; the way of a serpent upon a rock; the way of a ship in the midst of the sea; and the way of a man with a maid.
> PROVERBS. XXX. 19

Men are April when they woo, December when they wed.
> SHAKESPEARE—*As You Like It.* Act IV. Sc. 1

She's beautiful and therefore to be woo'd:
She is a woman, therefore to be won.
> SHAKESPEARE—*Henry VI.* Pt. I. Act V. Sc. 3

Sigh no more, ladies, sigh no more,
    Men were deceivers ever,
One foot in sea and one on shore;
    To one thing constant never.
> SHAKESPEARE—*Much Ado About Nothing.* Act II. Sc. 3

        O gentle Romeo,
If thou dost love, pronounce it faithfully.
Or if thou think'st I am too quickly won,
I'll frown and be perverse and say thee nay,
So thou wilt woo: but else, not for the world.
> SHAKESPEARE—*Romeo and Juliet.* Act II. Sc. 2

(See also FLIRTATION, KISS, LOVE, MATRIMONY, WOMAN.)

WORD

Words of truth and soberness.
> ACTS. XXVI. 25

Words of affection, howsoe'er expressed,
The latest spoken still are deem'd the best.
> JOANNA BAILLIE

A very great part of the mischiefs that vex this world arises from words.
> BURKE

Words writ in waters.
> GEORGE CHAPMAN—*Revenge for Honour*

Fair words butter no parsnips.
> JOHN CLARKE—*Paraemiologia*

Mum's the word.
> GEORGE COLMAN THE YOUNGER—Battle of Hexham

Words that weep, and tears that speak.
> COWLEY—*The Prophet*

Father is rather vulgar, my dear. The word Papa, besides, gives a pretty form to the lips. Papa, potatoes, poultry, prunes and prism are all very good words for the lips; especially prunes and prism.
> DICKENS—*Little Dorrit*

But words once spoke can never be recall'd.
> WENTWORTH DILLON

Let thy words be few.
> ECCLESIASTES. V. 2

Our words have wings, but fly not where we would.
> GEORGE ELIOT—*The Spanish Gypsy*

Let no man deceive you with vain words.

EPHESIANS. V. 6

Words are feminine; deeds are masculine.

BALTASAR GRACIÁN

How forcible are right words!

JOB. VI. 25

Who is this that darkeneth counsel by words without knowledge?

JOB. XXXVIII. 2

In the beginning was the Word, and the Word was with God, and the Word was God.

JOHN. I. 1

I am not yet so lost in lexicography, as to forget that words are the daughters of earth, and that things are the sons of heaven.

SAMUEL JOHNSON—Preface to His Dictionary

Words are the most powerful drug used by mankind.

KIPLING—Speech, 1923

We should have a great many fewer disputes in the world if words were taken for what they are, the signs of our ideas only, and not for things themselves.

LOCKE—Essay on the Human Understanding

Speaking words of endearment where words of comfort availed not.

LONGFELLOW—Evangeline

The word impossible is not in my dictionary.

NAPOLEON

Sticks and stones may break my bones,
But words can never harm me.

OLD ENGLISH RHYME

Words will build no walls.

PLUTARCH

A word spoken in good season, how good it is!

PROVERBS. XV. 23

A word fitly spoken is like apples of gold in pictures of silver.

PROVERBS. XXV. 11

The words of his mouth were smoother than butter, but war was in his heart; his words were softer than oil, yet were they drawn swords.

PSALMS. LV. 21

One of our defects as a nation is a tendency to use what have been called "weasel words." When a weasel sucks eggs the meat is sucked out of the egg. If you use a "weasel word" after another there is nothing left of the other.

THEODORE ROOSEVELT—Speech, 1916

My words fly up, my thoughts remain below:
Words without thoughts never to heaven go.

SHAKESPEARE—Hamlet. Act III. Sc. 3

But yesterday the word of Caesar might
Have stood against the world; now lies he there,
And none so poor to do him reverence.

SHAKESPEARE—Julius Caesar. Act III. Sc. 2

Taffeta phrases, silken terms precise,
Three-piled hyperboles, spruce affec-
    tation,
Figures pedantical.
    SHAKESPEARE—*Love's Labour's
    Lost.* Act V. Sc. 2

I sometimes hold it half a sin
    To put in words the grief I feel;
    For words, like Nature, half re-
    veal
And half conceal the Soul within.
    TENNYSON—*In Memoriam*

A word to the wise is sufficient.
    TERENCE

Hold fast the form of sound words.
    II TIMOTHY. I. 13

He utters empty words, he utters
sound without mind.
    VERGIL—*Aeneid*

You (Pindar) who possessed the
talent of speaking much without saying anything.
    VOLTAIRE

For of all sad words of tongue or pen,
The saddest are these: "It might have
    been!"
    WHITTIER—*Maud Muller*

(See also CONVERSATION, GOSSIP,
  ORATORY, SCANDAL, SPEECH
      TALK, TONGUE.)

WORK

When Adam dolve, and Eve span,
Who was then the gentleman?
    JOHN BALL—*Wat Tyler's
    Rebellion*

Tools were made and born were
    hands,
Every farmer understands.
    WILLIAM BLAKE—*Proverbs*

The best verse hasn't been rhymed
    yet,
    The best house hasn't been
    planned,
The highest peak hasn't been
    climbed yet,
    The mightiest rivers aren't
    spanned;
Don't worry and fret, faint-hearted,
    The chances have just begun
For the best jobs haven't been
    started,
    The best work hasn't been done.
    BERTON BRALEY—*No Chance*

All Nature seems at work, slugs
    leave their lair—
    The bees are stirring—birds are
    on the wing—
And Winter, slumbering in the open
    air,
    Wears on his smiling face a dream
    of Spring!
And I the while, the sole unbusy
    thing,
    Nor honey make, nor pair, nor
    build, nor sing.
    COLERIDGE—*Work Without
    Hope*

Every man's work shall be made
manifest.
    I CORINTHIANS. III. 13

Better to wear out than to rust out.
    BISHOP CUMBERLAND

The workers are the saviors of society, the redeemers of the race.
    EUGENE V. DEBS—Speech,
    1905

The Lord had a job for me, but I
    had so much to do,
I said, "You get somebody else—or
    wait till I get through."
I don't know how the Lord came
    out, but He seemed to get
    along:
But I felt kinda sneakin' like, 'cause
    I know'd I done Him wrong.
One day I needed the Lord—needed
    Him myself—needed Him right
    away,
And He never answered me at all,
    but I could hear Him say
Down in my accusin' heart, "Nigger,
    I'se got too much to do,
You get somebody else or wait till
    I get through."
    PAUL LAURENCE DUNBAR—
    The Lord Had a Job

All things are full of labour; man
cannot utter it: the eye is not satisfied with seeing, nor the ear filled
with hearing.
    ECCLESIASTES. I. 8

I never did anything worth doing
by accident, nor did any of my inventions come by accident; they
came by work.
    EDISON

It's all in the day's work.
    ENGLISH SAYING

A ploughman on his legs is higher
than a gentleman on his knees.
    FRANKLIN—*Poor Richard*

Handle your tools without mittens.
    FRANKLIN—*Poor Richard*

In every rank, or great or small,
'Tis industry supports us all.
    GAY—*Man, Cat, Dog, and Fly*

In the sweat of thy face shalt thou
eat bread.
    GENESIS. III. 19

When Darby saw the setting sun
He swung his scythe, and home he
    run,
Sat down, drank off his quart and
    said,
"My work is done, I'll go to bed."
"My work is done!" retorted Joan,
"My work is done! Your constant
    tone,
But hapless woman ne'er can say
'My work is done' till judgment
    day."
    ST. JOHN HONEYWOOD—*Darby
    and Joan*

All work and no play makes Jack
a dull boy.
    JAMES HOWELL

I like work; it fascinates me. I can
sit and look at it for hours. I love to
keep it by me: the idea of getting
rid of it nearly breaks my heart.
    JEROME K. JEROME—*Three
    Men in a Boat*

And only the Master shall praise us,
    and only the Master shall
    blame;
And no one shall work for money,
    and no one shall work for fame;
But each for the joy of the working,
    and each, in his separate star,
Shall draw the Thing as he sees It,
    for the God of Things as They
    Are!
    KIPLING—*L'Envoi.* In Seven
    Seas

No man is born into the world
    whose work
Is not born with him; there is al-
    ways work,

And tools to work withal, for those
who will;
And blessed are the horny hands of
toil!
LOWELL—*A Glance Behind the
Curtain*

The laborer is worthy of his hire.
LUKE. X. 7

Why do strong arms fatigue themselves with frivolous dumb-
bells?
To dig a vineyard is a worthier exercise for men.
MARTIAL

Many hands make light work.
WILLIAM PATTEN. 1547

A day's work is a day's work, neither
more nor less, and the man who does
it needs a day's sustenance, a night's
repose, and due leisure, whether he
be painter or ploughman.
GEORGE BERNARD SHAW—
—*Unsocial Socialist.*

How many a rustic Milton has passed
by,
Stifling the speechless longings of
his heart,
In unremitting drudgery and care!
How many a vulgar Cato has com-
pelled
His energies, no longer tameless
then,
To mould a pin, or fabricate a nail!
SHELLEY—*Queen Mab*

Heaven is blessed with perfect rest
but the blessing of earth is toil.
HENRY VAN DYKE—*Toiling of
Felix*

Too long, that some may rest,
Tired millions toil unblest.
WILLIAM WATSON—*New
National Anthem*

There will be little drudgery in this
better ordered world. Natural power
harnessed in machines will be the
general drudge. What drudgery is
inevitable will be done as a service
and duty for a few years or months
out of each life; it will not consume
nor degrade the whole life of anyone.
H. G. WELLS—*Outline of
History*

(See also ACTION, BUSINESS, DEEDS,
LABOR, OCCUPATION.)

WORLD

This is the best world, that we live
in,
To lend and to spend and to give in:
But to borrow, or beg, or to get a
man's own,
It is the worst world that ever was
known.
ANONYMOUS

This world's a bubble.
BACON

Believe everything you hear said of
the world; nothing is too impossibly
bad.
BALZAC

The world is like a board with holes
in it, and the square men have got
into the round holes, and the round
into the square.
BISHOP BERKELEY

The pomps and vanity of this wicked
world.
BOOK OF COMMON PRAYER

The year's at the Spring
  And day's at the morn;
    Morning's at seven;
      The hillside's dew-pearled;
The lark's on the wing;
  The snail's on the thorn:
    God's in his Heaven—
      All's right with the world!
    BROWNING—*Pippa Passes*

I have not loved the world, nor the
  world me;
I have not flatter'd its rank breath,
  nor bow'd
To its idolatries a patient knee.
    BYRON—*Childe Harold*

Socrates, indeed, when he was asked
of what country he called himself,
said, "Of the world"; for he considered himself an inhabitant and a
citizen of the whole world.
    CICERO

Such stuff the world is made of.
    COWPER—*Hope*

Come, follow me, and leave the
world to its babblings.
    DANTE

Good-bye, proud world! I'm going
  home;
Thou art not my friend; I am not
  thine.
    EMERSON—*Good-bye, Proud
    World!*

But in this world nothing is sure but
death and taxes.
    FRANKLIN—Letter to M. Leroy,
    1789

But it does move.
    GALILEO—Before the Inquisi-
    tion

The world is a beautiful book, but
of little use to him who cannot read
it.
    GOLDONI—*Pamela*

The nations are as a drop of a bucket.
    ISAIAH. XL. 15

World without end.
    ISAIAH. XLV. 17

It takes all sorts of people to make a
world.
    DOUGLAS JERROLD—*Story of a
    Feather*

If there is one beast in all the loath-
some fauna of civilization I hate and
despise, it is a man of the world.
    HENRY ARTHUR JONES—*The
    Liars*

The world is God's world, after all.
    KINGSLEY

The world goes up and the world
  goes down,
  And the sunshine follows the rain;
And yesterday's sneer and yesterday's
  frown
  Can never come over again,
  Sweet wife.
  No, never come over again.
    KINGSLEY—*Dolcino to Margaret*

If all the world must see the world
  As the world the world hath seen,
Then it were better for the world
  That the world had never been.
    LELAND—*The World and the
    World*

It is an ugly world. Offend
  Good people, how they wrangle,
The manners that they never mend,
  The characters they mangle.

They eat, and drink, and scheme, and plod,
And go to church on Sunday—
And many are afraid of God—
And more of Mrs. Grundy.
FREDERICK LOCKER-LAMPSON—
The Jester's Plea

Glorious indeed is the world of God around us, but more glorious the world of God within us. There lies the Land of Song; there lies the poet's native land.
LONGFELLOW—*Hyperion*

The world is full of beauty, as other worlds above,
And if we did our duty, it might be as full of love.
GERALD MASSEY—*This World*

This world is all a fleeting show,
For man's illusion given;
The smiles of joy, the tears of woe,
Deceitful shine, deceitful flow,—
There's nothing true but Heaven.
MOORE—*This World Is All a Fleeting Show*

Half the world does not know how the other half lives.
RABELAIS—*Pantagruel*

All nations and kindreds and people and tongues.
REVELATION. VII. 9

All the world's a stage,
And all the men and women merely players.
SHAKESPEARE—*Merry Wives of Windsor*. Act II. Sc. 2

Why, then, the world's mine oyster,
Which I with sword will open.
SHAKESPEARE—*Merry Wives of Windsor*. Act II. Sc. 2

You'll never have a quiet world till you knock the patriotism out of the human race.
GEORGE BERNARD SHAW—
O'Flaherty, V. C.

This world surely is wide enough to hold both thee and me.
LAURENCE STERNE—*Tristram Shandy*

There was all the world and his wife.
SWIFT—*Polite Conversation*

A mad world, my masters.
JOHN TAYLOR—*Western Voyage*

So many worlds, so much to do,
So little done, such things to be.
TENNYSON—*In Memoriam*

Everything is for the best in this best of all possible worlds.
VOLTAIRE—*Candide*

This world is a comedy to those who think, a tragedy to those who feel.
HORACE WALPOLE—Letter to Sir Horace Mann

(See also ACTING, CREATION, HUMANITY, LIFE, NATURE, SCIENCE, SOCIETY.)

WORRY
See SUFFERING

WORSHIP

It is only when men begin to worship that they begin to grow.
CALVIN COOLIDGE—Speech, 1922

And what greater calamity can fall upon a nation than the loss of worship.
EMERSON

Ay, call it holy ground,
  The soil where first they trod.
They have left unstained, what there
  they found—
    Freedom to worship God.
      Felicia D. Hemans—*The
      Landing of the Pilgrim Fathers*

Yet, if he would, man cannot live all
to this world. If not religious, he will
be superstitious. If he worship not
the true God, he will have his idols.
      Theodore Parker

(See also CHURCH, CHRISTIANITY,
FAITH, GOD, PRAYER, PREACHING,
RELIGION.)

WORTH

This was the penn'worth of his
thought.
      Butler—*Hudibras*

Nothing common can seem worthy
of you.
      Cicero to Caesar

We are valued either too highly or
not high enough; we are never taken
at our real worth.
      Marie Ebner-Eschenbach

The game is not worth the candle.
      French Proverb

Of whom the world was not worthy.
      Hebrews. XI. 38

Worth makes the man, and want of
  it the fellow;
The rest is all but leather and pru-
  nello.
      Pope—*Essay on Man*

It is easy enough to be prudent,
  When nothing tempts you to stray;
When without or within no voice of
  sin
    Is luring your soul away;

But it's only a negative virtue
  Until it is tried by fire,
And the life that is worth the honor
  of earth,
  Is the one that resists desire.
      Ella Wheeler Wilcox—
      Worth While

(See also CHARACTER, MERIT,
    SUCCESS.)

WOUND

What deep wounds ever closed without a scar?
The hearts bleed longest, and but
  heal to wear
That which disfigures it.
      Byron—*Childe Harold*

A certain Samaritan . . . bound up
his wounds, pouring in oil and wine.
      Luke. X. 33–34

I was wounded in the house of my
friends.
      Zechariah. XIII. 6

(See also AFFLICTION, CRUELTY,
  INJURY, PAIN, SOLDIER,
    SUFFERING, WAR.)

WRATH
See ANGER

WRITING

The reason why so few good books
are written is that so few people who
can write know anything.
      Walter Bagehot

Whatever we conceive well we express clearly.
      Boileau

Talent alone cannot make a writer.
There must be a man behind the
book.
      Emerson—*Representative Men*

If you wish to be a writer, write.
EPICTETUS

Writers seldom write the things they think. They simply write the things they think other folks think they think.
ELBERT HUBBARD

Think much, speak little, and write less.
ITALIAN PROVERB

Bad writers are those who try to express their own feeble ideas in the language of good ones.
G. C. LICHTENBERG

A man may write himself out of reputation when nobody else can do it.
THOMAS PAINE—*The Rights of Man*

(See also AUTHORSHIP, LITERATURE, PEN, POETRY.)

WRONG

The multitude is always in the wrong.
WENTWORTH DILLON

Two wrongs do not make a right.
ENGLISH PROVERB

Brother, brother; we are both in the wrong.
GAY—*Beggar's Opera*

It is better to suffer wrong than to do it, and happier to be sometimes cheated than not to trust.
SAMUEL JOHNSON

Truth forever on the scaffold, wrong forever on the throne.
LOWELL

The remedy for wrongs is to forget them.
SYRUS

(See also ERROR, INJURY, INSULT.)

YOUTH

Young men are fitter to invent than to judge; fitter for execution than for counsel; and fitter for new projects than for settled business.
BACON—*Of Youth and Age*

Our youth we can have but today;
We may always find time to grow old.
BISHOP BERKELEY

In the lexicon of youth, which fate reserves
For a bright manhood, there is no such word
As *fail.*
BULWER-LYTTON—*Richelieu*

Ah! happy years! once more who would not be a boy!
BYRON—*Childe Harold*

As I approve of a youth that has something of the old man in him, so I am no less pleased with an old man that has something of the youth. He that follows this rule may be old in body, but can never be so in mind.
CICERO

I remember my youth and the feeling that will never come back any more—the feeling that I could last forever, outlast the sea, the earth, and all men.
JOSEPH CONRAD—*Youth*

In youth we learn; in age we understand.
MARIE EBNER-ESCHENBACH

Youth will be served.
ENGLISH PROVERB

Reckless youth makes rueful age.
FRANKLIN

Forty is the old age of youth; fifty is the youth of old age.
FRENCH PROVERB

Yes, you may depend upon it he has the ability! He is the younger generation that stands ready to knock at my door—to make an end of Halvard Solness.
IBSEN—*The Master Builder*

Youth! youth! how buoyant are thy hopes! they turn,
Like marigolds, toward the sunny side.
JEAN INGELOW—*The Four Bridges*

All the world's a mass of folly,
Youth is gay, age melancholy:
Youth is spending, age is thrifty,
Mad at twenty, cold at fifty;
Man is nought but folly's slave,
From the cradle to the grave.
W. H. IRELAND—*Modern Ship of Fools*

Your old men shall dream dreams; your young men shall see visions.
JOEL. II. 28

When all the world is young, lad,
And all the trees are green;
And every goose a swan, lad,
And every lass a queen;
Then hey, for boot and horse, lad,
And round the world away;
Young blood must have its course, lad,
And every dog his day.
CHARLES KINGSLEY—*Water Babies*

Youth comes but once in a lifetime.
LONGFELLOW—*Hyperion*

How beautiful is youth! how bright it gleams
With its illusions, aspirations, dreams!
Book of Beginnings, Story without End,
Each maid a heroine, and each man a friend!
LONGFELLOW—*Morituri Salutamus*

The atrocious crime of being a young man.
WILLIAM PITT TO WALPOLE

We think our fathers fools, so wise we grow;
Our wiser sons, no doubt, will think us so.
POPE—*Essay on Criticism*

If youth but knew, and age were able,
Then poverty would be a fable.
PROVERB

Keep true to the dreams of thy youth.
SCHILLER

Crabbed age and youth cannot live together;
Youth is full of pleasance, age is full of care;
Youth like summer morn, age like winter weather;
Youth like summer brave, age like winter bare.
Youth is full sport, age's breath is short;
Youth is nimble, age is lame;
Youth is hot and bold, age is weak and cold;
Youth is wild, age is tame.

Age, I do abhor thee; youth, I do adore thee.
SHAKESPEARE—*The Passionate Pilgrim*

Live as long as you may, the first twenty years are the longest half of your life.
SOUTHEY

All sorts of allowances are made for the illusions of youth; and none, or almost none, for the disenchantments of age.
STEVENSON—*Virginibus Puerisque*

For God's sake give me the young man who has brains enough to make a fool of himself.
STEVENSON—*Crabbed Age*

(See also AGE, AMBITION, BABY-HOOD, CHILDHOOD, DREAMS, ENTHUSIASM, HOME, HOPE, INNOCENCE, PARENT, WAR, ZEAL.)

YUKON

There's a land where the mountains are nameless
And the rivers all run God knows where;
There are lives that are erring and aimless.
And deaths that just hang by a hair;
There are hardships that nobody reckons;
There are valleys unpeopled and still;
There's a land—oh, it beckons and beckons,
And I want to go back—and I will.
ROBERT W. SERVICE—*Spell of the Yukon*

ZEAL

There is no greater sign of a general decay of virtue in a nation, than a want of zeal in its inhabitants for the good of their country.
ADDISON—*Freeholder*

Through zeal knowledge is gotten, through lack of zeal knowledge is lost.
BUDDHA

It is good to be zealously affected always in a good thing.
GALATIANS. IV. 18

Blind zeal can only do harm.
MAGNUS GOTTFRIED LICHTWER

To be furious in religion is to be irreligiously religious.
WILLIAM PENN

My zeal hath consumed me.
PSALMS. CXIX. 139

Zeal is very blind, or badly regulated, when it encroaches upon the rights of others.
PASQUIER QUESNEL

A zeal of God, but not according to knowledge.
ROMANS. X. 2

Press bravely onward!—not in vain
Your generous trust in human kind;
The good which bloodshed could not gain
Your peaceful zeal shall find.
WHITTIER—*To the Reformers of England*

(See also AMBITION, ENTHUSIASM, LABOR, PERSEVERANCE, RESOLUTION, WORK, YOUTH.)

INDEX

A

Lear, Edward (1812–1888), English artist and writer of nonsense verse, 50, 193

Lebrun, Guillaume Pigault (1742–1835), French novelist, 309

Lee, Gerald Stanley (1862–1944), American educator, 7, 26, 180

Leibnitz, Gottfried Wilhelm, Baron von (1646–1716), German philosopher and mathematician, 103

Leigh, Henry Sambrooke (1837–1883), English poet and dramatist, 307

Leland, Charles Godfrey (1824–1903), American scholar and writer, 318

Lemierre, Antoine Marin (1723–1793), French dramatic poet, 108

L'Enclos, Ninon de (1620–1705), French beauty and wit, 16, 132

Lenin, Nikolay (1870–1924), Russian Soviet leader, 100, 130, 137, 240, 243

Leo XIII, (Gioacchino Pecci) (1810–1903), Pope (1878–1903), 13, 28, 151, 259, 268

Leopold, Duke of Anhalt-Dessau (1676–1747), Prussian field marshal, 299

Le Sage, Alain René (1668–1747), French novelist and dramatist, 226

Lessing, Gotthold Ephraim (1729–1781), German critic and dramatist, 17, 250

L'Estrange, Sir Roger (1616–1704), English journalist, 21, 226

Lewes, George Henry (1817–1878), English philosophical writer, 114, 246

Lewis, John Llewellyn (1880–   ), American labor leader, 145

Liancourt, Duc de, see La Rochefoucauld-Liancourt

Lichtenberg, G. C., 255, 321

Lichtwer, Magnus Gottfried (1719–1783), German fabulist, 57, 323

Liebknecht, Wilhelm (1826–1900), German socialist leader, 259

Lincoln, Abraham (1809–1865), 16th U.S. president, 28, 46, 58, 60, 69, 78, 82, 84, 97, 100, 101, 107, 111, 182, 193, 195, 196, 204, 219, 222, 241, 242, 256, 260, 299

Lindsay, Nicholas Vachel (1879–1931), American poet, 154

Lippmann, Walter (1889–   ), American journalist and author, 268

Livy, (Titus Livius) (59 B.C.–A.D. 17), Roman historian, 52, 79, 98, 284, 288, 289

Lloyd, J. William (1856–1940), American poet and socialist, 125

Locke, John (1632–1704), English philosopher, 145, 180, 222, 301, 314

Locker-Lampson, Frederick (1821–1895), English poet, 319

Logan, John (1748–1788), Scottish divine, 19

Longfellow, Henry Wadsworth (1807–1882), American poet, 1, 2, 5, 6, 7, 11, 19, 28, 30, 32, 34, 37, 56, 59, 62, 73, 80, 82, 93, 103, 119, 125, 134, 140, 154, 162, 174, 175, 184, 191, 192, 201, 209,

232, 240, 243, 245, 252, 261, 266, 267, 270, 289, 294, 303, 304, 306, 312, 314, 319, 322

Louis XIV (1638–1715), King of France, 111, 195, 211, 214, 243, 268

Lovelace, Richard (1618–1658), English poet, 123, 162, 220

Lover, Samuel (1797–1868), Irish song writer and painter, 67, 312

Lowell, James Russell (1819–1891), American poet, essayist, and diplomat, 2, 32, 33, 44, 50, 58, 81, 89, 93, 96, 104, 131, 135, 157, 176, 179, 196, 219, 221, 253, 256, 261, 278, 291, 299, 310, 317, 321

Lowndes, William (1652–1724), English statesman, 178

Luther, Martin (1483–1546), German leader of the Reformation, 25, 40, 46, 58, 70, 84, 107, 154, 162, 217, 234, 238, 291, 299, 301

Luxburg, Count Karl von (c. 1915), German diplomatist, 299

Lyly, John (1554?–1606), English dramatist and novelist, 17, 90, 192, 226, 270, 282

Lyttleton, George, 1st Baron Lyttleton (1709–1773), English poet and statesman, 21

Lytton, Edward Robert Bulwer, 1st Earl of Lytton, see Owen Meredith

Lytton, Lord, see Bulwer-Lytton

M

MacArthur, Douglas (1880–   ), American general, 7

Macaulay, Thomas Babington (1800–1859), English poet, critic, and historian, 9, 18, 44, 47, 60, 67, 100, 113, 180, 198, 210, 250, 251

Macy, Arthur (1842–1904), 91

McCrae, Lieut. Col. John (1872–1918), Canadian poet, 94, 299

McCreery, John Luckey (1835–1906), American journalist and verse writer, 56, 130

MacDonald, George (1824–1905), British poet and novelist, 8, 38, 221, 290, 292

MacFarren, G. (before 1580), 37

McFee, William (1881–   ), English-American novelist, 75

Machiavelli, Nicolo di Bernardo (1469–1527), Florentine statesman and political writer, 10, 49, 111, 133

Mackay, Charles (1814–1889), English poet and journalist, 56

McKinley, William (1843–1901), 25th U.S. president, 130

Macklin, Charles (1697–1797), English actor and dramatist, 226

MacLagan, Alexander (1818–1896), Scotch-Canadian poet, 299

MacPherson, James (1736–1796), Scottish poet, 273

P

Page, H. A. (1837–1905), English writer, 145

Page, Walter Hines (1855–1918), American editor, publisher, and diplomatist, 151

Paine, Thomas (1737–1809), English-born American political and theological writer, 18, 27, 40, 41, 45, 52, 112, 125, 177, 202, 236, 284, 294, 300, 321

Painter, William (1540?–1594), English writer, 240

Paley, William (1743–1805), English theologian and moralist, 258

Palgrave, Sir R. H. Inglis (1827–1919), English economist, 42

Panat, Charles Louis Étienne, Chevalier de (1762–1834), French naval officer, 150

Panin, 6, 189

Pardoe, Julia (1806–1862), English novelist, 244

Parker, Dorothy (1893–   ), American poet and satirist, 77, 92, 173

Parker, Edward Hazen (1823–1896), American physician, 239

Parker, George (1732–1800), English actor and lecturer, 90

Parker, Joseph (1830–1902), English divine, 79, 256

Parker, Theodore (1810–1860), American clergyman, 60, 112, 125, 128, 145, 320

Parton, Mrs. Sarah Payson (Fanny Fern) (1811–1872), American writer for children, 70

Pascal, Blaise (1623–1662), French philosopher and mathematician, 59, 69, 72, 97, 129, 132, 151, 193, 196, 231, 291

Pasteur, Louis (1822–1895), French biochemist, 305

Patten, William (c. 1548–1580), English historian, 317

Payne, John Howard (1791–1852), American author, 123

Peabody, Josephine Preston (1874–1922), American poet and dramatist, 288

Peacock, Thomas Love (1785–1866), English novelist and poet, 296

Peel, Sir Robert (1788–1850), English statesman, 196

Peele, George (1558–1597), English poet, 303

Penn, William (1614–1718), Quaker and founder of Pennsylvania, 25, 36, 68, 110, 135, 136, 141, 189, 200, 236, 240, 273, 280, 323

Penrose, Boise (1860–1921), American political leader, 195

Pepys, Samuel (1633–1703), English diarist, 16

Percy, Thomas (1729–1811), English prelate, 201

Pericles (495?–429 B.C.), Athenian statesman, 90, 284

Perry, Oliver Hazard (1785–1819), American naval commander, 295

Pershing, John Joseph (1860–1948), American general, 300

Peterson, Frederick (1859–   ), American physician and poet, 200

Petit-Senn, Jean Antoine (1792–1870), Swiss litterateur, 51, 117, 208

Petrarch, Francesco (1304–1374), Italian poet, 296

Phaedrus (1st century A.D.), Latin fabulist, 135

Phelps, Edward John (1822–1900), American publicist, 78

Philemon (c. 361–263 B.C.), Athenian comic poet, 87, 168

Philip II (382–336 B.C.), King of Macedonia, 113

Phillips, Wendell (1811–1884), American orator and reformer, 24, 30, 37, 59, 61, 86, 112, 118, 119, 128, 138, 166, 191, 208, 211, 214, 215, 221, 237, 241, 242, 250, 268

Philpots, Dr. Edward P., 131

Piis, Antoine Pierre Augustin de (1755–1832), French dramatist, 155

Pilpay (Bidpai), Oriental fabulist, 29

Pinckney, Charles Cotesworth (1746–1825), American statesman, 203

Pinero, Sir Arthur Wing (1855–1934), English dramatist, 103

Pitt, William, 1st Earl of Chatham (1708–1788), English statesman, 149, 169, 188, 214, 241, 292, 322

Pittacus of Mitylene (c. 652–569 B.C.), Greek statesman and poet, 284

Pius XI (1857–1939), Roman Pope, 86, 137, 297

Plato (428–347 B.C.), Greek philosopher, 22, 24, 45, 80, 107, 133, 162, 209, 247, 265, 268

Plautus, Titus Maccius (c. 254–184 B.C.), Roman comic dramatist, 64, 79, 82, 102, 115, 177, 212, 235, 249, 251, 265, 307

Pliny, Gaius Plinius Caecilius Secundus, the Younger (62–113), Latin letter writer and advocate, 151, 209

Pliny, Gaius Plinius Secundus, the Elder (23–79), Roman naturalist, 14, 20, 47, 123, 183, 253, 307

Plutarch (46?–120?), Greek biographer and moralist, 19, 35, 112, 275, 295, 314

Poe, Edgar Allan (1809–1849), American poet, critic, and story writer, 19, 67, 114, 136, 175, 209, 230, 243, 263

Poincelot, Achille (c. 1850), French philosopher, 278

Pollok, Robert (1798–1827), Scottish poet, 127

Pompadour, Mme. de (1721–1764), mistress of Louis XV, 103

Poole, Mary Pettibone, 53

Pope, Alexander (1688–1744), English poet and critic, 4, 21, 44, 50, 56, 63, 68, 72, 76, 78, 81, 82, 89, 96, 97, 98, 107, 123, 124, 125, 132, 138, 150, 155, 157, 162, 168, 172, 184, 187, 193, 194, 198,